AF615019

A DIRECTORY OF DEALERS IN SECONDHAND AND ANTIQUARIAN BOOKS

Uniform with this volume are—

BOOK DEALERS IN NORTH AMERICA

(A DIRECTORY OF DEALERS IN SECONDHAND AND ANTIQUARIAN BOOKS IN CANADA AND THE UNITED STATES OF AMERICA)

EUROPEAN BOOKDEALERS

(A DIRECTORY OF DEALERS IN SECONDHAND AND ANTIQUARIAN BOOKS IN EUROPE)

BOOK DEALERS IN INDIA PAKISTAN, SRI LANKA ETC

(A DIRECTORY OF DEALERS IN SECONDHAND AND ANTIQUARIAN BOOKS AND PERIODICALS IN THE S.W. ASIAN SUB-CONTINENT)

THE BOOKDEALERS' AND COLLECTORS' YEAR-BOOK AND DIARY

published each year in November
contains lists of additions and alterations
to all the above directories

A DIRECTORY OF DEALERS IN SECONDHAND AND ANTIQUARIAN BOOKS IN THE BRITISH ISLES

1984–86

LONDON: SHEPPARD PRESS

*First Published (*1951–52 *Edition) April,* 1951
Eleventh Edition (1984-86) April 1984

SHEPPARD PRESS LIMITED
RUSSELL CHAMBERS, COVENT GARDEN
LONDON, WC2E 8AX, ENGLAND

I.S.S.N. 0070–5411
I.S.B.N. 0 900661 32 1
DEWEY CLASSIFICATION
655.56

Printed by
Unwin Brothers Limited, Gresham Press
Old Woking, Surrey

CONTENTS

FOREWORD

The eleventh edition of this directory follows much the same pattern as previous issues: there have been a few minor changes, mainly in response to suggestions made by users, but the more radical proposals received from time to time have all been considered undesirable or impracticable.

One request often made is that new editions should be published more frequently. As regular users will know, the three principal booktrade directories from Sheppard Press are issued in sequence, one a year, so there is a gap of three years between new editions of each directory.

The number of new entrants to the trade, changes of address etc., and established firms ceasing business, seems to be increasing, and there is no doubt that a more frequent updating of the entries would be generally welcomed. Attempts have been made to do this, first by the issue of supplements (which had to be abandoned because they cost so much and could not be effectively distributed to directory users), and then in recent years by the inclusion of lists of alterations and additions in the trade year-book, but a revised directory would obviously be more convenient. Renewed consideration will be given to the possibility of reducing the period between editions to two years, and to whether such a change would be economically viable.

One change that will be noticed is the introduction of a second colour into the printing. This enlivens the title page, and can in future be used in advertisements, to bring a dealer's name and quality even more forcefully to the attention of potential customers.

The editors would be glad to receive a note of any errors or omissions that may be found, or any alterations that may be necessary. These will be included in the *Bookdealers' and Collectors' Yearbook and Diary* which is published every November.

THE BRITISH BOOK TRADE

NEW BOOKS

In the British Isles the marketing of new books is a very highly organized business, controlled mainly by the two principal trade associations concerned, those of the publishers and the booksellers.

THE PUBLISHERS ASSOCIATION (19 Bedford Square, London WC1B 3HJ. TN: (01) 580-6321, TA: Publasoc London. Secretary and Chief Executive: Clive Bradley) was established in 1896. It has about 320 member firms which between them account for all but a small percentage of the books published in Britain. The Association provides a forum for its members, and helps them operate effectively by providing essential background information about home and overseas markets, representing the industry's interests to British and foreign governments and national and international organisations, co-ordinating promotional activities, and providing help and advice on such matters as parliamentary legislation, taxation, libel, copyright, agreements, finance and credit, production, distribution, employee relations, training and development. Within the Association there are seven separate divisions; five of them are concerned with the special interests of publishers in particular fields (paperback books, children's books, educational books for schools, educational books for universities and colleges, and general books including religious books, book-clubs and maps), and the other two divisions deal with international matters and employment and training.

THE BOOKSELLERS ASSOCIATION OF GREAT BRITAIN AND IRELAND (154 Buckingham Palace Road, London SW1W 9TZ, TN: (01) 730-8214. Director: Tim Godfray) was founded in 1895 as the Associated Booksellers of Great Britain and Ireland and changed to its present name in 1948. It is not concerned with the secondhand or antiquarian trade, but its membership is open to all those engaged in the sale of new books. It has about 3,500 members, and there are fifteen regional branches in which members hold regular meetings. There are usually booksellers in a fairly substantial way of business, but there are altogether about 12,000 outlets in the United Kingdom and Ireland where books are sold, sometimes in very small quantities. The

Association is governed by an Annual Conference and a Council which meets six times a year, delegating much work to specialist committees, such as trade practice and training, and encouraging members to join groups concerned with college and university bookselling, religious bookselling, children's bookselling etc. The Charter Bookselling Scheme, Book Tokens, and a clearing house for the payment of accounts are some of the services provided for members; training courses for booksellers are also arranged and diplomas and certificates awarded. The Association is linked with similar bodies overseas through the International Community of Booksellers Associations, founded in 1956, and has a representative member on its council.

The two associations, through a joint advisory committee, consider all applications for inclusion in a directory maintained by the Publishers Association. This directory includes not only booksellers, but also certain other traders who sell books in one particular field only, such as gardening, motoring, arts and crafts etc.

Although, in fact, it confers no right to buy books at trade terms, entry in this directory is prized because most publishers (if their office systems are efficient enough) will allow discount only to firms listed there and to newsagents having a weekly newsbill with a recognized wholesaler.

Every trader who is allowed to buy books at a discount is required to sign the so-called Net Book Agreement. This is an undertaking entered into by booksellers that they will not sell any books that the publishers have declared to be "net" books to the public, including schools, libraries, and institutions at less than the prices fixed from time to time by the publishers.

The Net Book Agreement constitutes formal notice from each publisher who has signed it to each bookseller who has done so that a condition of supply is the maintenance of the retail price. If a breach of this condition is committed, the publisher may, through the courts, seek damages or an injunction or both. Most members of the Publishers Association have agreed that they will, in fact, do so, and have authorized the Association to act for them in such a case.

SECOND-HAND AND ANTIQUARIAN BOOKS

There is little organization and no control in the second-hand and antiquarian book trade. Even the two adjectives associated with it are not clearly defined, though it is generally understood that antiquarian books are those the value of which is partially attributable to their age as distinct from their contents; all other used books, which may be sought because they are cheaper or no longer obtainable new, are described as second-hand.

Anyone who is so minded can enter this branch of the trade without any formality at all, and indeed, book lovers and collectors, buying items for their own libraries and selling duplicate or unwanted copies, have sometimes, almost unwittingly, drifted into a habit of rather casual regular dealing. This sounds easy and pleasant, but to enter seriously into business and make a profit in any way commensurate with the work involved a great deal of expert knowledge is required.

There are two national trade associations for antiquarian book dealers.

THE ANTIQUARIAN BOOKSELLERS' ASSOCIATION

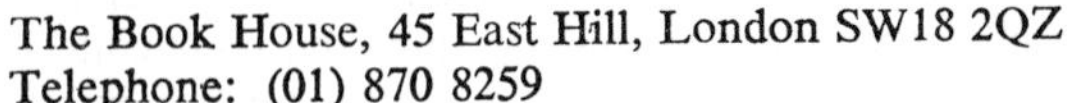
The Book House, 45 East Hill, London SW18 2QZ
Telephone: (01) 870 8259

The Antiquarian Booksellers' Association, founded in 1906, includes the leading dealers in antiquarian, fine, and scarce second-hand books throughout Great Britain as well as some other countries. It is the oldest of the eighteen similar associations scattered through Europe, Scandinavia, Japan, and the Americas which together form the International League of Antiquarian Booksellers.

The Association seeks to provide a comprehensive service to its members. It organises the well-known Antiquarian Book Fair each June at the Europa Hotel, Grosvenor Square, London, and Spring or Autumn fairs in Edinburgh, Cambridge or Bath. All members receive an informative newsletter each month and there is a fine reference library ready to answer their bibliographical queries. Their interests are further looked after by representatives sitting on various government bodies and dealing with such subjects as the export of manuscripts, the future of the British Library, the National Book League, postal charges, and the monitoring of V.A.T. and customs regulations both here and in the Common Market. The Association organises, throughout the year, a series of events; sporting, social, and educational; aimed at promoting friendship and understanding among colleagues at both national and international levels. There is a Benevolent Fund upon which members may call in times of financial difficulty.

There are various ways in which the Association looks after the interests of the general public. By requiring a good experience of the trade, and high professional standards and ethics, of all its members it ensures that the public may approach with confidence any dealer displaying the A.B.A. badge. In rare cases of difficulty or dispute the Association stands ready to arbitrate between dealer and client.

The public, especially institutions and public libraries, are further served by a sophisticated security system founded and developed by the Association and now copied throughout the world. It has already accounted for the apprehension of an impressive list of book-thieves and the recovery and restoration to their rightful owners of many hundreds of stolen books. A computor has recently been added to the system and work is in progress to develop it into a comprehensive global network.

From within its ranks the Antiquarian Booksellers' Association can produce experts on most aspects of bibliography and book-collecting and their collective expertise is available to the general public through the Association's office at The Book House, 45 East Hill, London SW18 2QZ, telephone: (01) 870 8259. The Secretary will be pleased to send a list of members upon request.

PROVINCIAL BOOKSELLERS FAIRS ASSOCIATION

60 Quarry Street,

Guildford, Surrey GU1 3UA.

The primary function of the P.B.F.A. is to organise Bookfairs throughout the country. In addition to its regular monthly London Bookfair, over 100 fairs and markets are organised in the Provinces each year. In this way it is intended that the widest possible market for members' books be obtained. Details of the fairs are published in the *Bookdealers' and Collectors' Year-book and Diary*.

Additionally it is the Association's aim to promote interest in antiquarian and secondhand books, encourage goodwill and to assist members and their dependants in times of distress through a Benevolent Fund.

Membership is now in excess of 600 and it is the largest antiquarian and secondhand trade association in the world. Both full and part time members of the book trade are eligible for membership and forms can be obtained from Mr. S. Brett, 111 Park Road, New Barnet, Hertfordshire EN4 9QR.

The P.B.F.A. is a non profit making organisation and all its officers and committee members are elected at the Annual General Meeting and are unpaid.

Calendars of the fairs are available from the Administrator. P.B.F.A. at the above address.

And there is also a small society for bookdealers' assistants.

SOCIETY OF ANTIQUARIAN BOOKSELLERS' EMPLOYEES (care of Roger D. Smith, Francis Edwards Limited, 83 Marylebone High Street, London W1M 4AL) popularly known as the "Bibliomites" founded in 1951 has a membership of fifty. It is mainly a social society, but educational visits are sometimes arranged. Membership is open to all employees in the antiquarian book trade.

Of course, many dealers have large and handsome premises, but a far greater number have more modest shops in the less expensive districts of their town, while hundreds run postal businesses from their private addresses, where the stock, often including rare and much sought after items, is stored in a spare room, or from overcrowded little stockrooms where the trade and general public are admitted only by appointment. How many of these dealers there are can only be guessed. This directory contains details of over 1,500. The editor has information about another hundred or so which for sufficient reasons (such as imminent removal to another address) have not been included. There well may be a hundred more making, say, 2,000 in all.

Dealers were asked to state the size of the stock that they normally carried; that is the number of books that a customer might expect to be able to inspect if he visited their premises. Most of them responded, and of the others users must form their own opinion. Stocks of less than two thousand volumes have been described as VERY SMALL; 2,000–5,000 as SMALL; 5,000–10,000 as MEDIUM; 10,000–20,000 as LARGE; and over twenty thousand as VERY LARGE. It must be emphasized, however, that these descriptions are rather arbitrary. A dealer who specializes in a particular subject and buys his stock carefully, perhaps one volume at a time, may feel justifiably proud if he can offer a choice from two thousand valuable items; on the other hand almost every bookseller will appreciate that by buying libraries and collections *en bloc* he can quickly amass a vast but mediocre stock. The total stock held by dealers in the British Isles can only be guessed, but it may be between fifteen and twenty million volumes.

Almost every dealer in second-hand and antiquarian books will try to obtain for a customer any required item which he has not in his stock. This is done through an elaborate system of reporting offers and requirements in trade journals. There are a number of these, but the best known are THE CLIQUE, which was started seventy years ago, and a more recently established competitor THE BOOKDEALER. Together they list about twenty thousand books required every week—over a million a year. Every week-end hundreds of booksellers go carefully through these lists reporting the books they have in stock to their colleagues who require them, who, in turn, as soon as they hear that one is available, quote it to their customer. Perhaps a word of advice may be given here: if a book is required, ask for it in as many shops as possible, but make it clear whether you wish the bookseller to advertise for it, and ask only one to do this. If a book buyer goes from shop to shop in an afternoon asking booksellers to see if they can get a copy of some book for him, the probability is that six advertisements for it will appear in the next week's trade journal; the law of supply and demand will begin to operate, and the man who has a copy will feel that he has put too low a price on a book that is so eagerly sought, and will increase it accordingly.

Booksellers whose principal business is in new books must, nearly always, maintain a general stock. There are a few in large towns that do not, but generally speaking if anyone requires any recently published book he goes to the nearest bookshop and it can be obtained as easily from there as from anywhere else; if it is not in stock it will come from the publishers in a few days at a known cost.

A distinctive feature of the second-hand book trade, however, is its high degree of specialization. Almost every dealer has his own particular interest, and some will be found who deal only in books on one subject, or indeed in the works of one author or group of authors. The small size of many of the units and the fact that they have no need for a high turnover to cover big overhead expenses makes this economically possible. If one requires a second-hand or antiquarian book he should go or write directly to the specialist. This directory is intended to provide a handy guide that will enable the booklover to do this with the minimum of trouble, and also, of course, to fill its place as an essential reference book for the trade.

R.D.

OVERSEAS ANTIQUARIAN BOOKSELLERS' ASSOCIATIONS

Australia and New Zealand

AUSTRALIAN AND NEW ZEALAND ASSOCIATION OF ANTIQUARIAN BOOKSELLERS, P.O. Box 356, Prahran, Victoria 3181, Australia. Founded 1977. 16 members. President: Kenneth Hince. Executive Secretary and Deputy President: Peter Arnold. Treasurer: Jack Bradstreet.

Austria

VERBAND DER ANTIQUARE OESTERREICHS, Gruenangergasse 4, A-1010 Wien. 1. TN: (0222) 52 15 35.

Belgium

SYNDICAT BELGE DE LA LIBRAIRIE ANCIENNE ET MODERNE, Rue de Chêne 21, B-1000 Bruxelles. TN (02) 513 0525. Founded 1948. 49 members. President Albert Van Loock. Vice-president: Jacques Van der Heyde. Secretary: J. Devroe. Treasurer: Claude Van Loock.

Brazil

ASSOCIACAO BRASILEIRA DE LIVREIROS ANTIQUARIOS, Rua Cosme Velho 800, BR-20,000, Rio de Janeiro ZC-01 Brazil.

Canada

ANTIQUARIAN BOOKSELLERS ASSOCIATION OF CANADA, 198 Queen Street West, Toronto, Ontario M5V 1Z2, Canada. President: John D. Townsend.

Denmark

DEN DANSKE ANTIKVARBOGHANDLER-FORENING, P.O. Box 2184. DK-1017K København. TN: (01) 157044. President: Peter Grosell. Founded 1920. 45 members.

Finland (Official languages are Finnish and Swedish)

SUOMEN ANTIKVARIAATTI YHDISTYS RY., P. Makasünikatu 6, Helsinki 13.

FINSKA ANTIKVARIAT FÖRENINGEN, Norra Magasinsgatan 6. Helsingfors 13.

France

SYNDICAT NATIONAL DE LA LIBRIARIE ANCIENNE ET MODERNE, 47 rue Saint-André des Arts, F-75006 Paris. Founded 1913. 300 members. President: Mme. Jeanne Laffitte.

Germany (Federal Republic)

VERBAND DEUTSCHER ANTIQUARE E.V. Die Vereinigung von Buchantiquaren, Autographen- und Graphikhändlern, Unterer Anger 15, D-8000 München 2. TN: (089) 26 38 55. Founded 1949. 240 members. President: Friedrich Zisska. Vice-president: Susanne Koppel. Treasurer: Edwin Vömel. Chairmen: Georg Sauer & Konrad Meuschel.

Italy

ASSOCIAZIONE LIBRAI ANTIQUARI D'ITALIA, Via Jacopo Nardi 6, 50132 Firenze. Founded 1947. 54 members. President: Dr. Renzo Rizzi. Treasurer: Pietro Chellini. Periodical: GAZZETTINO LIBRARIO, 6 issues a year.

Japan

THE ANTIQUARIAN BOOKSELLERS ASSOCIATION OF JAPAN, 29 San-ei-Cho, Shinjuku-ku, Tokyo 160. TN: 357-1411. Founded 1964. 26 members. President: Mitsuo Nitta. Vice-President Kimio Kohketsu. Treasurer: Shuichiro Inoue. Secretary: Takehiko Sakai.

Netherlands

NEDERLANDSCHE VEREENIGING VAN ANTIQUAREN, Kleine Houtstraat 60, 2011-DP Haarlem. TN: (023) 323986. Founded 1935. 82 members. President: A. Gerits. Secretary: F. W. Kuyper. Treasurer: E. M. Mulder.

Norway

NORSK ANTIKVARBOKHANDLERFORENING, Ullevålsveien 1, Oslo 1. TN: (02) 20 78 05. 8 members. President: Bjørn Ringstrøm.

Sweden

SVENSKA ANTIKVARIATFÖRENINGEN, Box 22549, S-104 22, Stockholm.

Switzerland

SYNDICAT DE LA LIBRAIRIE ANCIENNE ET DU COMMERCE DE L'ESTAMPE EN SUISSE, Schloss-Str. 6, FL-9490, Vaduz. TN: (075) 2 32 61. 72 members. President: Walter Alicke. Secretary: Elsbeth Haudenschild. Treasurer: Patrick Cramer.

United States of America

ANTIQUARIAN BOOKSELLERS ASSOCIATION OF AMERICA, 50 Rockefeller Plaza, New York, N.Y. 10020. TN: (212) 757 9395. Over 400 members. President: Elizabeth Woodburn. Vice-President: Louis Weinstein. Secretary: James Lowe. Treasurer: Raymond Wapner.

The badge of the INTERNATIONAL LEAGUE OF ANTIQUARIAN BOOKSELLERS (I.L.A.B.) to which most national associations belong.

CURRENT REFERENCE BOOKS

THE AFRICAN BOOK WORLD AND PRESS: A DIRECTORY. Third revised edition at £45.00. Published by Hans Zell Publishers, P.O. Box 56, Oxford OX1 3EL.

AFRICAN BOOKS IN PRINT, 1978. 2 vols. 1010pp. An index by author, title and subject of over 12,000 works in English, French and African languages. £60.00 the set. Edited Hans Zell. Published by Mansell, 6 All Saints Street, London N1 9RL.

AMERICAN BOOK PRICES CURRENT. 35,000 entries for books sold at auction, U.S.A., Canada, Europe, S. Africa and Australia. 1983, Vol. 89, 1,280pp. American Book Prices Current, P.O. Box 236, Washington CT 06793, U.S.A.

AMERICAN BOOK TRADE DIRECTORY. Lists every kind of book outlet, over 20,000 in 5,000 American and Canadian cities, also book wholesalers, clubs, libraries, publishers etc. 28th edition. Postpaid $89.95. Published by R. R. Bowker Company, 1180 Avenue of the Americas, New York 10036, U.S.A. Available from Kurmaparampil Building, Khrichy 686549, India.

AMERICAN BOOK TRADE IN INDIA: A Directory of Wholesale and Retail Booksellers, edited by Kunnuparampil P. Punnoose, $50. Published by Asian Bookmarket Information Services, 73-47-255th Street, Glen Oaks, New York 11004, U.S.A.

AMERICAN LIBRARY DIRECTORY, Lists 35,000 American and Canadian Libraries. Revised biennially. 35th edition. Published by R. R. Bowker Company, 1180 Avenue of the Americas, New York 10036, U.S.A.

AMERICAN PUBLISHER'S DIRECTORY. 1st edition 1978, 390pp. K. G. Saur, Shropshire House, 2-20 Capper Street, London WC1E 6JA.

ANNUAL REPORT of the American Rare Antiquarian and Out-of-Print Book Trade 1978/79. Edited by Denis Carbonneau. $9.95. Published by BCAR Publications, P.O. Box 50, Cooper Station, New York, N.Y. 10003, U.S.A.

BANGLADESH NATIONAL BIBLIOGRAPHY. Annually. Published by National Library of Bangladesh, 106 Central Road, Dacca 5, Bangladesh.

BOOK-AUCTION RECORDS. A priced and annotated record of books sold at auction in England, Europe and North America. Vol. 79 (1981-82). £50.00. Published annually by Wm. Dawson and Sons, Cannon House, Park Farm Road, Folkestone, Kent CT19 5EE, England.

BOOKDEALERS IN INDIA, PAKISTAN, SRI LANKA etc. A directory of dealers in secondhand and antiquarian books in the Southwest Asian sub-continent. First edition 1977. £3.50. Published by Sheppard Press Limited, P.O. Box 42, Russell Chambers, Covent Garden, London WC2E 8AX.

BOOKDEALERS IN NORTH AMERICA. A directory of dealers in secondhand and antiquarian books in Canada and the United States of America. Ninth edition. £10.50. Published by Sheppard Press Limited, P.O. Box 42, Russell Chambers, Covent Garden, London WC2E 8AX.

THE BOOKMAN'S GLOSSARY edited by Jean Peters, 6th edition. £19.00. Published by Bowker Publishing Co., P.O. Box 5, Epping CM16 4BU.

BOOKMAN'S GUIDE TO AMERICANA. Eighth Edition. By Norman Heard. £15.75. Published by The Scarecrow Press, Inc., Metuchen, New Jersey, U.S.A. Distributors: Bailey Bros. & Swinfen Ltd., Warner House, Folkestone, Kent.

BOOKMAN'S PRICE INDEX. Volumes 1 through 22 in print. Edited by Daniel F. McGrath. Published by Gale Research Company, Book Tower, Detroit, Michigan 48226, U.S.A. £125.00 per volume.

BOOKS IN PRINT. 1982-83. Lists 600,000 books in print from American publishers and distributors: Annually in October. Postpaid price in U.S.A. $149.50 for 6-volume set. Published by R. R. Bowker Company, 1180 Avenue of the Americas, New York, NY 10036, U.S.A.

THE BOOK TRADE IN CANADA. Published annually. The standard reference on the Canadian book industry, includes complete listings for publishers, distributors, booksellers, etc. £12.00. Ampersand Pubsishing Services, RR1, Caledon, Ontario L0N 1C0, Canada.

A BOOK WORLD DIRECTORY OF THE ARAB COUNTRIES, TURKEY AND IRAN. Compiled by Anthony Rudkin and Irene Butcher. Lists' Newspapers, Periodicals, Publishers, Libraries and Booksellers. £27.50. Published by Mansell, 6 All Saints' Street, London N1 9RL.

BRITISH BOOKS AND LIBRARIES. A series of eight tape/slide programmes. The British Council, 65 Davies Street, London W1Y 2AA. Distributed by Sweet and Maxwell.

BRITISH BOOKS IN PRINT. Lists books in print of British publishers. Annually in November. Post paid price in Britain £59.00, Overseas £67.00. Published by J. Whitaker and Sons Limited, 12 Dyott Street, London WC1A 1DF.

BRITISH NATIONAL BIBLIOGRAPHY. Records each week new British books with cumulations in last issue of month, two interim cumulations and annual volume. Published by the British Library Bibliographic Services Division, 2 Sherston Street, London W1V 4BH.

CUMULATIVE BOOK INDEX. A world list of books in the English language. Eleven issues a year and permanent bound annual cumulation. Bound four or five year cumulations through 1956; two years cumulations 1957 through 1968. Published by the H. W. Wilson Company, 950 University Avenue, Bronx, New York 10452, U.S.A.

A DIRECTORY OF LITERARY TERMS. By J. A. Cuddon. Published by Andre Deutsch Ltd., 105 Great Russell Street, London W.C.1. at £11.50.

DIRECTORY OF AMERICAN BOOK SPECIALISTS, 4th edition 1981. Published by Continental Publishing Co., 1261 Broadway, New York, NY 10001, U.S.A.

DIRECTORY OF AMERICAN BOOK WORKERS. Compiled by Renée Roff. $20.95 including postage. Published by Nicholas T. Smith, P.O. Box 66, Bronxville, NY 10708, U.S.A.

A DIRECTORY OF DEALERS IN SECONDHAND AND ANTIQUARIAN BOOKS IN THE BRITISH ISLES. 11th edition, (1984-86) £12.00. (N. America $25). Published by Sheppard Press, P.O. Box 42 Russell Chambers, Covent Garden, London WC2E 8AX.

DIRECTORY OF JAPANESE PUBLISHING AND BOOKSELLING. 2nd edition. £13.00. Published by the British Council, 65 Davies Street, London W1Y 2AA.

DIRECTORY OF PUBLISHING AND BOOKSELLING IN BRAZIL. Published by the British Council, 65 Davies Street, London W1Y 2AA. £10.50.

DIRECTORY OF THE INDIAN BOOK INDUSTRY. Edited by Dinkar Trivedi. Rs. 50. Published by New Order Book Co., Ellis Bridge, Ahmedabad 380006, India.

DIRECTORY OF PUBLISHING, in Great Britain, the Commonwealth, Ireland, South Africa and Pakistan 1982-83, £12.50. Cassell and Publishers Association, 8 Trident Way, Brent Road, Southall, Middlesex.

DIRECTORY OF SPECIALIZED AMERICAN BOOKDEALERS. 350pp. £10.25. Published by The Moretus Press, 274 Madison Avenue, New York, N.Y. 10016, U.S.A.

DIRECTORY OF SPECIALIST BOOKDEALERS IN THE UNITED KINGDOM HANDLING MAINLY NEW BOOKS. Second edition. Full descriptive entries for over 600 businesses, as well as listings of related directories. D4. 262pp, paper bound. £5.90. First supplement 1983. £3.50. Peter Marcan, 31 Rowliff Road, High Wycombe, Buckinghamshire.

EIGHTEENTH CENTURY BRITISH BOOKS, an author union catalogue extracted from the British Museum, Bodleian Library and University Library Cambridge Catalogues, by F. J. G. Robinson, G. Averley, D. R. Esslemont and P. J. Wallis. Published by Wm. Dawson & Sons, Cannon House, Folkestone, Kent. 1981. 5 vols. £1,250.00.

EUROPEAN BOOKDEALERS. A directory of dealers in secondhand and antiquarian books in the continent of Europe. Triennially, fifth edition £9.00 ($21). Published by Sheppard Press Limited, P.O. Box 42, Russell Chambers, Covent Garden, London WC2E 8AX.

FIRST PRINTINGS OF AMERICAN AUTHORS: Contributions Towards Descriptive Checklists. Four volumes. Matthew J. Bruccoli, Series Editor. C. E. Frazer Clark, Jr., Managing Editor. Richard Layman, Project Editor. Benjamin Franklin V, Associate Editor. 1,648 pages. Annotations; Author portraits; Reproductions of 3,000 title pages, dust jackets, and bindings; Cumulative index to volumes 1-4 in Vol. 4. $320.00 set. Published by Gale Research Co., Detroit, MI 48226.

GLAISTER'S GLOSSARY OF THE BOOK by Geoffrey Ashall Glaister. 548pp. 2nd edition. £50. Published by George Allen & Unwin, P.O. Box 18, Park Lane, Hemel Hempstead HP2 4TE.

INDEX TO THE STRAND MAGAZINE 1891-1950, by Geraldine Beare. Published by Greenwood Press, 88 Post Road West, P.O. Box 5007, Westport, CT 06881, U.S.A. $75.00 (U.K. and European orders to Westport Publications, 3 Henrietta Street, London WC2E 8LU).

GUIDE DES LIBRAIRES D'ANCIEN ET D'OCCASION par Denis Basane, donne l'adresse de 273 librairies. Editions Hubschmid et Bouret, Paris.

INTERNATIONAL BIBLIOGRAPHY OF REPRINTS/INTERNATIONALE BIBLIOGRAPHIE DER PRINTS. Band I, Books and Serials; Band II, Annuals and Periodicals. DM. 240,-. Published by K. G. Saur Verlag, München, Germany.

INTERNATIONAL BIBLIOGRAPHY OF THE BOOK TRADE AND LIBRARIANSHIP. 1981. DM. 148,-. K. G. Saur Verlag, München, Germany.

INTERNATIONAL BOOKS IN PRINT. 3rd edition. 1983. English language titles published outside the U.S.A. and U.K. 2 vols, 1,500pp, DM398,-. K. G. Saur, Verlag, München, Germany.

INTERNATIONAL DIRECTORY OF ANTIQUARIAN BOOKSELLERS. Published by I.L.A.B. A world list of members of organisations belonging to the International League of Antiquarian Booksellers. 7th edition 1980.

INTERNATIONAL DIRECTORY OF ARTS. Art Address Verlag, Müller G.m.b.H. & Co. KG., D-6000 Frankfurt an Main, 1. P.O. Box 2187.

INTERNATIONAL DIRECTORY OF BOOK COLLECTORS. 4th edition, £18.50. Published by the Trigon Press, 117 Kent House Road, Beckenham, Kent BR3 1JJ, England.

INTERNATIONAL DIRECTORY OF BOOKSELLERS. Lists more than 63,000 bookshops and wholesalers from 134 countries. £77.00. Available in U.K. and Commonwealth. Library Association Publishing, 7 Ridgmount Street, London WC1E 7AE.

INTERNATIONAL ISBN PUBLISHER'S DIRECTORY. 1980 Edition. 1,400pp. 55,000 publishers from 29 countries, £41.00. Published by J. Whitaker & Sons, 12 Dyott Street, London WC1A 1DF.

INTERNATIONAL LITERARY MARKET PLACE 1983-84. 551pp. £47.75. Bowker (New York), P.O. Box 5, Epping SM16 4BU.

INTERNATIONAL MAPS AND ATLASES IN PRINT. ed. Kenneth Winch $47.50. R. R. Bowker Company, New York.

JAHRBUCH DER AUKTIONSPREISE für Bücher, Handschriften und Autographen. Veröffentl. bei Dr. Ernst Hauswedell & Co., Rosenbergstrasse 113, D-7000 Stuttgart 1, Deutschland. Bericht über Bücher, Handschriften und Manuskripte, die auf Auktionen in Deutschland, Holland, Österreich und der Schweiz im Laufe eines Jahres gehandelt werden. Im Anhang eine Liste wichtiger Händler und ihrer Spezialitäten.

LIBRARIES IN THE UNITED KINGDOM AND THE REPUBLIC OF IRELAND. 9th edition. Compiled by Feona Hamilton, paper, £9.50. Library Association Publishing. 7 Ridgmount Street, London WC1E 7AE.

LIBROS EN VENTA. Supplement 1978. Lists 20,000 Spanish language books available. ed. Mary Turner. $42.50. R. R. Bowker, New York.

LES LIVRES DISPONIBLES. Index of French books in print. 5,020pp. listing over 237,625 French language books. Cercle de la Librairie, 35 rue Grégorie de Tours, F-75279, Paris. Cedex 06.

LYLE OFFICIAL BOOKS REVIEW 1980. Compiled and edited by Liz Taylor. £6.95. Published by Lyle Publications, Glenmayne, Galashiels, Scotland.

THE MARKET FOR BRITISH BOOKS IN FRANCE. The British Council, 65 Davies Street, London W1Y 2AA. 2nd edition, 1984.

MEDICAL BOOKS AND SERIALS IN PRINT 1982. 1,800pp. $62.50. Published by R. R. Bowker Company, New York.

BRITISH PAPERBACKS IN PRINT. A guide to over 50,000 paperback books in print in Great Britain. Published by J. Whitaker & Sons Limited, 12 Dyott Street, London WC1A 1DF, at £19.00 U.K., £21.50 Export.

PUBLISHERS IN THE UNITED KINGDOM AND THEIR ADDRESSES. A list of over 2,000 publishers, £2.25. Published by J. Whitaker & Sons Limited, 12 Dyott Street, London WC1A 1DF.

PUBLISHERS' INTERNATIONAL DIRECTORY, 10th edition 1983. DM348,-. Published by K. G. Saur Verlag, München, Germany.

PUBLISHERS WEEKLY YEARBOOK. 252pp. £34.75. Paperback £26.00. 1983 edition. Published by Bowker, New York, available from Bowker Publishing Co., P.O. Box 5, Epping, Essex CM16 4BU.

SCIENTIFIC, ENGINEERING AND MEDICAL SOCIETIES IN PRINT 1980-81. 4th edition. 525pp. $65.00. Published by R. R. Bowker Co., 1180 Avenue of the Americas, New York, N.Y. 10036, U.S.A.

A SHORT-TITLE CATALOGUE OF BOOKS PRINTED IN ENGLAND, SCOTLAND & IRELAND AND OF ENGLISH BOOKS PRINTED ABROAD, 1475-1640. Second revised and enlarged edition. Vol. 2: I-Z. By W. A. Jackson, F. S. Ferguson and Katharine F. Pantzer. Published by The Bibliographical Society, British Academy, Burlington House, Piccadilly, London W1V 0NS, at £70.00.

SUBJECT GUIDE TO BOOKS IN PRINT 1982-83. Published by R. R. Bowker Company, 1180 Avenue of the Americas, New York, N.Y. 10036. Classifies more than 500,000 non-fiction titles in-print of almost every American publisher under 62,500 subject headings. Issued annually, $99.50 for 3 volume set.

TASCHENBUCH DER AUKTIONSPREISE ALTER BÜCHER. Annual record of auction prices of old books in Germany, Austria and Switzerland. Volume 7 (Season 1981). £28.50. Published by S. Radtke, Aachen, Germany.

TITLES OF ENGLISH BOOKS AND OF FOREIGN BOOKS PRINTED IN ENGLAND. By A. F. Allison and V. F. Goldsmith. Published by Wm. Dawson & Sons Ltd., Cannon House, Folkestone, Kent. Vol. 1: 1475-1640. £10.00. Vol. 2: 1641-1700. £20.00.

ULRICH'S INTERNATIONAL PERIODICALS DIRECTORY 1982. (21st edition). Published by R. R. Bowker Company, 1180 Avenue of the Americas, New York, N.Y. 10036. A guide to over 67,000 world periodicals under 385 subject headings. Each entry tells where magazine is published, price, frequency of issue, where indexed or abstracted, whether it carries advertisements, book reviews, or any of twenty descriptive characteristics. 2 vols. $89.50.

UNIVERSITY LIBRARIES IN INDIA: A Guide for Direct Mail Promotion, edited by Kunnuparampil P. Punnoose, $25. Published by Asian Bookmarket Information Service, 73-47-255th Street, Glen Oaks, New York 11044, U.S.A. Available from Kunnuparampil Buildings, Kurichy 686549, India.

USED BOOK PRICE GUIDE. Standard reference work for pricing rare, scarce and used books. 2 volume set, paper bound $37, hard cover $45. Price Guide Publishers, 525 Kenmore Station, Kenmore, WA 98028, U.S.A.

VERZEICHNIS LIEFERBARER BÜCHER (German Books in Print) 1983, 13th edition. K. G. Saur, Shropshire House, 2-20 Capper Street, London WC1E 6JA.

WRITER'S MARKET. Published by Writer's Digest, 9933 Alliance Road, Cincinnati, OH 45242. 53rd annual edition, 1983. 936pp. $18.95.

WHITAKER'S CUMULATIVE BOOK LIST. A complete record of British book production. Four quarterly parts, one of which is the annual volume. £21.00. Published by J. Whitaker and Sons Limited, 12 Dyott Street, London WC1A 1DF.

WILLINGS PRESS GUIDE 1983. Facts on over 17,000 newspapers, periodicals and annuals, world wide. £25.00. Published by Thomas Skinner Directories. Windsor Court, East Grinstead House, East Grinstead, West Sussex RH19 1XE. TN: (0342) 26972.

WORLD GUIDE TO SPECIAL LIBRARIES, 1983. DM240,-, edited by Helga Lengenfelder. Published by K. G. Saur Verlag, München, Germany.

PERIODICALS

Literary Magazines and Book Trade Papers

THE AFRICAN BOOK PUBLISHING RECORD. Covers new and forthcoming African publications. Quarterly. £38.00 per annum. Published by Hans Zell Publishers, P.O. Box 56, Oxford OX1 3EL, England.

THE AMERICAN BOOK COLLECTOR. Six times a year. Annual subscription $18.50 (individual), $23.25 (institution). Editor: Anthony Fair. Published by Moretus Press, 274 Madison Avenue, New York, NY 10016.

ABMR (ANTIQUARIAN BOOK MONTHLY REVIEW). Monthly magazine containing articles, book reviews, auction reports and catalogue news. Editor: Jennifer Hainsworth. ABMR Publications Ltd., 52 St. Clement's, Oxford OX4 1AG. TN: (0865) 721615.

AB BOOKMANS WEEKLY: ANTIQUARIAN BOOKMAN. Founded 1948. Weekly and AB Bookmans Yearbooks (two parts). Editor and published: Jacob L. Chernofsky, AB Weekly, P.O. Box AB, Clifton, NJ 07015, U.S.A. Telephone (021) 772-0020.

ANTIQUES TRADE GAZETTE, 116 Long Acre, London WC2E 9PA. Weekly.

ANTIQUARIES JOURNAL, Established 1921, articles cover a wide variety of antiquarian subjects. Subscription £26.00 per annum. Oxford University Press, Journals Department, Walton Street, Oxford OX2 6DP. TN: (0865) 56767.

AUS DEM ANTIQUARIAT. Published from Römerstrasse 7. D-8000 München 40. TN: (089) 34 13 31. Monthly. Editor: Dr. Karl H. Pressler.

L'ARGUS DU LIVRE ANCIEN & MODERNE. Tous les trois mois. Description et prix des ouvrages passés en ventes publiques en France et à l'Etranger. Rédaction, 18 rue Dauphine, 76006 Paris, France.

THE BIBLIOTHECK, edited from Saint Andrews University Library. Bibliographical articles, notes and reviews of Scottish interest. Annual supplement lists books, reviews, essays and articles on Scottish literature published in the preceding year. Published by a Scottish Group of the Library Association from the National Library of Scotland, Edinburgh EH1 1EW.

THE BOOK COLLECTOR, 90 Great Russell Street, London WC1B 3PS. Telephone: 01-637 3029. Established 1952, Quarterly Subscription £15.00 ($35), plus post and packing £1.50 ($2.50).

THE BOOKDEALER. Trade weekly for secondhand and antiquarian books for sale and wanted. Published by Werner Shaw Limited, Suite 34, 26 Charing Cross Road, London WC2H 0DH. Telephone: (01) 240 5890.

THE BOOKSELLER. Weekly journal of the new book trade in Britain. Subscription £25.00 per annum. Published by J. Whitaker and Sons Limited, 12 Dyott Street, London WC1A 1DF. Telephone 01-836 8911.

BOOKS FROM FINLAND, quarterly English-language journal of writing from and about Finland. Subscription Fmk.80 per annum. Published by Helsinki University Library, P.O. Box 312, SF-00171, Helsinki 17.

BOOKS OF THE MONTH AND BOOKS TO COME. Monthly list of all books published in U.K. during the month and forthcoming publications for next two months. J. Whitaker & Sons, 12 Dyott Street, London WC1A 1DF.

BOOK WORLD ADVERTISER. Monthly. Articles, reviews and advertisements of books for sale and wanted. Published by Polybooks Ltd., 115 Old Street, London EC1V 9JR. TN: (01) 251 4995.

BÖRSENBLATT FÜR DEN DEUTSCHEN BUCHHANDEL (Angebotene und Gesuchte Bücher). Buchhändler-Vereinigung G.m.b.H., D-6000 Frankfurt am Main. Postfach 2404.

BRITISH BOOK NEWS, The British Council, 65 Davies Street, London W1Y 2AA. 01-499 8011.

BRITISH LIBRARY JOURNAL, Established 1975, a scholarly journal devoted to the study of the library's collections and to the historical archives preserved in the Department of Manuscripts. Oxford University Press, Journals Department, Walton Street, Oxford OX2 6DP. TN: (0865) 56767.

BULLETIN DU BIBLIOPHILE, 18 rue Dauphine, F-75006 Paris, France.

CLASSICAL QUARTERLY, Established 1907 (new series 1951), devoted to Greco-Roman antiquity in the English-speaking world. Oxford University Press, Journals Department, Walton Street, Oxford OX2 6DP. (0865) 56767.

CLASSICAL REVIEW, Established 1887 (new series 1951). Contains expert reviews of new work dealing with the literatures and civilisations of ancient Greece and Rome. Oxford University Press, Journals Department, Walton Street, Oxford OX2 6DP. TN: (0865) 56767.

THE CLIQUE. The antiquarian booksellers weekly. Established 1890. By subscription to booksellers only. Contains advertisements and lists of books wanted and for sale in Britain and elsewhere. Published by The Clique, c/o Stoate & Bishop (Printers), Saint James Square, Cheltenham, Glos. GL50 3PU. TN: (0242) 36741.

CONTEMPORARY REVIEW, 61 Carey Street, London WC2A 2JG. 01-242 3215. Incorporating THE FORTNIGHTLY founded 1866. Editor: Rosalind Wade.

CRITICAL QUARTERLY, Manchester University Press, Oxford Road, Manchester M13 9PL. 061-273 5539.

L'ESOPO, Revista trimestrale di bibliofilia. Mario Scognamizlio, via Rovello 1, 20121 Milano, Italy.

THE FICTION MAGAZINE, 5 Jeffreys Street, London, N.W.1. TN: (01) 267 2357.

FINE PRINT. A Review for the Arts of the Book. Quarterly, January, April, July and October. Published by Fine Print, P.O. Box 7741, San Francisco, CA 94120, U.S.A.

FOLIO QUARTERLY, Folio Society Ltd., 202 Great Suffolk Street, London SE1 1PR. 01-407 7411.

GAZZETTINO LIBRARIO. Richieste ed offerte di libri antichi e moderni. Pubblicazione bimestrale. Gazzettino Librario, Via J. Nardi 6, 50132 Firenze, Italy.

GREECE AND ROME, Established 1931, (new series 1954), places the main emphasis on the literary evaluation of the major authors, both Greek and Roman. Oxford University Press, Journals Department, Walton Street, Oxford OX2 6DP. TN: (0865) 56767.

INDEX ON CENSORSHIP, 39C Highbury Place, London N5 1QX.

INDIAN PUBLISHER AND BOOKSELLER. In English, monthly. Rs. 15 per annum. Published by Popular Book Depot, Dr Bhadkamkar Marg, Bombay 400007, India.

THE LIBRARY. Transactions of the Bibliographical Society, quarterly, £20 per annum. Oxford University Press, Journals Department, Walton Street, Oxford OX2 6DP.

LIBRARY ASSOCIATION RARE BOOKS GROUP NEWSLETTER, Editor: Dr Brian Hillyard, National Library of Scotland, George IV Bridge, Edinburgh EH1 1EW. Correspondence about subscriptions to Miss J. Archibald, English Antiquarian Section, British Library Reference Division, Great Russell Street, London WC1B 3DG.

THE LISTENER, BBC, 35 Marylebone High Street, London W1M 4AA. (01) 580 5577.

LITERARY MARKET REVIEW. In English, Quarterly. U.S. $5.00 per annum. Published from Kunnuparampil Buildings, Kurichy 686549, Kottayam District, Kerala, India.

THE LITERARY REVIEW, 27 Goodge Street, London W1P 1FD. TN: (01) 636 3992. Telex: 919034. Editor: Gillian Greenwood.

THE LONDON MAGAZINE, 30 Thurloe Place, London, S.W.7 Telephone: (01) 589 0618.

LONDON REVEIW OF BOOKS, 6a Bedford Square, London, W.C.1.

MINIATURE BOOK NEWS, 16 Dromara Road, St. Louis, Missouri 63124, U.S.A.

NEW STATESMAN, 14-16 Farringdon Lane, London EC1R 3AU. Telephone: (01) 253 2001.

NEW YORK REVIEW OF BOOKS, 250 West 57th Street, New York, NY 10107, U.S.A.

PUBLISHER'S WEEKLY. Weekly reports of new books published; promotion, market and foreign book news, etc. Enlarged Spring and Falls numbers, containing information and announcements on publishing programmes. Published by R. R. Bowker Co., 1180 Avenue of the Americas, New York, NY 10036, U.S.A.

QUILL AND QUIRE, Journal of the Canadian Book Trade, 56 The Esplanade, (Suite 213), Toronto, Ontario M5E 1A7. TN: (416) 364 3333.

THE SPECTATOR, 56 Doughty Street, London WC1N 2LL. 01-405 1706. Publishes each week a Books Wanted column as free service for book collectors.

TAAB WEEKLY, THE LIBRARY BOOKSELLER. P.O. Box 239, W.O.B. West Orange, NJ 07052, U.S.A. Founded 1944. Provides the antiquarian bookseller with a direct link to libraries and private buyers. Publisher: Albert Saifer.

THE TIMES LITERARY SUPPLEMENT. Published by Times Newspapers Ltd., Priory House, Saint John's Lane, London EC1M 4BX. TN: (01) 253 3000. Telex: 264971.

TRIBUNE, 306 Grays Inn Road, London WC1X 8DY. (01) 278 0911.

ABBREVIATIONS

The following are some of the abbreviations commonly used within the book trade. Frequently they will be employed without punctuation. Confusion can result from improper and over-use of abbreviation, and for the reporting of expensive items it is recommended that all words be clearly written, or type-written, in full. A list of abbreviations used will be found at the beginning of most catalogues.

A.B.A.	Antiquarian Booksellers' Association
A.B.A.A.	Antiquarian Booksellers' Association of America

A.D.	Autograph document
A.D.s.	Autograph document, signed
A.e.g.	All edges gilt
A.L.	Autograph letter, not signed
A.D.*	Autograph document, with seal
A.L.s.	Autograph letter, signed
a.v.	Authorised version
B.A.R.	Book Auction Records
Bd.	Bound
Bdg.	Binding
Bds.	Boards
B.L.	Black letter
C., ca.	Circa (approximately)
C. & p.	Collated and perfect
Cat.	Catalogue
Cent.	Century
Cf.	Calf
C.I.F.	Cost, insurance and freight
Cl.	Cloth
Col(d).	Colour(ed)
C.O.D.	Cash on delivery
Cont.	Contemporary
C.O.R.	Cash on receipt
Cr. 8vo.	Crown octavo
d.e.	Deckle edges
Dec.	Decorated
D-j., d-w.	Dust jacket, dust wrapper
E.D.L.	Edition de luxe
Edn.	Edition
Endp., e.p.	Endpaper(s)
Eng., engr.	Engraved, engraving
Ex-lib.	Ex-library
Facs.	Facsimile
Fcp.	Foolscap
F.	Fine
F., ff.	Folio, folios
Fo., fol.	Folio (book size)
F.O.B.	Free on board
Fp., front.	Frontispiece
Free	Post free
G.	Good
G., gt.	Gilt edges
G.L.	Gothic letter
Hf. bd.	Half bound
Illum.	Illuminated
Ill(s).	Illustrated, illustration(s)
Imp.	Imperial
Impft.	Imperfect
Inscr.	Inscribed, inscription
Ital.	Italic letter
Lea.	Leather

Lev.	Levant morocco	q.v.	Quod vide (which see)
Ll.	Leaves	Qto.	Quarto
L.P.	Large paper	Rev.	Revised
M.	Mint	Rom.	Roman letter
Mco., mor.	Morocco	S.L.	Sine loco (without place)
M.e.	Marbled edges	Sgd.	Signed
M.S.(S.)	Manuscript(s)	Sig.	Signature
N.d.	No date	S.N.	Sine nomine (without name of printer)
n. ed.	New edition		
n.p.	No place (of publication)	Spr.	Sprinkled
		T.e.g.	Top edge gilt
Ob., obl.	Oblong	Thk.	Thick
Oct.	Octavo	T.L.s.	Typed letter, signed
O.p.	Out of print	T.p.	Title-page
P.	Page	T.S.	Typescript
P.f.	Post free	unbd.	Unbound
Pict.	Pictorial	uncut	Uncut (pages not trimmed)
Pl(s).	Plate(s)		
Port.	Portrait	und.	Undated
P.P.	Printed privately	V.d.	Various dates
Pp.	Pages	V.g.	Very good
Prelims.	Preliminary pages	Vol.	Volume
Pseud.	Pseudonym(ous)	W.a.f.	With all faults
Ptd.	Printed	Wraps.	Wrappers

SIZE OF BOOKS

These are only approximate, as trimming varies

	Octavo (8vo.)		Quarto (4to.)	
	Inches	*Centimetres*	*Inches*	*Centimetres*
FOOLSCAP	6¾×4½	17.1×10.7	8½×6¾	21.5×17.1
CROWN	7½×5	19.0×12.7	10 ×7½	25.4×19.0
LARGE POST	8¼×5¼	20.9×13.3	10½×8¼	26.6×20.9
DEMY	8¾×5	22.2×14.2	11¼×8¾	28.5×22.2
MEDIUM	9 ×5¾	22.8×14.6	11½×9	29.2×22.8
ROYAL	10 ×6¼	25.4×15.8	12½×10	31.7×25.4
SUPER ROYAL	10 ×6¾	25.4×17.1	13½×10	34.2×25.4
IMPERIAL	11 ×7½	27.9×19.0	15 ×11	38.0×27.9
FOOLSCAP FOLIO		34.2×21.5	13½×8½	

SERVICES AND SUPPLIES

BOOK AUCTIONEERS

NOEL D. ABEL, 32 Norwich Road, Watton, Norfolk. 0953 881204.

ALDRIDGES OF BATH, The Auction Galleries, 130/132 Walcot Street, Bath, Avon. (0225) 62830.

BARNARD & LEARMONT, 18 Bathurst Walk, Richings Park, Iver, Bucks. 0753 652024.

BIDDLE & WEBB, Ladywood Middleway, Birmingham B16 0PP. TN: (021) 455 8042.

BLOOMSBURY BOOK AUCTIONS, 6A Bedford Square, London, W.C.1.

BONHAMS, Montpelier Galleries, Montpelier St., Knightsbridge, London SW7 1HH. 01-584 9161. Five auctions a year. Contact Christopher Johnston with enquiries.

BUCKELL & BALLARD (FINE ARTS), 49 Parsons Street, Banbury, Oxon. OX16 8PF. (0295) 53197.

BURSTOW & HEWETT, 12-13 High Street, Battle, Sussex. TN: (04246) 2374.

H. C. CHAPMAN & SON, The Auction Mart, North Street, Scarborough, Yorkshire YO11 1DL. TN: (0723) 72424.

CHRISTIE'S, 8 King Street, St. James's, London SW1Y 6QT. (01) 839 9060.

CHRISTIE'S & EDMISTON'S, 164-166 Bath Street, Glasgow G2 4TG. TN: (041) 332 8134.

CHRISTIE'S SOUTH KENSINGTON LTD., 85 Old Brompton Road, London SW7 3JS. (01) 581 2231. Telex: 922061.

CUBITT & WEST FINE ART AUCTION GALLERIES, Millmead, Guildford, Surrey. (0483) 504030.

DREWEATT, WATSON & BARTON, Donnington Priory, Donnington, Newbury, Berks. RG13 2JE. TN: (0635) 31234. Telex: 848580.

EDDISONS, Argus Chambers, Broadway, Bradford, West Yorkshire BD1 1HH. (0274) 734101. Telex: 55169.

EKINS DILLEY & HANDLEY, The Salerooms, The Market, St. Ives, Cambs. 0480 68144.

GARROD TURNER, 50 St. Nicholas Street, Ipswich, Suffolk. 0473 54664.

GEERING & COLYER, Hawkhurst, Kent TN18 4AD. TN: (05805) 3181.

GLENDINING & CO., Blenstock House, 7 Blenheim Street, New Bond Street, London W1Y 9LD. 01-493 2445.

GRAVES SON & PILCHER, 71 Church Road, Hove, Sussex BN3 2GL. 0273 735266.

JOHN P. GRAY & SON LTD., 10 Green Street, Cambridge. TN: (0223) 350 862.

GROUNDS & CO., 2 Nene Quay, Wisbech, Cambs. PE13 1AG. (0945) 585041.

HAMMOND & CO., Cambridge Place, Cambridge CB2 1NS. TN: (0223) 356067.

HARMERS OF LONDON STAMP AUCTIONEERS LTD., 41 New Bond Street, London W1A 4EH. TN: (01) 629 0218.

HARVEY'S AUCTIONS LTD., 14-18 Neal Street, London WC2H 9LZ. TN: (01) 240 1464.

HEATHCOTE BALL & CO., 47 New Walk, Leicester LE1 6TE. 0533 544001.

HONITON GALLERIES, LAURENCE & MARTIN TAYLOR, High Street, Honiton, Devon. 0404 2404.

RAYMOND P. INMAN, The Auction Galleries, 35 Temple Street, Brighton, Sussex BN1 3BH. 0273 774777.

JOLLY'S OF BATH (see Phillips & Jolly's).

LAMBERT & FOSTER, 77 Commercial Road, Paddock Wood, Near Tonbridge, Kent TN12 6DR. 089 283 2325.

W. H. LANE & SON, The Central Auction Rooms, 67 Morab Road, Penzance, Cornwall. (0736) 61447, and The Central Auction Rooms, Kinterbury House, Saint Andrew's Cross, Plymouth, Devon. (0752) 669298; and the Central Auction Rooms, Belmoit, Wadebridge, Cornwall. (020 881) 2059.

LAWRENCE FINE ART OF CREWKERNE, Auctioneers & Valuers, South Street, Crewkerne, Somerset TA18 8AB. (0460) 73041.

LOCKE & ENGLAND, 1 & 2 Euston Place, Leamington Spa, Warks. CV32 4LW. 0926 27988.

GEORGE MEALY & SONS, The Square, Castlecomer, Co. Kilkenny, Ireland. 056 41229 (through operator), and 2 & 3 Proby's Lane, Dublin.

MESSENGER MAY BAVERSTOCK, 93 High Street, Godalming, Surrey GU7 1AL. (048 68) 23567.

MOORE, ALLEN & INNOCENT, 33 Castle Street, Cirencester, Gloucestershire GL7 1QD. (0285) 2862.

MORPHETS OF HARROGATE, 4-6 Albert Street, Harrogate, N. Yorkshire HG1 1JL. (0423) 502282.

D. M. NESBIT & CO., Southsea Salerooms, 7 Clarendon Road, Southsea, Portsmouth, Hants. PO5 2ED. (0705) 820785.

NICHOLAS, 12 High Street, Streatley, Berkshire RG8 9HY. TN: Goring 872318.

OUTHWAITE & LITHERLAND, Kingsway Galleries, Fontenoy Street, Liverpool L3 2BE. (051) 236 6561.

OXBORROWS, ARNOTT & CALVER, 14 Church Street, Woodbridge, Suffolk IP12 IDH. (03943) 2244.

PARKINS, 18 Malden Road, Cheam, Surrey. (01) 644 6127. Books included in first Monday sale each month.

PARSONS WELCH & COWELL, 129 High Street, Sevenoaks, Kent. (0732) 451211.

PEARSONS, 99 Fleet Road, Fleet, Hants. (02514) 3166, and Walcote Chambers, High Street, Winchester, Hampshire GU13 8PL. (0962) 64444.

PHILLIPS FINE ART AUCTIONEERS, 98 Sauchiehall Street, Glasgow. (041) 332 3386.

PHILLIPS, 17a East Parade, Leeds, Yorkshire LS1 2BU. (0532) 448011.

PHILLIPS & JOLLYS, Auction Rooms of Bath, 1 Old King Street, Bath, Avon BA1 1DD. (0225) 310609.

PHILLIPS IN KNOWLE, The Old House, Station Road, Knowle, Solihull, West Midlands B93 0HT. (056 45) 6151.

PHILLIPS IN SCOTLAND, 65 George Street, Edinburgh EH2 2JL. 031 225 2266, and 98 Sauchiehall Street, Glasgow G2 3DQ. 041 332 3386.

PHILLIPS (OXFORD), 39 Park End Street, Oxford OX1 1JD. (0865) 723524.

PHILLIPS, Blenstock House, 7 Blenheim Street, London W1Y 0AS. (01) 629 6602.

PHILLIPS WEST 2, 10 Salem Road, London W2 4BU. (01) 221 5303.

RENDELLS, 13 Market Street, Newton Abbot, Devon. (0626) 3881.

RUSSELL, BALDWIN & BRIGHT, Ryelands Road, Leominster, Herefordshire. (0568) 3897.

SANDOE, LUCE, PANES, Chipping Manor Salerooms, The Estate Offices, Wotton under Edge, Glos. GL12 7HD. (0453) 843193.

SOTHEBY HUMBERTS, Magdalene House, Taunton, Somerset. (0823) 88441.

SOTHEBY'S, Pulborough, Sussex RH20 1AJ. TN: (07982) 3831.

SOTHEBY PARKE BERNET & CO., Bloomfield Place, off New Bond Street, London W1A 2AA. (01) 493 8080.

SOTHEBY'S, Fine Art Auctioneers, 112 George Street, Edinburgh EH2 4LH. (031) 226 7201, also at 146 West Regent Street, Glasgow G2 2RQ. (041) 221-4817.

HENRY SPENCER & SONS, 20 The Square, Retford, Nottinghamshire DN22 6DJ. TN: (0777) 708633, and at Sheffield, South Yorkshire, Leeds, West Yorkshire, and Saint Annes, Lancashire.

TAVINER'S OF BRISTOL, Prewett Street, Bristol BS1 6PB. 0272 25996.

TAYLOR, LANE & CREBER, The Western Auction Rooms, 38 North Hill, Plymouth, Devon PL4 8EQ. (0752) 670700.

THOMSON, RODDICK & LAURIE, 24 Lowther Street, Carlisle, Cumbria. (0228) 28939.

WALLIS & WALLIS, Regency House, 1 Albion Street, Lewes, Sussex BN7 2NJ. (07916) 3137. Telex: 896691.

THOMAS WATSON & SON, Northumberland Street, Darlington, Co. Durham. (0325) 62555 and 62559.

WEST LONDON AUCTIONS, 7-21 King Street, Acton, London, W.3. TN: (01) 993 1355.

WHITTON & LAING, Devon & Exeter Auction Galleries, 32 Okehampton Street, Exeter, Devon. (0392) 52621.

P. F. WINDIBANK, 18-20 Reigate Road, Dorking, Surrey RH4 1SG. (0306) 884556.

WINGETT & SON, 24-25 Chester Street, Wrexham, Clwyd LL13 8BP. (0978) 353553.

WOOLLEY & WALLIS, The Castle Auction Mart, 51 Castle Street, Salisbury, Wiltshire SP1 2SU. (0722) 21711.

CRAFT BOOKBINDERS

The following are able to undertake the repair and rebinding of old books. It is recommended that full details of binding style, materials, etc., be discussed with the binder before any work is ordered, and that an estimate be obtained both as to likely cost and time required for completion.

F. F. ALLSOPP & CO. LTD., Union Road, Nottingham. (0602) 57631.

JENNY ASTE & TREVOR LLOYD, 7 Grape Lane, York. TN: (0904) 21243. *Binding, restoration and conservation.*

R. & H. ATKINSON, 15a Pennyfarthing Street, Salisbury, Wiltshire. (0722) 29474.

ANTHONY BARON, 116 Shirland Road, London W9 2BT. (01) 286 2793.

GEORGE BAYNTUN, Manvers Street, Bath, Avon BA1 1JW. (0225) 66000.

BELL BOOKS (JANE GORE) LTD., 16 Junction Road, Ealing, London W5 4XL. (01) 568 0957.

THE BOOKENDS BINDERY, 1b Orleston Road, London N7 8LQ. (01) 607 0511.

CLIVE BOVILL, Millers Lea, Mill Hill, Swaffham Prior, Cambridge CB5 0JZ. *Fine bindings, gold tooling, conservation.*

FIONA CAMPBELL, 158 Lambeth Road, London, S.E.1. (01) 928 1633.

CHARLTON BINDERS, 63 St. Francis Road, Keynsham, Bristol BS18 2DX. (027 56) 4820.

DELRUE BOOKBINDERS, Ruthin Craft Centre, Park Street, Ruthin, Clwyd, Wales LL15 1BB. TN: Ruthin 4911. Old style hand bookbinding.

DUNN & WILSON LTD., Bellevue Bindery, Falkirk, FK1 4HP, Scotland. (0324) 21591.

THE EDDINGTON BINDERY LTD., Hungerford, Berkshire RG17 0PL. (0488) 82275.

A. H. FAIRHURST, 23a Raincliffe Avenue, Scarborough YO12 5BU. (0723) 72780.

KENNY GALWAY FINE BINDING LTD., 178 Salthill, Galway, Ireland. (091) 22752.

GREEN STREET BINDERY, Green Street, Oxford OX4 1YB. TN: (0865) 43540. Fiie binding, restoration, preservation.

JOHN HENDERSON, 70 Micklegate, York YO1 1LF. (0904) 24414.

ROBERT HARTNELL LIMITED, Victoria Square, Bodmin, Cornwall. TN: (0208) 3266. Fine leather binders; collectors and trade editions. TN: Amulree 225. Craft bookbinding, restoring.

HUNTER & FOULIS LTD., Bridgeside Works, McDonald Road, Edinburgh EH7 4NP, Scotland. (031) 556 7947.

A. W. LUMSDEN, Edgefield Industrial Easte, Loanhead, Edinburgh EH20 9TB, Scotland. (031) 440 0726.

MRS. KEITH LUMSDEN, Scotston, Amulree, Near Dunkeld, Perthshire. TN: Amulree 225.

ALFRED MALTBY & SON LTD., 28 & 30 Saint Michael's Street, Oxford OX1 2EB. (0865) 43413.

W. T. MORRELL & CO. LTD., 4-7 Nottingham Court, Shorts' Gardens, London, W.C.2. 01-836 6066.

MUIR & MUIR, The Workshop, 14A Stoneham Street, Coggeshall, Essex CO6 1TT. TN: (0376) 61730.

PETER NEWBOLT, High Street, Cley, Holt, Norfolk. TN: Cley 740469.

JOHN F. NEWMAN & SON LTD., 13 Belvedere Court, Dublin 1, Eire. TN: 743548.

MR. PICKWICK OF TOWCESTER, Lavender Cottage, Shutlanger, Towcester. 0604 862 006.

E. A. NEALE, LTD., Eaglescliffe Industrial Easte, Stockton, Cleveland. (0642) 784 560.

OMEGA BINDERY, 56a Goose Street, Beckington, Bath, Avon BA3 6SS. (0373) 83463.

PERIOD BOOKBINDERS, Lower Bristol Road, Twerton, Bath, Avon BA2 9ES. (0225) 20698.

S. J. PUGH BOOKBINDING, 116 Gosford Street, Coventry CV1 5DL. TN: (0203) 20813. Fine binding, conservation, repairs.

B. RILEY & CO. LTD., Red Doles Lane, Leeds Road, Huddersfield, West Yorkshire HD2 1YE. (0484) 34323/4.

F. SANGORSKI & G. SUTCLIFFE LTD., 1-5 Poland Street, London W1V 4LJ. TN: (01) 437 2252.

MICHAEL SASSEN, 145 Golders Green Road, Londoi, N.W.11.

HENRY SOTHERAN LTD., 2-5 Sackville Street, London W1X 2PD. (01) 734 1150 and (01) 734 0308.

THE STUDIO BINDERY, 4 Park Road, New Malden KT4 8NS. Props., Keith Houghton and John Norman. TN: (01) 949 2664.

SYMINGTON BOOKBINDERS, 41 Low Petergate, York YO1 2HT. TN: (0904) 33995. *Restoration of books & manuscripts, binding and repairs.*

E. A. WEEKS & SON, 168 North Gower Street, London, N.W.1. (01) 387 4674. Fine craft hand bookbinders.

A. WINSTANLEY, 213 Devizes Road, Salisbury, Wiltshire SP2 9LT. (0722) 4998. Antiquarian Book Restorer.

ZAEHNSDORF LTD., 175r Bermondsey Street, London, S.E.1. (01) 407 1244.

PACKING MATERIALS SUPPLIERS

ABBOTT'S PACKAGING LTD., Gordon House, Oakleigh Road South, New Southgate, London N11 1HL. 01-368 1266. *Jiffy bags* and *Easy-wrap*, also at Buckingham Road, Brackley, Northants N13 5EN. 0280 702791, and Homefield Road, Haverhill, Suffolk CB9 8QP. TN: (0440) 705541.

AJBB PLASTICS LIMITED, Osborn Way, Station Road, Hook, Basingstoke, Hants. (025) 672-2706. *Plastic bags, sheet and tubular film.*

A. J. BROWN BROUGH & Co., 1, 2 and 3 Dufferin Street, London EC1Y 8SD. TN: (01) 638 8085; also at 64-66 Duke Street, Liverpool L1 5AD. TN: (051) 709 3872, and 42 Tower Street, Leicester LE1 6WT. TN: (0533) 554256.

CENTRAL PACKAGING LTD., 78 Milton Trading Estate, Abingdon, Oxon OX14 4TD. 0235 834686. *"Corrosheet" self-sealing corrugated boards.*

SAMUEL JONES & CO. LTD., 165-177 The Broadway, Wimbledon, London SW19 1NE. 01-542 8511. *Sealing tapes etc.*

W. MacCARTHY & SONS LTD., St. Brigid's Works, 310-326 St. James Road, London SE1 5LB. 01-237 1946. *Cardboard box and container manufacturers.*

M. PETRUSHKIN LTD., Petapak Works, Sugar House Lane, London E15 2PQ. 01-534 7744. *Packing envelopes for books.*

BOOKCASES AND DISPLAY EQUIPMENT SUPPLIERS

BALMFORTH ENGINEERING LTD., Library Systems Division, Dallow Road, Luton LU1 1TE, Beds. 0582 31171. *Book shelving.*

BOOKS & BOOKCASES, 46 Malden Road, London NW5. TN: (01) 485 6045.

J. GLOVER & SONS LTD., Bridge Works, Kingston Road, Leatherhead, Surrey. TN: (0372) 373475. *Metal "Bookstacks".*

E. P. JOSEPH LTD., Supremacy House, Hurstwood Road, London NW11 0AR. TN: (01) 458 5656. *Perspex display stands for books.*

MODERN MERCHANDISING SERVICES LTD., P.O. Box 17, Vicarage Street, Oldbury, Warley, West Midlands B68 8HG. TN: (021) 552 2696. *Bookshop and display equipment.*

POINT EIGHT LTD., Shaw Road, Dudley, West Midlands DY2 8TP. TN: (0384) 58670. *Bookshop and display equipment.*

SIMPLEX, High Street, Oldland, Bristol BS15 6TA. 027 588 2279. *Wooden shelving, storage units and bookcases.*

TOP STONE, 29 Station Road, Harpenden, Hertfordshire AL5 4XB. TN: (058 27) 64510. *Display stands etc., trolleys.*

SHIPPING AGENTS

DAWSON ROYLE & WILLAN, 437 North Woolwich Road, Silvertown, London E16 2BS. TN: (01) 474 4060; also at Havelock Chambers, Queens Terrace, Southampton SO1 1BP. TN: (0703) 333845 and 14-15 Church Green East, Redditch, Worcestershire B98 8BP. TN: (0527) 62691.

THOMAS MEADOWS & CO. LTD., Horton Road, Colnbrook, Slough, Bucks SL3 0BG. TN: Colnbrook 3100.

UNITED CARGO CONTAINERS LTD., Sterling Trading Estate, Rainham Road South, Dagenham, Essex RM10 8TX. 01-592 0102.

CATALOGUE PRINTERS

THE DOLPHIN PRESS, Edison House, Fullerton Road, Glenrothes, Fife, Scotland. TN: (0592) 743014.

ROBERT STOCKWELL LTD., Baden Place, Crosby Row, London SE1 1YP. 01-403 3377. *Antiquarian booksellers' catalogue a speciality.*

LIONEL HALTER, 7 Hale Lane, Mill Lane, London NW7 3NU. *Printing service to the book trade.*

PRINTING SERVICES, N. F. and E. Bell, Croyde, Church Crescent, Finchley, London N3 1BE. Printing and photocopying service to the trade with discount. TN: (01) 346 3618.

COLOURERS, FRAMERS, CLEANERS OF MAPS AND PRINTS

BLACKMAN HARVEY LIMITED, 29 Earlham Street, London, WC2H 9LE. TN: (01) 836 1904. *Framing, restoring. Original print gallery.*

Mrs. P. A. BLUNT, Timberley, 48 Hillside Road, Ashtead, Surrey. TN: (27) 74909. *Colouring artist, maps and prints.*

CALLIGRAPHICA, 130 Farley Road, Selsdon, South Croydon CR2 7NE. *Bookplates designed and printed.*

ALAN CLARKE, 64 Battersea Park Road, London, S.W.11. TN: 01-622 1674. *Cleaning and colouring of prints.*

EXPORT GALLERIES, Penn Barn, By the Pond, Elm Road, Penn, Buckinghamshire HP10 8LU. TN: Penn (049 481) 5691. *Mount suppliers to the trade.*

A. H. FAIRHURST, 23A Raincliffe Avenue, Scarborough YO12 5BU. *Paper restoration (books, maps, prints), colouring, mount cutting, etc.*

THE FINCHLEY BOOKSHOP, 13 Long Lane, London N3 2PR. Prop: M. N. Keene. TN: 01-349 2597. *Pictures framed and mounts cut, trade and retail.*

CLAIRE D. LOWEN, B.A., 3 Herm Close, Newcastle under Lyme, Staffordshire ST5 3LS. TN: (0782) 621716. *Professional colouring of maps and prints.*

HERITAGE FINE ART, 10 Barley Mow Passage, Chiswick, London W4 4PH. TN: (01) 994 6477. Telex 8811418. *Cleaning and colouring of maps and prints, mount cutting, hand line and wash, framing.*

PERIWINKLE PRESS, Chequers Hill, Doddington, Sittingbourne, Kent ME9 0BN. TN: Doddington 246. *Picture frame makers; mount cutters; picture restorers.*

PRINTED PAGE, 2 and 3 Bridge Street, Winchester, Hampshire SO23 9BH. TN: (0962) 54072. *Framing, mount cutting, restoration and conservation of maps, prints, watercolours etc., hand colouring.*

NICOLA B. PIROZEK, 9 Minster Yard, York YO1 2HH. TN: (0904) 35609. *Paper conservation and restoration (books, maps, prints, drawings, water colours).*

E. PHIPPS, The Glasshouse, 11 Lettice Street, London SW6. TN: (01) 736 9498. *Mount cutting, colourist.*

ALAN AND MAUREEN PURSER, 12 Peverells Road, Chandlers Ford, Hampshire. TN: Chandlers Ford 61815. *Colouring and mounting of antique maps and prints.*

R. & B. MOUNT SERVICES, Kent Cottage, High Street, Staplehurst, Kent. *Mount cutters to the trade.*

R.S.D. FINE ARTS, 12 Wallbridge, Stroud, Gloucestershire. *Mounting and framing.*

THE STUDIO BOOKSHOP, 17 Broad Street, Alresford, Hampshire. TN: (096 273) 2188. Prop: Laurence Oxley. Est: 1949. *Restoration and cleaning of oil paintings and prints; frame makers, trade and retail.*

SUPPLIERS OF MATERIALS AND TOOLS FOR BINDING AND RESTORING BOOKS ETC.

Some suppliers whose products are well known and widely used have supplied the following details:

ANTIFOX, P.O. Box 28, Guildford, Surrey GU5 0JN.
ANTIFOX, a preparation and rinse to remove foxing (brown rust-like spots or stains) from books and prints. £2.50 post free.

ANTIOCH U.K. LIMITED, Faraday Road, London Road, Industrial Estate, Newbury, Berkshire RG13 2AD. TN: (0635) 44397. BOOKPLATES, BOOKMARKS etc.

EDGAR BACKUS LIMITED, 44-46 Cank Street, Leicester LE1 5GU. Telephone: (0533) 58137.
BACKUS LEATHER BINDING POLISH, cleans and restores leather bindings. Sold in 500ml. tins (U.K. only).
BACKUS BOOKCLOTH CLEANER, restores and cleans buckram, linen, art and other bookcloths. Sold in 500ml. tins (U.K. only).

SUSAN DONCASTER, Duchy Manor Mill, Hazzards Hill Mere, Warminster, Wiltshire BA12 5ER. TN: (0747) 860965.
DUTCH GILT AND PRINTED AND COMBED PASTE PAPERS, sample envelope and colour swatch, £1.00.
BOXES, covered in decorated paper for display purposes and storage boxes for prints, drawing, books etc.

FALKINER FINE PAPERS LIMITED, 117 Long Acre, London WC2E 9PA. Telephone: 01-240 2339.
PAPERS, wide selection of papers for repairs, marbled papers and coloured end papers.
LEATHERS AND BOOKCLOTHS for repairs and binding.
BOOKS on conservation and restoration of books etc., all items can be supplied by post.

GWASG BOASE, 7 Russell Place, Monmouth, Gwent NP5 3EB, Wales. Telephone: (0600) 5076.
BOOKPLATES, hand set and printed.

J. HEWIT AND SONS LIMITED, 97 Saint John Street, London EC1M 4AT. Telephone: 01-253 6082.
LEATHER CLEANING AND PRESERVING DRESSING, a non-ionic synthetic wax with properties similar to beeswax. Sold in 500ml. bottles.
BOOKBINDERS' TOOLS AND SUPPLIES, adhesive (paste, glue, P.V.C.), bone folders, brass type and type holders, brushes, knives, papers (marbled etc.), presses, tapes, threads
BINDING LEATHERS, basil, calf, goatskin, moroccos, pigskin, skivers, etc., in a wide range of colours.
BOOKCLOTHS, buckram, linen, cloth, mull, etc.

ALFRED MALTBY AND SON LIMITED, 28-30 Saint Michael's Street, Oxford OX1 2EB. Telephone: (0865) 43413.
FORTIFICUIR, book leather dressing.

BDH CHEMICALS LIMITED, Broom Road, Poole, Dorset BH12 4NN. Telephone: (0202) 745520. (Formerly Hopkin and Williams).
LEATHER DRESSING SOLUTION, made to British Museum formula. Sold in 500ml. tins, sufficient for treating about 200 average sized books.
POTASSIUM LACTATE SOLUTION, used to stabilise leather bindings against chemical decay. Sold in 500ml. packs, can be diluted with nine volumes of water to make solution for use.

MELROSE GATE FANCY PAPERS, 64 Heslington Road, York YO1 5AT. (Prop.: Mark Whittaker).
MARBLED PAPERS for antiquarian book restoration.

MITCHELL AND MALIK LIMITED, Duchy Manor Mill, Hazzards Hill, Mere, Wiltshire BA12 5ER. Telephone: (0747) 860965.
HAND-MARBLED PAPER, for restoration, facsimile, limited editions etc. Available in 36 designs, sheets 20x25 inches, minimum order by post is ten sheets. Visits by appointment.

ARTHUR RICH AND PARTNERS LIMITED, 42 Mount Pleasant Drive, Belper, Derbyshire DE5 2TH. Telephone: (077 382) 3907. Royal Warrant Holders for the supply of Leather Dressings to H.M. the Queen.
PLIANTINE TRANSPLANT LEATHER PRESERVER AND DRESSING, a liquid to lubricate leather fibres and restore flexibility to old leather book bindings. 'Standard' for grain side (can be polished), 'Special' for flesh side of skin. Sold in 500ml. and in 1, 2.5 and 5 litre tins.
PLIANCREME LEATHER DRESSING CREAM a concentrated aqueous emulsion with same basic ingredients as Pliantine Standard with the addi-

tion of a fungicide. Not suitable for old books where water could have a detrimental effect on the leather. Sold in jars, 175g, 300g and 630g. PLIANTEX CONSERVATION AGENT, an inert liquid which penetrates leather and on evaporation of the solvent leaves a clear film that protects individual fibres from further decay or spreading of the fungus that causes 'red rot', and gives support to any weakened structure. The film can re removed, if desred, even years later by a solvent called PLIANSOLVE. Sold in 500ml. and in 1, 2.5 and 5 litre tins.

RUSSELL BOOKCRAFTS, 94 Bancroft, Hitchin, Hertfordshire SG5 1NQ. Telephone: (0462) 59711. General suppliers to bookbinders, archivists and librarians.
DEACIDIFICATION. Materials for deacidification of books and documents by the vapour phase process using Cyclohexylamine Carbonate (C.H.C.) which neutralizes the acid in dry paper. Available in three forms: sachets of loose powder 10g, tablets, ½g, and impregnated sheets of paper 10x8 inches (254x203mm).
BOOSBINDERS' AND ARCHIVISTS' TOOLS AND SUPPLIES, fully equipped binders' benches, wooden and metal presses, adhesives (glue, paste, cold plastic etc.), agate burnishers, awls, bodkins, bone folders, British Museum formula dressing, sold in 85g. bottles, brushes, glass paper, guillotine, hemp, knives, shears, tapes.
BINDING LEATHERS, Oasis Nigerian goat, morocco, calf, white pigskin, sheepskin and skiver; parchment, vellum.
BOOKCLOTHS, BOARDS AND PAPERS (end and cover, including Cockerell hand-marbled, Ingres, Sylvia series etc.).

T. N. WALDRON LIMITED, Avon Works, Great William Street, Stratford upon Avon, Warwickshire. Telephone: (0789) 292126.
BOOK CORNERS. Corners of paper-covered metal to protect books in transit. Available in multiples of 100.

GEOGRAPHICAL SECTION

EXPLANATORY NOTE

The information given, if available, for each entry is:

Name of firm and postal address.

Name of proprietor if different from foregoing (Prop:).

Telephone Exchange and number (TN:) and telegraphic address (TA:) Date the business was established (Est:).

Type of premises occupied. If described as a shop they are, unless otherwise stated, open to the public and members of the trade without appointment during normal business hours. If described as a storeroom or private premises, information as to whether an appointment is necessary or not is added. Most business premises in the British Isles close early (about midday) on one day in the week, and where applicable this is shewn.

Type and size of business. The size of the normal stock of second-hand (sec.) or antiquarian (antiq.) books; also whether the firm deals in new books, and if any other business is carried on.

The subjects, if any, in which the business specializes (spec:). Whether catalogues are issued, and if so, on what subjects, and how often, (cata:).

Languages, other than English, in which correspondence can be conducted (corresp:)

Name and address of Bankers and account number (B:)

If the firm is a member of any of the following associations—

ABA —Antiquarian Booksellers Association (Int.)
BA —Booksellers Association of G.B. & I.
NBL —National Book League
PBFA —Provincial Booksellers Fairs Association
PA —Publishers Association.

MAP OF THE BRITISH ISLES SHEWING DIVISION INTO AREAS

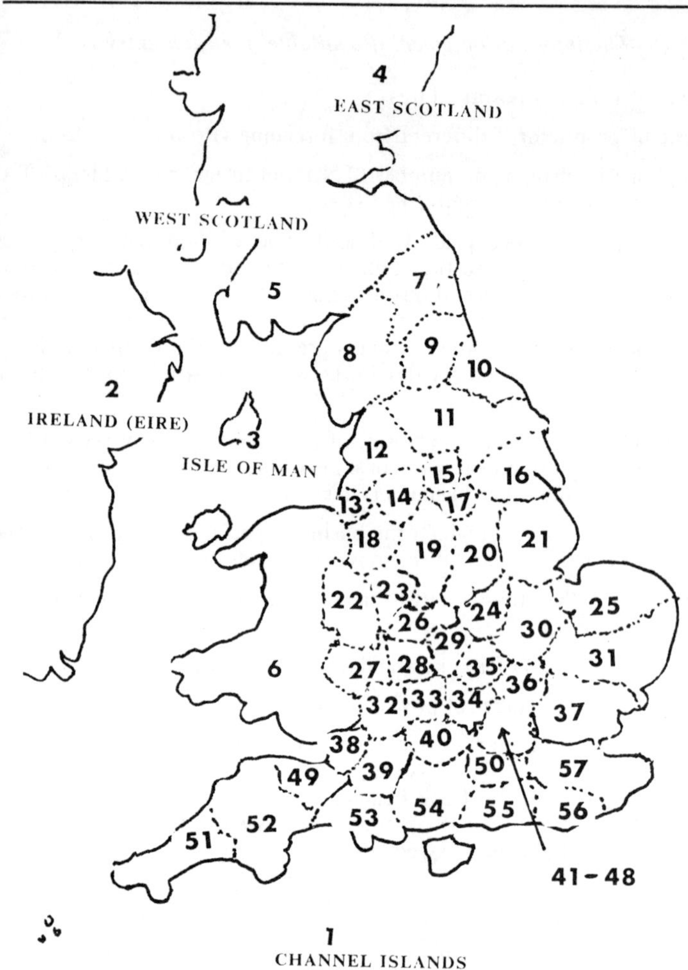

The above map shews the Areas into which the British Isles have been divided for the purpose of this Directory. The names of the Areas are given on the facing page, while any town or village can be located from the Index which follows.

GEOGRAPHICAL SECTION

The geographical section of this directory has been arranged in areas, so that, from any part of the British Isles, it can be seen at a glance what dealers there are within easy travelling distance. The map opposite shews the general arrangement of the areas; an index of towns and villages follows overleaf.

AREAS

1. THE CHANNEL ISLANDS
2. IRELAND (EIRE)
3. THE ISLE OF MAN
4. EAST SCOTLAND
5. WEST SCOTLAND
6. WALES (CYMRU)
7. NORTHUMBERLAND
8. CUMBRIA
9. TYNE AND WEAR AND COUNTY DURHAM
10. CLEVELAND
11. NORTH YORKSHIRE
12. LANCASHIRE
13. MERSEYSIDE
14. GREATER MANCHESTER
15. WEST YORKSHIRE
16. HUMBERSIDE
17. SOUTH YORKSHIRE
18. CHESHIRE
19. DERBYSHIRE
20. NOTTINGHAMSHIRE
21. LINCOLNSHIRE
22. SHROPSHIRE (SALOP)
23. STAFFORDSHIRE
24. LEICESTERSHIRE
25. NORFOLK
26. WEST MIDLANDS
27. HEREFORD AND WORCESTERSHIRE
28. WARWICKSHIRE
29. NORTHAMPTONSHIRE
30. CAMBRIDGESHIRE
31. SUFFOLK
32. GLOUCESTERSHIRE
33. OXFORDSHIRE (OXON)
34. BUCKINGHAMSHIRE
35. BEDFORDSHIRE
36. HERTFORSHIRE
37. ESSEX
38. AVON (BRISTOL AREA)
39. WILTSHIRE
40. BERKSHIRE
41. LONDON EAST
42. LONDON EAST CENTRAL
43. LONDON NORTH, AND NORTH MIDDLESEX
44. LONDON NORTH WEST AND MIDDLESEX
45. LONDON SOUTH EAST
46. LONDON SOUTH WEST
47. LONDON WEST
48. LONDON WEST CENTRAL
49. SOMERSET
50. SURREY
51. CORNWALL
52. DEVON
53. DORSET
54. HAMPSHIRE
55. WEST SUSSEX
56. EAST SUSSEX
57. KENT

---

58. AUSTRALIA
59. NEW ZEALAND
60. SOUTHERN AFRICA
61. WEST AFRICA
62. EAST AFRICA
63. SOUTH EAST ASIA

INDEX OF TOWNS AND VILLAGES

The Index numbers refer to areas in the geographical Section

A LIST OF DEALERS IN SECONDHAND AND ANTIQUARIAN BOOKS ARRANGED GEOGRAPHICALLY

01. THE CHANNEL ISLANDS

SAINT HELIER, JERSEY — SAINT PETER PORT, GUERNSEY

BUTTON'S LTD, 21 Smith Street, Saint Peter Port, Guernsey, C.I. Prop: P.L. Button. TN: (0481) 25955. Est: 1973. Shop. Large stock sec. and antiq, also new books. Spec: Local topography, biography, (including Victor Hugo), and fiction; modern out-of-print authors. B: National Westminster Bank, Saint Peter Port, Guernsey, C.I. A/c No. 60-09-20/06090699.

CHANNEL ISLANDS GALLERIES LIMITED, Island Craft Centre, Trinity Square, Saint Peter Port, Guernsey, C.I. Prop: Geoffrey P. Gavey and Mrs. Christine M. Gavey. TN: (0481) 23247 or (0481) 47337 (Home). Est: 1967. Shop, early closing Thursday. Very small stock secondhand and antiq. books; also art dealers and picture mounting and framing. Spec: antique books and prints, maps, sea charts, paintings etc. relating to Channel Islands. Corresp: Français, Deutsch. B: National Westminster Bank, High Street, Saint Peter Port, Guernsey.

STEVENS-COX, Birling, Mount Durand, Saint Peter Port, Guernsey, Channel Islands. Est: 1930. Storeroom, appointment necessary. Very large sec. and antiq. stock; also maps, prints and paintings. Spec: archaeology, agriculture, history, Dorset and Somerset, world topography, English literature. Cata: general, 2 a year, 20p. per annum.

THE GUERNSEY BOOKSHOP, 11 Contrée Mansell, St. Peter Port, Guernsey, C.I. Prop: Mrs. Gwen Baker. TN: 0481-25553. Est: 1980. Shop, closed Thursday afternoons. Small stock used. Spec: Channel Islands, Women's history. Back-numbers of journals stocked and new books. Cata: 1 a year. Corresp: Français. B: Williams and Glyn's Bank Ltd., 22 High Street, St. Peter Port, Guernsey. Account 12077545.

HILGROVE BOOKS, 22B HILGROVE STREET, SAINT HELIER, JERSEY, CHANNEL ISLANDS. TN: 0534-31947. Est: 1941. Small general sec. and antiq. stock, also new books. Spec: Channel Islands. Cata: infrequently. B.A.

THESAURUS [JERSEY] LIMITED, 20 SAND STREET, SAINT HELIER, JERSEY, C.I. Prop: Irene Creaton. Est: 1981. Shop, open weekdays 08.30 to 18.00 hrs. Stock of 3,000 antiq. vols.

THESAURUS [JERSEY] LIMITED, 30 SAND STREET, SAINT HELIER, JERSEY, C.I. Prop: Irene Creaton, TN: 37045. Est: 1974. Shop. Very large stock sec. and antiq. Spec: Channel Islands, Victor Hugo, Edmund Blampied. Cata: 1 a year. Corresp: Français. B: Midland Bank, Library Place, St. Helier, Jersey. Account 91226061.

THESAURUS [JERSEY] LIMITED, 1 SUNSHINE AVENUE, SAINT HELIER, JERSEY, C.I. Prop: Irene Creaton. TN: 77016. Est: 1979. Shop and stockrooms, open Thursday and Saturday: appointment advisable. Very large stock sec. and antiq. Spec: modern first editions. Corresp: Français. Cata: annually. B: Midland Bank, Library Place, Saint Helier. Account 91226061.

THESAURUS [JERSEY] LIMITED, 15–16 TUDOR HOUSE, MILL STREET, SAINT PETER PORT, GUERNSEY, C.I. Prop: Irene Creaton. TN: 20217. Est: 1977. Shop, closed Monday and Thursday afternoons. Very large stock sec. and antiq. Corresp: Français. Cata: annually. B: William and Glyn's Bank Ltd., 22 High Street, Saint Peter Port, Guernsey. Account 12046887.

02. IRELAND (EIRE)

ACHILL, CO. MAYO
BALLYDEHOB, CO. CORK
BALLYNAHINCH, CO. DOWN
BELFAST (BEAL FEIRSDE), NORTHERN IRELAND
BLACKROCK (CARRAIG DHUBH), CO. DUBLIN
CASTLEBAR, CO. MAYO
CASTLETOWNROCHE (BAILE CHAISLEAIN AN ROISTIGH), CO. CORK
COLERAINE, CO. LONDONDERRY
CORK (CORCAIGH), CO. CORK
CRUMLIN, CO. ANTRIM
DROGHEDA, CO. LOUTH
DUBLIN (BAILE ATHA CLIATH)
DUN LAOGHAIRE, CO. DUBLIN
GALWAY (AN GHAILLIMH), CO. GALWAY
JORDANSTOW, CO. ANTRIM
LISBURN, CO. ANTRIM
KILKENNY (CILL CHOINNIGH), CO. KILKENNY
TRAMORE, CO. WATERFORD
WESTPORT, CO. MAYO
WICKLOW, CO. WICKLOW

THE ANTIQUARIAN BOOKSHOP, 9 Queen Street, Tramore, Co. Waterford, Eire. Prop: Padraig S. Cuddihy. TN: (051) 86196. Est: 1978. Shop, closed on Thursdays. Small stock sec. and antiq. Spec: Irish interest and Provincial imprints, rare maps, some back numbers of journals. Corresp: Deutsch, Français, Erse. Cata: occasionally. B: Allied Irish Banks, Strand Street, Tramore, Co. Waterford. Account 02773255.

THE BELL GALLERY, 13 Adelaide Park, Belfast BT9, Northern Ireland. Prop: James Nelson Bell. TN: Belfast 662998. Est: 1965. Art gallery, early closing Saturday. Some new, and small sec. and antiq. stock: also dealer and framer. Spec: material on Ireland. Fine Art Trade Guild.

MRS. I.J. BURLINGHAM, 11 Geneva Gardens, Stranmillis Road, Belfast BT9 5FY, Northern Ireland. TN: (0232) 661753, (after 18.00 hrs. only). Private premises. Small stock sec. and antiq. Spec: Irish, theology, cricket & golf, juvenile, travel & exploration.

CARRAIG BOOKS, 25 Newton Avenue, Blackrock, Co. Dublin, Eire. Prop: A.E. Day. TN: Dublin 882575. Est: 1968. Shop and storeroom, early closing Saturday. Some new, and medium sec. and antiq. stock. Spec: Irish interest, Manx, Catholic, occult, political. Cata: on foregoing, frequently.

CATHAIR BOOKS, GLENCREST, GREENHILL ROAD, WICKLOW, EIRE. TN: Wicklow (0404) 9466. Prop: E. Mallon and K. Gallen. Est: 1975. Private premises; appointment necessary. Medium stock of sec. and antiq. books, maps. Spec: Ireland. Cata: 4 a year.

THE COLERAINE BOOKSHOP, 5 STONE ROW, COLERAINE, NORTHERN IRELAND. Prop: W.J.B. and R.J. McClements. TN: (0265) 52557. Est: 1976. Shop, closed Thursdays. Medium stock sec. and antiq. also some new of local interest. Corresp: Français, Español, Deutsch. B: Northern Bank, Coleraine.

CURRAUN BOOKS. BELFARSAD, CURRAUN, ACHILL, CO. MAYO, EIRE. Prop: Mrs. Stevens-Vulto. TN: Achill Sound 94. Shop, open on Sunday, closed on Monday. Small stock sec. and antiq. P.B.F.A.

DAVIDSON BOOKS, 34 BROOMHILL ROAD, SPA, BALLYNAHINCH, CO. DOWN, NORTHERN IRELAND. Prop: Arthur Davidson. TN: (0238) 562502. Est: 1958. Private premises; appointment necessary. Medium stock sec. and antiq. Spec: Irish interest, topography, literature etc. Cata: 2 or 3 a year. B: Northern Bank, High Street, Ballynahinch.

DE BÚRCA RARE BOOKS, MOUNT GORDON, CASTLEBAR, CO. MAYO, EIRE. Prop: Eamonn De Búrca. TN: Castlebar 21958. Est: 1980. Private premises; appointment necessary. Small stock sec. and antiq. Spec: books of Irish interest. Corresp: Irish. B: Bank of Ireland, Castlebar, County Mayo, Ireland. Also Bank of Ireland, High Street, Birmingham.

EMERALD ISLE BOOKS, 539 ANTRIM ROAD, BELFAST, BT15 3BU, NORTHERN IRELAND. Prop: Mr. and Mrs. John Gamble. TN: Belfast 771798. TA: Aldus Belfast. Est: 1963. Private premises; appointment preferred. Large stock antiq. Spec: Irish interest, fine and rare, 18th to 20th century literature, architecture, theology, economics, travel. Cata: about 2 a year.

FALKNER GRIERSON & COMPANY LIMITED, 53 PEMBROKE ROAD, DUBLIN 4, EIRE. TN: Dublin 684216. Private premises; appointment necessary. Medium antiq. stock. Spec: English and Continental literature and science before 1840. Cata: on foregoing, 4 a year. A.B.A.

FEEHAN & COMPANY LIMITED, 2 BRIDGE STREET, CORK, EIRE. Prop: Sean Feehan and Captain J.M. Feehan. TN: 26079. Est: 1965. Shop, closed Saturday except by appointment. Large sec. and antiq. stock. Spec: Ireland, Irish topography and travel, views and prints. Cata: on foregoing, 8–12 a year.

JAMES O'D. FENNING, 12 GLENVIEW, ROCHESTOWN, DUN LAOGHAIRE, CO. DUBLIN, EIRE. Prop: Jim and Chris. Fenning. TN: (01) 852805, (Ansafone). TA: Fenbooks, Dublin. Est: 1969. Private premises; appointment necessary. Small stock general antiquarian Books. Cata: 6 a year. A.B.A.

FIGGIS RARE BOOKS, 53 PEMBROKE ROAD, DUBLIN 4, EIRE. Prop: Neville Figgis. TN: 609491. TA: Tomes, Dublin. Est: 1974. Private premises; appointment necessary. Medium stock antiq. books. Spec: Irish literature, English literature to 1840, travels. Cata: 4 a year. B: Coutts, 440 Strand, London W.C.2. Account 180002. A.B.A.

GREENE & COMPANY, 16 CLARE STREET, DUBLIN 2, EIRE. Prop: H.S. Pembrey. TN: Dublin 762554. Est: 1843. Shop, early closing Saturday. New, and very large sec. and antiq. stock. N.B.L. B.A.

FRED HANNA LIMITED, 27, 28 & 29 NASSAU STREET, DUBLIN 2, EIRE. TN: Dublin 771255. TA: Hanna Bookseller Dublin. Est: 1860. Shops, early closing Saturday. New, and large sec. and antiq. stock. Spec: Ireland, fine bindings. B: Allied Irish Banks, College Green, Dublin 2. B.A.

C.P. HYLAND, THE OLD RECTORY, WALLSTOWN, CASTLETOWNROCHE, MALLOW, CO. CORK, EIRE. TN: Mallow (022) 25217. TA: Hylibris. Est: 1965. Private House; appointment necessary. Stock sec. and antiq. Spec: books relating to Ireland. Cata: Irish, monthly; 2 a year. B: Bank of Ireland, Doneraile, Co. Cork. Account 29536714. Bank of Ireland, 2 Lombard Street, London, EC3P 2EU. Account 49860722.

JIRI BOOKS, 11 MILL ROAD, LISBURN, NORTHERN IRELAND. Prop: Mrs. C.M.J. Swindall. TN: (023 126) 443. Est: 1978. Private premises; appointment necessary. Small stock sec. and antiq. Spec: Irish Interest. B: Ulster Bank, University Road, Belfast.

KENNY'S BOOKSHOP AND ART GALLERY, HIGH STREET, GALWAY, EIRE. TN: (091) 62739, 61041 and 61021. Shop, open weekdays 9.00 to 18.000 hrs. Very large sec. and antiq. stock; also prints, maps and original paintings, binding. Spec: Irish interest, literature and periodicals. Cata: on foregoing, 12 a year. M: A.B.A.

LEE BOOK STORE, 10 LAVITTS QUAY, CORK, EIRE. Prop: P.G. McSweeney, TN: (021) 22307. Est: 1944. Shop. Medium stock sec. and antiq. Spec: Irish interest.

R.A. MARTIN, 83 CRUMLIN ROAD, SEACASH, CRUMLIN, CO. ANTRIM, NORTHERN IRELAND. TN: (08494) 53453. Est: 1982. Private premises; postal business only. Very small stock sec. and antiq. Spec: Big Game hunting, field sports, ornithology, natural history. Bi-monthly lists issued. B: Trustee Savings Bank, Main Street, Antrim.

NAUGHTON BOOKSELLERS, 8 MARINE TERRACE, DUN LAOGHAIRE, CO. DUBLIN, EIRE. Prop: S. and R. Naughton. TN: 804392. Est: 1976. Shop, open Monday-Saturday 9.30–17.30. Medium stock sec. and antiq. Spec: books of Irish interest.

NEPTUNE GALLERY LIMITED, 4 SOUTH WILLIAM STREET, DUBLIN 2, EIRE. Prop: Law and Arnold. TN 715021. Shop; early closing Saturday. Small stock antiq. Spec: Irish interest. Irish Antique Dealers Association.

ROBERTS BOOKS, SAINT KIERANS STREET, KILKENNY, EIRE. Prop: D.M. Roberts. TN: 0409-5054. Est: 1976. Shop. Spec: Irish interest, back numbers of journals stocked. Corresp: Deutsch, Français, Erse. B: Allied Irish Banks, Terenure, Dublin 6.

P. & B. ROWAN, CARLTON HOUSE, 92 MALONE ROAD, BELFAST, BT9 5HP, NORTHERN IRELAND. Prop: Peter Rowan. TN: Belfast 666448. Est: 1973. Private premises; appointment necessary. Large stock sec. and antiq. books. Spec: Irish interest, history, literature; history of science and technology and medicine; economics, philosophy, law, travel and exploration, rare. Cata: 3 or 4 a year. Corresp: Français.

SALT HOUSE ANTIQUES LIMITED, WELLINGTON QUAY, DROGHEDA, EIRE. Director: Peter Lennon. TN: Drogheda (041) 7888. Est: 1968. Shop. Medium stock sec. books; also maps, prints and antiques.

SCHULL BOOKS, Ballydehob, Co. Cork, Eire. Prop: Barbara Millgate and Jack O'Connell. TN: Skibbereen (028) 37317. Est: 1981. Private premises; appointment necessary. Medium stock sec. and antiq. Spec: Irish interest. Cata: 4 a year. Corresp: Français, Deutsch, Irish (Gaelic). B: Allied Irish Banks Ltd., Schull, County Cork, Ireland.

ENA WELLS, 7 Glenkeen Avenue, Jordanstown, Co. Antrim, Northern Ireland. TN: White Abbey (0231) 61275. Est: 1979. Private premises; appointment necessary. Small stock sec. and antiq. Spec: Irish interest, prints, topography.

WESTPORT HOUSE COUNTRY ESTATE, Westport, Co. Mayo, Eire. Prop: Jeremy Lord Altamont. TN: Westport 171. Est: 1969. Shop. Small stock sec. and antiq. books; also antiques and art centre. Spec: Irish interest.

03. ISLE OF MAN

EAST FOXDALE

CARNEGIE'S ANTIQUARIAN FINE AND RARE BOOKS, Knockrushen House, Scarlett, Castletown, Isle of Man. Prop: I.H. Carnegie. TN: (0624) 82 4287.

DAVID I. HELSBY, Brooklands, Cornelly, Archalagan, East Foxdale, Isle of Man. TN: Isle of Man 851-125. Est: 1964. Private premises; appointment necessary Small sec. and antiq. stock, also new. Spec: Manx literature, Victoriana, postcards, maps. Cata: general, 1 a year. Corresp: Cymraeg.

04. EAST SCOTLAND

Regions of Grampians, Tayside, Central, Fife, Lothian and Border.

ABERDEEN, ABERDEENSHIRE
ABERNETHY, PERTHSHIRE
DUNDEE, ANGUS
EDINBURGH
ELLON, ABERDEENSHIRE
GALASHIELS, PERTHSHIRE
INNERLEITHEN, PEEBLESHIRE
KIRKCALDY, FIFE
KIRKMICHAEL, PERTHSHIRE
LEITHOLM BY COLDSTREAM, BERWICKSHIRE
METHIL, FIFE
MONTROSE, ANGUS
NEWPORT ON TAY, FIFE
PERTH, PERTHSHIRE
PITLOCHRY, PERTHSHIRE
SAINT ANDREWS, FIFE
STROMNESS, ORKNEY
STONEHAVEN, KINCARDINESHIRE
STRATH TAY, PERTHSHIRE
WEST LINTON, PEEBLES-SHIRE

ABERDEEN RARE BOOKS, SLAINS HOUSE, COLLIESTON, ELLON, ABERDEENSHIRE AB4 9RT. Prop: A.J. Campbell. TN: (035 887) 275. Est: 1977. Private premises; appointment necessary. Medium stock, antiq. Scottish interest and agriculture only, also old journals. Cata: 4 a year. M: P.B.F.A.

JOY ALLAN, 24 CAMERON STREET, STONEHAVEN AB3 2HS. TN: 63588. Est: 1974. Shop, closed on Fridays. Small stock sec. and antiq. also antiques. B: Clydesdale Bank, West End Branch, Union Street, Aberdeen. Account 115527.

BARROW BOOKS LIMITED, LEITHOLM BY COLDSTREAM, BERWICKSHIRE TD12 4JN. Prop: Cyril Barrow. TN: Leitholm 277. Est: 1961. Office and store; appointment necessary. Medium stock sec. and antiq. books. Spec: politics, social sciences and social welfare. Cata: 6 a year.

B. & R. BAXTER, THE 647 GALLERY, 647 King Street, Aberdeen AB2 1SB. TN: 45416. Est: 1974. Shop, open 2-8 pm during week; occasionally on a Saturday. Very small stock sec. and antiq. Spec: poetry and plays, also back-numbers of journals and new books, paintings, prints and pottery of B. Baxter. Corresp: Deutsch, Français. B: Trustee Savings Bank, St. Machar Branch, 28 School Road, AB2 1TY.

PETER BELL, 31 Nelson Street, Edinburgh EH3 6LJ. Est: 1980. Stockroom open by appointment, Medium stock sec. and antiq. Spec: theology, history and literature, 19th century biography, Victorian age. Cata: regularly on above subjects. M: P.B.F.A.

BILLSON OF SAINT ANDREWS, 15 Greyfriars Gardens, Saint Andrews, Fife KY16 9DE. Prop: Bill and David Waugh. TN: (0334) 75063.

JAMES G. BISSET LIMITED, 12–14 Upperkirkgate, Aberdeen AB9 1BG. Prop: University Booksellers, Oxford. TN: Aberdeen 53528/9. Est: 1869. Shop, no early closing. Small sec. and antiq stock, also university booksellers and stationery. A.B.A. B.A. N.B.L.

BOOKFARE, 8 Victoria Street, Edinburgh EH1 2HG. Prop: A.C.I. Naylor. TN: (031) 225-9237. Est: 1977. Shop. Small sec. and antiq. stock, with an emphasis on literature. Occasional lists issued. Corresp: Français. B: Midland Bank, 62 Castle Street, Liverpool L69 2BQ. M: P.B.F.A.

BOOKRANGER, 14 Hepburn Gardens, Saint Andrews, Fife. Prop: James W.B. Laing. TN: Saint Andrews 5066. Est: 1969. Private premises, appointment necessary. Medium sec. and antiq. stock. Spec: English literature, illustrated, curios. Cata: general, 3 a year.

THE BORDER BOOKSHOP, 64 High Street, Galashiels, Selkirkshire. Prop: Ronald C. Hodges. TN: (0896) 57269 Est: 1981. Shop, closed Wednesday afternoons. Medium stock seq. and antiq. also new books. Spec: Scottish history and topography; gypsy books (non-fiction); field sports. Cata: 3 a year. B: Clydesdale Bank, High Street, Galashiels. M: P.B.F.A.

BOUQUINISTE, 31 Market Street, Saint Andrews, Fife. Prop: A. and W. Anderson. TN: (0334) 76724. Est: 1982. Shop, closed Thursdays. Medium stock sec. and antiq. Corresp: Français. B: Clydesdale Bank, Anstruther, Fife. M: P.B.F.A.

BROUGHTON BOOKSHOP, 49a Broughton Street, Edinburgh EH1 3RJ. Prop: P. Galinsky. Est: 1971. Shop. Medium sec. and antiq. stock.

NORMAN BURNS, Bridge Street, Dunkeld, Perthshire. TN: (03502) 282 Shop.

CATHAY BOOKS, 12 Chapel Street, Edinburgh. Prop: Malcolm James Wylie. TN: (031) 667-0164. Est: 1977. Shop. Medium stock sec. and antiq. general with emphasis on Far East and Scottish interest. M: P.B.F.A.

CHRISTINE CROSS BOOKS, 166 Kirkland Walk, Methil, Fife KY8 2AG. TN: (0333) 26555. Est: 1982. Private premises: appointment necessary. Very small stock sec. and antiq. Spec: travel and topography; illustrated. B: Trustee Savings Bank, Methil, Fife.

DUNDAS BOOKSHOP, 23A Dundas Street, Edinburgh EH3 6QG. Prop: Margaret S. Duncan. TN: (031) 556-4591. Est: 1965. Shop, closed Wednesdays (except in Summer). Small sec. and antiq. Stock. Cata: general. Corresp: Français, Deutsch, Italiano, Español. B: Bank of Scotland, 64 George Street, Edinburgh. Account 00315028.

DUNOLLIE FINE ARTS, 12 Townsend Place, Kirkcaldy, Fife KY1 1HB. Prop: Alexander McNeill. TN: (0592) 263370. Est: 1970. Private house; appointment necessary. Small stock sec. and antiq. Spec: modern firsts, illustrated including juvenile, art reference. B: Clydesdale Bank, Kirkcaldy. Account 245245.

ALEX M. FRIZZELL, Castlelaw, West Linton, Peebles-shire. TN: (0968) 60450. Est: 1952. Private premises; appointment necessary. Medium stock sec. and antiq. books. Spec: private press; Scottish. Cata: Scottish, 8 a year. B: Bank of Scotland, 69 George St. Edinburgh EH2 2JP. Account 00303864. National Giro: Account 126740003. A.B.A., P.B.F.A.

JAMES GALL, 49 Anderson Avenue, Aberdeen AB2 2LR. TN: Aberdeen 0224-491716. Est: 1941. Private premises, open normal business hours. Very small sec. and antiq. stock. Spec: field sports, racing, horses, foxhunting, old boys books, Magnets Gems, Greyfriars Holiday Annuals. etc., books searched for.

GRANGE BOOKSHOP, 186–188 Causewayside, Edinburgh EH9 1PN. Prop: William Blair. TN: (031) 667-2759. Est: 1956. Shop, closed all day Tuesday. Large sec. and antiq. stock. Spec: Scottish history & literature, folklore, topography. A.B.A.

JOHN GRANT, 13C & 15A Dundas Street, Edinburgh EH3 6QG. Prop: Ian and Senga Grant. TN: (031) 556 9698. TA: Books Edinburgh. Est: 1874. Shop, closed all day Monday. Medium stock sec. and antiq. books; also printsellers. Spec: Scottish interest; 18th century literature. Cata: 3 a year. A.B.A.

HAWTHORN BOOKS, 3 West Cross Causeway, Edinburgh. Prop: Margaret Jameson. TN: (031) 669-4283. Est: 1980. Shop, Small stock sec. and antiq.

JOHN HOOKER, Cortes, Kirk Wynd, Abernethy, Perthshire PH2 9JD. TN: (073) 885-325. Est: 1981. Private premises; appointment necessary. Small stock sec. and antiq. Spec: Scottish interest; modern first editions. Cata: 6 a year. B: Royal Bank of Scotland, Newburgh, Fife. M: P.B.F.A.

G. & M. HUGHES 19 Graham Place, Stromness, Orkney KW16 3BZ. Gordon and Maureen Hughes. TN: Stromness (0856) 850428. Est: 1979. Shop. Medium stock used. Spec: Orkney and Shetland, Caithness. Old postcards also stocked. Cata: Occasionally. M: P.B.F.A.

SPIKE HUGHES RARE BOOKS, Leithen Bank, Leithen Road, Innerleithen, Peeblesshire EH44 6HY. Prop: Spike Hughes. TN: (0896) 830019. Est: 1981. Private premises; appointment essential. Small stock sec. and antiq. Spec: English literature; Scottish philosophy and history. Cata: 8 a year. M: A.B.A.

D.W. HYSLOP, 17 19 Guthrie Street, Edinburgh EH1 1VG. TN: (031) 225-4061. Est: 1924. Shop, open afternoons. Medium stock sec. and antiq books.

THE INVERNESS SECONDHAND BOOK SHOP, Grants Close, High Street, Inverness. Prop: Charles Leakey. TN: (0463)-239947. Est: 1979. Shop. Medium stock sec. and antiq. Spec: Scottish interest. B: Clydesdale Bank, Queensgate, Inverness.

JAY BOOKS, 1 Roull Grove, Edinburgh EH12 7JP. Prop: D.J. Brayford. TN: 031-334-1844. Est: 1977. Private premises; appointment necessary. Small stock used. Spec: science, natural history and gardening. No other books stocked. Cata: 4 times a year. Corresp:

Deutsch, Français. B: Royal Bank of Scotland, 239 St. John's Road, Edinburgh, EH12 7XB. Account 00114339. M: P.B.F.A.

JEROME BOOKS, 6 WESTERN TERRACE, EDINBURGH EH12 5QF. Prop: John Hems. TN: (031) 337-2113. Est: 1970. Private premises; appointment necessary. Medium stock sec. and antiq. Spec: scholarly, antiquarian and illustrated. Corresp: Français, Español. B: Bank of Scotland, 69 George Street, Edinburgh EH2.

SUSAN JORDAN BOOKS, 9 GEORGE STREET, MONTROSE, ANGUS. Est: 1982. Shop, open only on Saturdays. Small stock sec. and antiq. Spec: East Scotland. Corresp: Français. B: Royal Bank of Scotland, High Street, Montrose.

LORIEN BOOKS, LORIEN, GLEN DERBY, KIRKMICHAEL, PERTHSHIRE PH10 7NA. Prop: Leslie Johnston. TN: Strathardle (025 081) 318. Est: 1974. Private premises; appointment necessary. Small stock sec. and antiq. books. Cata: 6 a year.
Also at 17 LESLIE STREET, BLAIRGOWRIE.

DOMHNALL MacCORMAIG, 18 BABERTON MAINS COURT, EDINBURGH EH14 3ER. TN: (031) 442 1201. Est: 1974. Private premises; appointment necessary. Very small stock sec. and antiq. books. Spec: Scottish Gaelic; Topography Highlands and Islands; Celtic studies (Scotland, Ireland, Wales, Isle of Man, Brittany). Cata: monthly

R. AND B.D. MacCUTCHEON, 30 SPITTAL STREET, STIRLING. TN: (0786) 61771. Shop.

McNAUGHTAN'S BOOKSHOP, 3A HADDINGTON PLACE, EDINBURGH EH7 4AE. Prop: Elizabeth A. Strong. TN: (031) 556-5897. Est: 1957. Shop, closed Monday. Very large sec. and antiq. stock. Spec: early children's, travel, topography, literature, arts, Scottish. Corresp: Français, Deutsch. A.B.A., P.B.F.A.

MAIR WILKES BOOKS, 3 SAINT MARY'S LANE, NEWPORT-ON-TAY, FIFE. Prop: James Mair and Alan Wilkes. TN: Newport-on-Tay 542352 or 542167. Est: 1970. Stockroom, open Saturdays or by appointment. Medium sec. and antiq. stock. Spec: psychology, Scotland (topography, history, literature). Cata: psychology, Scottish topography and general, 4 a year.

DOUGLAS MASON, 84 BARNTON PLACE, GLENROTHES, FIFE. TN: (0592) 758766. Private premises; appointment necessary.

KENNETH N.W. PAGE, 41 DUNDAS STREET, EDINBURGH EH3 6QQ. TN: (031) 556 6560. Est: 1972. Shop. Large stock sec. and antiq. books. Cata: fortnightly.

Also at 8 BARCLAY TERRACE, EDINBURGH EH10 4HP. TN: 031-228 1815

PERTH BOOKSHOP, 3A ABBOT STREET, PERTH. Prop: Leslie J.W. Fraser. TN: (0738) 33970. Shop, closed Mondays. Medium stock sec. and antiq. Spec: non-fiction, Scottish interest.

THE QUARTO BOOKSHOP, 8, GOLF PLACE, SAINT ANDREWS, FIFE KY16 9JA. Prop: M. Squires and J. Hopgood. TN: St. Andrews (0334) 74616. Est: 1969. Shop, medium sec and antiq. stock, also paperbacks. Spec: golf, Scottish books, St. Andrews and Fife. Corresp: French. B: Clydesdale Bank, Saint Andrews.

ALAN RANKIN, 72 DUNDAS STREET, EDINBURGH EH3 6QZ. TN: (031) 556-3705. Est: 1962. Private premises; appointment necessary. Small sec. and antiq. stock. Spec: scholarly and antiquarian. Cata: general occasionally.

SECOND EDITION, 9 HOWARD STREET, EDINBURGH. Prop: Mrs. Maureen E. Smith. TN: (031) 552-1850. Est: 1979. Shop. Large stock sec. and antiq. Spec: Literature, travel and Penguins. Corresp: Español. B: Royal Bank of Scotland PLC., Canonmills, Edinburgh.

G. AND I. SMITH, 25 MORNINGSIDE DRIVE, EDINBURGH EH10 5LZ. Prop: Gordon and Irene Smith. TN: (031-447) 6091 (evenings only). Est: 1980. Shop, closed on Mondays. Open on other days between 11.30 am-6.00 pm. Medium stock used. Spec: Scottish, archaeology. Cata: Occasionally. B: Royal Bank of Scotland, Ediburgh. Comiston Road Branch. Account 261183.

SPEIR BOOK SERVICE, OLD BALLECHIN, STRATH TAY, BY PITLOCHRY, PERTHSHIRE. Prop: Alasdair Steven. TN: Strath Tay (088-74) 319. Private premises; appointment preferable. Medium stock sec. and antiq. books. Spec: Scottish interest. Cata: occasionally.

THE SWINGS BOOKSHOP, 207–213 LOCHEE ROAD, DUNDEE DD2 2PJ. Prop: D.G. Garland. Est: 1964. Shop, no early closing. Large sec. and antiq. stock. Spec. Africana, travel, Scottish subjects, modern first editions.

JAMES THIN 53-59 SOUTH BRIDGE, EDINBURGH EH1 1YS. TN: (031) 556-6743. TA: Bookman Edinburgh. Est: 1848. Shop, early closing Saturday. Medium second-hand, and antiquarian stock: also new books. Spec: Scottish illustrated, travel. Cata: general, 3 a year. Corresp: Français, Deutsch. B: Royal Bank of Scotland, North Bridge, Edinburgh. N.B.L. B.A. A.B.A.

JOHN UPDIKE, 7 SAINT BERNARD'S ROW, EDINBURGH EH4 1HW. Prop: J.S. Watson and E.G. Nairn. TN: (031) 332-1650. Est: 1964. Bookrooms in office premises: prior 'phone call advisable. Large stock 19th and 20th century first editions, English, Scottish and American literature: illustrated books, private press books, fine bindings. Cata: occasionally. A.B.A.

WEST PORT BOOKS. 151 WEST PORT, EDINBURGH EH3 9OP. Prop: H.N. Barrott. TN: (031) 229 4431. Est: 1977. Shop. Medium sec. and antiq. stock. P.B.F.A.

G.R. AND M WINRAM, 32 ROSEMOUNT PLACE, ABERDEEN AB2 4XB. Prop: Mrs M. Winram. TN: 630673. Shop, closed Wednesday all day. Small stock sec. and antiq. Spec: local Scottish. B: Clydesdale Bank, 133 King Street, Aberdeen.

05. WEST SCOTLAND

Regions of Dumfries and Galloway, Strathclyde and Highlands

AYR, AYRSHIRE
CASTLE DOUGLAS, KIRKUDBRIGHTSHIRE
DUMFRIES, DUMFRIESSHIRE
FORTROSE, ROSS-SHIRE
GLASGOW, STRATHCLYDE
INVERNESS, INVERNESS-SHIRE
KILMARNOCK, AYRSHIRE
LARKHALL, LANARKSHIRE
LOCHMABEN, DUMFRIESSHIRE
MAUCHLINE, AYRSHIRE
NEWTON STEWART, WIGTOWNSHIRE
PAISLEY, RENFREWSHIRE
RHU, DUNBARTONSHIRE

ACORN BOOKS, 12 FORTEVIOT GARDENS, GARLIESTON, NEWTON STEWART DG8 8BL. Est: 1982. Private premises; postal business only. Small stock sec. and antiq. Spec: gardening, natural history. Cata: occasionally.

AILSA BOOKS, 10 WALKER STREET, PAISLEY. Prop: David McGarry. TN: 041-887-9446. Est: 1970. Shop. Medium stock used. Spec: Scottish. B: Bank of Scotland, 130 West Nile Street, Glasgow. Account 00675216. M: P.B.F.A.

IAN ANDERSON, 24 RAE STREET, DUMFRIES. TN: (0387) 64660. Private premises: appointment necessary. Medium stock sec. and antiq. Spec: Scottish. Cata: regular. M: P.B.F.A.

THE BOOKSHOP, 138 RENFIELD STREET, GLASGOW G2. Prop: Abdul Majid. TN: 041 332 7791. Est: 1960. Shop and stockroom. Large stock. Spec: arts and Scottish. Corresp: Deutsch, Français. B: The Bank of Scotland, 55 Bath Street, Glasgow G2 2DJ. Account 00169040.

BUITTLE BOOKS, KIRKSYDE, BUITTLE, CASTLE DOUGLAS. Prop: Mrs. H.F. Bell. TN: (0556) 610288. Private premises; appointment necessary. Small stock sec. and antiq. Spec: Scottish.

R.J.W. COLEBY, BARRASHEAD HOUSE, LOCHMABEN, DUMFRIESSHIRE DG11 1QF. Prop: R.J.W. Coleby. TN: (038 781) 601. Est 1970. Private premises with bookrooms attached; appointment necessary. Sec. and antiq., also new books. Spec: angling, shooting, Big Game, falconry, field sports and related natural history. C: 2 a year (charged).

CORN EXCHANGE BOOKSHOP, CORN EXCHANGE, STIRLING. Prop: B.R. and E.M.B. Young. TN: (0786) 3967. Shop, closed Wednesdays. Small sec. and antiq. stock. Spec: local history and topography.

ROBERT CROZIER, 2 PARK VIEW, LARKHALL, LANARKSHIRE ML9 2JJ. TN: 883272. Est: 1975. Private premises; appointment necessary. Small stock sec. and antiq. also new books. Theology only. Cata: 4 a year.

BENNY GILLIES, 31 VICTORIA STREET, KIRKPATRICK DURHAM, CASTLE DOUGLAS, KIRKCUDBRIGHTSHIRE DG7 3HQ. TN: (055 665) 412. Est: 1979. Private premises; appointment advisable. Small stock sec. and antiq. Spec: Scottish interest, especially Dumfries and Galloway; anything to do with countryside and natural history, also prints and maps. Cata: occasionally. Corresp: Français, M: P.B.F.A.

GILMOREHILL BOOKS, 43 BANK STREET, HILLHEAD, GLASGOW. Prop: Gerard McGonigle. TN: (041) 339-7504. Shop. Spec: literature, Scottish, sets, art.

LAIDIR LEISURE [BOOK SECTION], 2 ALBANY QUAD, SPRINGBOIG, GLASGOW. Prop: D. Webster, Jnr. TN: (041) 774 3236. Est: 1958. Mail order business only. Very small stock sec. and antiq. also new books. Spec: physical education, sports, etc.

McLAREN BOOKS, ARDENCONNEL COTTAGE, CHURCH ROAD, RHU, DUNBARTONSHIRE G84 8RW. Prop: George M.O. Newlands. TN: (0436) 820487 or 6453. Est: 1976. Private premises; postal business only, but shop at 13 East King Street, Helensburgh, Dunbartonshire, TN: (0436) 6453, open Thursdays, Fridays and Saturdays or by appointment. Medium stock sec. and antiq. Spec: naval and maritime, Scottish interest. Cata: 8 a year. M: P.B.F.A.

BRUCE MARSHALL, GARSTANG, STAIR, NEAR MAUCHLINE, AYRSHIRE. TN: Trabboch 283 and Ayr 284505. Est: 1972. Private premises; appointment necessary. Medium stock sec. and antiq. Spec: atlases, travel and topography, natural history. Cata: 3 a year. A.B.A.

B. MARSHALL, 24 River Street, Ayr, Ayrshire. TN: Ayr 84505. Est: 1976. Shop, early closing Wednesdays. Medium sec. and antiq. stock. Spec: travel and local topography. Cata: 2 a year.

RICHARD ROBERTS, 8 Main Road, Waterside, Kilmarnock, Ayrshire KA3 6JB. Prop: Richard Roberts. TN: (05 606) 349. Est: 1976. Private premises; appointment necessary. Medium stock sec. and antiq. Spec: mathematics and Scottish. Cata: 5 a year. B: Clydesdale Bank, The Foregate, Kilmarnock. A/c 2046 5255.

JOHN SMITH & SON [GLASGOW] LTD., 57 Saint Vincent Street, Glasgow G2 5TB. TN: (041) 221-7472. Shop. Large stock sec. and antiq. Maps and prints. M: A.B.A. Catalogues issued.

S.S. STANSFIELD, 3 Castle Street, Fortrose, Ross-shire IV10 8TH TN: Fortrose (0381) 20579. Est: 1967. Private premises, appointment necessary. Small sec. and antiq. stock. Scottish books of all types only. Cata: on foregoing, monthly.

VOLTAIRE & ROUSSEAU, 12–14 Otago Lane, Kelvinbridge, Glasgow G11 7QY. Prop: Joseph McGonigle. TN: (041) 339-1811. Shop. Medium stock sec. and antiq.

06. WALES (CYMRU)

The Welsh names of towns usually known by English names, are shown in brackets

DYFED

ABERYSTWYTH
CARDIGAN (ABERTEIFI)
CARMARTHEN (CAERFYRDDIN)
CRYMMYCH
HAVERFORDWEST (HWLFFORDD)
LLANWRDA

CLWYD

COLWYN BAY (BAE COLWYN)
MOLD (YR WYDDGRUG)
OLD COLWYN (HEN COLWYN)
PRESTATYN
WREXHAM (WRECSAM)

GWYNEDD

BARMOUTH (ABERMO)
CAERNARFON
DOLGELLAU
HOLYHEAD (CAERGYBI)
LLANDUDNO
LLANGEFNI
MOELFRE

GWENT

ABERGAVENNY (Y FENNI)
CHEPSTOW (CAS-GWENT)
MONMOUTH (TREFYNWY)
NEWPORT (CASNEWYDD)
USK (BRYNBUGA)

POWYS

HAY ON WYE (Y GELLI)
LLANDRINDOD WELLS
MACHYNLLETH
NEWTOWN (Y DRENEWYDD)
PRESTEIGN (LLANANDRAS)

GLAMORGAN (MORGANWG)

CARDIFF (CAERDYDD)
SWANSEA (ABERTAWE)

ALBANY BOOKS, 113 Albany Road, Cardiff CF2 3NS. Prop: John Barrett, TN: (0222) 498802. Est: 1974. Shop, early closing Wednesday. Medium stock sec. and antiq. also new books, prints and maps. Spec: Welsh topography; chess.

THE ALBATROSS BOOKSHOP, 12 MARINERS SQUARE, HAVERFORDWEST, PEMBROKESHIRE, DYFED. Prop: Michael Whitelock. TN: (06467) 475. (after hours). Est: 1983. Shop: open Mondays and Fridays. Small stock sec. and antiq. Spec: ornithology, topography (especially local), art, church plate. Cata: 1 or 2 a year. B: Barclays Bank PLC., Main Street, Pembroke, Dyfed.

ANGLESEY BOOKS, 5 CHURCH STREET, LLANGEFNI, ANGLESEY, GWYNEDD. Prop: Jack Baines. TN: (0407) 810121. Est: 1980. Shop, closed Tuesday afternoon. Medium stock sec. and antiq. Spec: mountaineering, Himalayan exploration. Cata: 2 or 3 a year. Corresp: Cymraeg. B: Midland Bank, Rhosneigr, Anglesey, Gwynedd. M: P.B.F.A.

S.E. ARTHUR, 4 TY BRITH GARDENS, USK, GWENT NP5 1BY. TN: Usk 3368. Est: 1975. Private premises; appointment necessary. Very small stock, sec. and antiq. Spec: Acts of Parliament, golf. Cata: Lists occasionally.

ASHLEY BOOKS, RHYCHYDWR, CRYMMYCH, DYFED SA41 3RB. Prop: Mrs. Anne Oldham. TN: (023 973) 371. Est: 1966. Private premises; appointment necessary. Very small stock sec. and antiq. also new books and publishing. Spec: caving, potholing, speleology, cave art. Cata: on speleology, weekly.

J. GEOFFREY ASPIN, THE RARE BOOK SHOP, 27 CASTLE STREET, HAY-ON-WYE, POWYS, VIA HEREFORD HR3 5DF. TN: 0497-820-437. Est: 1972. Shop, closed on Tuesdays. Open only during afternoons in winter. Medium stock antiquarian and used. Spec: French books, all periods, old and rare Bibles and Prayer books. Cata: 3 a year. Corresp: Français. B: Barclays Bank, 23 High Street, Royston, Herts SG8 9AB. Account 30129488.

BAY BOOKSHOP, 14 SEAVIEW ROAD, COLWYN BAY, CLWYD. Prop: R. & R. Morley, B.A. (Hons). TN: (0492) 31642. Est. 1961 (shop since 1973). Medium stock sec. and antiq. also new books and postcards. Shop, open every day in Summer; early closing Wednesday from September to June.

MARY BLAND, AUGOP, EVENJOBB, NEAR PRESTEIGN, POWYS. TN: (054 76) 218. Est: 1978. Private premises; appointment necessary. Small stock sec. and antiq. Spec: gardening and botany. Cata: 1 or 2 a year. B: Barclays Bank, Broad Street, Knighton, Powys. M: P.B.F.A.

RICHARD BOOTH [BOOKSELLER] LIMITED, FRANK LEWIS HOUSE, HAY ON WYE, VIA HEREFORD. TN: Hay on Wye 820 322. TA: Castlebook, Hay on Wye. Est: 1958. 2 shops and storerooms and Hay Castle. Very large stock of sec. and antiq. books, also new books, prints and water-colours, design, art, architecture. General stock, especially English literature, natural history, science and technology, military, medical, American genealogy, theology, topography sets, remainders. Cata: quarterly, general list.

JANET BOX, LLANFACHRAETH, HOLYHEAD, GWYNEDD. Prop: Mrs. J.A. Box. TN: (0407) 740374. Est: 1982. Private premises; appointment necessary. Very small stock sec. and antiq. Spec: Africana; Middle East. Cata: 6 a year. Corresp: Français. B: Lloyds Bank, Boston Street, Holyhead.

THE BRIDGE BOOKSHOP, P.O. BOX 15, VICARAGE HILL, WREXHAM, CLWYD. Prop: Mr. and Mrs. W.A. Williams. TN: Wrexham 59968. Est: 1978. Shop, closed half days on Wednesdays. Small stock used. Spec: local and Welsh history. New books also stocked. Cata: 3 a year. Corresp: Cymraeg. B: Barclays Bank, High Street, Wrexham.

MRS. D. BUDGE, 61 UPPER WATERLOO ROAD, PENYLAN, CARDIFF CF3 7BL. TN: (0222) 485369. Est: 1960. Shop, closed all day Mondays and Tuesdays. Small stock sec. and antiq. books. Spec: arts, antiques, crafts, collecting. Cata: quarterly. B: Barclays Bank, 86 Queens Road, Clifton, Bristol. Account 60222321. P.B.F.A.

THE CARDIGAN BOOK CENTRE, 1 ROYAL OAK, QUAY STREET, CARDIGAN SA43 1HR. Prop: Mrs. Frances Mason. TN: Cardigan (0239) 612704. Storeroom, open normal business hours, closed Wednesdays. Large sec. and antiq. stock, also new books, stationery and old maps & prints. Spec: topography, politics, maps and prints. Cata: general, occasionally. B: National Westminster Bank, High St., Cardigan, Dyfed. Account 02308525.

THE CERAMIC BOOK COMPANY, 4 SAINT JOHNS ROAD, NEWPORT, GWENT NPT 8GH. Prop: Simcox and Coombes. TN: Newport 71561. TA: Dressings Newport-Gwent. Stockroom; appointment necessary. Medium sec. and antiq. stock. Spec: ceramics, Welsh porcelain, fine arts. Also publishers of ceramics books. B: Lloyds Bank, Maindee, Newport, Gwent. Account 0218794.

CHARLES STREET BOOKSHOP, 50 CHARLES STREET, CARDIFF. Prop: C.R. Mitchell. TN: (0222) 388423. Est: 1981. Shop. Medium stock sec. and antiq. Spec: Welsh interest. Corresp: Français, Deutsch, Cymraeg. B: Co-operative Bank, The Hayes, Cardiff. M: P.B.F.A.

CHRISTMAS ARCHIVES, WASSAIL HOUSE, 64 SEVERN ROAD, CANTON, CARDIFF CF1 9EA. PROP: MARIA HUBERT VON STAUFER. TN: 0222-41120. Est: 1978. Private premises; appointment necessary. Small stock used. Spec: Christmas, children's, magazines, Icons and illuminations, photography. Cata: annually. Corresp: Deutsch, Français, Español. Enquiries in Dutch, Swedish and Polish understood. B: National Westminster Bank, Cowbridge Road, Canton, Cardiff.

THE CLOCKTOWER BOOKSHOP, THE PAVEMENT, HAY-ON-WYE, POWYS, VIA HEREFORD HR3 5BU. Prop: Kemys and Sally Forwood. TN: Hay-on-Wye 820 539. Est: 1978. Shop. Medium stock sec. and antiq. Spec: natural history, literature and topography. Corresp: Français. B: Barclays Bank Broad Street, Hay-on-Wye. Account 90262978.

COCH-Y-BONDDU BOOKS, COEDCAE, PENEGOES, MACHYNLLETH, POWYS. Prop: Paul Morgan. TN: (0654) 2837. Est: 1982. Private premises; appointment preferable. Small stock sec. and antiq. Spec: fishing, field sport, countryside. Cata: 3 a year.

CRATCHIT'S BOOKSHOP, 22A LAMMAS STREET, CARMARTHEN, DYFED. Prop: M. Yaffey. TN: (0269) 870537. Home. Est: 1978. Shop, closed Monday and Thursday. Small stock sec. and antiq. Spec: Welsh topography. Corresp: Cymraeg, Français, Deutsch.

JIM CRONIN, 84 MONTHERMER ROAD, CATHAYS, CARDIFF CF2 4QY. Prop: J.T. Cronin. TN: (0222) 485271 evenings. Est: 1977. Shop, early closing Wednesdays. Very small stock sec. and antiq. books, also sheet music and records (78 & 45 r.p.m. & LPs). Spec: music theory and history: musical magazines.

DOGGIE HUBBARD'S BOOKSHOP, FFYNNON CADNO, PONTERWYD, ABERYSTWYTH, DYFED. Prop: Clifford L.B. Hubbard, F.I.A.L., TN: (0970) 85224. Est: 1972. Private premises; appointment necessary. Large stock sec. and antiq. Spec: dogs: all cynological subjects in all languages, also new books on dogs. Corresp: Cymraeg, Français, Deutsch. B: National Westminster Bank, 2 Water Lane, Bakewell, Derbyshire. M: A.B.A.

DYLANS BOOKSTORE, SALUBRIOUS PASSAGE, SWANSEA, WEST GLAMORGAN. Prop: J.M. Towns. TN: 55255 and 297800 (Home). Est: 1970. Shop and stockroom; closed half day on Thursdays. Spec: Welsh history and topography, Dylan Thomas, Gypsies. Cata: occasionally. Corresp: Français. B: National Westminster Bank, Belle Vue Way, Swansea. Account 01637541. M: P.B.F.A.

J.M. FARRINGDON, ARIEL HOUSE, 8 HADLAND TERRACE, WEST CROSS, SWANSEA SA3 5TT. TN: (0792) 405267. Est: 1970. Private premises; strictly by appointment. Small stock sec. & antiq. Spec: bells, carillons, bellringing, 18th and 20th century English literature, also publishers. Cata: 2 a year. B: National Westminster Bank, 528 Mumbles Road, Mumbles, Swansea. Account: 02008815.

GALLOWAY LIMITED, PIER STREET, ABERYSTWYTH, DYFED SY23 2LR. TN: Aberystwyth 612563. Shop, early closing Wednesday. Large sec. and antiq. stock; also new books and stationery. H.M.S.O. Agents. B.A., N.B.L.

JUDITH GARDNER CHILDREN'S BOOKS, TOLL COTTAGE, PONTVAEN, HAY ON WYE, POWYS HR3 5EW. Prop: Mrs. J.M. Gardner. Est: 1981. Private premises with showroom; appointment preferable. Very small stock sec. and antiq. Children's literature only. Lists on request. Corresp: Français, Deutsch.

S. HAMILTON, PARC, CAIO, LLANWRDA, DYFED SA19 8PF. TN: (055 85) 405. Est: 1968. Private premises; postal business only. Small stock sec. and antiq. Spec: Sherlockiana. Cata: 2 a year.

THE HAY CINEMA BOOKSHOP, CASTLE STREET, HAY-ON-WYE, VIA HEREFORD. Prop: Greg Coombes. TN: (0497) 820071. Telex: 95596 (ref. Pharos). Est: 1982. Shop, open every day including Sundays. Very large stock sec. and antiq. Cata: 12 a year. Corresp: Français, Deutsch. B: Midland Bank P.L.C., High Town, Hay-on-Wye via Hereford HR3 5AE.

HAY-ON-WYE BOOKSELLERS, CROWN HOUSE, 8 HIGH TOWN, HAY-ON-WYE, HEREFORD. Prop: M.A. Bullock. TN: (0497) 820875. Est: 1980. Shop. B: National Westminster Bank, Orford Road, Hay-on-Wye, Hereford. A/c No. 05335426.

HAY-ON-WYE BOOK SERVICES LTD., THE COTTAGE, CAE MAWR LANE, HAY-ON-WYE, HEREFORD. Prop: M.A. Bullock and J.E. Jordan. TN: (0497) 820 131. Est: 1981. Warehouse and showrooms. Sec. and antiq. stock. Spec: natural history, field sports, dogs. Mainly remainders. B: Barclays Bank, Broad Street, Hay-on-Wye, Hereford. A/c. No. 00221171.

HOURGLASS BOOKS, 6 DEW STREET, HAVERFORDWEST, DYFED. Prop: Peter Abrams. Shop: small stock sec. and antiq.

DAVID E. HUGHES, 21 MADOC STREET, LLANDUDNO. TN: 77700. Est: 1968. Shop, closed on Wednesdays. Medium stock used. B: Midland Bank, Mostyn Street, Llandudno.

J.P. WILLIAMS JONES, MAESGWYN, ELDON SQUARE, DOLGELLAU, GWYNEDD. TN: (0341) 422520. Est: 1980. Shop, closed on Wednesdays; appointment necessary. Very small stock used. Spec: Welsh interest, mountaineering, modern fiction. Cata: occasionally. Corresp: Cymraeg. B: Midland Bank, Eldon Square, Dolgellau, Gwynedd. Account 71011456. M: B.A.

H.K. LOCKYER [BOOKSELLERS], PRIORY BOOKSHOP, MONK STREET, ABERGAVENNY, GWENT NP7 5NP. Prop: H.K. Lockyer and Mrs. L.M. Fitzgerald. TN: Abergavenny (0873) 5825 and Little Mill (049 528) 286. Est: 1970. Shop. Large stock sec. and antiq. also new books. Spec: horses, dogs, field sports, livestock and agriculture, South Wales and Welsh Border topography, antiques and collecting.

LOTUS PRESS LIMITED, MOELFRE, ANGLESEY LL72 8HU. Prop: Alan Darby. TN: Moelfre (024888) 423. Telex: 61208. Est: 1973. Private premises; postal business only. Very small stock sec. and antiq. also new books. Spec: Africa and Asia. Corresp: Français. Cata: several a year. B: Midland Bank, 47 High Street, Bromsgrove, Worcestershire B61 8AW. M: Publishers' Association.

MONNOW BOOKS, 9 WHITECROSS STREET, MONMOUTH, GWENT NP5 3BY. Prop: John Clark. TN: (0600) 2347. Est: 1983. Shop, closed Thursdays. Small stock sec. and antiq. Spec: antiquarian Welsh topography. Corresp: Français. B: Midland Bank, Monmouth. M: P.B.F.A.

D.M. NEWBAND, DREFOR COTTAGE, NEAR NEWTOWN, POWYS SY16 4PQ. TN: (0686) 88205. Est: 1983. Private premises; appointment necessary. Very small stock sec. and antiq. Spec: railways and related transport. B: Lloyds Bank, Welshpool, Powys.

OUT-OF-PRINT BOOK SERVICE, 17 FAIRWATER GROVE EAST, CARDIFF. Prop: L. Foulkes. TN: (0222) 569488. Est: 1973. Private premises; postal business only. Search service; explanatory leaflet available on receipt of s.a.e. B: Barclays Bank, 410 Cowbridge Road East, Cardiff CF5 1WZ.

PALACE BOOKS, POOL STREET, CAERNARFON, GWYNEDD, NORTH WALES. Prop: David Jarvis. TN: (0286) 4892. Shop; early closing Thursday afternoons in winter. Also viewing by appointment possible. Large stock sec. and antiq. Spec: Welsh interest, mountaineering.

LESLIE & PATRICIA PARRIS, THE CORNER HOUSE, HILLCREST AVENUE, LLANDRINDOD WELLS, POWYS LD1 6DL. TN: (0597) 3175. Est: 1970 Shop at 1 Craig Road, Llandrindod Wells, TN: (0597) 3484. Medium stock sec. and antiq. books. Spec: card games, British and foreign royalty. Cata: 8 a year.

RIVER WYE BOOKSELLERS, 14 HIGH TOWN, HAY-ON-WYE, POWYS, VIA HEREFORD. Prop: Mr. and Mrs. M.A. Bullock. TN: Hay-on-Wye (0497) 820875. Est: 1977. Shop, open seven days a week. Large stock used. Spec: illustrated books. Cata: annually. B: National Westminster Bank, Oxford Road, Hay-on-Wye. Account 05332605.

TOM LLOYD-ROBERTS, OLD COURT HOUSE, CAERWYS, MOLD, CLWYD CH7 5BB. TN: (0352) 720276. Private premises; stock can be seen 10.00 to 18.00 Monday to Friday or by appointment. Large stock sec. and antiq. also new books and bookbinding. Spec: Wales, topography, travel, literature, bindings. Cata: 5 or 6 a year. A.B.A., N.B.L.

SEAFARER BOOKS, 24 MARKET COURTYARD, RIVERSIDE, HAVERFORDWEST, DYFED. Prop: D.R. and S.M. Saunders. TN: Home: after 18.00 hrs. (0646) 600675. Est: 1980. Shop, closed Thursday afternoon. Small stock sec. and antiq. also new books. Spec: maritime. Cata: 3 a year. B: Barclays Bank, High Street, Haverfordwest.

SOUTH WIND PRESS, THE MOUNTAIN BOOKSHOP, MELIDEN, PRESTATYN, CLWYD. Prop: Mrs. D. Wild-Rice. TN: Prestatyn 4777. Est: 1974. Private premises; appointment necessary. Small stock sec. Spec: modern first editions. books. Cata: fortnightly.

BRIAN STEVENS, 3 CHURCH STREET, MONMOUTH, GWENT NP5 3BX. TN: Monmouth 3701. Est: 1968. Shop, closed Thursdays. Very small stock sec. and antiq. also new books and antique prints and maps. Spec: history and topography, Gwent and Wales generally.

E. WYN THOMAS, OLD QUARRY, MINERS' LANE, OLD COLWYN, CLWYD. TN: (0492) 515336. Est: 1947. Shop, closed Wednesdays. Small stock sec. and antiq. also new books. Spec: Natural history; Welsh interest, fiction and non-fiction. Corresp: Cymraeg, Français.

WALSALL HOUSE, WALSALL HOUSE, CHURCH STREET, BARMOUTH, GWYNEDD. Prop: R.I. and S. Huxter. TN: (0341) 280194. Est: 1982. Shop, closed Wednesdays in Winter. Medium stock sec. and antiq. Spec: stage magic; celebrity autographs. Cata: occasionally.

MARK WESTWOOD, LITTLE MILL, GLASBURY, near HAY ON WYE, VIA HEREFORD. TN: Glasbury 436. Est: 1975. Private premises; appointment necessary. Small stock sec. and antiq. Spec: science, medicine, technology, Wales, ballooning. Cata: 6 a year. A.B.A.

YESTERDAY'S NEWS, 43 DUNDONALD ROAD, COLWYN BAY, CLWYD LL29 7RE. Prop: Elfed Jones. TN: Colwyn Bay (0492) 31195. Est: 1959. House premises; stock can be seen normal business hours. 100,000 newspapers, periodicals, comics, documents, diaries etc., (17th century to 1960's. Corresp: Français, Deutsch. B: Barclays Bank, Colwyn Bay. Account 00523550.

YSTWYTH BOOKS, 7 PRINCESS STREET, ABERYSTWYTH, DYFED SY23 1DX. Prop: P.T. Hinde, B.Sc. TN: (0970) 617511. Est: 1976. Shop, closed on Wednesdays. Medium stock. Spec: history, technology, economic industrial history. Welsh interest books. Small stock of journals and medium stock of new books. Corresp: Cymraeg Francçais. B: National Westminster Bank, North Parade Aberystwyth. M: B.A.

07. NORTHUMBERLAND

BELFORD
BELLINGHAM
BERWICK ON TWEED
FELTON
HEXHAM
MORPETH
WARTON

BOOKWORMS, 6 High Street, Belford, Northumberland NH70 7ND. TN: (066 83) 755. Shop. Est: 1983. Sec. and Antiq. rare and out-of-print books

LORRAINE GOODINSON, Cragwell House, Hesleyside, Bellingham, Hexham, Northumberland. TN: (0660) 20345. Private premises; appointment necessary. Very small stock sec. and antiq.

HENCOTES ANTIQUES AND BOOKS, 8 Hencotes, Hexham, Northumberland NE46 3EJ. Prop: J.D. and G.H. Clayton. TN: (0434) 604803 after 18.00 hrs. Shop: 605971. Est: 1972. Shop, early closing Thursdays. Small stock sec. and antiq. books; also antiques.

INTECH BOOKS, 14 Bracken Ridge, Morpeth, Northumberland NE61 3SY. Prop: Mrs. C. Wilkinson. TN: (0670) 519102. Est: 1981. Private premises; appointment necessary. Very small stock sec. and antiq. also new books. Spec: transport, British topography. B: Barclays Bank, Chesterfield.

K.G. McDONALD, Fell Cottage, Felton, Northumberland NE65 9PZ. TN: Felton 504. Est: 1978. Private house; appointment necessary. Small stock of general books and forestry, some journals. Corresp: Français, Español. Cata: rarely. B: National Westminster Bank, 38 Saint Mary's Place, Newcastle-on-Tyne. Account 92179924.

JULIE MacGREGOR, 48, Bridge Street, Berwick upon Tweed, Northumberland TD15 1AQ. TN: Berwick (0289) 307749. Shop. Small stock sec. and antiq. books. Spec: maritime, local history.

ALAN MORRISON, 4 Warton Cottages, Warton, near Rothbury, Northumberland. Private premises; appointment necessary. Medium stock sec. and antiq.

08. CUMBRIA

ALSTON	HOLMROOK
AMBLESIDE	KENDAL
BARROW IN FURNESS	KESWICK
CARLISLE	PENRITH
CARTMEL	SEASCALE
COCKERMOUTH	SEDBURGH
GRANGE OVER SANDS	

MARGARET ARMSTRONG, 22 Brandlehow Crescent, Keswick, Cumbria CA12 4JE. TN: (0596) 74555.

BERNICIA BOOKS, Clarghyll Hall, Alston, Cumbria CA9 3NF. Prop: W. G. Wilson. TN: Alston (0498) 81701. Est: 1974. Private premises; appointment necessary. Small stock sec. & antiq: Spec: 19th century travel and minor novelists; political history. Corresp: Français. B: Lloyds Bank, 3 Allendale Terrace, Tynemouth, NE30 4RA. Account 0017545.

BOOK COTTAGE BOOKS, Book Cottage, Braithwaite, Keswick, Cumbria CA12 5SY. Prop: Timothy Walsh. TN: Braithwaite 275. Est: 1974. House and barn, customers welcome normal business hours. Medium stock sec. books. Spec: national history, trees and forests, history, travel, general, fiction also a Café in summer. Corresp: Gaelic (Scots). B: National Westminster, Main Street, Keswick. Account 07013302.

BOOKCASE, 28 Castle Street, Carlisle, Cumbria. Prop: Mrs. G. Matthews. TN: 44560. Est: 1978. Shop. Large stock sec. and antiq. Spec: local history and Cumbria. B: Midland Bank, King Street, Wigton. Account 01014552.

THE BOOK HOUSE, Grey Garth, Ravenstonedale, Kirkby Stephen, Cumbria CA17 4NQ. Prop: Christopher and Mary Irwin. Medium stock sec. and antiq. Spec: industrial history, railway and transport history.

MAURICE DODD BOOKSELLER, 112 Warwick Road, Carlisle, Cumbria CA1 1LF. Prop: G.W. & V.A. Keates and R.J. McRoberts. TN: 22087. Est: 1945. Private House; stock can be seen any time in business hours or after hours by appointment. Large stock sec. and antiq. also stocks prints and pictures. B: Barclays Bank, Devonshire Street, Carlisle. Account: 30332623. M: P.B.F.A.

DUNDAS GALLERIES, 18 Fisher Street, Carlisle. Prop: Jenni and Charles Sleath. (0228) 37341 & 34715. Shop. Medium stock sec. and antiq. M: P.B.F.A. Also Art Gallery, Antiques, Coffee House.

FINE ART CATALOGUES, The Hollies, Port Carlisle, Nr. Carlisle, Cumbria CA5 5BU. Prop: Michael Bennett. TN: 096-55-51398. Est: 1973. Private house and stockroom; appointment necessary. Medium stock of sec. and antiq. Spcc: books of reference material on British art and artists. Back-numbers of journals. Cata: 4-6 a year.

ANNE FITZSIMONS, THE RETREAT, THE GREEN, WETHERAL, CARLISLE, CUMBRIA CA4 8ET. Prop: Anne FitzSimons. (0228) 60675. Est: 1978. Private premises; appointment necessary. Very small stock sec. and antiq. Spec: Books ephemera, memorabilia, concerning the Performing Arts. Cata: 3 or 4 a year. M: P.B.F.A.

GRAYLING BOOKS, LYVENNET, CROSBY RAVENSWORTH, PENRITH, CUMBRIA CA10 3JP. Prop: David A.H. Grayling. TN: Ravenworth 282. Est: 1970. Private premises; appointment necessary. Medium stock sec. and antiq. books. Spec: field sports, Big Game, Deer, natural history. Cata: 6 a year.

R.F.G. HOLLETT AND SON, 6 FINKLE STREET, SEDBERGH, CUMBRIA LA10 5BZ. TN: Sedbergh (0587) 20298 & 20286. Shop; appointment advisable. Large antiq. stock. Spec: natural history, travel & topography, fine arts. M: A.B.A.

EWEN KERR, 1 NEW ROAD, KENDAL LA9 4AY. TN: (0539) 20659. TA: Kerr Bookseller Kendal. Est: 1935. Shop and storerooms, closed all day Thursday. Large sec. and antiq. stock. Spec: Lake District, A.B.A.

NORMAN KERR, CARTMEL, GRANGE OVER SANDS, CUMBRIA LA11 6PX. Prop: N.M. and H. Kerr. TN: (044 854) 247. Est: 1933. Private premises; appointment essential. Large sec. and antiq. stock. Spec: Railways, maritime and naval, aviation, automobiles, transport and engineering, natural history. M: A.B.A., P.B.F.A.

THE LITTLE BOOKSHOP, 1 CHEAPSIDE, AMBLESIDE, CUMBRIA LA12 0AB. Prop: Marion Hebden. TN: (096-63) 32094. Shop. Medium sec. and antiq. stock.

E.A. MARSHALL & DAUGHTERS, ISEL COTTAGE, ISEL, NEAR COCKERMOUTH, CUMBRIA CA13 0QG. TN: (09404) 608. Est: 1968. Postal business but dealers welcome by appointment. Very small stock sec. and antiq. books. Spec: Lake District and Cumbrian topography.

MICHAEL MOON'S BOOKSHOP, 41–43 ROPER STREET, WHITEHAVEN, CUMBRIA. Prop: Michael and Sylvia Moon. TN: Whitehaven 62936. Est: 1967. Shop, office and warehouse (own offstreet car park), closed all day Wednesday. Large stock sec. and antiq. also publishers of local topography, and some journals. Spec: Cumbriana. Cata: 3–4 a year. B: Midland Bank, Lowther Street, Whitehaven. Account 81025619. M: A.B.A., P.F.B.A.

MOSTLY BOOKS, 247 RAWLINSON STREET, BARROW-IN-FURNESS, CUMBRIA LA1 4DW. Prop: Harvey Leeson. TN: (0229) 36808 or 25097. Est: 1981. Shop: closed Monday. Telephone if coming from a distance. Small stock sec. and antiq.

SAINT ANDREWS BOOKSHOP, SAINT ANDREWS VIEW, PENRITH, CUMBRIA. Prop: A.G. Vines. TN: Penrith 64455. Shop, early closing Wednesdays. Small stock sec. and antiq. also new books. B.A.

PETER BAIN SMITH, Bank Court, Market Square, Cartmel. (044854) 369. Shop: closed Monday and Tuesday in winter. Spec: children's books and local topography.

STRICKLANDGATE ANTIQUES, 138 Stricklandgate, Kendal, Cumbria LA9 4QG. Prop: D. Grayling and D. Woodeson. TN: Kendal 26644. Est: 1979. Shop, open from 10.30 am-2.30 pm daily except Thursdays. Small stock sec. and antiq. also antiques. Corresp: Deutsch, Français. B: Midland Bank. Account 71003291. M: P.B.F.A.

EDWARD PAGET-TOMLINSON, 1a Market Street, Ulverston, Cumbria LA12 7AY. TN: Buckland Newton (030 05) 414. Est: 1978. Shop, closed on Wesnesdays. Small stock sec. and antiq. Spec: local history, topography, maritime. Corresp: Français. B: National Westminster Bank, 2 Queen Street, Ulverston, LA12 7AX. Account: 05214300.

TRADING POST, 34 Derby Street, Barrow-in-Furness, Cumbria LA13 9TQ. Prop: Alan R. Beattie. TN: (0229) 29722. Private Premises, mail order only. Spec: The American West.

D. ARNOLD VARTY, Church Street, Ambleside, Cumbria LA22 0BU. Prop: Derrick Arnold Varty. TN: (0966) 33313. TA: Varty Ambleside 33313. Est: 1946. Shop, early closing Thursdays. Small stock sec. and antiq. Also duplicating service. Spec: Cumbria and Lake District. Cata: occasionally.

D.R. WINKWORTH, The Printing House, 102 Main Street, Cockermouth. TN: (0900) 824984. Shop: early closing Thursday. Medium stock sec. and antiq. Spec: Lake District, climbing, printing.

VIVIAN WRIGHT, Fennelsyke, Raughton Head, Carlisle, Cumbria. TN: (069 96) 431. House premises; telephone for appointment. Small stock sec. and antiq. books. Spec: Cumbria; modern architecture and design. Cata: 4 or 5 a year. M: P.B.F.A.

09. TYNE AND WEAR AND COUNTY DURHAM

CONSETT	NEWCASTLE UPON TYNE
CROOK	NORTH SHIELDS
DARLINGTON	ROWLANDS GILL
DURHAM	SOUTH SHIELDS
GATESHEAD	

ADAB BOOKS, Moody's Yard, Claypath, Durham DH1 1RG. Prop: D.M. Roper. TN: (0385) 63309. Est: 1971. Private premises; appointment necessary. Small stock sec. and antiq. books. Spec: oriental subjects (Asia, Middle East, North Africa). Cata: 6 a year.

BARBICAN BOOKROOM, 28 Market Place, Durham, TN: (0385) 63041. Spec: Theology.

BEWICK BOOKS, 14 Clayton Road, Jesmond, Newcastle 2. Prop: A.V. Seaton. TN: (0632) 812711. Est: 1982. Shop. Small stock sec. and antiq. Spec. North East material, Bewick items, caricature and comic books. Corresp: Francais. B: Barclays Bank, Park View, Whitley Bay.

THE BOOKSTALL, The New Markets, Durham City. Prop: R.J. Dickinson. TN: (0385) 61491. Est: 1929. Bookstall, open on Fridays and Saturdays between 9 am–5 pm. Medium Stock. Spec: Modern first editions, pre 1700 imprints. Also sells coins, stamps and pictures. Corresp: Français, Italiano, Russian, Español.

CORSTOPHINE GALLERY, 1 Clayton Park Square, Jesmond, Newcastle upon Tyne 2. TN: (0632) 812763. Shop, small stock of sec. and antiq. books, also postcards, posters, prints.

DAVIS BOOKS LIMITED, 140 Westgate Road, Newcastle upon Tyne. Prop: E. Davis, S.B. Davis and J. Sneddon. TN: (0632) 614580. Est: 1981. Shop. Large stock sec. and antiq. also remainders. Spec: arts and humanities. Cata: occasionally. B: Midland Bank, Grainger Street, Newcastle upon Tyne. M: P.B.F.A.

ALAN GODFREY, 57–58 Spoor Street, Dunston, Gateshead NE11 9BD. TN: Dunston 608546. Est: 1977. Private premises; appointment necessary. Small stock used. Spec: ordnance survey maps. Cata: occasionally. B: Lloyds Bank, Dunston. Account 0109050.

KEEL ROW BOOKS, 11 Fenwick Terrace, Preston Road, North Shields, Tyne and Wear. Prop: A. and L. Rickard. TN: (0632) 595105. Shop, closed Wednesdays. Large stock sec. and antiq. M: P.B.F.A.

JOAN LAMBERT, 24 Beechwood Avenue, Darlington DL3 7HP. TN: (0325) 54485. Private premises; appointment necessary. Medium stock sec. and antiq. Spec: children's books; topography. M: P.B.F.A.

RICHARD OLEY, 6 Station Road, South Shields, Tyne and Wear NE33 1ED. TN: (0632) 551963. Est: 1980. Shop, usually closed Tuesday and Wednesday. Small stock sec. and antiq. Spec: maritime, topography, modern first editions, science.

PAST AND PRESENT, 44 Bondgate, Darlington. Prop: W.A. Vokes. Est: 1973. Shop, early closing Wednesday. Medium sec. and antiq. stock. Cata: 4 a year.

W. ROBINSON [NEWCASTLE] LIMITED, 49–53 Grainger Market, Newcastle upon Tyne NE1 5QQ. TN: (0632) 322978. Est: 1881. Shop, early closing Wednesday. Large sec. stock. A.B.A. B.A.

R.J. SCOTT, 26a Coniscliffe Road, Darlington, County Durham. TN: 63911 & 53767. Est: 1936. Shop, early closing Wednesdays. Large stock sec. and antiq. books; also prints and water colours. Spec: Extra illustrated, colourplate books. A.B.A.
(*Also at* 91 High Northgate, Darlington and warehouse at Feethams Hill, Darlington).

J. SHOTTON, The Bookshop, 89 Elvet Bridge, Durham DH1 3AG. TN: (0385) 64597. Est: 1967. Shop, Small stock sec. and antiq. books; also prints and maps. Cata: general. Annually. M: A.B.A.

FRANK SMITH, 40A Heaton Road, Newcastle upon Tyne NE6 1SD. TN: (0632) 656333. Est: 1981. Storeroom, open Thursday, Friday and Saturday or by appointment. Small stock sec. and antiq. books on maritime, naval, shipbuilding, yachting and aviation only. M: P.B.F.A.

ROBERT D. STEEDMAN, 9 Grey Street, Newcastle upon Tyne NE1 6EE. TN: (0632) 326561. TA: Biblio Newcastle upon Tyne. Est: 1907. Shop, early closing Saturday. Medium sec. and antiq. stock, some new. Cata: occasionally. A.B.A. I.L.A.B. B.A.

THORNE'S BOOKSHOP, Percy Street, Newcastle upon Tyne. TN: (0632) 326421. Shop. Stock of sec. books mainly academic, educational and remainders; also new books.

TIMESLIP, 20 PINK LANE, NEWCASTLE UPON TYNE. Prop: Ray Thompson and Chris Moir. TN: (0632) 328616 Est: 1978. Shop: medium stock sed. and antiq., also new books. Spec: science fiction, fantasy, comics, movies, nostalgia. B: Yorkshire Bank, Pilgrim Street, Newcastle upon Tyne.

JOHN TURTON, 1 AND 2 COCHRANE TERRACE, WILLINGTON, CROOK, COUNTY DURHAM. TN: (0388) 745770. Est: 1978. Private premises; appointment necessary. Large stock sec. and antiq. Spec: topography and history especially North-eastern England. Cata: 4 to 6 a year. B: Co-operative Bank, Saddler Street, Durham.

UNIVERSITY BOOKSHOP [SPCK], 55–57 SADDLER STREET, DURHAM DH1 3EJ. TN: (0385) 42095. Shop. Very large stock sec. and antiq. Spec: history, North Country topography, theology. New books also stocked. Cata: 2-3 a year. M: P.B.F.A., B.A., N.B.L.

IAN WATSON, 31 DENE AVENUE, ROWLANDS GILL, TYNE AND WEAR NE39 1DY. TN: Rowlands Gill 2883. Private premises; appointment necessary. Very small stock sec. and antiq. books, also antique maps and prints: colouring and mounting service to the trade. Spec: topographical and sporting. Cata: occasionally.

JOHN M.W. WHITTAKER, 51 WESTERN HILL, DURHAM DH1 4RJ. TN: (0385) 43202. Est: 1982. Private premises; appointment necessary. Very small stock sec. and antiq. Spec: Association Football, Rugby Football, Cricket. Cata: occasionally. Corresp: Français, Deutsch.

M.N. WRIGHT, 137 HEDONSLEY ROAD, CONSETT, COUNTY DURHAM. TN: (0207-50) 5560. Private premises; appointment necessary. Small stock sec. and antiq. Cata: occasionally.

10. CLEVELAND

GREAT AYTON YARM
STOCKTON

CHRISTOPHER G. CASSON, 22 Gilpin House, Claymont Court, Norton, Cleveland. TN: (0642) 581964.

RICHARD FAIRCLOUGH, 20 Worsall Road, Yarm, Cleveland TS15 9DF. TN: (0642) 782881. Est: 1971. Private premises; appointment necessary. Very small sec. stock. English literature, modern first and limited editions, private press books. Cata: 8 a year.

THE GREAT AYTON BOOKSHOP, 47 High Street, Great Ayton, Cleveland. Prop: Madalyn S. Jones. TN: Great Ayton 723358. Est: 1979. Shop, closed on Monday and Wednesday afternoons. Small stock sec. and antiq. Also sells children's paperbacks and toys both old and new. B: Midland Bank, 33 Corporation Road, Middlesbrough, Cleveland. Account 51015168. M: P.B.F.A.

THE NORTON BOOKSHOP, 66 Bishopston Lane, Stockton, Cleveland. Prop: Christopher Casson. TN: (0642) 601676. Est: 1983. Shop. Small stock sec. and antiq. Spec: English and American literature. B: National Westminster Bank, The Green, Norton, Cleveland. M: P.B.F.A. and P.L.A.

11. NORTH YORKSHIRE

ALLERTHORPE
FULFORD
HARROGATE
RICHMOND
RIPON
SCARBOROUGH
SETTLE
SKIPTON IN CRAVEN
THIRSK
WHITBY
YORK

THE BAR BOOKSTORE, UNIT A1, CHAPMAN'S YARD, WATERHOUSE LANE, SCARBOROUGH, NORTH YORKSHIRE YO11 1DP. Prop: Rory Brierley. Est: 1976. Shop, closed Mondays. Medium stock sec. and antiq. also new books. Spec: Rosicrucian; Tao. Cata: occasionally. Corresp: Français. B: National Westminster Bank, Westborough, Scarborough.

BARBICAN BOOKSHOP, 1 FRANKLIN ROAD, HARROGATE. TN: Harrogate (0423) 55620. Est: 1976. Shop, closed Wednesdays. Medium stock sec. and antiq. Also new books. Spec: theology and topography.

BARBICAN BOOKSHOP, 24 FOSSGATE, YORK. Prop: Christian Literature Stalls Limited. TN: York (0904) 53643. Est: 1967. Shop. New and very large sec. and antiq. stock. Spec: theology, topography. topography. Cata: occasionally. B.A., P.B.F.A.
Also at WALMGATE BAR, YORK.) SHOP. Medium sec. and antiq. stock.

FRED BETTLEY BOOKSHOP, ZETLAND CINEMA, VICTORIA ROAD, RICHMOND, NORTH YORKSHIRE. TN: 3528. Est: 1975. Shop, closed on Mondays. Small stock sec. and antiq. Corresp: Français. B: Midland Bank, Richmond, North Yorkshire. Account 51038443.

BOER WAR BOOKS, 10 SAINT GEORGE'S PLACE, YORK YO2 2DR. Prop: R.G. Hackett. TN: (0904) 54698 and 51711. Small stock sec. and antiq. on Boer War/South African material. Also books on wine. Appointment preferred.

THE BOX OF DELIGHTS, 25 OTLEY STREET, SKIPTON, NORTH YORKSHIRE BD23 1DY. Prop: Sheila Coe. TN: 60111. Est: 1979. Shop, open 11 am-5.30 pm except on Tuesdays and Thursdays. Small stock sec. and antiq. Spec: Children's books, detective fiction, ephemera. A few remainders of new books and bric-a-brac and collectors items. B: Yorkshire Bank, Skipton. Account 17765459.

MICHAEL COLE OF YORK, 41 FOSSGATE, YORK YO1 2TF. TN: (0904) 31752. Est: 1979. Shop, open irregular hours throughout the week. Small stock, sec. and antiq.

CRAVEN BOOKS, 23 NEWMARKET STREET, SKIPTON IN CRAVEN, NORTH YORKSHIRE BD23 2JE. Prop: Miss M.G. Fluck and Miss K. Farey. TN: Skipton (0756) 2677. Est: 1961. Shop, closed Tuesday and first and last Monday of month. Small sec. and antiq. Stock. Spec: Northern topography, maps and prints. M: A.B.A.

RICHARD DALBY, 4 WESTBOURNE PARK, SCARBOROUGH, NORTH YORKSHIRE YO12 4AT. TN: (0723) 77049. Private premises, appointment necessary, (stockroom). Small stock sec. and antiq. Spec: Literature, fantasy fiction, juvenalia, cinema. Cata: 6 a year. M: P.B.F.A.

DORIC HOUSE BOOKS, FLAT 1, OAKMERE, WEAPONNESS PARK, SCARBOROUGH YO11 2UB. Prop: N.H. Godsmark. TN: (0723) 352819. Est: 1980. Private premises; appointment necessary. Very small stock sec. and antiq. Spec: 18th and 19th century literature; Johnsoniana; architecture; 19th century colourplate and illustrated. Cata: occasionally. Corresp: Español. B: Barclays Bank, High Row, Darlington. M: P.B.F.A.

E. ELLIS, SAINT MARGARET'S BOOKSHOP, 10–11 KIRKGATE, RIPON, NORTH YORKSHIRE HG4 1PA. TN: (0765) 2877. Est: 1948. Top floor of shop, early closing Wednesday. Medium sec. and antiq. stock, also new books. Cata: occasionally. B.A.

FIVE OWLS BOOKSHOP, 28 VICTORIA ROAD, RICHMOND, NORTH YORKSHIRE DL10 4AS. Prop: Valerie Alderson. TN: (0748) 3648. Est: 1983. Shop, closed Mondays. Medium stock sec. and antiq. Cata: occasionally. Corresp: Français, Deutsch. B: Midland Bank, Market Place, Richmond, Yorkshire DL10 4QQ.

T. R. FRANCIS, 4 NEWBIGGIN, MALTON, YORK YO17 0JF. TN: Whitwell on the Hill 420. Shop, closed Monday afternoons and Thursdays. Medium stock sec. and antiq. Spec: English literature; Yorkshire Topography; fine bindings. B: Lloyds Bank, Market Weighton, York. M: P.B.F.A.

FULFORD BOOKSHOP AND CARTOON GALLERY, 90 Main Street, Fulford, York. Prop: Jack Duncan. TN: (0904) 641389. Est: 1982. Shop, closed Mondays. Large stock sec. and antiq. Spec: British, American and European literature; fine sets; Folio Society; theatre; cartoon and caricature. B: Barclays Bank, Boston Spa, Wetherby, West Yorkshire. M: P.B.F.A.

GARD BOOKS, P.O. Box 59, York YO2 1PQ. Prop: Philip Titcombe. TN: (0904) 27614. Medium sec. and antiq. stock. Spec: music, literary and autograph material. B: Midland Bank, 13 Parliament St, York. Corresp: Français, Deutsch. P.B.F.A.

THOMAS C. GODFREY LIMITED, 32 Stonegate, York YO1 2AP. TN: (0904) 24531. TA: Godfreys York. Est: *c.*1895. Shop: new, and very large sec. and antiq. stock also new books, library & school supplies. Cata: 1 a year. B: Barclays Bank, Mansion House, York. B.A. A.B.A. N.B.L. general and special lists. B.A. A.B.A. N.B.L.

GOODRAMGATE BOOKS, MAPS AND PRINTS, 58 Goodramgate, York. TN: (0484) 46833. Shop: Sec. and Antiq. Spec: topography/travel, natural history, fine bindings. Also maps and prints.

HAMBLETON BOOKS, 43 Market Place, Thirsk, North Yorkshire YO7 1HA. Prop: Anne Turner. TN: (0845) 22343. Est: 1978. Shop, closed on Wednesdays. Small stock sec. and antiq. Also new books. Spec: geology. Corresp: Français, Español. M: B.A., B: Barclays Bank, Market Place, Thirsk.

HANOVER BOOKS, 8 Hunter Street, Whitby, North Yorkshire. Prop: G.E. and E.M. Shipley. TN: Whitby 603587. Est: 1972. Shop, closed Wednesdays (and Mondays in Winter). Large sec. and antiq. stock. Spec: Whitby, North Yorkshire, North Country generally. Corresp: Français, Deutsch.

HARROGATE BOOKSHOP, 29 Cheltenham Crescent, Harrogat Prop: I.W. Linford (Music) and C.A. Winder. TN: (0423) 50047 Est: 1978. Shop. Medium stock used. Spec: literature, poetry, music, theatre, history, motoring, racing and field sports. Back-numbers of journals stocked. M: P.B.F.A.

JOHN R. HOGGARTH, Thorneywaite House, Glaisdale, Whitby, North Yorkshire YO21 2QU. TN: (0947) 87338. Est: 1978. Private premises; appointment necessary. Very small stock sec. and antiq. Spec: Scouting, Guiding, Baden-Powells, Mafeking. Cata: monthly.

INCH'S BOOKS, 3 Saint Paul's Square, York YO2 4BD. Prop: Peter Inch and Janette Ray. TN: (0904) 29770. Est: 1979. Private premises; appointment necessary. Very small stock sec. and antiq. Spec: modern art and design, architecture, town planning, film, photography, social history. Cata: 4 a year. Corresp: Français, Español. B: National Westminster Bank, Hebden Bridge, West Yorkshire. M: P.B.F.A.

K. BOOKS, WAPLINGTON HALL, ALLERTHORPE, YORK YO4 4RS. Prop: B.J. and S.M. Kaye, M.J. Rose, TN: Pocklington (075 92) 2142. Est: 1966. Private premises; postal business only. Very large sec. and antiq stock. Spec: Africa, Asia, Australia, European topography, history, natural history; classics; 16th and 17th century books. Cata: on foregoing bi-monthly, each with 1,000 items.

W.H. LEALMAN, 11 WINDSOR STREET, YORK YO2 1DN. TN: York (0904) 33630 Postal business only. Very small sec. and antiq. stock. Spec: sporting, especially horse racing and breeding.

McDOWELL & STERN LIMITED, 3 AND 5 GRAPE LANE, YORK. Prop: Daniel McDowell and Dr. Jeffrey Stern. TN: York 22000. Cables: MACSTER, York. Est: 1971. Shop. Large stock antiq. books, also maps and prints. Spec: science, technology, medicine, natural history and economics. Cata: 4 a year. Corresp: Franais, Deutsch. B: National Westminster Bank, Coney St, York. Account 99917580. P.B.F.A.

PHILIP MARTIN MUSIC BOOKS, 22 HUNTINGDON ROAD, YORK YO3 7RL. Prop: Martin and Eleanor Dreyer. TN: York (0904) 36111. Est: 1976. Private premises; appointment preferable. Medium stock sec. and antiq. books; also new books. Music and books on music only. Cata: 4 a year. Corresp: Français, Deutsch, Italiano. B: Barclays Bank, York. Account 40703192.

ARCHIE MILES LIMITED, SOUTHFIELD, WILSILL, NEAR PATELEY BRIDGE, HARROGATE, NORTH YORKSHIRE. Prop: John and Cynthia Linsley. TN: (0423) 711166. Est: 1870. Private premises; appointment necessary. Medium stock sec. and antiq. Spec: 19th and 20th century illustrated. English literature; topography. Cata: occasionally. Corresp: Français. B: Midland Bank, 88 Town Street, Horsforth, Leeds LS18 4AR. M: P.B.F.A.

THE MINSTER GATE BOOKSHOP, 8 MINSTER GATES, YORK, YO1 2HL. Prop: N.D. Wallace. TN: (0904) 21812. Est: 1970. Shop, no early closing. Large stock sec. and antiq. books. Spec: modern literature, folklore, history and arts. Cata: General occasionally.

NANBOOKS, UNDERCLIFFE COTTAGE, DUKE STREET, SETTLE, NORTH YORKSHIRE BD24 9DN. Prop: Mrs. N.M. Midgley. TN: Settle 3324. Est: 1954. Shop, open Tuesdays, Fridays and Saturdays only. Very small sec. and antiq. stock; main business antiques.

O'FLYNN ANTIQUARIAN BOOKSELLERS, 35 MICKLEGATE, YORK, NORTH YORKSHIRE. TN: (0904) 641404. Shop: very large stock sec. and antiq. Spec: Scottish, early printed books, incuabula, manuscripts, classical texts. Cata: About 6 a year. C: Français, Deutsch, Italiano, Polish.

PANDION BOOKS, 81 MOORSIDE DALE, RIPON, NORTH YORKSHIRE HG4 2RY. Prop: L. and P.L. Wray. TN: (0765) 4500. Est: 1980. Private House; appointment necessary. Very small stock sec. and antiq. Spec: natural history, books illustrated by Charles Tunnicliffe and B.B. Cata: quarterly. B: Barclays Bank, Skipton.

PINDERS BOOKSHOP, THE SHAMBLES, 10 SANDGATE, WHITBY, NORTH YORKSHIRE. Prop: P. Pinder. TN: Whitby (0947) 603379. Est: 1974. Shop. Small stock sec. and antiq. and new books to order; also small antiques.

POST HORN BOOKS, GIGGLESWICK, SETTLE, NORTH YORKSHIRE BD24 0BA. Prop: Mrs. B.H. Panton. TN: Settle 3438. Est: 1976. Shop, closed all day Mondays. Medium stock sec. and antiq. books. Spec: mountaineering, caving; Yorkshire topography.

POTTERTON BOOKS, 8 Montpellier Parade, Harrogate, North Yorkshire. Prop: Mrs. Clare Jameson. TN: (0423) 521439. Shop. Medium stock sec. and antiq. Spec: architecture, the fine and decorative arts, collecting, antiques. Cata: 4 a year. M: P.B.F.A., L.A.P.A.D.A.

RIPPON BOOKSHOP, 6 Station Bridge, Harrogate, North Yorkshire. Prop: James T. Rawson. TN: (0423) 501835. Est: 1982. Shop. Medium stock sec. and antiq. Spec: local histories, Yorkshire topography. Lists available. B: Midland Bank, 7 Prospect Crescent, Harrogate.

SAINT MARY'S BOOKS, 3 Saint Mary's Lane, York. Prop: Paul Roberts. TN: (0904) 26970. Est: 1980. Private premises; appointment necessary. Very small stock sec. and antiq. Spec: modern first editions, especially 20th century. Cata: 2 a year. B: Barclays Bank. Booker, High Wycombe, Bucks. Account 80773131. M: P.B.F.A.

SCARBOROUGH MILITARIA, 73 Castle Road, Scarborough, North Yorkshire. Prop: G.D. Stephenson. TN: (0723) 61147. Est: 1976. Shop, (closed on Thursdays during Winter). Small stock sec. and antiq. books; also new books, stamps, coins, postcards, militaria. Spec: military books, and books on collecting. Cata: 3 a year.

YORK

The numbers below refer to positions indicated on the map opposite. For full details, please turn to the North Yorkshire section; for bookbinders, main entries are in the specialist section at the front of the guide.

BOOKSHOPS & BOOKSELLERS

1. Barbican Bookshop.
2. Boer War Books.
3. Michael Cole of York.
4. Jack Duncan Books.
5. Gard Books (not on map).
6. Goodramgate Books.
7. Inch's Books.
8. McDowell & Stern Ltd.
9. Phillip Martin Music Books.
10. Minster Gates Bookshop.
11. O'Flynn Antiquarian Booksellers.
12. Pandion Books.
13. Ken Spelman. A.B.A.
14. Colin Stillwell (Books).
15. Taikoo Books.
16. Yesterday's Paper.
17. Thomas C. Godfrey Ltd. A.B.A.
18. S.P.C.K. Bookshop.

BOOKBINDERS, ETC.

A. Jenny Aste.
B. John Henderson.
C. Melrosegate Fancy Papers.
D. Nicola B. Pirozek.
E. Symington Bookbinders.

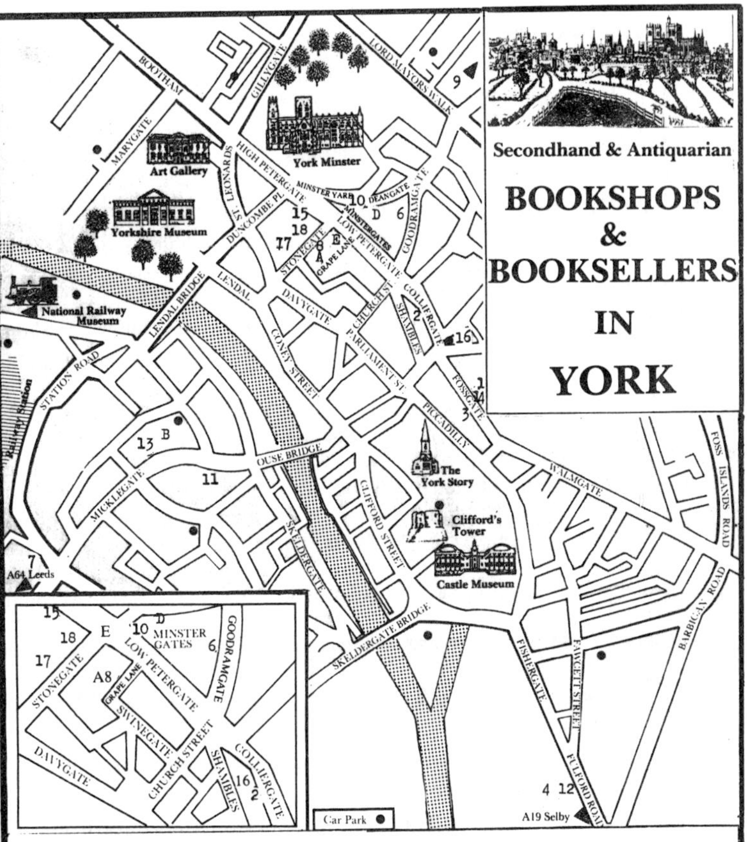

As one of the earliest centres of printing in Britain outside London, it is appropriate that York today is the centre of the antiquarian book-trade in the North of England.

York offers the Book Collecter:

- Eighteen Antiquarian Booksellers with over 300,000 books for sale. Most of the shops are within a short walk of each other, and there is a specialist dealer on most subjects.
- Three bookbinders, a paper restorer and a papermaker. Free quotations are given on request.
- Easy access—York is two hours from London, two hours from Edinburgh by train; with close proximity to A1 and M1.
- The largest Antiquarian Book Fair, outside London, is held in York each year.
- Catalogues produced by members will be sent free on request.
- Special "Book Weekends" on particular themes, with exhibitions, lectures, talks, etc. are projected—write for further details.
- A leaflet containing full details of all the antiquarian and secondhand booksellers in the city is available from: –

The Hon. Secretary
York Antiquarian Booksellers
25 Fossgate
York YO1 2TA.
Tel: (0904) 27467

SEA BOOKS, 1 CAMBRIDGE STREET, HARROGATE, NORTH YORKSHIRE. Prop: John Courtney. TN: (0423) 500341 (evenings only). Est: 1980. Shop, closed on Mondays and Tuesdays. Small stock sec. and antiq. Maritime and General. B: Lloyds Bank, Newton Abbot, Devon and Harrogate, North Yorkshire.

S.P.C.K. BOOKSHOP, 42 STONEGATE, YORK YO1 2AT. TN: (0904) 54176. Shop. Small stock sec. and antiq. Spec: theology, history and literature also new books. M: B.A. N.B.L.

SCORESBY HOUSE BOOKSHOP, 13 FLOWERGATE, WHITBY, NORTH YORKSHIRE. Prop: A.R. Hattersley. TN: Whitby (0947) 605116. Shop, open 9.00 to 17.00 hrs. Monday to Saturday. Medium stock sec. and antiq. books.

KEN SPELMAN, 70 MICKLEGATE, YORK YO1 1LF. Prop: Peter B. Miller. TN: (0904) 24414. TA: Spelman York. Est: 1948. Stock of 50,000 sec. and antiq. books. Spec: fine arts, literature, history and topography. Cata: annual specialist art catalogues and general lists. Corresp: Français. B: Midland Bank, 13 Parliament St, York. Account 91039164. European-American Bank: topography. Corresp: Français. B: Midland Bank, 13 Parliament St, York. Account 91039164. European-American Bank: 10 Hanover Sq, New York 10015. Account 2841490.

STEPPING STONES BOOKSHOP, LEALHOLME, near WHITBY, NORTH YORKSHIRE. Prop: P. Timbrell. TN: Lealholme (0947) 60382. Est: 1970. Shop. Stock of 12,000 volumes sec. and antiq. books and also small country bygones.

COLIN STILLWELL [BOOKS], 25 FOSSGATE, YORK YO1 2TA. TN: (0904) 27467. Est: 1979. Shop, open Mondays to Saturdays, 10.00 am–5.30 pm. Medium stock secondhand. Spec: Modern English and American literature and history. Cata: occasionally. Corresp: Français. B: National Westminster Bank, Coney Street, York. Account 99833506. M: P.B.F.A.

TAIKOO BOOKS LIMITED, 29 HIGH PETERGATE, YORK YO1 2HP, NORTH YORKSHIRE. Prop: D.A. Chilton. TN: (0904) 641-213. Est: 1978. Shop and stockroom. Small stock sec. and antiq. Spec: Africana, Middle East, India and Asia, big game, mountaineering, and Polar. Cata: 2 or 3 a year. B: National Westminster Bank PLC., Market Street, York. M: York Antiquarian Booksellers.

YESTERDAY'S PAPER, 102 WALMGATE, YORK. Prop: Fiona Clewlow. TN: (0904) 27715. Est: 1978. Shop, closed Monday, Tuesday and Wednesday. Small stock sec. and antiq. Spec: printed ephemera, comics and children's books. B: Williams and Glyns Bank, Nessgate, York. M: P.B.F.A., Ephemera Society.

12. LANCASHIRE

BLACKPOOL
BURNLEY
BURY
CARNFORTH
CHORLEY
DARWEN
LANCASTER
LYTHAM SAINT ANNES
OLDHAM
PRESTON
TODMORDEN
WIGAN

THE BORDER BOOKSHOP, 61A HALIFAX ROAD, TODMORDEN, OL14 5BB. Prop: Victor H. Collinge. TN: (070-681) 4721. Est: 1980. Shop and stockroom, closed on Tuesdays. Medium stock. New books also stocked. B: National Westminster Bank, Bacup, Lancashire. Account 01021702.

THE CARNFORTH BOOKSHOP LIMITED, 38–42 MARKET STREET, CARNFORTH LA5 9JX. Prop: Mr. P.J. Horrobin. TN: (0524) 734588. Est: 1977. Shop. Very large stock of secondhand in three adjacent shops. New books and stationery also stocked. Cata: occasionally. B: Lloyds Bank, Market Street, Lancaster. M: B.A.

CLIFTON BOOKS, 5 Dicconson Street, Wigan, Lancashire. Prop: D.M. Shaw. TN: (0942) 36716. Est: 1969. Shop, open 6 days a week. Small stock sec. and antiq. Spec: maps and prints. Cata: occasionally. P.B.F.A.

BOB DOBSON, 3 Staining Rise, Staining, Blackpool FY3 0BU. TN: (0253) 886103. Est: 1969. Private house; appointment necessary. Very small stock sec. and antiq. Spec: Lancashire, Yorkshire and Cheshire. Cata: 2 a year. B: Yorkshire Bank, Corporation Street, Blackpool. Account 24486141.

EXPORT BOOK COMPANY, P.O. Box 57, Preston PR1 1PA. Sec. and antiq. stock. A.B.A.

HALEWOOD & SONS, 37 Friargate, Preston, Lancashire, PR1 2AT. TN: Preston (0772) 52603. Est: 1867. Shop, early closing Thursday. New, and very large sec. and antiq. stock. Spec: Africa, America, Australia. Cata: general. A.B.A. B.A.

C.M. AND G. HARDING, 31 Riley Avenue, Lytham St. Annes FY8 1HZ. TN: (0253) 725138. Est: 1970. Private premises; appointment necessary. Small stock used. B: Barclays Bank, Lytham St. Annes. M: P.B.F.A.

BETTINA JONES, 30 Beryl Avenue, Tottington, Bury, Lancashire BL8 3NF. TN: (020488) 2950. Est: 1965. Private premises: appointment necessary. Small stock sec. and antiq. Spec: Scottish books, including fiction. Cata: 4 a year. B: Midland Bank, 437 Bury New Road, Preswich, Manchester M25 5AF.

W.B. MCCORMACK 2 Lower Church Street, Lancaster LA1 1NP. TN: 36405. Est: 1979. Shop, open Thursday, Friday and Saturday or by appointment. Medium stock sec. and antiq. books, autograph letters and historical documents; also prints and maps. Cata: 1 or 2 a year. B: Midland Bank, 35 Market Street, Lancaster LA1 1JQ Account 51095692.

PENDLESIDE BOOKS, Rhoslyn, Fence, near Burnley BB12 9QB. Prop: Mr. and Mrs. E. Sutcliffe. TN: (0282) 65617. Private premises;

appointment necessary. Small stock sec. and antiq. books. Spec: Lancashire and Yorkshire; farming and natural history. Cata.

PRESTON BOOK COMPANY, 68 FRIARGATE, PRESTON, LANCASHIRE, PR1 2ED. Prop: M.H. Halewood. TN: Broughton 862347. Est: 1952. Shop and storeroom, early closing Thursday. New, and very large sec. and antiq. stock. Spec: atlases, Colonial travel, topography. Cata: general, 1 a year. Corresp: Français. B.A.

HARTLE B. RIGBY, PASTURES HOUSE, SCOUTHEAD, OLDHAM OL4 4AS. Prop: Mrs. Betty Rigby. TN: (061) 665 3486. Est: 1975. Private premises; appointment necessary. Small stock sec. and antiq. Spec: cookery, herbals. P.B.F.A.

HEDRIC W. TYSON, 21–29 SAINT MARY'S PARADE, LANCASTER LA1 1YX. TN: Lancaster 68022. Est: 1971. Shop, no early closing. Medium sec. and antiq. stock. Spec: Lancashire and Furness topography. Cata: 2 a year. Corresp: Français, Español, Polski. B: William and Glyn's Bank, Grove Street, Wilmslow, Cheshire. Account 13228563. 2 a year.

R. & J.A. WHITTLE, THE COTTAGE BOOKSHOP, 5 HILL STREET, CHORLEY, LANCASHIRE PR7 1AX. Prop: Ray and Avril Whittle. TN: (025) 726-9280. Est: 1982. Shop, closed Wednesdays. Small stock sec. and antiq. and new books. Spec: Reference and technical books on applied art, crafts and design including needlework. Cata: 3 a year. Corresp: Français. B: Midland Bank, Chorley.

GERRY WOLSTENHOLME, 22 ELIZABETH STREET, BLACKPOOL FY1 3JD. TN: (0253) 24316. Private premises; appointment advisable. Medium stock sec. and antiq. books; Spec: literature, cricket. Cata: 6 a year.

13. MERSEYSIDE

BIRKENHEAD
BOOTLE
LIVERPOOL
MORETON
SOUTHPORT

BOOTLE BOOKSHOP, 350 STANLEY ROAD, BOOTLE. Prop: Liverpool Book Company. T.N: 051-933-4787. Est: 1978. Shop. Very large stock, sec. and antiq.

C.K. BROADHURST & COMPANY LIMITED, 5 & 7 MARKET STREET, SOUTHPORT PR8 1HD. TN: Southport 32064 and 34110. TA: Literaria Southport. Est: 1926. Shop, early closing Tuesday. Very large sec. and antiq. stock. A.B.A. N.B.L. B.A.

IAIN CAMPBELL, 22 GAMBIER TERRACE, LIVERPOOL 1. TN: (051 708) 7438 & (051-494) 0162. Stockroom. By appointment at any reasonable time. Medium stock sec. & antiq. Spec: food and wine, British topography, maritime, 19th century school text books, Ian Fleming prints and ephemera. Back numbers of journals and a few new books. Corresp: French. B: Midland Bank, 4 Dale Street, Liverpool 1. Account 21057332. M: P.B.F.A.

THE CROSBY BOOKSHOP, 39 CROSBY ROAD NORTH, CROSBY, LIVERPOOL LL22 LQB. Prop: Peter Lovering. TN: (051 920) 7738. Est: 1976. Shop. Large stock sec. and antiq. books also prints. B.A.

HAZELDENE BOOKSHOP, 61 RENSHAW STREET, LIVERPOOL, MERSEYSIDE L1 2SJ. Prop: A.H. and L.G. Elliot. TN: (051) 708-8780. Est: 1974. Shop, also by appointment. Medium stock sec. and antiq. also new books. Spec: modern first editions. Cata: 8 a year. B: National Westminster, University Branch, Oxford Street, Liverpool.

ERIC LANDER, 369 LEASOWE ROAD, MORETON, WIRRAL, MERSEYSIDE L46 2RE. Prop: Gillian Lander. TN: (051 638) 3235. Est: 1947. Shop, private premises; appointment necessary. Small stock sec. and antiq. books; also some new books. Spec: shipping. Cata: 4 a year. B: Midland Bank, Wallasey Village, Merseyside.

THE LYVER GALLERY, 8 HACKINS HEY, LIVERPOOL L2 2AW. Prop: Paul Breen (Fine Art) Limited. TN: (051 236) 7524. Est: 1978 (ex Paul Breen 1970). Shop, closed on Saturdays. Very small stock sec. and antiq. also maps and prints, new books and periodicals. Cata: annually. B: National Westminster Bank, Great Crosby, Cooks Road Branch, Liverpool L23 2TD. Account 09115684. M: Fine Art Trade Guild and L.A.P.A.D.A.

OUT OF PRINT BOOKSHOP, 97 RENSHAW STREET, LIVERPOOL L1 4HN. Prop: J. Burns and E. Singleton. TN: (051) 708 9700. Est: 1979. Shop. Medium stock sec. and antiq. Spec: English literature, shipping, local history. B: Barclays Bank, 99 Bold Street, Liverpool 1 44HN. Account 90679836.

R.G. PARKER, 287 OLD CHESTER ROAD, ROCK FERRY, BIRKENHEAD. Est: 1929. Private premises, appointment necessary. Small sec. and antiq. stock. Cata: subject lists.

PARKINSONS, 357 LORD STREET, SOUTHPORT, AND 24 PRINCES STREET, SOUTHPORT, MERSEYSIDE. Prop: K.A. and J. Parkinson. TN: (0704) 31244. Est: 1978. 2 shops, closed Mondays and Tuesdays. Medium stock sec. and antiq. Cata: Infrequently. Corresp: Deutsch. B: Williams & Glyn's Bank, Lord Street, Southport, Merseyside.

JOHN D. ROLES, 55 MOUNT PLEASANT, WATERLOO, LIVERPOOL L22 5PL. TN: (051 920) 6801. Est: 1959. Shop; appointment advised. Large sec. and antiq. stock. Corresp: Español, Urdu. B: Barclays Bank, Exchange, Old Hall Street, Liverpool 3. Account 70804053.

ROSEMARY BOOKS, 27 CEDAR STREET, SOUTHPORT, MERSEYSIDE PR8 6NQ. Prop: Miss Eileen Golborn. TN: (0704) 42134. Est: 1983. Private premises; appointment necessary. Small stock sec. and antiq. Spec: Girls' fiction. Cata: 3 a year, juveniles and 2 a year adult books. B: National Westminster Bank, 130 Lord Street, Southport

THE STRAND BOOKSHOP, 374 STANLEY ROAD, BOOTLE, LIVERPOOL, MERSEYSIDE L20 5AD. Prop: Liverpool Book Co. TN: (051 922) 8995. Est: 1969. Shop. Large stock sec. and antiq. books. B: Williams and Glyn's Bank, Chapel Lane, Formby, Merseyside. Account 11826199.

WATERSTONS OF LIVERPOOL, 32 BERRY STREET, LIVERPOOL 1 L1 4JQ. Prop: William J. Waterston. TN: 709-4501. Est: 1930. Shops and stockrooms, open daily 9 am-4.30 pm. Very large stock sec. and antiq. Spec: English literature, theology, topography. B: Midland Bank, Bold Street, Liverpool. Account 30839167.

14. GREATER MANCHESTER

BOLTON	PRESTWICH
CHORLTON ON MEDLOCK	ROCHDALE
DIDSBURY	RUSHOLME
LEVENSHULME	SALE
OLDHAM	STOCKPORT

J.F. BLOOD & SONS, 99 WILMSLOW ROAD, RUSHOLME, MANCHESTER M14 5SU. Props: Frank & Fred Blood. TN: (061) 224-2446. Est: 1927. Shop, early closing Wednesday. Very small sec. and antiq. stock; also antiques. Spec: collecting subjects

BOLTON BOOK CENTRE, 12 BARK STREET, (BRIDGE STREET) BOLTON, LANCASHIRE. Prop: G.Hall. TN: 061-764-3406. Est: 1976. Shop, open on Saturdays only between 11 am and 4 pm. Large stock used. Spec: Lancashire. Cata: occasionally.

BOOKS, 30 CROSS STREET, SALE, MANCHESTER M33 1AE. Prop: T.P. Sever. TN: (061) 962-9646. Est: 1981. Shop: early closing Wednesday afternoon. Sec. and antiq. stock.

BROWZERS, 14 WARWICK STREET, PRESTWICH, MANCHESTER, LANCASHIRE. Prop: Alan and Maureen Seddon. (061) 798 0626. Est: 1980 (Shop 1983). Shop, also by appointment. Small stock sec. and antiq. B: Co-operative Bank, Balloon Street, Manchester.

M. & R. CLARK, 67 LOWTHER ROAD, PRESWICH, MANCHESTER M25 8GP. TN: (061) 798-9123. Est: 1981. Very small stock sec. and antiq. by appointment, private premises. Spec: Gardening, Natural History. Cata: 3 or 4 a year. Co-operative Bank, Balloon Street, Manchester.

GEOFFREY CLIFTON'S THEATRE BOOKSHOP PICCADILLY PLAZA, YORK STREET, MANCHESTER M1 4AH. TN: 061-236-2537. Est: 1979. Shop, closed on Mondays. Very small stock used. Spec: Theatre, cinema, dance, circus, puppetry, broadcasting. Back-numbers of journals stocked and new books and periodicals. Cata: 2 a year. Corresp: Français. B: National Westminster Bank, Manchester Road, Denton, Manchester M34 2PB. Account 01054007. M: P.B.F.A. *also* (evenings) The Contact University Theatre, Devas Street, Manchester M15 6JA.

S.M. AND R. DU FEU, 287 STAMFORD STREET, ASHTON UNDER LYNE, CHESHIRE. Est: 1950. Stockroom, open Friday and Saturday 11.00 to 16.00 hrs.
also at 120A MOTTRAM ROAD, HYDE, CHESHIRE. (061) 368-7258) but appointment necessary for these premises.

GARRICK BOOKSHOP, 8 TO 10 WELLINGTON ROAD SOUTH, STOCKPORT, CHESHIRE SK4 1AD. Prop: P.S. Aird and A.J. Garnett. TN: (061 480) 4346. Est: about 1935. Shop. Very large stock sec. and antiq. books; also new books. Spec: local; natural history; illustrated books. B.A.

GIBBS BOOKSHOP LIMITED, 10 CHARLOTTE STREET, MANCHESTER M1 4FL. TN: (061) 236-7179. Est: 1922. Shop, no early closing. Large sec. stock.

GOLDEN DAWN BOOKS, 35 ATWOOD ROAD, MANCHESTER M20 0TA. Prop: B.A. Bender. TN: (061) 434 1308. Est: 1982. Small stock sec. and antiq. also new to order. Private premises, appointment necessary. Spec: occult books and tarot. Cata: 3 or 4 a year. B: National Westminster, 35 King Street, Manchester N20 2NP.

GRENVILLE STREET BOOKSHOP, 105 GRENVILLE STREET, EDGELEY, STOCKPORT SK3 9ET. Prop: Joseph Anthony Heacock. TN: (061) 4771909. Est: 1978. Shop, closed on Mondays. Large stock used. B: Barclays Bank, Stockport.

GEORGE KELSALL, THE BOOKSHOP, 22 CHURCH STREET, LITTLEBOROUGH, LANCASHIRE, OL15 9AA. TN: Littleborough 70244 & 79767 (Home). Est: 1979. Shop. Medium stock sec. and antiq. books. Also some new. Spec: topography of Yorkshire, Lancashire and Lake District. Corresp: Français, Español.

McGILL'S BOOKSHOP, 184 OXFORD ROAD, CHORLTON ON MEDLOCK, MANCHESTER M13 9QQ. Prop: James P. McGill. TN: (061 273) 4736. Est: 1966 Shop. Large general sec. and antiq. stock. Spec: juvenile.

MARATHON BOOKS, 23 GREENWAY CLOSE, SALE, CHESHIRE. Prop: Richard Bond. TN: (061) 969-4594. Est: 1980. Private premises; postal business only. Very small stock sec. and antiq. Spec: track and field athletics, distance running, Olympic Games. Cata: 1 a year. B: Williams and Glynns Bank, Piccadilly Station Approach, Manchester.

MOORLAND BOOKS, UNIT 5, ALEXANDER CRAFT CENTRE, HIGH STREET, UPPERMILL, OLDHAM, GREATER MANCHESTER. Prop: Alan Shaw and George Bennett. TN: Saddleworth (045 77) 5214 and 3095. Est: 1981. Shop, closed Mondays and Tuesdays. Small stock sec. and antiq. B: National Westminster Bank, Chew Valley Road, Greenfield, Oldham.

E.J. MORTEN [BOOKSELLERS] LIMITED, 2, 4, 6, 8 AND 9 WARBURTON STREET, DIDSBURY, MANCHESTER M20 0RA. TN: (061 445) 7629. Directors: Eric J. Morten and S. Pryce. Est: 1959. Shops and showrooms. Very large sec. and antiq. stock, also new books. Spec: English literature; bindings; topography. Cata: 2 a year. A.B.A., B.A., N.B.L., P.B.F.A.
also at DUNDONALD ROAD, DIDSBURY, MANCHESTER

ROCHDALE BOOK COMPANY, 399 OLDHAM ROAD, ROCHDALE, LANCASHIRE OL16 5LN. TN: (0706) 31136 and 58300. Est: 1971. Shop; telephone for appointment advisable. Large stock general sec. and antiq. books. Strong section on Lancashire topography and dialect.

SHAWS BOOKSHOP LIMITED, 11 POLICE STREET, MANCHESTER M2 7LQ. TN: (061) 834-7587. Est: 1930. Shop and stockroom. Very large stock sec. and antiq. also picture framing and restoring. Spec: antiquarian, maps, prints, local and topographical. Corresp: Français, Deutsch, Español, Italiano. B: National Westminster Bank, 35 King Street, Manchester. Account 01006533. M: A.B.A.

ALAN SMITH, 15 OAKLAND AVENUE, DIALSTONE LANE, STOCKPORT, CHESHIRE. TN: (061) 483 2547. Est: 1982. Private premises; postal business only. Very small stock sec. and antiq. Spec: modern literature, illustrated books, 1940's imprints. Cata: 3 a year. B: National Westminster Bank, Bramhall, Cheshire. A/c 0606 2954. M: P.B.F.A.

L. WALTON, 41 WOODLAND ROAD, LEVENSHULME, MANCHESTER M19 2GW. TN: (061 224) 6630. Est: 1967. Private premises; appointment necessary. Very small stock sec. and antiq. Spec: maps, prints, early photography. Cata: 3 or 4 a year.

15. WEST YORKSHIRE

BATLEY	HUDDERSFIELD
BRADFORD	ILKLEY
HALIFAX	LEEDS
HOLMFIRTH	SHIPLEY

ALMAR BOOKS, 10 Commercial Road, Kirkstall, Leeds LS5 3AQ. Prop: Alan and Marjorie Jones. TN: (0532) 780937. Est: 1974. Shop, closed Monday mornings and all day Wednesdays. Medium stock sec. and antiq. books. M: P.B.F.A.

AMPERSAND BOOKS, 2 West View, Wells Prop: Megan and Michael Dawson. TN: (0943) 608925. Est: 1982. Private premises, postal business only. Medium stock sec. and antiq. Spec: art, architecture, childrens illustrated books, particularly moveables, pre-1939. Cata: periodically. B: National Westminster, The Grove, Ilkley.

ELAINE BEARDSELL, TOLL HOUSE BOOKSHOP, 32–34 HUDDERSFIELD ROAD, HOLMFIRTH, HUDDERSFIELD. TN: Holmfirth 686541. Shop, closed Mondays. Stock sec. and antiq. Books, also coffee and cakes.

DAVID AND CHRIS BLAND, 20 BELVOIR GARDENS, SKIRCOAT GREEN, HALIFAX, YORKSHIRE. TN: (0422) 51212. Est: 1976. Private premises; appointment necessary. Very small stock sec. and antiq. books. Spec: folk music and folklore. Cata: occasionally.

THE COLLECTOR, 36 THE COLONNADE, PIECE HALL, HALIFAX, WEST YORKSHIRE. Prop: Peter C. Nicholls and T. Ian Wilkinson. TN: (0274) 45126 (Evenings only). Est: 1978. Shop, closed Thursdays but open Sundays; also by appointment. Small stock sec. and antiq. Cata: 4 a year. Corresp: Français, Deutsch, Italiano, Polski. B: Barclays Bank, Market Street, Bradford, West Yorkshire.

A.G. CRAM, 23 KINGSLEY AVENUE, ADEL, LEEDS LS16 7NY. Prop: A.G. Cram. TN: (0532) 674207. Est: 1982. Small stock sec. and antiq. Private premises, appointment necessary. Spec: mountaineering, Lake District, science, and antiquarian. Cata: 3 a year. M: PBFA.

FALCON BOOKS OF SALTAIRE, 13/13A VICTORIA ROAD, SALTAIRE, BRADFORD BD18 3LQ. Prop: Clive Woods. TN: (0274) 584275. Est: 1982. Shop; also by appointment. Large stock sec. and antiq. Spec: modern first editions and Yorkshire topography. B: Co-Operative Bank, Vicar Lane, Leeds LS1 1HJ.

FINE BOOKS OF ILKLEY, 41 MANLEY ROAD, ILKLEY LS29 8QP. Prop: Dr. F.P. Williams. TN: 0943-600168. Est: 1979. Private premises; appointment necessary. Small stock used. Spec: Asia, Africa, 19th century topographical guides, railway and technical. Cata: annually. B: Midland Bank, Holbeck Branch, Sweet Street, Leeds, LS11 9AZ. Account 11021575. M: P.B.F.A.

O.M. FORD, 26 MELTHAM ROAD, LOCKWOOD, HUDDERSFIELD, WEST YORKSHIRE. TN: (0484) 32878. Est: 1960. Shop. Large stock sec. and antiq. books.

HARRY HAYES, 48 TRAFALGAR STREET, BATLEY, WEST YORKSHIRE WF17 7HA. TN: (0924) 474298. Est: 1955. Shop. Small sec. and antiq. stock and new books. Spec: philately and postal history. The world's largest stock of philatelic literature. Cata: 3 a year. B: Yorkshire Bank, Market Place, Heckmondwike, Yorks. Account 32962845.

K. & J. HOWE, 14 NEW STATION STREET, OFF BOAR LANE, LEEDS. Prop: K.C. Howe. Est: 1983. Shop. Small stock sec. and antiq. Spec: travel, topography (British) and first editions. B: Lloyds Bank, Park Row, Leeds.

HYDE PARK BOOKSHOP, 8 AND 10 HEADINGLEY LANE, LEEDS 6. Prop: D. and B. Fairburn. TN: (0532) 782689. Est: 1967. Shop. Very large stock sec. and antiq. books. Spec: colourplate books; engraved view books, art reference books. Cata: 12 a year. Corresp: Français, Deutsch. B: Midland Bank, Hyde Park, Leeds. Account 50344621. P.B.F.A.

J.K. BOOKS [SPORTING], 90 SHAY LANE, OVENDEN, HALIFAX, WEST YORKSHIRE. Prop: James Kenny. TN: (0422) 58771. Est: 1982. Private premises, appointment necessary. Small stock sec. and antiq. Spec: Hunting, racing, the horse, field sports and sporting. Cata: 2 a year. B: Lloyds Bank, Halifax. M: Trade member of the British Field Sports Society.

ALEX G. JACKSON, 91 GREAT GEORGE STREET, LEEDS LS1 3BS. TN: (0532) 51689. TA: Printbook Leeds. Warehouse, appointment necessary. Very large stock sec. and antiq. books, prints, maps and ephemera. Spec: atlases, maps, colour plate books, steel engraved and other view books, prints, topography.

JACKSONS OF ILKLEY, 22 Parish Ghyll Road, Ilkley, West Yorkshire. Prop: Kate and Tom Jackson. TN: 0943 601947. Est: 1983. Private premises; appointment necessary. Small stock sec. and antiq. Spec: Children's books and books on food and drink, wine, herbals, etc. Cata: 6 a year. B: National Westminster Bank, The Grove, Ilkley, West Yorkshire 12

JAMES MILES [LEEDS] LIMITED, 80 Woodhouse Lane, Leeds LS2 8AB. TN: (0532) 455327. Est: 1870. Shop. Large sec. and antiq. stock. *Also at* 74 Basinghall Street, (off the Headrow). Large Remainder and Bargain Books stock. *and at* 53 Great George Street, by appointment only. Medium stock antiq.

MOORHEAD BOOKS, Suffield Cottage, Moorhead, Gildersome, Leeds LS27 7BA. Prop: Frank Spicer. TN: (097 330) 852264. Est: 1966. Private premises; appointment necessary. Very large stock sec. and antiq. books. Spec: Wine and food; illustrated books; topography. Cata: 2 or 3 a year. B: Midland Bank, 1 Hick Lane, Batley, West Yorkshire. N.B.L.

PENDRAGON BOOKS, 10 CHURCH STREET, ILKLEY, WEST RIDING, YORKSHIRE. Prop: John Killeen. TN: (0943) 607124. Est: 1976. Shop, closed on Wednesdays. Large stock sec. and antiq. Spec: Yorkshire topography, fine antiquarian books on most subjects. Back-numbers of journals stocked. Corresp: Français. B: Lloyds Bank, Brook Street, Ilkley. Account 1052531. M: P.B.F.A.

THE POET'S BOOKSHOP, 20 SKIPTON ROAD, ILKLEY, YORKSHIRE. Prop: Professor Cyril L. Riley, Ph.D. TN: Burley in Wharfdale 863081. Est: 1966. Shop, closed Tuesdays. Large sec. and antiq. stock; also some new books. B: Yorkshire Bank, The Grove, Ilkley.

STEVE RIBBONS, 7 OAKTREE AVENUE, SCHOLES, HOLMFIRTH, WEST YORKSHIRE. Prop: Steve Ribbons. TN: (0484) 684043. Private premises; appointment necessary. Very small stock sec. and antiq. Spec: dog books and related subjects, especially field sports. Cata: 2 a year.

S.P.C.K. BOOKSHOP, 14 NORTH PARADE, BRADFORD BD1 3HY. TN: 0274-28669. Shop. Small stock sec. and antiq. Also new books. Spec: theology, history, literature. M: B.A., N.B.L.

VINTAGE MOTORSHOP, 500 BRADFORD ROAD, BATLEY, WEST YORKSHIRE, WF17 5JY. Prop: R. Hunt. TN: 0924- 470773. Est: 1976. Shop, open between 11.00 and 5 pm except on Mondays, Tuesdays and Wednesdays. Small stock sec. Spec: motoring books and a few railway and aviation titles. Also some motoring magazines and new books on motoring. M: P.B.F.A.

WALKER'S BOOKSHOP, 28 ARNDALE CENTRE, HEADINGLEY, LEEDS LS6 2UG. Directors: Mrs. P.J.Jackson, Mrs. F.C. Middleton-Walker, Mrs. L. Waddilove, Mrs. C. Cowley and Mrs. M. Kemp. TN: (0532) 751319. Shop. Small antiq. stock; also large stock new books. Spec: Yorkshire topography. C.B.A. N.B.L.

PAUL WILSON [BOOKS]. 15 WILLOW STREET, GIRLINGTON, BRADFORD, WEST YORKSHIRE BD8 9NJ. Prop: Paul Wilson. TN: (0274) 42331. Est: 1982. Private Premises; appointment necessary. Very small stock sec. and antiq. Spec: Africa and the Middle East, especially the Sudan. Cata: 3 a year. Corresp: Français. B: Co-Operative Bank PLC., P.O. Box 10, 41 Vicar Lane, Leeds LS1 1HJ. M: P.B.F.A.

C.G. WOODS, 13 AND 13A VICTORIA ROAD, SALTAIRE, SHIPLEY, WEST YORKSHIRE BD18 3LQ. Est: 1978. Private premises; appointment necessary. Medium stock sec. and antiq. Spec: British and foreign topography, especially Yorkshire. Cata: occasionally.

16. HUMBERSIDE

BEVERLEY
BRIDLINGTON
CLEETHORPES
GOOLE
HULL
SCUNTHORPE

EASTGATE BOOKSHOP, 11 EASTGATE, BEVERLEY, EAST YORKSHIRE HU17 0DR. Prop: R.B. Roper. TN: (0482) 868579. Est: 1983. Shop and stockroom, closed Mondays. Medium stock seq. and antiq. and remainders

GOOD NEWS BOOKSHOP LIMITED, 67 WRIGHT STREET, HULL HU2 8JD. Prop: Humberside Good News Trust. TN: (0482) 28135. Est: 1971. Shop. Large stock sec. and antiq., also new books on theology. Spec: theology, main Protestant. B.A. B: T.S.B. George Street, Hull. Account 03599053.

HUMBER BOOKS, 688 BEVERLEY ROAD, HULL, NORTH HUMBERSIDE, HU6 7JH. Prop: Peter M. Cresswell. TN: (0482) 802239. Est: 1972.

Private premises; appointment necessary. Very small stock sec. and antiq. Books. Spec: 16th and 17th century theology and Bibles. Cata: 3 or 4 a year (free on request, airmailed abroad). B: Barclays Bank, 18 Cottingham Road, Hull.

J.L. BOOK EXCHANGE, 72 HILDERTHORPE ROAD, BRIDLINGTON YO15 3BQ. Prop: John Ledraw. TN: 601285. Est: 1971. Shop. Medium stock sec. and antiq. also new books. P.B.F.A.

K BOOKS OF HULL, 15 AND 17 HEPWORTH'S ARCADE, SILVER STREET, HULL, YORKSHIRE. Prop: Kaye (Books) Limited. TN: (0482) 26457. Est: 1946. Shop. Very large sec. and antiq. stock. Cata: monthly.

LAFAYETTE BOOKSELLERS, 6 HIGH STREET, CLEETHORPES, SOUTH HUMBERSIDE. TN: (0472) 699244 (day) and (050 781) 363 (evening). Open Tuesday, Thursday, Friday, Saturday. In summer open every day

PHILIP MORRIS, 31 HIGHGATE, BEVERLEY, NORTH HUMBERSIDE HU17 0N. Prop: Philip Morris. TN: (0482) 869453. Est: 1975. Shop: closed Monday. Large stock sec. and antiq. Spec: philosophy. Cata: 2 a year. B: Lloyds Bank, Newland Avenue, Hull. A/c. No. 0248378. M: P.B.F.A.

MR. PYE [BOOKS], 47 HAILGATE, HOWDEN, GOOLE DN14 7ST. Prop: M.S. and E.J. Kemp. TN: Howden 30309. Est: 1979. Private house, appointment necessary. Small stock sec. and antiq. Spec: modern first editions, illustrated, juvenile, Yorkshire topography. Cata: 6 a year. B: National Westminster Bank, Boothferry Road, Goole.
Also at 19A BRIDGEGATE, HOWDEN-GOOLE.

QUEST BOOKS, 51 WOOD LANE, BEVERLEY, EAST YORKSHIRE HU17 8BS. Prop: Dr. Peter Burridge. TN: (0482) 868860. Private premises; postal business only. Very small stock sec. and antiq. Spec: scientific travel, especially in the Near East, Byzantine studies, archaeology and architecture. Cata: 3 a year.

SARAWAK BOOKS, 11 EAST CLOSE, BEVERLEY HU17 7JN. Prop: R.B. Roper. TN: (0482) 861870. Private premises; postal business only. Small stock. Spec: Borneo, bookbinding and books about books. Cata: General lists occasionally. B: Barclays Bank, Beverly.

WHITE RABBIT BOOKSHOP, 47 NORTH BAR WITHIN, BEVERLEY, EAST YORKSHIRE Manager: Lenore Showler. TN: (0492) 885913. Est: 1975. Shop, closed all day Thursdays in winter. Medium stock sec. and antiq. books; also some new, mainly reprints, gift cards and papers. P.B.F.A.

RICHARD AND JANE WILLIAMS, 17 North Street, Winterton, Scunthorpe, South Humberside. Prop: Richard and Jane Williams. TN: 0724 733788. Est: 1975. Private Premises; appointment necessary. Medium stock sec, and antiq. Spec: collectable paperbacks, Penguins, crime and science fiction. Cata: Frequent. Corresp: Français. B: Trustee Savings Bank, Scunthorpe.

17. SOUTH YORKSHIRE

DONCASTER
ROTHERHAM
SHEFFIELD
WENTWORTH

ROD AND MARGOT ARMITAGE, 51 SAINT LAWRENCE ROAD, SHEFFIELD, SOUTH YORKSHIRE S9 1SB. TN: (0742) 448396. Est: 1981. Private premises; appointment necessary. Medium stock sec. and antiq. Spec: true crime, juveniles, railways. Cata: 2 a year on true crime. Corresp: Deutsch, Español, Français.

BARNARD GALLERY, GRANGE FARM, EVERTON, DONCASTER. TN: (077 786) 324. Est: 1956. Private premises; appointment necessary. Small sec. and antiq. stock; also prints and maps.

CHANTREY BOOKS, 24 COBNAR ROAD, SHEFFIELD S8 8QB. Prop: C. and R. Brightman. TN: (0742) 748958. Est: 1980. Private Premises; postal business only. Very small stock sec. and antiq. Spec: gardening, natural history, country life. Cata: Approximately 4 a year

T.E. & J. FRANKS, 30 RERESBY CRESCENT, ROTHERHAM S60 4DW. TN: (0709) 541166. Private premises; appointment necessary. Very small stock sec. and antiq. B: National Girobank, Bootle. GIR 0AA 60-640-8002.

MRS. THELMA HARRISON, 25 CLAYFIELDS, WENTWORTH, near ROTHERHAM S62 7TD. TN: Barnsley (0226) 742097. Private premises, appointment necessary. Small sec. and antiq. stock. Spec: education, juveniles, social sciences. All pre 1900.

ALAN HILL BOOKS, 130 WHITHAM ROAD, SHEFFIELD, S10 2SR. TN: 665768, 747721. Est: 1980. Shop. Large stock sec. and antiq. also prints and maps. Spec: local topography, cricket. B: National Westminster Bank, Market Place, Chesterfield, Derbyshire. Account 80210317. M: P.B.F.A.

LINDEN BOOKS, 43 BROXHOLME LANE, DONCASTER, SOUTH YORKSHIRE. Prop: G.H. Hill. TN: (0302) 69910. (Shop), 23784 (Theology Dept.). and 69910. Est: 1973. Shop, closed Mondays and Thursdays. Small stock sec. and antiq.. Spec: theology. Cata: theology, 4 a year. Incorporates the Theological Book Trust.

RAILWAYANA LIMITED, 745 ABBEYDALE ROAD, SHEFFIELD S7 2BG. Prop: B. Hinchliffe. TN: Sheffield (0742) 550602. Est: 1969. Shop, closed Monday. Medium stock sec. and antiq. stock on Railways. trams, buses and canals: also relics, records and photographs relating to these, also new books. Subjects. Cata: on foregoing, occasional. Corresp: Français. B: Lloyds Bank, 771 Abbeydale Road, Sheffield 7. Account 0099462.

RARE AND RACY, 164–166 DEVONSHIRE STREET, SHEFFIELD S3 7SG. Est: 1969. Shop. Large stock sec. and antiq. books; also new and secondhand records,
also at 278 SOUTH ROAD, WALKLEY, SHEFFIELD S6 3TB. antiq. Books, maps and prints. Spec: Yorkshire, Derbyshire material.

SWAN ANTIQUES, 4 SWAN STREET, BAWTRY, near DONCASTER, YORKSHIRE. Prop: F.W. Laywood, Shop, no early closing. Small sec. and antiq. stock. Spec: Yorkshire topography.

JOHN R. WRIGLEY, 185 THE WHEEL, ECCLESFIELD, SHEFFIELD S30 3ZA. Prop: John R. Wrigley and B. Wrigley. TN: (0742) 460275. Est: 1961. Postal business only. Medium stock sec. and antiq. books. Cata: 'The Greenlist' fortnightly.

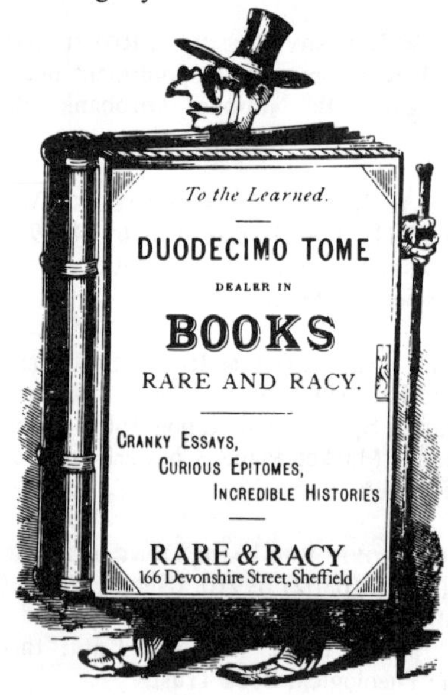

18. CHESHIRE

ALDERLEY EDGE	HYDE
ALTRINCHAM	KNUTSFORD
CHEADLE	MACCLESFIELD
CHESTER	NANTWICH
CREWE	NORTHWICH
HALE	TARPORLEY
HOYLAKE	WARRINGTON

ABACUS BOOKS, 24 REGENT ROAD, ALTRINCHAM, CHESHIRE. Prop: C.D. Lawton. TN: (061 928) 5108. Shop, closed Mondays and Wednesdays. Medium sec. and antiq. stock. B: Williams and Glynn's Bank, Altrincham, Cheshire.

THE BOOKSHOP, 64A PARK ROAD, HALE, CHESHIRE. TN: (0625) 533913. Prop: Miss S.A. Lawrence and M.E. Aumomer. Est: 1975. Shop, open Saturdays 10.00–17.00. Very small stock sec. and antiq. books on Cheshire and Derbyshire. All correspondence to 5 Park Road, Wilmslow SK9 5BT. M: P.B.F.A.

GEOFF. BOOTH, HILLTOP AVENUE, CHEADLE HULME, CHEADLE, CHESHIRE SK0 7HN. Prop: Geoff. Booth. TN: (061) 485-4246. Est: 1981. Private premises; appointment necessary. Very small stock sec. and antiq. also a few new. Spec: steam railways, "B.B." books, true crime, old conjuring items. Cata: Very occasionally. Corresp: Français. Lists from foreign dealers welcomed. B: Williams & Glyn's Bank Ltd., 14/16 The Mall, Sale, Cheshire.

BRIANT BOOKS, 94 QUARRY LANE, KELSALL, TARPORLEY, CHESHIRE. Prop: S.J. Jones. TN: (0829) 51804. Est: 1980. Private premises; appointment necessary. Very small stock sec. and antiq. Spec: ornithology and general natural history. Cata: 2 or 3 a year. B: National Westminster Bank, High Street, Runcorn, Cheshire. Account number 93501986. M: P.B.F.A.

BRIDGEWATER BOOKS, 28 SUNDERLAND STREET, MACCLESFIELD, CHESHIRE. Prop: R.J. Bisknell. TN: (0625) 24763.

COPNAL BOOKS, 320 BROAD STREET, CREWE, CHESHIRE. Prop: P. Ollerhead. TN: 585622. Est: 1980. Private premises; appointment necessary. Very small stock sec. and antiq., also small stock of new religious books. Corresp: Français. M: B.A.

DICKINSON BOOKS, 4 CHILTERN ROAD, CULCHETH, WARRINGTON WA3 4LH. Prop: J.J. and W. Dickinson. (092) 576-3791. Est: 1978. Private premises; appointment necessary. Very small sec. stock. Spec: mountaineering, guides, also journals, prints and maps. Back-numbers of journals. Cata: 6 a year.

CLIFFORD ALAN ELMER, 8 BALMORAL AVENUE, CHEADLE HULME, CHEADLE, CHESHIRE, SK8 5EQ. TN: 061 485 7064. Est: 1978. Private house; postal only. Small stock sec. and antiq. Spec: true crime and criminology only. Cata: 6 a year.

EASTGATE BOOKS, 11 CITY WALLS, CHESTER CH1 1LD. Prop: K.M. Williams. TN: (0244) 26486. Est: 1966. Shop. Medium stock sec. and antiq. stock; also small antiques and glass.

RAYMOND P. HEPNER, 'HAYRAKER', MOSS LANE, MERE, NEAR KNUTSFORD, CHESHIRE. TN: Knutsford 54550. Private premises; appointment necessary. Medium sec. and antiq. stock; very large stock prints and ordnance survey maps. Spec: books on natural history and related subjects; topography; illustrated.
Also at LION GALLERY AND BOOKSHOP, 15A MINSHULL STREET, KNUTSFORD. TN: Knutsford 52915.

C.R. JOHNSON 1 GREENBANK HOUSE, ALBERT SQUARE, BOWDON, ALTRINCHAM, CHESHIRE. TN: (061 941) 1710. Est: 1970. Private premises; appointment necessary. Small stock sec. and antiq. books. Spec: literature, rare and fine before 1900, literary collections, fiction before 1800. Cata: 1 a year.

ELIZABETH KNOWLES, FRANDLEY FARM, ANTROBUS, NEAR NORTHWICH, CHESHIRE, CW9 6JB. TN: Northwich (0606) 891265. Est: 1971. Private premises; postal business only. Very small stock sec. and rare books. Spec: Art, antiques, illustrated.

MARINE BOOKS, "NILCOPTRA", 3 MARINE ROAD, HOYLAKE, WIRRAL, CHESHIRE L47 2AS. Prop: Michael Nash. TN: (051) 632-5365. Est: 1983. Private premises; appointment necessary. Medium stock sec. and antiq. Spec: maritime and naval, Lord Nelson/Lady Hamilton, and topography and history of the Wirral Peninsula. Cata: 1 or 2 a year, on the first two categories. B: National Westminster Bank PLC, 6 The Quadrant, Hoylake, Wirral, Cheshire. M: P.B.F.A.

JOHN MARTIN, 14 WALKER LANE, HYDE, CHESHIRE. Prop: John Martin. TN: (061) 368 1406. Est: 1980. Stockroom; by appointment only. Small stock. Spec: non fiction. B: Williams and Glyn's Bank, Midland, Workington, Hyde. M: P.B.F.A.

MORTEN'S BOOKSHOPS LIMITED, 50-52 CHESTERGATE, MACCLESFIELD. Prop: E.J. Morten and S. Pryce. TN: (0625) 23679. Shop. Medium stock sec. and antiq. also new books. Spec: English literature, fine books, local history. Cata: 1 a year. Corresp: Français. B: National Westminster Bank, Didsbury, Manchester. M: A.B.A. P.B.F.A. B.A.

RICHARD A. NICHOLSON, 25 WATERGATE STREET, CHESTER CH1 2LB. TN: Chester 26818 (STD 0244). Est: 1963. Shop, no early closing. Large stock of antique maps and prints of all parts of the world. Cata: on foregoing, monthly, illustrated.

STANDFAST BOOKS, 26 ALBERT SQUARE, BOWDEN, ALTRINCHAM, CHESHIRE WA14 2ND. Prop: Robin and Carol Booth. TN: (061) 928 4907. Est: 1980. Private premises; appointment necessary. Small stock of sec. and antiq. Spec: John Buchan, history. Cata: about 3 a year. Corresp: Français, Deutsch. B: Lloyds Bank, P.O. Box 10, 46–48 High Street, Newcastle, Staffordshire ST5 1QY. M: P.B.F.A.

HENRY WILSON, 14 BROOMHEATH LANE, TARVIN, CHESTER CH3 8HB. TN: (0829) 40693.

19. DERBYSHIRE

ASHBOURNE
CHESTERFIELD
CROMFORD
DERBY
LITTLEOVER
MATLOCK

R.F. BARRETT, The Bookshop, 3 Eyre Street, Clay Cross, Chesterfield, Derbyshire. Prop: R.F. Barrett. TN: (0246) 865880. Est: 1980. Shop, closed Wednesdays. Medium stock sec. and antiq. Spec: Derbyshire and the Peak District. Cata: Occasionally.

HONEYFIELDS BOOKS, 5 Hazel Close, Ashbourne, Berbyshire DE6 1HX. Prop: Mrs A.C. Davies. TN: (0335) 43823.

GRANT JARVIS, Hy-Brasail, Ribor Road, Matlock, Derbyshire, DG4 5JB. Prop: Grant Jarvis. TN: 55322. Est: 1979. Private premises; appointment necessary. Small stock sec. and antiq. also back-numbers of journals. Spec: mountaineering. Cata: 2 or 3 a year.

LAURA'S BOOKSHOP, 58 Osmaston Road, Derby DE1 2HZ. Prop: Laura J. and Ronald B. Crooks. TN: (0332) 47094. Est: 1969. Shop, closed Mondays and Wednesdays (large car park at rear of shop). Medium stock sec. and antiq. also large stock of antiquarian maps and prints. Spec: Derbyshire topography and history; illustrated books

JOHN O'REILLY - MOUNTAIN BOOKS, 85 and 87 King Street, Derby DE1 3EE. TN: Derby 365650. Est: 1972. Shop. Very small stock sec. and antiq. also back-numbers of journals, new books and periodicals and mountaineering equipment. Spec: mountaineering, caving, polar, Himalayan travel. Cata: 3 or 4 a year. B: Lloyds Bank, The Spot, 40 Osmaston Road, Derby. M: P.B.F.A.

JOHN E. PHILLIPS 11 Corfe Close, Littleover, Derby DE3 7HW. TN: (0332) 768605. Fine and rare books.

SCARTHIN BOOKS, The Promenade, Scarthin, Cromford, Derbyshire DE4 3QF. Prop: Dr. D.J. Mitchell. TN: (062 982) 3272. Est: 1974. Shop, open Sunday afternoon. Large stock sec. and antiq. books; also new books. Spec: industrial history, juvenile, Derbyshire, Alison Uttley. B.A.

TILLEYS BOOKSHOP, 29/31 SOUTH STREET, NEW WHITTINGTON, CHESTERFIELD, DERBYSHIRE. Prop: A.G.J. and A.A.J. Tilley. TN: (0246) 473047. Est: 1979. Shop; normal hours except Thursday, 9am–3pm, also closed daily for lunch 1.30–3pm. Also by appointment. Large stock sec. and antiq. also periodicals, newspapers, cigarette cards. B: National Giro.

20. NOTTINGHAMSHIRE

NEWARK
NOTTINGHAM
RADCLIFFE ON TRENT
SUTTON IN ASHFIELD

THE BOOK SHELF, 16 ALBERT STREET, MANSFIELD, NOTTINGHAMSHIRE. Prop: F.B. & S. Payton. TN: Mansfield (0623) 648231. Est: 1980. Shop, closed on Wednesdays. Medium stock sec. and antiq. also some new and remainders. Spec: topography, natural history, gardening, country matters, railways, collecting. Cata: irregularly. Corresp: Deutsch. B: Barclays Bank, Main Street, Hucknall, Nottinghamshire. Account 40705829.

THE BOOKSHOP, 4 STATION ROAD, SANDIACRE, NEAR NOTTINGHAM NG10 5BG. Prop: Ian H.R. Cowley. TN: (0602) 393379. Est: 1962. Shop. Large stock sec. and antiq. B: National Westminster Bank, Thurland Street, Nottlngham. M: A.B.A.

HEATHER COWLEY BOOKSHOP AND GALLERY, 233 TO 237 MANSFIELD ROAD, NOTTINGHAM NG1 3FT. Prop: Heather Cowley TN: (0602) 473836. Est: 1962. Shop, but appointment preferred. Large stock sec. and antiq. books; also maps and prints and picture framing. Spec: old books, bindings; scholarly; topography. A.B.A., N.B.L. Fine Art Trade Guild. (Car park and back entrance is at 240 North Sherwood Street).

IAN H. R. COWLEY, THE BOOKSHOP, 4 STATION ROAD, SANDIACRE, DERBYSHIRE, NG10 5HU. (Near Junction 25 on the M1.) TN: (0602) 393379. Est. 1962. Shop, open between 9.30 am and 5 pm or by appointment. Medium stock, sec. and antiq. Spec: antiquarian books, binding, literature, topography and other subjects. B: National Westminster Bank, Thurland Street, Nottingham, NG1 3DT, Account 97108421.

NIAL DEVITT BOOKS, 133 MANSFIELD ROAD, NOTTINGHAM NG1 3FQ. Prop: Nial Devitt. TN: (0602) 413923. Est: 1976. Shop, also by appointment. Medium stock sec. and antiq. Spec: D.H. Lawrence, Nottinghamshire topography, arts and crafts, travel. Cata: Occasionally. Corresp: Français. B: National Westminster Bank, 10, The Square, Keyworth, Nottingham NG12 5JT. M: P.B.F.A.

CLIFFORD GILL, SPRINGFIELD LODGE, ROLLESTON, NEWARK, NOTTINGHAMSHIRE NG23 5SH. TN: Southwell 81-3104. Est: 1978. Private House; postal business only. Very small stock sec. and antiq. Spec: Kate Greenaway.

E.G. GLOVER 20 CHATSWORTH, SUTTON-IN-ASHFIELD, NOTTINGHAMSHIRE NG17 4GG. TN: (0623) 59352. Sec. and antiq. Spec: travels, Australiana.

SUE AND TONY GRAVES, "BOOKS", 34 ALFRETON ROAD, NOTTINGHAM. Prop: A.H. and S.M. Greaves. Est: 1979. Shop: medium stock sec. and antiq. Spec: military (arms, armour, equipment). Also new books. Cata: rarely.

JERMY AND WESTERMAN, 199–201 MANSFIELD ROAD, NOTTINGHAM NG1 3FS. Prop: P.R. Jermy and R.I. Westerman. TN: 0602 474522. Est: 1977. Shop, open during normal business hours. Medium stock sec. and antiq. also postcards and cigarette cards. Spec: Nottinghamshire topography, English literature, illustrated. M: P.B.F.A

ROBERT W. MORRELL, 443 MEADOW LANE, NOTTINGHAM NG2 3GB. Est: 1967. Private premises, appointment necessary. Small sec. and antiq. stock. Spec: 19th century, freethought, secularism. Cata: freethought, geology, malacology. 2 a year.

TRENTWOOD INTERNATIONAL LIMITED, 6 GRANTHAM ROAD, RADCLIFFE ON TRENT, NOTTINGHAM NG12 2HD. Prop: Mr. & Mrs. H. Boehm. TN: (06073) 3530. Telex: 37412 (shared). Est: 1970. Private premises; appointment necessary. Small stock sec. and antiq. books. Spec: export business in continental books and prints, also arts. Cata: occasionally. Corresp: Français, Deutsch. P.B.F.A.

21. LINCOLNSHIRE

BILLINGHAY	HOLBEACH
BOSTON	LINCOLN
BOURNE	LONG SUTTON
CAISTOR	LOUTH
EAST BARKWITH	SPALDING
GAINSBOROUGH	STAMFORD
GRANTHAM	TEALBY

BOOKS ETC., 3B WHARF ROAD, STAMFORD, LINCOLNSHIRE. Prop: A. & B. Schein. TN: Stamford 54980. Est: 1978. Shop, open between 10.30-5.30 pm daily; Sunday afternoons during Summer. Small stock sec. and antiq. also postcards, stamps, ephemera and old games. Spec: Americana, topographical, illustrated children's books from 1830's to 1910, philatelic related books. Cata: occasionally. Corresp: Deutsch, Français.

DEREK CROOK RARE BOOKS, BRITANNIA CENTRE, BEAUMONT STREET, GAINSBOROUGH, LINCOLNSHIRE. Prop: Derek Crook. TN: (0427) 5976. Est: 1980. Stockroom; appointment necessary. Medium stock sec. and antiq. Spec: Lincolnshire, North Nottinghamshire, South Humberside. Cata: 2 or 3 a year. Corresp: Français, Deutsch. B: Barclays Bank, Siver Street, Gainsborough, Lincolnshire. M: National Book League.

FOREST BOOKS, KNIPTON, GRANTHAM, LINCOLNSHIRE. Prop: W.R.H. Laywood. TN: (0476) 870224. Est: 1979. Private premises; appointment necessary. Large stock sec. and antiq. Spec: Bibliography, Bookbinding. Cata: 6 a year. B: Lloyds Bank, Grantham, 1 Saint Peter's Hill, Grantham, Lincolnshire. M: P.B.F.A.

T.B. & J.N. GRAY, THE OLD MARKET GARDEN, TEALBY, MARKET RASEN, LINCOLN LN8 3YB. TN: (067 383) 436. Est: 1973. House premises; open normal business hours. Small stock sec. and antiq. books. Spec: Middle East; agriculture; country subjects. Cata: occasionally.

HARLEQUIN GALLERY 20, 21 AND 22 STEEP HILL, LINCOLN. Prop: Richard West-Skinn. TN: Lincoln 22589 and Wragby 858294. Shop and storerooms; appointment necessary to view antiquarian stock. Very large sec. and antiq. stock, some new, also antiquarian fine art. Bookcases and Library Furniture. Spec: 19th century, ephemera, prints, natural sciences, English literature. Cata: general, 4 a year.

LAFAYETTE BOOKSELLERS, 6/8 CORNMARKET, LOUTH, LINCOLNSHIRE LN11 9PY. TN: (0507) 606856 (day) and (050 781) 363 (evening). Open Tuesday, Wednesday, Friday, Saturday.

ANTHONY W. LAYWOOD, KNIPTON, GRANTHAM, LINCOLNSHIRE NG32 1RF. TN: (0476) 870224. Est: 1965. Private premises; appointment advisable. Medium stock sec. and antiq. books. Spec: English books before 1850. Cata: 4 to 6 a year. A.B.A.

JAMES M&CBRIDE, 23 WALCOTT ROAD, BILLINGHAY, LINCOLNSHIRE LN4 4EG. TN: (0526) 860508. Private premises; appointment necessary. Small stock sec. and antiq. books. Spec: Middle East; archaeology, classical. B: Lloyds Bank, Sleaford, Lincolnshire. Account 0301065.

PILGRIM BOOKS, 7 RED LION STREET, BOSTON, LINCOLNSHIRE. Prop: R.H. Smith and J.H. Murgatroyd. TN: (0284) 84704. Shop. Small stock sec. and antiq. B: Midland Bank, Boston, Lincolnshire.

MICHAEL PRIOR, 34 FEN END LANE, SPALDING, LINCOLNSHIRE PE12 6AD. TN: (0775) 61851. Est: 1970. Private premises; appointment necessary. Small stock sec. and antiq. books, also new books and old cigarette cards. Spec: naval and maritime. Corresp: Français. B: Barclays Bank, Hall Place, Spalding. Account 50735329. Cata: 6 a year.

ALEXANDER ROGOYSKI (OLD AND RARE BOOKS), 22 MARKET STREET, LONG SUTTON, NEAR SPALDING, LINCOLNSHIRE PE12 9DF. Prop: Alexander Rogoyski. TN: (0406) 364111. Est. 1964. Private premises, appointment advisable. Small stock sec. and antiq. Spec: Continental Books, mainly pre-1800. Cata: On foregoing, occasionally. M: A.B.A.

S.P.C.K., 36 STEEP HILL, LINCOLN LN2 1LU. TN: (0522) 27486. Shop, closed on Mondays. Small stock sec. and antiq. also new books. Spec: theology. M: B.A., N.B.L.

STAFFORD'S BOOKS, ASH HOUSE, 40 RASEN ROAD, TEALBY, MARKET RASEN, LINCOLNSHIRE LN8 3XL. Prop: F., G. and T. Stafford. TN: (067) 383 557 Est: 1979. Private premises; appointment necessary. Small stock sec. and antiq. Spec: Children's Illustrated, English Literature. B: Midland Bank, Louth, Lincolnshire. M: P.B.F.A.

STANILAND [BOOKSELLERS], 4 SAINT GEORGE'S STREET, STAMFORD, LINCOLNSHIRE, PE9 2BJ. Prop: M.F. and M.G. Staniland. TN: Stamford 55800. Est: 1972 (in Oxfordshire). Shop, closed on Thursdays. By appointment at other times. Medium stock sec. and antiq. also old postcards. Spec: local topography. Cata: 2 a year. Corresp: Français.

ANDREW STEWART, 14 MIDDLE STREET, RIPPINGALE, BOURNE, LINCOLNSHIRE PE10 0SU. Est: 1978. Stockroom; appointment necessary. Very small stock sec. and antiq. books. Spec: early printing, incunabular, theology. Cata: 2 a year. Corresp: Deutsch, Français, Español. B: Midland Bank, Market Bosworth. Account 21019279. M: P.B.F.A.

JAMES C. & THE HON. JENNIFER SULLIVAN, 11 WEST BOURNE GROVE, LINCOLN. TN: (0522) 42310. Private premises; appointment necessary. Est: 1947. Medium sec. and antiq. stock. Spec: fine and scholarly books, 16th to 20th centuries. Cata: general. M: A.B.A., N.B.L.

K. WHYLD, Moorland House, Kelsey Road, Caistor, Lincolnshire, LN7 6SF. TN: (0472) 851374. Est: 1975. Private premises; appointment preferable. Small stock sec. and antiq. books. Spec: chess. Cata: 2 a year.

22. SHROPSHIRE (SALOP)

BRIDGNORTH	MUCH WENLOCK
CLUNTON	SHIFNAL
CRAVEN ARMS	SHREWSBURY
LUDLOW	TELFORD
LYDBURY NORTH	WHITCHURCH

BLACK HILL BOOKS, THE WAIN HOUSE, BLACK HILL, CLUNTON, CRAVEN ARMS SY7 0JD. Prop: Jean M. Smith and Guy N. Smith. TN: (058-84) 551. Est: 1972. Private premises; appointment necessary. Very large stock of fine first editions in science fiction, fantasy, horror, pulp magazines 1920–60. Cata: 8 a year. B: Midland Bank, 49 Market Street, Lichfield WS13 6LB. Account 41032178.

BOOKSTACK, 2 CASTLE TERRACE, BRIDGNORTH, SHROPSHIRE WV16 4AH. Prop: Mrs. E.A. Anderton. TN: (074 62) 3896. Est: 1975. Private premises. Mail order and Booksearch from this address. Shops at Bookstack, The Lodge, Wightwick Manor (National Trust) near Wolverhampton, West Midlands and at 8 Bank Street, Bridgnorth, Shropshire.

CANDLE LANE BOOKS, 28 PRINCESS STREET, SHREWSBURY, SALOP SY1 1LW. Prop: John and Margaret Thornhill. TN: (0743) 65301. Est: 1974. Shop, early closing Thursdays. Large stock sec. and antiq. books.

NIGEL COLLINS [FINE BOOKS], 20 MARKET PLACE, SHIFNAL, SHROPSHIRE TF11 9AZ. Prop: Nigel Collins and John Constable. TN: Telford 460351. Est: 1978. Shop, closed Mondays and Thursdays. Small stock sec. and antiq. also new books on art subjects. Spec: 19th and 20th century art and illustrated books, English literature, George Orwell.

THE COUNTRY BOOKSHOP, 23 WATERGATE STREET, WHITCHURCH, SHROPSHIRE. Prop: Ann and Kent Nielsen. TN: (0948) 5196. Shop; closed Wednesdays. Medium stock sec. and antiq. also new books.

L.G. HEYWOOD, USHER HOUSE, 30 MILL STREET, LUDLOW, SHROPSHIRE. Prop: L.G. Heywood. TN: (0584) 2658. Est: 1983. Private premises; appointment necessary. Small stock sec. and antiq. Spec: bibliography, illustrated books, Wales and the marches. Corresp: Français, Welsh. B: Midland Bank, 10 Bull Ring, Ludlow, Shropshire.

WILLIAM C. HUXLEY, THE BOOK CORNER, WELLINGTON MARKET, SALOP TF1 1DT. TN: (0743) 4506. Est: 1975. Shop, open Tuesdays, Thursdays and Saturdays. Small stock sec. and antiq. books, also a few publishers' remainders.

THE KINGS' BOOKSHOP, 139 CORVE STREET, LUDLOW, SHROPSHIRE. Prop: J.R.Y. and R.H. King. TN: (0584) 3761. Est: 1976. Shop, closed Thursday afternoons. Medium stock sec. and antiq. books. Spec: military history. Cata: general, occasionally.

P.J. MEAD, 2B WILMORE STREET, MUCH WENLOCK, SHROPSHIRE TF13 6RH. Prop: Philip Mead. (0952) 727058 & 727591. Est: 1978. Shop; early closing Wednesday. Also viewing by appointment. Small stock sec. and antiq. Spec: fine binding, Shropshire topography, Wilfred Owen, Mary Webb. Corresp: Français, Deutsch. B: Barclays Bank, High Street, Much Wenlock. M: P.B.F.A.

NELSON'S BOOKROOM, LYDBURY NORTH, SHROPSHIRE SY7 8AS. Prop: L.B. Walker. TN: (058 88) 219. Est: 1955. Postal business only, strictly no callers. Large sec. and antiq. stock. Spec: theology, all religions. Cata: on foregoing, occasionally.

OFFA'S DYKE BOOKS, 9 BELL LANE, LUDLOW, SHROPSHIRE. Prop: S.R. Bainbridge. TN: (0584) 3854. Est: 1972. Stockroom; open business hours but prior phonecall advised. Small stock sec. and antiq. Spec: literature, 18th-20th century. Cata: occasionally. Corresp: Français, Deutsch, Dutch. B: Barclays Bank, Corvedale Road, Craven Arms, Salop.

'Q' BOOKS, 28 HIGH STREET, IRONBRIDGE, TELFORD, SALOP TF8 7AD. Prop: Ian Hall. TN: (0952) 45 2769. Est 1978. Shop, closed Monday. Small stock sec. and antiq. Spec: architecture and allied arts, Ironbridge and the Industrial Revolution, Shropshire. Cata: 4 a year. B: Lloyds Bank PLC., 28A High Street, Tettenhall, Wolverhampton. M: P.B.F.A.

FRANK TURNER RARE BOOKS, c/o BARCLAYS BANK, KING STREET, LUDLOW, SHROPSHIRE. Est: 1972. Postal business only. Very small stock sec. and antiq. Spec: rare printed works pre-1840; 17th and 18th century cartography, topography, social and political comment; rural life, any period.

23. STAFFORDSHIRE

BIDDULPH
BREWOOD
BURTON ON TRENT
LEEK
LICHFIELD
NEWCASTLE UNDER LYME
STAFFORD
STOKE ON TRENT
TAMWORTH

ALBION GALLERIES, 8 ALBION STREET, HANLEY, STOKE-ON-TRENT ST1 1QH. Prop: R. Bladen. TN: Stoke-on-Trent 21051 (STD 0782). Est: 1969. Shop, closed Thursdays. Large sec. and antiq. stock, also new books and prints. Spec: local histories, family histories, fine bindings, topograph. Cata: on foregoing and general, 4 a year. P.B.F.A.

ANTIQUARIAN BOOK CENTRE, 104–110 HOPE STREET, HANLEY, STOKE-ON-TRENT ST1 5DA. Prop: Keith W. Fisher. TN: (0782) 261352. Est: 1970. Shop. Medium stock sec. and antiq. books. B: Midland Bank, Burslem, Stoke-on-Trent. Account 20344192.

BITS, BOBS AND BOOKS, CRANMERE COURT, WALSALL ROAD, LICHFIELD, WS13 6RF. Prop: Michael J. and Mrs. Denise A. Abrahams. TN: Lichfield (05432) 56200. Private premises; appointment necessary. Medium stock sec. and antiq. books. Spec: Staffordshire Topography: early postal history and coaching; early children's; sporting. B: National Westminster Bank, 47 Market Street, Lichfield. M: P.B.F.A.

BRIDGE-END BOOKSHOP, 198 BEARWOOD HILL ROAD, WINSHILL, BURTON-ON-TRENT, STAFFORDSHIRE. Prop: Pete Stancer. TN: Burton (0283) 46743 (home). Est: 1971. Shop, closed Tuesdays and Thursdays. Medium sec. and antiq. stock; also British and American comics, magazines and ephemera. B: National Giro 49 678 9104.

CARTOGRAPHICS, 49 GRANGE ROAD, BIDDULPH, STOKE ON TRENT. Prop: R.J. and S.W. Dean. TN: (0782) 513449. Est: 1969. Private Premises; appointment necessary. Medium stock sec. and antiq. maps and plans. Spec: maps and plans mainly of Great Britain, with related literature; the ordnance survey. Cata: 2 or 3 a year. B: Midland Bank PLC., 8 High Street, Manchester.

G. & J. CHESTERS, 23 MORRIS HILL, POLESWORTH, TAMWORTH, STAFFORDSHIRE B78 1JT. Prop: Geoff. and Jean Chesters. TN: (0827) 892828. Est: 1970. Private premises; appointment necessary. Small sec. and antiq. stock. Spec: British topography. Cata: occasionally. B: Midland Bank, Atherstone. Account 30232998.

HARTSHILL BOOKS, 439 HARTSHILL ROAD, STOKE ON TRENT ST4 6AB. Prop: Michael, Aline and Robert Downie. TN: 618130. Est: 1974. Shop. Medium stock sec. and antiq. also new books. Spec: science fiction and American comics. Cata: occasionally. Corresp: Français. B: Lloyds Bank, 41 High Street, Newcastle under Lyme. Account 0277032.

HUTTON BOOKS, BARNFIELD, THE PAVEMENT, BREWOOD, STAFFORD ST19 9BZ. Prop: Patrick and Felicity Hutton. TN: (0902) 850229. Est: 1977. Stockroom, open daily but appointment advisable. Medium stock sec. and antiq. books. Lists issued occasionally. Corresp: Français, Deutsch. B: Barclays Bank, Chapel Ash, Wolverhampton.

THE NEEDWOOD BOOKSHOP, 55 NEW STREET, BURTON-ON-TRENT, STAFFORDSHIRE DE14 3QY. Prop: C.R. Shepard and Mrs. D.M. Hall. TN: (0283) 41641. Est: 1974. Shop. Large sec. and antiq. stock. Cata: 3 or 4 a year.

NEWCASTLE BOOKSALES, 23 BARRACKS ROAD, NEWCASTLE UNDER LYME, STAFFORDSHIRE. Prop: Nigel and Glenice Woolliscroft. TN: (0782) 636460. Est: 1982. Shop; closed Thursday. Medium stock sec. and antiq. Spec: ordnance survey maps. Also new books stocked. B: Barclays Bank PLC., Town Road, Hanley, Stoke on Trent, Staffordshire.

ROBERT A. PICKEN, 11 GAOL ROAD, STAFFORD. TN: (0785) 53425. Est: 1979. Shop, closed Wednesdays. Small stock sec. and antiq. books. B: Midland Bank, 155 Stratford Road, Birmingham B11 1RB.

L. ROYDEN SMITH [BOOKS], FAREWELL LANE, BURNTWOOD, WEST MIDLANDS WS7 9DP. TN: (054 36) 2217. Est: 1972. Shop, open Wednesdays and Saturdays or by appointment. (3 miles from Lichfield). Large stock sec. and antiq. books, also new books and antiques.

STAFFS EDUCATIONAL BOOK COMPANY, 4 AND 6 DAM STREET, LICHFIELD, STAFFORDSHIRE WS13 6AA. Prop: G.B. Morton. TN: (054 32) 24093. Shop. Very large stock sec. and antiq. books. Spec: Classics; Shop. Very large stock sec. and antiq. books. Spec: Classics; Johnsoniana; Midlands topography. M: A.B.A., B.A.

R.G. WRAGG, 319 CHEADLE ROAD, CHEDDLETON, NEAR LEEK, STAFFORDSHIRE ST13 7BG. TN: (0538) 360044. Est: 1971. Private premises; appointment necessary. Very small stock sec. and antiq. books. Spec: local history, travel, atlases, topography, plate books. B: National Westminster Bank, 24 Derby St., Leek, ST13 5AF. Account 9162935. P.B.F.A.

24. LEICESTERSHIRE

ASHBY DE LA ZOUCH
BIRSTALL
COLEORTON
LEICESTER
LOUGHBOROUGH
MARKET HARBOROUGH
MELTON MOWBRAY
OADBY
OAKHAM
RUTLAND
THURCASTON
UPPINGHAM

EDGAR BACKUS LIMITED, 44–46 Cank Street, Leicester LE1 5GU. Directors: H.T.H. Taylor and M.R. Taylor. TN: (0533) 58137. Est: 1914. Shop, closed all day Mondays: but appointment preferable. Small stock sec. and antiq. books; also new books, maps, prints and Backus book cloth cleaner and leather binding polish. Spec: Leicestershire and Rutland material, natural history. M: B.A.

BREWHOUSE PRESS, The Orchard, Wymondham, Melton Mowbray, Leicestershire LE14 2AZ. Prop: T.C. Hickman. TN: (057 284) 274. Est: 1961. Private premises; appointment necessary. Very small stock sec. and antiq. books, also publishing. Spec: limited editions. Cata: very occasionally.

COTTAGE BOOKS, Gelsmoor, Coleorton, Leicestershire. Prop: J.M. Cropley. Est: 1970. Postal business only. Very small stock sec. and antiq. books. Spec: rural life, country crafts, gypsies, British folklore, agriculture, rural architecture. Cata: bimonthly, charged on subscription.

COUNTY BOOKSHOP, 34 Northgate, Oakham, Rutland, Leicestershire LE15 6AX. Prop: Anthony Marshall. TN: (0572) 2403. Est: 1979. Shop. Medium stock sec. and antiq. books and prints. Spec: women, feminism etc. Corresp: Français, Deutsch, Italiano, Español. B: Barclays Bank, High Street, Uppingham, Nr. Oakham. Account 50119911. M: P.B.F.A.

HENRY V.B. CROPLEY, Gelsmoor, Coleorton, Leicestershire. Est: 1970. Private premises; appointment essential. Very small stock, exclusively English and European manuscripts of the 17th to 19th centuries. Cata: 1 a year, charged.

CYCLAMEN BOOKS, P.O.Box 69, Leicester LE1 9EW. Prop: Y. and Mrs. D. Abramski. TN: (0533) 551795. TA: Cyclabook, Leicester. Est: 1976. Private premises; postal business only. Very large stock sec. and antiq. books, also back-numbers of journals. Social and political movements; East European politics and history; Judaica and Hebraica; Languages (Russian, Polish, French, Italian, German, Yiddish). Corresp: Français.

MRS. REBECCA DEARMAN, 90 CHARLES STREET, LEICESTER. TN: (0533) 21009. Shop. Very large stock sec. and antiq. also coins and medals. Cata: 4 a year.

HENRY FREER, 16 SYCAMORE ROAD, BIRSTALL, LEICESTER LE4 4LT. TN: Leicester 674719. Est: 1920: Private premises, appointment necessary. Small sec. stock. Spec: rare, limited editions, privately printed.

GOLDMARK BOOKS, 14 ORANGE STREET, UPPINGHAM, LEICESTERSHIRE. Prop: Mike and Sue Goldmark. TN: (0572) 822 694. Est: 1982. Shop; early closing Thursday. Also by appointment. Very large stock sec. and antiq., also a few new books and remainders. Spec: literature, history (especially medieval), Rutland topography. Cata: very occasionally. Corresp: Français, Deutsch, Italiano, Espanol. B: Barclays Bank, Old Fletton, Peterborough.

SIMON M. GREEN, MARCUSH, BLACKSMITH'S END, STATHERN, MELTON MOWBRAY, LEICESTERSHIRE LE14 4EZ. TN: (0949) 60705.

G.K. HADFIELD, BLACKBROOK HILL HOUSE, TICKOW LANE, SHEPSHED, LOUGHBOROUGH LE12 9EY. Prop: G.K. Hadfield. TN: (0509)

503014. Est: 1974. Business premises; stock can be seen at any time Monday to Saturday. Small stock sec. and antiq. books also new books, antique clocks and clock parts. Spec: horology (clocks, watches, chronometers) lathes, turning, automata; astronomy. Cata: frequently. Corresp: Français, Deutsch. B: Barclays Bank, Old Market Square, Nottingham.

M. HORNSBY, 36 BURTON ROAD, ASHBY-DE-LA-ZOUCH, LEICESTERSHIRE. TN: Ashby 6734. Shop, closed Mondays and Wednesdays except by appointment. Medium stock sec. and antiq. Spec: economics, politics, labour, pre-20th century periodicals.

IAN KILGOUR, ALL SAINTS ROAD, THURCASTON, LEICESTERSHIRE LE7 7JD. Prop: Ian Kilgour. TN: (0533) 350025. Private premises; appointment necessary. Small stock sec. and antiq. Spec: field sports and country life. Cata: approximately 4 a year. B: National Westminster Bank, 659 Loughborough Road, Birstall, Leicester.

R.L. LEETE, LEICESTERSHIRE SPORTING GALLERY & BROWN JACK BOOKSHOP, 78 MAIN STREET, LUBENHAM, near MARKET HARBOROUGH, LEICESTERSHIRE. Est: 1954. Shop and storeroom, closed Thursdays, (free parking opposite shop). Medium stock sec. and antiq. books; also maps and prints and oil paintings. Spec: sporting books, horse-racing, hunting, birds, fishing, local history and topography; golf, racing, cricket prints, spy cartoons etc., old horse brasses.

Private address: The Avenals, 87 Lubenham Hill, Market Harborough, TN: (0858) 65787.

ALFRED LENTON, 27 SAINT NICHOLAS PLACE, LEICESTER LE1 4LD. TN: Leicester 27827 (STD 0533). Est: 1942. Shop, no early closing. Medium sec. and antiq. stock. Spec: the arts, finely printed and illustrated, history, literature, natural history, science, sport, travel. Cata: general, occasionally.

MAYNARD AND BRADLEY, 48 EDENDALE ROAD, MELTON MOWBRAY, LEICESTERSHIRE. Also shop at ROYAL ARCADE, SILVER STREET, LEICESTER. TN: (0533) 532712. TN: (0664) 66842. Medium sec. and antiq. stock, also prints and maps. Private premises; appointment necessary. Cata: several a year. Corresp: Francais, Deutsch, Espanol. P.B.F.A.

Also at ERMINE COTTAGE, WASHDYKE CAVE, FULBECK, NEAR GRANTHAM.

MURRAY'S LIMITED, 23 LOSEBY LANE, LEICESTER. Prop: E.J. Feaks. TN: Leicester 20360. Est: *c.* 1890. Shop, early closing Thursday. New, and small sec. stock. A.B.A.

NORTHSTEAD BOOKS, 88 FAIRSTONE HILL, OADBY, LEICESTER. Prop: F.I. and A.M. Glenton. TN: (0533) 714508. Est: 1979. Private premises; appointment necessary. Very small stock sec. and antiq. Spec: 19th and 20th century literature. Cata: Very occasionally. B: National Westminster Bank, The Parade, Oadby, Leicester.

THE RUTLAND BOOKSHOP, 13 HIGH STREET WEST, UPPINGHAM, RUTLAND. Prop: Mr. and Mrs. Edward Baines. TN: Uppingham 823450. Est: 1977. Shop, open Tuesdays, Wednesdays and Fridays (a.m.). Medium stock sec. and antiq. Spec: fox hunting, public schools. Corresp: Français, Deutsch. B: Barclays Bank, High Street West, Uppingham. Account 60777005.
Also at CHEYNE LANE, STAMFORD, LINCOLNSHIRE.

S.P.C.K., 68 High Street, Leicester LE1 5YP. TN: (0533) 26161. Shop; closed on Mondays. Small stock sec. and antiq. also new books and periodicals. Spec: theology. M: B.A., N.B.L.

JOHN SPEED [MAPS], 36 Woodstock Close, Burbage, Hinckley LE10 2EG. TN: (0455) 618343, office (0455) 39556. Est: 1974. Spec: atlases and topographical books.

25. NORFOLK

BLAKENEY	NORWICH
DISS	SUSTEAD
FAKENHAM	SWANTON ABBOT
GREAT YARMOUTH	WELLS NEXT THE SEA
HOLT	WYMONDHAM
KING'S LYNN	

BAVERSTOCK BOOKS [AND BYGONES], 31 Lynn Road, Snettisham, Near King's Lynn, Norfolk. Prop: Beryl Baverstock. TN: (0485) 41680. Est: 1983. Shop; closed Tuesdays and Thursdays but appointments can be made for these days. Very small stock sec. and antiq. B: National Westminster Bank, High Street, Heacham, King's Lynn, Norfolk.

BLACKBORO'BOOKSHOP, Blackborough End, near King's Lynn, Norfolk PE32 1SL. Prop: Joy Rohan. TN: (0553) 5230. Est: 1976. Shop; stock can be seen Saturdays or by appointment. Small stock sec. and antiq. books.

THOMAS CROWE, 77 Upper Saint Giles Street, Norwich, Norfolk NR2 1AB. TN: (0603) 21962. Est: 1900. Shop, early closing Saturdays. Large sec. and antiq. stock. Spec: fine; colourplate books; voyages and travel; bound sets. Cata: rare books, 3 a year. A.B.A.

HOWARD FEARS BOOKS, 13 Bedford Street, Norwich, Norfolk. TN: Norwich 614459. TA: Books, Norwich. Est: 1980. Shop. Medium stocks sec. and antiq. Spec: finely bound sets and single volumes, topography, literature and illustrated books, maps. Cata: occasionally. B: Barclays Bank, Norwich.

DAVID FERROW, 77 Howard Street South, Great Yarmouth, Norfolk NR30 1LN TN: Great Yarmouth (0493) 63800 (Private: Great Yarmouth 662247). Est: 1940. Shop, closed Thursday. Very large sec. and antiq. stock, some new. Spec: local items, fine and out of print books on all subjects. A.B.A. N.B.L.

JENIFER FROST, Hill House, Gresham, Norwich NR11 8RB. TN: Matlaske 338. Private premises; postal business only. Very small stock sec. and antiq. Spec: embroidery, knitting, crochet, lace. Cata: 3 a year. Corresp: Français. B: Midland Bank, 8 Kings Road, Southsea, Hampshire PO5 3AH. Account 61017152.

SIMON GOUGH BOOKS, 3 Fish Hill, Holt, Norfolk. TN: (026 371) 2650 or (026 387) 603 and 2761. TA: Books, Holt. Est: 1976. Shop. Large stock sec. and antiq. books. Spec: natural history (birds); East Anglia; modern firsts, illustrated books, topography, finely bound sets. Cata: 4 a year. Corresp: Français, Italiano, Español. B: Coutts & Co., 15 Lombard Street, London EC3V 9AU.

PAUL GRINKE [AND WAVENEY BOOKS], Sustead Old Hall, Sustead, Norfolk NR11 8RU. Prop: Paul Grinke. TN: (026 377) 247. TA: Bookshelf, Norwich. Est: 1968. Private premises; appointment necessary. Very small stock sec. and antiq. Spec: art, architecture, English and Continental books before 1800; East Anglian topography. Cata: 2 or 3 a year. B: Coutts & Co., 10 Mount Street, London W1. M: A.B.A., P.B.F.A.

ELKIN MATHEWS, Scriveners, Cley Road, Blakeney, Norfolk NR25 7NL. Prop: Barbara Muir. TN: (0263) 740475. Est: 1880. Private premises. Small stock sec. and antiq. books. Spec: illustrated, natural history, English literature, sociology. Corresp: Français. B: Barclays Bank, High Street, Holt. Account 00618513.
Also at 14a Stoneham Street, Coggeshall, Essex CO6 1TT. TN: (0376) 61730.

MERRION BOOK COMPANY, Wickmere House, Wickmere, Norfolk NR11 7JE. Prop: Noel Bolingbroke-Kent. Est: 1965. Private premises; appointment necessary. Medium stock sec. and antiq. books. Cata.

.E. OLIVER, Malt Cottage, Croft Yard, Wells-Next-The-Sea, Norfolk. Prop: J.E. Oliver. TN: (0328) 711128. Est: 1978. Private premises; appointment necessary. Very small stock sec. and antiq. Also new books. Spec: natural history, M: P.B.F.A.

THE SAXON BOOKSHOP, 12A SAINT NICHOLAS STREET, DISS, NORFOLK. Prop: Mrs. P. Besley. TN: (0379) 2441. Est: 1978. Shop, closed Tuesdays. Large stock sec. and antiq. Corresp: Français. M: P.B.F.A.

SCIENTIFIC ANGLIAN BOOKSHOP, 30–30A SAINT BENEDICT STREET, NORWICH NR2 4AQ. Prop: N.B. Peake. TN: (0603) 24079. Est: 1965. Shop, closed mornings Mondays and Thursdays. Stock of over 60,000 sec. and antiq. also publishers' remainders. Spec: Norfolk topography, geology, archaeology, transport. Corresp: Français, Deutsch, Greek. B: National Westminster Bank, 45 London St., Norwich. Account 66167272.

G.B. & C. SCURFIELD, 1 WELLS ROAD, FAKENHAM, NORFOLK NR21 9EG. TN: (0328) 2450. Est: 1969. Shop, closed Wednesdays. Large sec and antiq. stock; also paperbacks. Spec: out-of-print fiction, poetry, children's books. B.A.

HAMISH RILEY-SMITH, SWANTON ABBOT HALL, SWANTON ABBOT NORFOLK NR10 5DJ. TN: (069 269) 244. Telex: 975 114 (EABANK G.). TA: Rileybooks, Norwich. Private premises; appointment necessary. Small stock rare books and manuscripts from 15th to 20th century. Early books printed in Arabic; Islamic science and medicine rare economics, philosophy and social sciences. Cata: 2 a year.

M. & A.C. THOMPSON, UNIT 3, 1 TOWN GREEN, WYMONDHAM NORFOLK NR18 0PN. Prop: A.C. Thompson. TN: (0953) 602244 Est: 1975 (at Poringland). Shop; closed Wednesday. Medium stock sec. and antiq. Cata: 4 a year. Corresp: Français. B: Barclays Bank Saint Stephens Branch, Red Lion Street, Norwich.

S.P.C.K., 19 POTTERGATE, NORWICH NR2 1DS. TN: (0603) 27332. Shop Medium stock sec. and antiq. also some new books. Spec: theology history, literature. M: B.A. N.B.L.

DAPHNE STEEL, 94 TENNYSON ROAD, KING'S LYNN, NORFOLK PE3 5NG. TN: King's Lynn 71712. Est: 1961. Private premises appointment necessary. Very small stock sec. and antiq.

TORC BOOKS 9 HALL ROAD, SNETTISHAM, KING'S LYNN, NORFOLK Prop: Heather Shepperd. TN: Dersingham 41188. Est: 1977. Shop closed Tuesdays and Thursdays. Large stock sec. and antiq. books. M P.B.F.A.

TURRET HOUSE BOOKS 27 Middleton Street, Wymondham, Norfolk Prop: lHugh and Rosemary Morgan. TN: (0953) 603462 Est: 1972. Shop, but appointment advisable. Very small sec. and antiq. stock. Spec: scientific and medical; the microscope. M: P.B.F.A.

WESTLEGATE BOOKSHOP, 10 All Saints' Green, Norwich, Norfolk. TN: Norwich 22569. Shop, early closing Thursday. Very large sec. and antiq. stock; also antiques. Spec: topography of Norfolk. A.B.A.

26. WEST MIDLANDS

BIRMINGHAM	SOLIHULL
COVENTRY	STOURBRIDGE
DUDLEY	SUTTON COLDFIELD
GREET	WALSALL
HALESOWEN	WARLEY
HARBORNE	WOLVERHAMPTON

J.G. ADAMS, 32 Cropthorne Road, Shirley, Solihull, B90 3JN. TN: (021) 744-1754. Est: 1941. Private premises, appointment necessary. Very small sec. and antiq. stock, also new. Spec: books and periodicals on railways. Cata: railways, rarely. B: Barclays Bank, Stratford Road, Shirley, Solihull.

BEECH BOOKS, 28b Oldbury Road, Rowley Regis, Warley, West Midlands B65 0JN. Prop: Kenneth Ernest Allen. TN: (021) 559 9822. Est: 1979. Shop, open Mondays, Fridays and Saturdays. Small stock sec. and antiq. also used records. Cata: occasionally. B: Barclays Bank, Church Square, Oldbury, Warley, West Midlands.

BIRMINGHAM BOOKSHOP, 567 Bristol Road, Selly Oak, Birmingham B29 6AF. Prop: I.K. and S.C. Watson. TN: (021) 472 8556 and (021) 426 2766. Est: 1976. Shop. Medium stock sec. and antiq. books; also back-numbers of periodicals. On A38 Road, near Birmingham University. Corresp: Français.

G.W.M. BLEWETT, 44 Wolverhampton Street, Dudley, West Midlands DY1 1DT. TN: Dudley 54112. Est: 1951. Shop, early closing Wednesday. New, and small sec. stock. B.A.

BLITZGEIST OF HARBORNE, 189 High Street, Harborne, Birmingham. Prop: J. Overbeck. TN: (021) 426 4122. Est: 1981.

Shop. Medium stock sec. and antiq., also new books. Spec: military, occult, collecting. B: National Westminster, Harborne.

BOOKSTACK AT THE LODGE, The Lodge, Wightwick Manor, Near Wolverhampton, West Midlands. Prop: Mrs. E.A. Anderton. Bookroom, open Thursdays & Saturdays (except in February) and Wednesday afternoons May to Sept. Medium stock sec. and antiq. books. Spec: Victorian and Edwardian art, literature; gardening, architecture; social life. Wightwick Manor is a National Trust Property and the bookroom will open when the house is open to the public. All enquiries to Bookstack, Bridgnorth, Shropshire. (TN: Bridgnorth (07462) 3896).

THE BOOK WARREN, P.O. Box 115, Wolverhampton WV6 8EG. Prop: Anita Jones. TN: Wolverhampton (0902) 763202. Private premises; postal and telephone business only. Small stock sec. and antiq. Spec: children's, illustrated gardening, cookery and country life. Cata: on specialities 4 a year: general occasionally.

BRACKEN BOOKS, 380 Birmingham Road, Wylde Green, Sutton Coldfield, West Midlands B72 1YH. Prop: A.G.M. Hill. TN: (021 373) 8958. Est: 1975. Shop and storeroom. Small stock sec. and antiq. books, also some new.

V.J. BULMAN, 53 Bath Road, Wolverhampton WV1 4EL. TN: (0902) 21055. Est: 1967. Shop, closed Mondays. Large stock sec. and antiq. stock. Spec: art, Black Country and Staffordshire topography.

CLENT BOOKS, 52 Summer Hill, Halesowen, West Midlands. Prop: Ivor Simpson. (021) 550 0309. Est: 1977. Shop; closed Wednesdays; Saturdays closes 4.30pm. Small stock sec. and antiq. Spec: history, local history, topography, natural history.

COMPTON BOOKS. 18 Upper Green, Tettenhall, Wolverhampton WV6 8QH. Prop: R. & B. Compton. TN: (0902) 753098. Shop (entrance through tearooms and upstairs). Closed Monday all day and Wednesday afternoons. Medium stock sec. and antiq. Spec: theology, missions, law.

ANTHONY DYSON, 57 Saint John's Road, Oldbury, Warley, West Midlands B68 9SA. TN: (021) 544 5386. Est: 1973. Private premises; appointment necessary. Small stock sec. and antiq. books. Spec: detective fiction, modern literature, music, fashion & costume. Cata: monthly.

PETER ELLIS-BOOKSELLER, 272 FOX HOLLIES ROAD, BIRMINGHAM B27 7PT. TN: 707 7968. Est: 1981. Shop. Medium stock sec. and antiq. M: P.B.F.A.

DAVID ESPLIN, 7 OAKLAND ROAD, MOSELEY, BIRMINGHAM 13. TN: (021) 449 7916. Est: 1978. Private premises; appointment necessary. Very small stock sec. and antiq. Spec: history of science, medicine and technology. Cata: 4 a year. B: Trustee Savings Bank, City Branch, Birmingham 72. Account 11803860. M: P.B.F.A.

GOSFORD BOOKS, 116 GOSFORD STREET, COVENTRY CV1 5DL. TN: (0203) 20813. Est: 1977. Shop. Medium stock sec. and antiq. also bookbinding and restoration. Spec: philosophy.

FRANK GREENWOOD, 7 WAVERLEY GARDENS, WOMBOURNE, WOLVERHAMPTON WV5 9EB. TN: (0902) 895496. Private premises; appointment necessary. Very small stock sec. and antiq. books. Spec: French. Corresp: Français. B: Barclays Bank, Gravel Hill, Wombourne.

THE HAGLEY BOOKSHELF, 30 CAVENDISH DRIVE, WEST HAGLEY, STOURBRIDGE DY9 0LS. Prop: Margaret Rankin. TN: (0562) 884816. Est: 1981. Private premises; appointment necessary. Very small stock sec. and antiq. Corresp: Français. B: Barclays Bank, West Hagley, Stourbridge, West Midlands.

HUDSON'S BOOKSHOPS LIMITED, HUDSON'S UNIVERSITY BOOKSHOP, THE NEW REFECTORY, UNIVERSITY OF BIRMINGHAM, BIRMINGHAM B15 2TP. TN: (021) 472-3034 and 3035. Est: 1962. Shop, closed Saturday. Very small sec. stock, also new. Spec: scientific textbooks. B.A.

MAGPIE BOOKS, 470 STAFFORD ROAD, OXLEY, WOLVERHAMPTON, WEST MIDLANDS WV10 6AR. Prop: Nina Tranter. TN: (0902) 783/03 (7.30 am–9.30 am, Mon–Fri only). Est 1083. Private premises; appointment necessary. Very small stock sec. and antiq. natural history only. B: National Westminster Bank, 2 Three Tuns Lane Parade, Ford Houses, Wolverhampton.

MAXWELL'S, 22 SHAFTMOOR LANE, ACOCKS GREEN, BIRMINGHAM B27 7RS. Prop: M.L. and C.M. Prickett. TN: (021) 706 8379 & (021) 777 6448. Est: 1947. Shop, no early closing. Large sec. and antiq. stock; also glass, china and antiques.

MIDDLETON'S BOOK SHOP, 230 AND 232 WARWICK ROAD, GREET, BIRMINGHAM B11 2NB. Prop: R. Middleton. TN: (021) 772 3575. Est: 1974. Shop, closed Mondays. Medium stock sec. and antiq. books. M: P.B.F.A.

A.J. MOBBS, 65 BROADSTONE AVENUE, WALSALL, WEST MIDLANDS WS3 1JA. Prop: A.J. Mobbs. TN: (0922) 77281. Est: 1982. Private premises; appointment necessary. Very small stock sec. and antiq. also new books. Spec: natural history, especially herpetology, ornithology and entomology. B: Midland Bank, The Bridge, Walsall, West Midlands.

P AND P BOOKS, 27 LOVE LANE, OLDSWINFORD, STOURBRIDGE, WEST MIDLANDS DY8 2DA. Prop: J.S. Pizey. TN: (038) 43 3845. Est: 1982. Private premises; appointment necessary. Very small stock sec. and antiq. Spec: literature, poetry, topography, natural history. Cata: occasional. Corresp: Français. B: Lloyds Bank, Gosta Green Branch, Birmingham B4 7HZ. M: P.B.F.A.

DAVID TEMPERLEY, 19 ROTTON PARK ROAD, EDGBASTON, BIRMINGHAM B16 9JH. TN: (021) 454 0135. Est: 1969. Private premises; appointment necessary. Medium sec. and antiq. stock. Spec: the arts, fine illustrated books of all periods, rare bindings, early children's books, topography (especially West Midlands), natural history, travel, old and rare playing cards.

P.J. WALCOT, 60 SUNNYBANK ROAD, SUTTON COLDFIELD, WEST MIDLANDS B73 5RJ. Prop: P.J. Walcot. TN: (021) 382 6381. Est: 1980. Private premises; appointment necessary. Small stock sec. and antiq. Spec: Polar exploration and travel.

STEPHEN WYCHERLEY, 508 BRISTOL ROAD, SELLY OAK, BIRMINGHAM B29 6BD. TN: (021) 471 1006. Est: 1971. Shop, closed Wednesdays. Large stock sec. and antiq. books. Spec: literature and the humanities, travel, illustrated, folklore and street literature. Cata: occasionally. P.B.F.A.

27. HEREFORDSHIRE AND WORCESTERSHIRE

BEWDLEY
BROADWAY
BROMSGROVE
BROMYARD
DROITWICH
EVESHAM
HAY-ON-WYE (SEE POWYS WALES)
HEREFORD
KIDDERMINSTER
LEDBURY
MALVERN
ROSS-ON-WYE
UPTON ON SEVERN
WORCESTER

ARENA BOOKS, Shelsley Beauchamp, Worcester, WR6 6RH. Prop: V.J. Packwood. TN: (08865) 266. Private premises and stockroom; appointment necessary. Very small stock sec. and antiq. Spec: theatre and associated subjects. Back numbers of journals also stocked. Cata: 3 a year. Corresp: Français. B: Barclays Bank, 42 High Street, Stourport-on-Severn, Worcestershire. Account 90120758. M: P.B.F.A.

ATKINS AND SON, The Lea, Ross-on-Wye, Hereford. Prop: A.I. Atkins. TN: (0989) 81404. Est: 1962. Stockroom; appointment necessary. Large stock sec. and antiq. B: American Commercial Bank, Ventura, California.

BATELEUR BOOKS, Perryfield, Sollers Hope, Hereford HR1 4RN. Prop: P.W. Francis. TN: (098 986) 226. Est: 1971. Private premises; appointment necessary. Very small stock sec. and antiq. books. Spec: Africa. Cata: 2 a year.

A.K. BENNETT, 15 Foley Street, Hereford HR1 2SG. TN: (0432) 270630. Private premises; appointment necessary. Very small sec. and antiq. stock. Spec: erotica, sexology

JOHN BEVAN, Saint Francis, Great Doward, Ross-on-Wye, Herefordshire, HR9 6DY. TN: (0600) 890878. Private premises and stockroom; appointment necessary. Small stock sec. and antiq. Spec: Roman Catholic literature, Greek and Latin classics. Cata: 4 a year.

THE BOOK END, 10 The Square, Bromyard, Herefordshire. Prop: K.I. Duncan. TN: (0885) 82515. Est: 1983. Shop; closed Monday all day and Tuesday afternoons. Also by appointment. Medium stock sec. and antiq. Corresp: Polski. B: Williams and Glyn's Bank, High Street, Bromyard.

BOOKS AND EPHEMERA, 44 New Street, Worcester. Prop: Norman Low. Est: 1980. Shop. Medium stock sec. and antiq. books. Spec: Scottish interest. Cata: 6 a year. B: Barclays Bank, High Street, Worcester. Account 20585688.

BOOKWORMS, 81 Port Street, Evesham, Worcestershire. Prop: J.E. Slaughter and C.J. Garratt. TN: Evesham 45509. Est: 1971. Shop, closed Mondays. Medium sec. and antiq. stock. Cata: occasionally

ANDREW BOYLE [BOOKSELLERS] LIMITED 21 Friar Street, Worcester. Prop: Mrs. P. Leeming. TN: (0905) 23893. Incorporated 1954. Shop, closed most Saturdays; appointment advisable. Very large sec. and antiq. stock. Cata: 6 a year. M: A.B.A., P.B.F.A.

GOLDEN AGE BOOKS, Valldemosa, 28 Saint Peter's Road, Malvern, Worcestershire WR14 1QS. Prop: Tony Byatt. Est: 1981. Private premises; postal business only. Very small stock Theological books only, also deals in Golden Age Postcards. Spec: English Bible translations, paraphrases, parts, text criticism and history. Cata: occasional. Also irregular auctions of Bibles. M: Postcard Traders Association (P.T.A.)

GRANT BOOKS, Victoria Square, Droitwich, Worcestershire. Prop: Shirley and Bob Grant. TN: (029 923) 680 or (0905) 778155. Est: 1973. Offices; appointment desirable. Stock sec. and antiq. books, also new books on golf and publishers of golf books. Spec: golf, Worcestershire. Cata: golf, 3 a year. P.B.F.A.

GERALD GUNTON, 87 London Road, Worcester. Prop: Gerald Gunton. TN: (0905) 354903. Est: 1982. Private premises, postal business only. Small stock sec. and antiq. Spec: Gypsy and archaeology. Cata: 2 a month. B: Barclays Bank, Cathedral Branch, Worcester. P.B.F.A.

GEORGE J. HARRIS, "Heathview", Habberley Road, Bewdley, Worcestershire. Prop: George J. Harris. TN: (0299) 40 2413. Est: 1977. Private premises; appointment necessary. Small stock sec. and antiq. Spec: natural history, modern firsts, Henry Williamson, Worcestershire local items. B: National Westminster Bank, High Street, Kidderminster. M: P.B.F.A.

THE HEREFORD BOOKSHOP LIMITED, 24 & 25 Church Street, Hereford HR1 2LR. Prop: Paul and Valerie Latcham. TN: (0432) 57617. Est: 1974. Shop. Small sec. and antiq. stock, also new books. Spec: local topography. Corresp: Español. B: Barclays Bank, 8–9 Hanover Square, London W1A 4ZW. Account 60441481. BA.

HOLDFAST BOOKS, 54 Old Street, Upton-on-Severn, Worcestershire WR8 0HW. Prop: Tony Hopwood. TN: (06846) 2134. Est: 1980. Shop, open Wednesday, Friday, Saturday; also by appointment. Small stock sec. and antiq. Spec: vintage technology, especially electrical and radio and heat engines. Corresp: Français, Deutsch. B: Midland Bank, 22 High Street, Upton-on-Severn. M: P.B.F.A.

HOLLAND BROTHERS, Barn House, New Street, Ledbury, Herefordshire HR8 2DX. Prop: L.M. and R.P. Holland. TN: (0531) 2825. Est: 1894. Private premises, appointment necessary. Medium sec. and antiq. stock. Spec: antiquarian; fine. Cata antiquarian, 3 a year. A.B.A.

LANDSMANS BOOKSHOP LIMITED, BUCKENHILL, BROMYARD, HEREFORDSHIRE. Prop: K.J. Stewart. TN: Bromyard (0885) 83420. Est: 1945. Offices in private premises, open normal business hours to public and trade. New, and small sec. and antiq. stock. Spec: agriculture and horticulture. Cata: new books only, annually, B.A. N.B.L.

MACKINTOSH BOOKS, THE LOWER HOUSE, STONEY LANE, TARDEBIGGE, BROMSGROVE, WORCESTERSHIRE B60 1LY. Prop: Mrs. D.J. Price. TN: Bromsgrove 71204. Est: 1973. Private premises; appointment necessary. Small stock sec. and antiq. Spec: local history, the countryside. Cata: occasionally. B: Lloyds Bank, 4 The Cross, Worcester. M: A.B.A. P.B.F.A.

THE MALVERN BOOKSHOP, 7 ABBEY ROAD (AT THE PRIORY STEPS), MALVERN, WORCESTERSHIRE. Prop: R.A.H. Lechmere and A.J. Lechmere. TN: Malvern 5915. Shop, early closing Wednesday. Large sec. stock.

B. MORTON AND M. JONES, DOWNWOOD, DUSTHOUSE LANE, BROMSGROVE, WORCESTERSHIRE. Prop: Mrs. B. Morton and Mrs. M. Jones. TN: (0527) 73449 and 73797. Est: 1978. Private premises; appointment necessary. Medium stock sec. and antiq. Spec: topography, especially Worcestershire & Midlands, natural history, children's, illustrated, literature and modern first editions. Cata: 5 or 6 a year. B: National Westminster Bank, High Street, Bromsgrove. M: P.B.F.A.

Also at 10 HARTFORD ROAD, BROMSGROVE.

PIERPOINT GALLERY, 10 CHURCH STREET, HEREFORD HR1 2LR. Prop: A.G. Beaver. TN: Hereford (0432) 367002. Est: 1968. Shop, closed Thursday. Medium sec. and antiq. stock, also maps and prints.

JAMES PLACE, TOWER FARM HOUSE, COW HONEYBOURNE, near EVESHAM, WORCESTERSHIRE. TN: Evesham 830488. Est: 1945. Storeroom, appointment advisable. Medium sec. and antiq. stock.

SABRINA BOOKS, 66 BARBOURNE ROAD, WORCESTER. Prop: C.R. Postle. TN: Worcester 20816. Est: 1962. Shop. Small stock sec. and antiq. books.

KENNETH TOMKINSON LIMITED [BEWDLEY FINE BOOKS] MIDDLE HABBERLEY, KIDDERMINSTER. TN: (0562) 743333. Est: 1975 Shop, appointment advisable. Medium sec. and antiq. stock. Spec incunabula, typography, private press books, bindings; local history Worcestershire and Shropshire and illustrated. Cata: 2 a year. Corresp Français, Deutsch. B: Midland Bank, Church Street, Kidderminster.

STRATFORD TREVERS, HB The Green, Broadway. TN: (038 681) 3668. Shop, early closing Thursdays. Medium stock sec. and antiq. books. M: A.B.A., N.B.L.

28. WARWICKSHIRE

ALCESTER
KENILWORTH
LEAMINGTON SPA
STUDLEY
STRATFORD UPON AVON
WARWICK

DUNCAN M. ALLSOP, 26 Smith Street, Warwick. TN: (0926) 493266. Est: 1966. Shop. Large stock sec. and antiq. books. Spec: Warwickshire topography. Cata: 4 a year. M. A.B.A.

K.A.F. BREWIN, 13 Gunners Lane, Studley, Warwickshire B80 7LX. TN: (052 785) 2098. Est: 1973. Storeroom; appointment necessary (business is mainly postal). Very small stock sec. and antiq. books; also new books. Spec: transport history; Midlands topography. Cata: transport, general about 2 a year.

BROWNE'S BOOKSHOP, 44 Railway Terrace, Rugby, Warwickshire. Prop: H. Browne Shop, early closing Wednesdays. Medium stock sec. and antiq. books. B: Trustee Savings Bank, Regent Street, Rugby

COFFEEBOOKS, 15 Meer Street, Stratford-upon-Avon, Warwickshire. Prop: L.W. Bailey and R.C. Pierce. TN: (0789) 66204 or 205441 (home). Est: 1950s. Shops. Very large stock sec. and antiq. books; some publishers' remainders and coffee. Spec: Shakespeare, Bruce Bairnsfather, Warwickshire topography. Cata: 3 or 4 a year. Corresp: Français, Italiano. B: National Giro 40 914 9004. M: B.A.
(*Also at* 29 Henley Street, Stratford-upon-Avon).

MRS. MARGARET DUCKWORTH, 169 Rugby Road, Milverton, Leamington Spa, Warwickshire CV32 6DP. Prop: Mrs. Margaret Duckworth. TN: (0926) 38345. Est: 1973. Private premises; appointment necessary. Small stock sec. and antiq., also new books and periodicals. B: National Westminster Bank PLC, 168 Parade Branch, Leamington Spa, Warwickshire CV32 4AF.

MASET BOOKS, 37 Henry Street, Kenilworth, Warwickshire CV8 2HL. Prop: Mrs. Susan Twigger. TN: (0926) 511808. Est: 1982. Private House; appointment necessary. Very small stock sec. and antiq. Spec: book-finding service, natural history, field sports, royalty, cookery, Warwickshire. Cata: 6 a year. Corresp: Deutsch, Français, Italiano. B: National Giro Bank, A/c 46-354-4005.

N.B. PAINE, 14 Portland Street, Leamington Spa, Warwickshire. TN: (0926) 883404. Est: 1983. Private premises; appointment necessary. Small stock sec. and antiq. Spec: dowsing, earth mysteries, archaeology and related subjects. Cata: 4 a year approx. B: Lloyds Bank, PLC, Leamington Spa, Warwickshire.

PIERS-GIBBONS BOOKS, 1 Radford House Cottages, 22 Lewis Road, Radford Semele, Leamington Spa, Warwickshire CV31 1UB. Prop: R.H. Gibbons. TN: (0926) 30914. Est: 1983. Private premises; appointment necessary. Very small stock sec. and antiq. Some new books. Spec: medieval history, (English and European), Anglo-Saxon studies. Cata: 4 a year. Corresp: Français, Deutsch. B: National Westminster Bank, 59 The Parade, Leamington Spa. M: P.B.F.A.

PORTLAND BOOKS, 5 Spencer Street, Leamington Spa, Warwickshire. Prop: Jan Weddup. TN: (0926) 38793. Est: 1974. Shop. Medium stock sec. and antiq. books. Spec: English literature.

IAN K. PUGH BOOKS, Warwick Antique Centre, 22 High Street, Warwick CV34 4AP. TN: Warwick 491382.

P.R. AND V. SABIN, April Cottage, Coughton Lane, Coughton, Alcester, Warwickshire B49 5HN. Prop: Paul and Vivien Sabin. TN: (0789) 762661. Private premises; appointment essential. Medium stock sec. and antiq. books; also large stock antique maps. Spec: Warwickshire and Worcestershire topography; cartography, atlases and maps of the Midland Counties of England. Cata: occasional lists.

NORMAN SLATER LIMITED, 70 Leam Terrace, Leamington Spa, Warwickshire CV31 1DG. Est: 1950. Postal business only. Small stock sec. and antiq. books. Spec: topography; archaeology; Roman history. Cata: occasionally

ROBERT VAUGHAN, 20 Chapel Street, Stratford-upon-Avon, Warwickshire. TN: (0789) 205312. Est: 1953. Shop. Large stock sec. and antiq. books. Spec: first and fine editions, of English literature, theatre and other performing arts, Shakespeareana. M: A.B.A.

29. NORTHAMPTONSHIRE

BRACKLEY
BRIXWORTH
KETTERING
NORTHAMPTON
OUNDLE
TOWCESTER
WELLINGBOROUGH

ARS ARTIS, School House, Clopton, Kettering, Northamptonshire. Prop: G.B. Lowe, M.A. and H.J. Lowe, M.A. TN: (080 15) 257. Est: 1965. Converted school premises; appointment necessary. Very large sec. and antiq. stock also new books; Deals in books on art only. Cata: 5 a year.

THE DOVE BOOKSHOP, 18/18A Cambridge Street, Wellingborough, Northamptonshire NN8 1DJ. Prop: John Paul Bolton. TN: (0933) 78049. Est: 1982. Shop, closed Thursday afternoons. Small stock sec. and antiq. books, also new books. Corresp: Français. B: Midland Bank, High Street, Rushden, Northamptonshire. M: B.A., and Wellingborough Chamber of Trade.

GUNNETT BOOKS, 128 Northampton Road, Brixworth, Northampton. Prop: Mr. and Mrs. B.R. Gunnett. TN: (0604) 880057. Est: 1983. Shop, closed Mondays. Also by appointment. Very small stock sec. and antiq. Spec: general non-fiction and modern first editions. B: Barclays Bank PLC, 18 The Drapery, Northampton NN1 2HH.

CARL HOWARD OF WELLINGBOROUGH, 84 Cedar Way, Wellingborough, Northamptonshire. Prop: Carl Howard. TN: (0933) 67808. Est: 1980. Private premises; appointment necessary. Very small stock sec. and antiq. also some new books. Spec: Cricket. Cata: 1 or 2 a year. B: Yorkshire Bank, Sheep Street, Wellingborough, Northamptonshire.

R.A. MARRIOTT, 24 Thirlestane Road, Far Cotton, Northampton NN4 9HD. TN: (0604) 65190. Private premises; postal business only. Small stock rare and antiq. Spec: astronomy.

THE OLD HALL BOOKSHOP, 32 Market Place, Brackley. Prop: John Townsend and Lady Juliet, Townsend. TN: (0280) 704146. Shop. Large stock sec. and antiq. books. B: Lloyds Bank, Brackley. Account 0175606. M: P.B.F.A.

PARK BOOK SHOP. 12 Park Road, Wellingborough, Northamptonshire NN8 4PG. Prop: Mrs. J.A. Foster. TN: (0933) 222592. Shop, closed Thursdays. Medium stock sec. and antiq.

MR. PICKWICK OF TOWCESTER, Lavender Cottage, Shutlanger, Towcester, Northamptonshire. Prop: William Mayes. TN: (0604) 862006. Est: 1972. Postal business only. Very large stock sec. and antiq. books. Spec: Charles Dickens. Worldwide bookfinding service. N.B.L.

THE PUDDING BOWL, 4 North Street, Oundle, Peterborough, Northamptonshire. Prop: Brian E. Rice. TN: (0832) 73404/72611. Est: 1966. Shop, closed Wednesdays. Medium stock sec. and antiq. Spec: Northamptonshire. Corresp: Français, Deutsch. B: Barclays Bank, Thrayston, Northamptonshire.

WOOTTON-BILLINGHAM. 79 Saint Giles Street, Northampton NN1 1JF. Prop: David J. Veryard. TN: (0604/34531. Est: 1896. Shop. About 60,000 volumes general sec. and antiq. books. Spec: Bibles; theology of 16th and 17th centuries. Account 09005943.

30. CAMBRIDGESHIRE

CAMBRIDGE
CASTOR
COTTENHAM
ELY
GREAT SHELFORD
HUNTINGDON
LITTLE ABINGTON
LODE
PETERBOROUGH
SAINT IVES
WISBECH

ABINGTON BOOKS, LITTLE ABINGTON, CAMBRIDGESHIRE CB1 6BQ. Prop: J. Haldane. TN: (01) 267 2701. Est: 1971. Private premises, appointments in London. Small sec. and antiq. stock, also new. Spec: books on Oriental and other carpets, classical tapestries, Eastern embroideries, the Eastern countries that make carpets (especially Central Asia) and their crafts. Cata: on foregoing, occasionally. Corresp: Deutsch, Français. A.B.A.

DAVID BICKERSTETH, 38 FULBROOKE ROAD, CAMBRIDGE CB3 9EE. TN: Cambridge 352291. Est: 1967. Private premises, appointment necessary. Small sec. and antiq. stock. A.B.A.

BLUNTISHAM BOOKS, OAK HOUSE, EAST STREET, BLUNTISHAM, HUNTINGDON, CAMBRIDGESHIRE PE17 3LS. Prop: D.W.H. and S.A. Walton. TN: (0487) 840449. Private premises; postal business only. Spec: Antarctic, Arctic.

THE BOOKROOM, 13A SAINT ELIGIUS STREET, CAMBRIDGE CB2 1HS. Prop: E.A. Searle. TN: Cambridge 69694 (STD 0223). Est: 1974. Shop, closed Saturday. Small sec. and antiq. stock. Lists, occasionally. M: A.B.A.

BRACTON BOOKS, 25 LODE ROAD, LODE, CAMBRIDGE CB5 9ER. Prop: Mrs. S.J. Harrison. Est: 1981. Private premises; postal business only. Spec: anthropology, travel, early law, social history. Cata: every 2 or 3 months. B: National Girobank.

CHESTERTON BOOKS, 1 ARBURY ROAD, CAMBRIDGE CB4 2JB. Prop: Philip Lund. TN: (0223) 61367. Est: 1983. Private premises; appointment necessary. Very small stock, sec. and antiq. Spec: theology.

PETER CLAY, CHAPEL COLLECTORS CENTRE, CHURCH HILL, CASTOR, NEAR PETERBOROUGH, CAMBRIDGESHIRE. Prop: Peter Clay. TN: (0733) 267169. Est: 1982. Shop (converted chapel), closed Wednesdays and Thursdays. Medium stock sec. and antiq. Spec: Northamptonshire and Fenland topography, prints and maps. B: Midland Bank Ltd., North Street, Bourne, Lincolnshire.

CLEARWATER BOOKS, 21 Burstellars, Saint Ives, Huntingdon, Cambridgeshire PE17 4XX. Prop: Stephen Francis Clarke. TN: (0480) 68613. Est: 1972. Private premises; postal business only. Small stock sec. and antiq. Spec: modern first editions, rural life, folklore. Cata: 6 a year. B: Barclays Bank, The Pavement, Saint Ives, Huntingdon. Account 10271616. M: P.B.F.A.

G. DAVID, 3 & 16 Saint Edward's Passage, Cambridge CB2 3PJ. TN: (0223) 354619. Est: 1896. Two shops, closed Thursdays. Large sec. and antiq. stock and publishers' remainders. Spec: antiquarian. M: A.B.A., B.A.

DEIGHTON BELL & COMPANY, 13, Trinity Street, Cambridge CB2 1TD. Prop: Wm. Dawson and Sons Limited. TN: (0223) 353939. TA: Deightons Cambridge. Est: 1700. Shop, closed Saturday afternoons. Very large stock of fine and rare antiquarian books. Spec: travel, topography; English literature; typography; Classics. Cata: 4 to 6 a year. A.B.A.

EQUUS, 99 King Street, Cambridge CB1 1LD. Prop: Caroline Burt. (0223) 66999. Small stock sec. and antiq. Spec: the horse (books on racing, hunting, polo etc.)

GALLOWAY & PORTER LIMITED, 30 SIDNEY STREET, CAMBRIDGE CB2 3HS. TN: Cambridge 67876. TA: Books Cambridge. Est: 1900. Shop and four floors. Closed Saturday. New, and large sec. and antiq. stock. Spec: Greek, Latin, philosophy, mathematics, theology, humanities. A.B.A. B.A. N.B.L.

NIGEL GARWOOD, 58 MAIN STREET, HARTFORD, HUNTINGDON, CAMBS. PE18 7XZ. Prop: Nigel Garwood, Rainer G. Voigt. TN: (0480) 54887 Est: 1977. Private premises; appointment necessary. Medium stock sec. and antiq. Spec: colourplate books, music and opera, foreign travel and topography, especially European and Americana, antique maps and prints. Cata: 2 a year. Corresp: Français, Deutsch. M: P.B.F.A.

DEREK GIBBONS, c/o THE GALLERY, 8 KING'S PARADE, CAMBRIDGE CB2 1ST. TN: (0223) 312913 & 68169. Spec: early children's and illustrated books. A.B.A.

ERIC GOLDING, 11 AND 12 NORTH BRINK, WISBECH, CAMBRIDGESHIRE PE13 1JR. TN: Wisbech 582927. Est: 1971. Storeroom, appointment necessary. Very large sec. and antiq. stock. Spec: juvenile, 19th century, Africa.

J.C.G. HAMMOND, CROWN POINT, 33 WATERSIDE, ELY, CAMBRIDGE CB7 4AU. Prop: J.C.G. and M.I.E. Hammond. TN: (0353) 4365. Est. 1970. Shop, open on Saturdays and by arrangement. Medium stock sec. and antiq. books on criminology and related subjects. Cata: 4 a year. P.B.F.A.

HAWTHORN BOOKS, 14 HIGH STREET, BRAMPTON, HUNTINGDON CAMBRIDGESHIRE. Prop: Mrs Nora Aldridge. TN: (0480) 53207. Est 1980. Private premises; appointment necessary. Small stock sec. and antiq. Spec: modern first editions, contemporary poetry, P.G Wodehouse, literature. Cata: 6 a year, approximately. B: Lloyds Bank Ltd., Huntingdon, Cambridgeshire. M: P.B.F.A.

ROBERT HICKS: BOOKSELLER, 5 SAINT JOHN ROAD, OLD FLETTON PETERBOROUGH PE2 8BL. Prop: Robert Hicks. TN: (0733) 65996 Est: 1980. Private premises; appointment necessary, also posta business. Very small stock sec. and antiq. Spec: rare, sec. and antiq books on Japan (Art, history, literature, Scholarly studies, religion) Cata: 2 a year.

W.A. LEE, 90 SAINT MARY'S STREET, ELY, CAMBRIDGESHIRE. TN: El 3483. Est: 1938. Storeroom, appointment necessary. Large antic stock. Spec: science, travel, art, music, colour plate books. Cata: o foregoing, several a year. A.B.A.

ADAM MILLS RARE BOOKS, 328 High Street, Cottenham, Cambridge. Prop: Adam Mills. TN: (0954) 50106. Est: 1981. Private premises; appointment necessary. Small stock sec. and antiq. Spec: 19th century English literature, modern fine printing and illustrated books. Catalogues. Corresp: Français. B: Barclays Bank, Chesterton Road, Cambridge.

PETER MOORE, P.O. Box 66, 200a Perne Road, Cambridge CB1 3PD. TN: 211846. TA: Antipodes, Cambridge, England. Est: 1970 in Canberra. Office premises; postal and by appointment. Small stock sec. and antiq. some back numbers of journals also a few new books. Spec: Australasia and the Pacific. Cata: 3 or 4 a year. B: National Westminster Bank. 26 Trinity Street, Cambridge, CB2 1TH. M: A.B.A. P.B.F.A., N.B.L.

JEAN PAIN, 34 TRINITY STREET, CAMBRIDGE CB2 1TB. Prop: J.D. Pain TN: (0223) 358279. Est: 1968. Shop. Medium stock sec. and antiq. books; also old maps and prints. Corresp: Deutsch, Français, Español, Italiano. A.B.A., P.B.F.A. *Also Gallery at* 9 KINGS PARADE, CAMBRIDGE.

FRANK T. POPELEY, 27 WESTBROOK PARK ROAD, WOODSTON, PETERBOROUGH PE2 9JG. TN: (0733) 62386. Private premises; postal business only. Very small stock sec. and antiq. also some back numbers of journals. Spec: Africa especially Kenya and Tanzania. Cata: 3 a year. B: Barclays Bank, Western Trust and Savings, Plymouth, Devon PL1 1SE. Account 22425705.

B RICE, 4 NORTH STREET, OUNDLE, PETERBOROUGH, CAMBRIDGESHIRE TN: (083 22) 3404. Shop, early closing Wednesdays. Medium sec. and antiq. stock; also coins and antiques. Spec: Northamptonshire.

JOHN ROBERTSHAW, 5 FELLOWES DRIVE, RAMSEY, HUNTINGDON, CAMBRIDGESHIRE PE17 1BE. Prop: John Robertshaw. TN: (0487) 81330. Est: 1983. Private premises: appointment necessary. Medium stock sec. and antiq. Cata: 6 a year. Corresp: Français, Deutsch. B: Barclays Bank, Market Hill, Huntingdon, Cambridgeshire. M: P.B.F.A.

SIDDELEY & HAMMOND LIMITED, 19 CLARENDON STREET, CAMBRIDGE CB1 1JU. Prop: Miss Kay Hammond. TN: (0223) 50325. Est: 1976. Private Premises; appointment necessary. Medium stock sec. and antiq. books. Spec: Theatre; English literature; illustrated books; modern firsts and limited editions. Cata: 4 a year. B: Midland Bank, Cambridge. Account 31026682 P.B.F.A.

PETER WOOD, 20 STONEHILL ROAD, GREAT SHELFORD, CAMBRIDGE CB2 5JL. TN: (0223) 842419. Private premises; appointment necessary. Medium stock sec. and antiq. books. Spec: theatre and all performing arts. Cata: 4 or 5 a year.

31. SUFFOLK

- BECCLES
- BILDESTON
- BOXFORD
- BURES
- BURY SAINT EDMUNDS
- CLARE
- EYE
- FRAMLINGHAM
- HALESWORTH
- IPSWICH
- LAVENHAM
- LOWESTOFT
- MONKS ELEIGH
- NEWMARKET
- SAXMUNDHAM
- SUDBURY
- WOODBRIDGE

GARETH ADAMSON AND ASSOCIATES, 108 High Street, Newmarket, Suffolk CB8 8JP. Prop: Gareth Adamson. TN: 0638-68934. Bookrooms; appointment necessary. Medium stock used. Spec: illustrators, ephemera, social history, juvenile. Cata: 8 a year. B: Lloyds, University Branch, Cambridge. Account 0019229. M: A.B.A. The Ephemera Society.

ARCADE BOOK CENTRE, 178 London Road North, Lowestoft, Suffolk NR32 4PW. Prop: Laurence Gall. TN: 84919. Est: 1979. Shop. Large stock sec. also publisher's remainders. B: Barclays Bank, London Road North, Lowestoft.

R.G. ARCHER, 91 High Street, Lavenham, Suffolk CO10 9PZ. TN: 247229. Est: 1971. Shop. Open seven days a week. Large stock sec. and antiq. books. Cata: 1 a year. B: Midland Bank, Market Hill, Sudbury. Account 91024566.

JAMES CARTERS BOOKSHOP, 160 High Street, Newmarket, Suffolk CB8 9AG. Prop: Mrs Janet Carters. TN: (0638) 61787. Est: 1978. Shop; closed on Mondays. Large stock sec. Spec: all aspects of the horse including racing and breeding. Cata: occasionally. B: National Westminster Bank. High Street, Newmarket.

G. CAWTHORN, The Bookshop, New Street, Sudbury, Suffolk CO10 6JB. Prop: T.M. and G. Cawthorn. TN: (078 73) 72075. Est: 1975. Shop, closed Mondays and Wednesdays. Medium stock sec. and antiq. books.

COLLEGE GATEWAY BOOKSHOP, [CLAUDE COX OLD & RARE BOOKS], 3/5 Silent Street, Ipswich IP1 1TF. Prop: C.W., J. and A.B. Cox. TN: (0473) 54776. TA: BIBLIOCOX SAXMUNDHAM. Est: 1944. Shop, closed Wednesdays. Large stock sec. and antiq. Spec: Suffolk books, maps and prints, printing and the art of the book, literature, history, natural history, topography and travel. Cata: 6 a year. M: A.B.A., P.B.F.A., B.A.

R.I. DONALD, 4 PEACOCK CLOSE, CARLTON COLVILLE, LOWESTOFT, SUFFOLK NR33 8BH. Prop: R.I. Donald. TN: (0502) 512207. Est: 1971. Private premises; appointment only. Very small stock sec. and antiq. Spec: military history. Cata: occasional lists. B: Lloyds Bank, London Road North, Lowestoft, Suffolk.

BRENDA E. EBSWORTH, WAVENEY ANTIQUES CENTRE, SALTGATE, BECCLES, SUFFOLK. Prop: Mrs. B.E. Ebsworth. TN: (0502) 722691. Est: 1980. Shop. Small stock sec. and antiq. Spec: 20th century art and literature, East Anglia and Broads items. B: Lloyds Bank, Southwold, Suffolk.

A.W. & R.S. EEKHOUT, ORCHARD FARM, BEDINGFIELD, EYE, SUFFOLK. TN: (072876) 338. Est: 1965. Private premises; appointment necessary. Small stock sec. and antiq. books; also some new books, prints, water colours etc. Spec: topography; illustrated books.

FIRESIDE BOOKS, "COPPINS", IXWORTH ROAD, HONINGTON, NEAR BURY SAINT EDMUNDS, SUFFOLK IP31 1QY. Prop: Ken and Pat Schulz. TN: (035 96) 8240. Est: 1973. Private premises; appointment necessary. Very small stock sec. and antiq. and new books. Spec: lacemaking and embroidery. Cata: occasionally.

THE GLOBE BOOKSHOP, 21 Saint Margarets Green, Ipswich, Suffolk. Prop: D. Wright. Est: 1975. Shop. Small stock sec. and antiq. books.

MAJOR IAIN GRAHAME, Daws Hill, Lamarsh, Bures, Suffolk CO8 5EX. TN: (078-729) 213. TA: Dawshall, Bures. Est: 1979. Private premises; appointment necessary. Very small stock sec. and antiq. Spec: natural history, sport, Africana. Cata: 3–4 a year. Corresp: Français. B: Lloyds Bank, Sudbury, Suffolk. Account 0097054.

ROSALIND HEATH BOOKS, The Cottage, The Street, Monks Eleigh, Suffolk. Prop: Rosalind Heath. TN: (0449) 740 898. Est: 1981. Private premises; appointment necessary. Small stock sec. and antiq. Spec: illustrated books, modern first editions. Cata: infrequently. Corresp: Français. B: Barclays Bank Ltd., High Street, Hadleigh, Suffolk. M: P.B.F.A.

MRS. A. KENT, 19 Market Hill, Framlingham, Near Woodbridge, Suffolk IP13 9BB. TN: (0728) 723046. Est: 1974. Open weekdays except Wednesdays or by appointment. Small stock sec. and antiq. books, also old postcards and sheet music. Spec: detective fiction. B: Lloyds Bank, 3 King Street, Saffron Walden, Essex.

.W. AND C.R. LAMB, Talbot House, 158 Denmark Road, Lowestoft, Suffolk NR32 2EL. TN: (0502) 64306. Est: 1972. Postal business only. Small stock sec. and antiq. books. Spec: Latin, Greek; Japan; East Anglia. Cata: 2 or 3 a year.

AITH LEGG, The Guildhall, Bookroom, Church Street, Eye, Suffolk IP23 7BD. TN: (0379) 870193. Est: 1970. Shop, open Fridays and Saturdays or by appointment. Small stock sec. and antiq. also some new books. Spec: costume, social history; cookery, crafts, (especially needlework & lace); collecting, postcards and other ephemera. M: P.B.F.A.

. & M. LORFORD, Vine Cottage, Duke Street, Hintlesham, Ipswich, Suffolk IP8 3PL. Prop: Michael Lorford. TN: Hintlesham 379. Est: 1953. Private premises, appointment necessary. Small sec. and antiq. stock. Cata: general, occasionally.

MAINMAST BOOKS, SAXMUNDHAM, SUFFOLK IP17 1JB. Prop: John P.F.H. Cook. TN: (0728) 2359. Private premises; postal business only. Medium stock sec. and antiq. also new books and back-numbers of journals. Spec: maritime and allied subjects only. Cata: 2 a year. Corresp: Français, Deutsch. B: Midland Bank: Saxmundham. Account 71012223.

JOHN MEAD, POST BOX NO. C06 5DX, BELSIZE COTTAGE, 3 BROAD STREET, BOXFORD, SUFFOLK. Prop: John Mead. TN: (0787) 210421. Est: 1974. Private premises; appointment necessary. Small stock sec. and antiq. Spec: agriculture, sociology and biography. Cata: occasionally. Corresp: Français, Deutsch. B: Barclays Bank PLC, University of Essex, Wivenhoe Park, Colchester, Essex.

ELIZABETH NELSON, "ROSSLYN", THE GREEN, BARROW, SUFFOLK IP9 5AA. ALSO SAINT JOHN'S ANTIQUES CENTRE, BURY SAINT EDMUNDS. Prop: Elizabeth Nelson. TN: (0284) 910502. Est: 1982. Shop, also private premises; business hours and by appointment. Small stock sec. and antiq.

C.D. PARAMOR, 25 SAINT MARY'S SQUARE, NEWMARKET, SUFFOLK CB8 0HZ. TN: (0638) 664416. Est: 1974. Private premises: postal business only. Very small stock sec. and antiq. books. Spec: Gilbert and Sullivan, entertainments and related subjects. Cata: entertainments, 4 to 6 a year.

PATRICK QUORN, 21B QUAY STREET, HALESWORTH, SUFFOLK. TN (098 67) 4278. Est: 1977. Shop, open Fridays and Saturdays or by appointment. Medium stock sec. and antiq. Spec: military, aviation and naval history, jazz. Cata: 4 a year. Corresp: Français, Español. B: Lloyds Bank, Thoroughfare, Halesworth, Suffolk. Account 0010778. M: P.B.F.A.

JOHN ROLPH, THE COACH-HOUSE BOOKSTORE, MANOR HOUSE, PAKEFIELD STREET, LOWESTOFT, SUFFOLK NR33 0JT. TN: Lowestoft 2039. Est: 1952. Shop, closed Monday and Thursday, Medium sec. and antiq. stock. Spec: modern first editions, Victoriana, Edwardiana, children's books.

EILEEN RYLEY, 104 RISBYGATE STREET, BURY SAINT EDMUNDS, SUFFOLK. Prop: Mrs. Eileen Williams. TN: (0284) 62490. Est: 1973. Shop, closed Mondays and Tuesdays. Small stock sec. and antiq. books. Spec: local topography; children's books; English literature. Cata: local topography and children's books, occasionally.

GRAHAM K. SCOTT 68–69 SAINT JOHN'S STREET, BURY SAINT EDMUNDS, SUFFOLK IP33 1SJ. TN: (0284) 3933. TA: Antiquaria, Bury Saint Edmunds. Est: 1976. Shop, closed Thursdays. Large stock sec. and antiq. books. Spec: history, biography, architecture, military, Penguin books. M: A.B.A.

SHERLOCKS, 11 DUKE STREET, BILDESTON, SUFFOLK. Prop: P.D. Sherlock. TN: (0449) 740397. Est: 1971. Stockroom; appointment necessary. Small stock sec. and antiq. Spec: travel, 20th century wood engravers. B: National Westminster Bank, 25 High Street, Colchester. M: P.B.F.A.

PETER TRINDER, MALTING LANE, CLARE, SUFFOLK CO10 8NW. TN: (0787) 277130. Est: 1975. Shop. Very large stock sec. and antiq. books and some new. Spec: topography, architecture. Cata: occasionally. B: Lloyds Bank. Chesterton Road, Cambridge. Account 202456. P.B.F.A.

R.E. & G.B. WAY, BRETTONS, BURROUGH GREEN, NEWMARKET, SUFFOLK CB8 9NA. Prop: G.B. Way. TN: (063 876) 217. Est: 1958. House premises; appointment preferable. Large stock sec. and antiq. books. Spec: horses, hunting, racing, shooting, big game and all field sports. Cata: occasionally. A.B.A.

E.T. WEBSTER, WESTWOOD LODGE, BLYTHBURGH, HALESWORTH, SUFFOLK. TN: Blythburgh 539. Est: 1900. Private premises; appointment necessary. Medium stock sec. and antiq. Spec: 16th to 18th century English literature, early juveniles, poetry. Cata.

NICHOLAS WILLMOTT BOOKSELLER, 11 ALPE STREET, IPSWICH, SUFFOLK IP1 3NZ. Prop: Nicholas Willmott and Judith Wayne. TN: (0473) 59139. Private premises; appointment necessary. Medium stock sec. and antiq. Spec: English literature especially humour and Penguin books. Cata: occasional informal lists.

WISE OWL BOOKS [THE BURY BOOKSHOP], 28/28A, HATTER STREET, BURY ST. EDMUNDS, SUFFOLK. Prop: Colin Lewsey. TN: Sudbury 79947. Est: Business: 1976. Shop: 1980. Shop. Medium stock sec. and antiq. also back numbers of journals and new books and periodicals. Corresp: Deutsch, Svenska, Danske. B: Midland Bank, Bury St. Edmunds. M: P.B.F.A., B.A.

YOXFORD BOOKSHOP, High Street, Yoxford, Saxmundham, Suffolk. Prop: Phyllis Packer. TN: (072 877) 309. Est: 1974. Shop, open Easter to September, weekdays; October to Easter Thursdays. to Saturdays. Medium stock sec. and antiq. books. Cata: occasionally mainly to interest to colleges and universities.

32. GLOUCESTERSHIRE

BOURTON ON THE WATER
CHELTENHAM
CHIPPING CAMPDEN
CIRENCESTER
GLOUCESTER
LECHLADE
MORETON IN MARSH
NAILSWORTH
NEWHHAM
STROUD
TEWKESBURY
UPPER LYDBROOK
WINCHCOMBE

ABBEY ANTIQUARIAN BOOKS, Abbey Old House, Cowl Lane, Winchcombe, Near Cheltenham, Gloucestershire GL54 5RA. Prop: Christopher John Aeschlimann. TN: (0242) 602589. Est: 1978, Private premises, with display window on Abbey Terrace in central Winchcombe; appointment necessary. Medium stock sec. and antiq. Spec: print illustrated books 1550–1860; fables, Emblem books, children's books. Lists can be prepared. Corresp: Deutsch, Français. B: Payments can be in sterling, U.S. dollars, Swiss Francs, West German D.M. M: P.B.F.A.

AURORA BOOKS, The Bothy, Puckrup, Tewkesbury, Gloucester. Prop: Jean and Philip Syed. TN: (0684) 294001. Est: 1963. Private premises; appointment necessary. Small stock sec. and antiq. books, also some prints. Spec: English literature. Cata: 4 a year.

BARRIE'S BOOKSHOP, 4 Montpellier Walk, Cheltenham, Gloucestershire GL50 1SD. Prop: Peter and Martin Barrie. TN: (0242) 515813. TA: Barbook, Cheltenham. Shop, Antiquarian Department, First Floor, by appointment only. Medium antiq. stock. A.B.A.

THE BOOKSHOP, 2 Victoria Street, Bourton on the Water, Gloucestershire GL54 2BU. Prop: Stephen and Bridget Swann. TN: (0451) 20154. Large stock sec. & antiq. books, prints and maps.

CHURCH STREET GALLERY, Waite House, 71 Church Street, Tewkesbury, Gloucestershire. Prop: F.W. Taylor. TN: (0684) 295990. Est: 1973. Shop. Very small stock sec. and antiq. books, also fine antique furniture, ceramics and silver. Spec: collecting subjects particularly ceramics, English, continental and oriental.

FOUR SHIRE BOOKS, 17 High Street, Moreton-in-Marsh, Gloucestershire GL56 0EA. Prop: Hazel and David Potten. TN: (0608) 51451. Est: 1981. Shop, closed Monday all day and Wednesday afternoons. Small stock sec. and antiq., also new books. Spec: the Cotswolds, embroidery. Cata: 6 a year. B: Midland Bank PLC, Moreton-in-Marsh, Gloucestershire.

GREENSLEEVES-BOOKS, 23 ALL SAINTS VILLAS ROAD, CHELTENHAM, GLOUCESTERSHIRE GL52 2HB. Prop: N.F.R. Rose. TN: (0242) 516273. Est: 1982. Stockroom and private premises; appointment necessary. Very small stock sec. and antiq. Spec: occult, new age. C: 4–6 a year. Corresp: Français, Deutsch. B: Williams & Glyns Bank, The Promenade, Cheltenham.

ALAN HANCOX, 101 PROMENADE, CHELTENHAM, GLOUCESTERSHIRE. TN: Cheltenham 513204 Est: 1949. Shop storeroom, early closing Wednesday. Large sec. and antiq. stock. Spec: scholarly literature, first editions and rare books.

ALEXANDER HERIOT & CO. LIMITED, P.O. BOX 1, NORTHLEACH, CHELTENHAM, GLOUCESTERSHIRE. Prop: J. Fleming. TN: Northleach 530. TA: Alborak, Cheltenham. Est: 1974. Private premises; appointment necessary. Very small stock sec. and antiq. also new books. Spec: Arab horse. B: Bank of Scotland, 30 Bishopsgate. London E.C.1.

HERMES BOOKS, 10 SUFFOLK ROAD, CHELTENHAM, GLOUCESTERSHIRE GL50 2AQ. Prop: Andrew Fountain. TN: (0242) 41095. Shop, business hours, also by appointment. Medium stock sec. and antiq. Spec: occult, mythology, Eastern philosophies, freemasonry, astrology. Cata: 4 a year. B: Lloyds Bank, Bath Road, Cheltenham.

HEYNES BOOKSHOP, 40 CLARENCE STREET, CHELTENHAM, GLOUCESTERSHIRE. Prop: S.E. Martin. Est: 1919. Shop, closed Wednesdays. Large sec. stock.

IAN HODGKINS AND COMPANY LIMITED, MOUNT VERNON, BUTTEROW, RODBOROUGH, STROUD, GLOUCESTERSHIRE GL5 2LP. Prop: I.G. Kenyon-Hodgkins, C. & A. Yablon, M. Paisner, I. Hoy. TN: Stroud 4270. Est: 1974. Private premises; appointment necessary.

Small stock sec. and antiq. also publishers. Spec: Pre-Raphaelites, Brontë family, Bloomsbury Group, illustrated books of 19th century. Cata: 4-6 a year. M: A.B.A., P.B.F.A.

HORSE AND GROOM BOOKSHOP, 310 SAINT GEORGE'S PLACE, CHELTENHAM, GLOUCESTERSHIRE. Prop: John Ball. Est: 1982. Shop, early closing Wednesday. Small stock sec. and antiq. B: National Westminster Bank, Promenade, Cheltenham.

MRS. PEGGY LEAVER [BOOKFINDING SERVICE], MINERVA COTTAGE, SPRING GARDENS, LECHLADE, GLOUCESTERSHIRE GL7 3AY. TN: (0367) 52791. Est: 1971. Private premises; postal business only. Small stock sec. and antiq. Cata: occasionally. B: Lloyds Bank Ltd., Brunel Centre, 82 Regent Street, Swindon, Wilts SN1 1JY. M: P.B.F.A.

LECHLADE BOOKSHOP, 5 OAK STREET, LECHLADE, GLOUCESTERSHIRE GL7 3AX. Prop: Peggy and Norman Leaver. TN: (0367) 52791 (Home) after 18.00 hrs. Est: 1971. Shop, closed Mondays. Medium stock sec. and antiq. books.

R.R. & V.C. MERRITT, 174 OLD BATH ROAD, CHELTENHAM, GLOUCESTERSHIRE GL53 7DR. Prop: Valerie C. Merritt. TN: (0242) 514664. Est: 1975. Private premises; appointment necessary. Very small stock sec. and antiq. books. Spec: natural history, (geology, palaeontology, mineralogy,) metallurgy, mining, general science, gardening. Cata: 1 a year.

NEWNHAM BOOKSHOP, CENTRAL HOUSE, HIGH STREET, NEWNHAM, GLOUCESTERSHIRE GL14 1AB. Prop: Roger H. Orman. TN: (059 455) 324. Est: 1983. Shop, open Mon-Sat June-September, Thurs-Sat the rest of the year. Also by appointment. Spec: Folio Society, Forest of Dean. Cata: occasional. Also Folio Society, occasional. Corresp: Français. M: P.B.F.A.

SERIF BOOKS, Harrow House, Chipping Campden, Gloucestershire GL55 6DY. Prop: Seumas Stewart. TN: (0386) 840558. Est: 1961. Shop, early closing Thursday; or by appointment. Medium sec. and antiq. stock. Spec: natural history, agriculture, the country. Cata: natural history and general, occasionally. Corresp: Français, Italiano. B: Midland Bank, The Square, Chipping Campden. Account 00724610.

THOEMMES ANTIQUARIAN BOOKS, 1a College Court, Gloucester, Gloucestershire GL1 2NJ. Prop: R. Thoemmes. TN: (0452) 500776. Telex: 437244 CMINTL. Est: 1981. Office: appointment necessary. Small stock sec. and antiq. Spec: philosophy and related subjects, German. Cata: 5 a year, also lists. Corresp: Deutsch, Français. B: Midland Bank, 241 Cheltenham Road, Bristol 6. Account 01041568. National-Bank, Essen. BLZ 360 200 30 Konto Nr. 224 431 005. M: P.B.F.A.

THOMPSON'S BOOK SHOP, Dunstall House, Park Street, Cirencester GL7 2BX. Prop: J.M.H. and S.V. Thompson. TN: (0285) 5239. Est: 1978. Shop, closed on Mondays. Medium stock sec. and antiq. also back-numbers of journals. Spec: architecture. Cata: 3 a year. B: Lloyds Bank, Cirencester. Account 0499089.

P. THREDDER [BOOKS], Bourtswell Cottage, The Bourts, Upper Lydbrook, Gloucestershire GL17 9QB. Prop: Philip Thredder. TN: (0594) 60187. Est: 1978. Private premises; postal business only. Spec: Forest of Dean, Gloucestershire. Cata: occasional. B: Lloyds, Cinderford, Forest of Dean. M: P.B.F.A.

ALAN & JOAN TUCKER, The Bookshop, Station Road, Stroud, Gloucester GL5 3AP. TN: (045 36) 4738. Est: 1962. Shop, open daily except on Thursdays. Large stock sec. and antiq. also new books in Children's bookshop and new Bookshop located in same street. Cata:

3 a year. Corresp: Français. B: National Westminster Bank, George Street, Stroud. Account 98417827. M: B.A.

VALENTINE'S BOOKSHOP, 6A BRIDGE STREET, NAILSWORTH, GLOUCESTERSHIRE GL6 0AA. Prop: Richard Valentine. TN: (045383) 2483. Est: 1980. Shop, sometimes closed all day Mondays and half day Thursdays. Medium stock sec. and antiq. Cata: occasionally.

ADRIAN WALKER, 6 CULVER STREET, NEWENT, GLOUCESTERSHIRE GL18 1DA. TN: (0531) 821816. Est: 1965. M: P.B.F.A.
Also at THE FALCONRY CENTRE, NEWENT. TN: (0531) 820286. Spec: falconry and hawking, birds of prey, conservation.

PAUL WELLER LIMITED, 1 DOLLAR STREET, CIRENCESTER, GLOUCESTERSHIRE GL7 2AJ. TN: (0285) 2764 and 4460. TA: Weller Books. Est: 1970. Shop. Large stock sec. and antiq. books; also new books. M: B.A.

ROBERT B. WILSON, 56 BATH ROAD, CHELTENHAM, GLOUCESTERSHIRE. Prop: R.B. Wilson. TN: (0242) 24684. Est: 1976. Stockroom. Small stock sec. and antiq. Cata: 1 a year. B: Midland Bank, 1 Montpellier Terrace, Cheltenham, Gloucestershire.

DAVID WRAY, FORTUNES WELL, SHEEPSCOMBE, STROUD, GLOUCESTERSHIRE GL6 7RL. TN: Painswick 812386. (STD 0452). Est: 1969. Storeroom, appointment necessary. Small sec. and antiq. stock. Spec: country books of all periods.

33. OXFORDSHIRE (OXON.)

ABINGDON
BANBURY
BICESTER
BLOXHAM
BURFORD
CHURCH ENSTONE
CHURCH HANBOROUGH
CUMNOR
EAST HAGBOURNE
EYNSHAM
FARINGDON
HENLEY-ON-THAMES
HORSPATH
KIDLINGTON
LONG HANBOROUGH
OXFORD
SANDFORD SAINT MARTIN
WALLINGFORD

ARTEMIS BOOKS, 76 COWLEY ROAD, OXFORD, OX4 1JB. Prop: Diana Burfield. TN: Oxford 726 909. Est: 1980. Shop, closed Mondays. Medium stock sec. and antiq. books. Spec: social sciences and humanities. Cata: occasionally. Corresp: Français. B: Lloyds Bank, 181 Cowley Road, Oxford OX4 1UX. Account 0058813.

BANBURY BOOKSHOP, White Lion Walk, Banbury, Oxon OX16 8UD. Prop: Dianne Coles. TN: (0295) 52002 & 50731. Est: 1975. Shop. Small stock sec. and antiq. books; also new books. Corresp: Français, Russian. B: Lloyds Bank, High Street, Banbury. Account 0280931. M: B.A.

BENNETT AND KERR BOOKS, 99 The Causeway, Steventon, Near Abingdon, Oxfordshire OX13 6SJ. Prop: Edmund Bennett and Andrew Kerr. TN: (0235) 832587. Est: 1982. Private premises, appointment necessary. Medium stock sec. and antiq., also a few new books. Spec: English literature, art, history, private press and first editions. Cata: every 2 to 4 months. Corresp: Français, Italiano, Dutch. B: National Westminster Bank, 11 Market Place, Abingdon, Oxfordshire. M: P.B.F.A.

THE BICESTER BOOKSHOP LIMITED, 5 Kingsley Road, Bicester, Oxon. Managing Director: J. Hanks. TN: (086 92) 41852. Est: 1971. Shop, closed Thursdays. Medium stock of sec. and antiq. books on Aviation, Railways and woodworking crafts (no general stock); also new books. Cata: occasionally. B.A. N.B.L.

B.H. BLACKWELL LIMITED, 48–51 Broad Street, Oxford OX1 3BU. TN: (0865) 49111. TA: Books Oxford. Shop. Very large stock of sec. and new books. Cata: on various subjects at frequent intervals. B.A. A.D.A. N.B.L.

BLACKWELL'S RARE BOOKS, Fyfield Manor, Fyfield, Abingdon, Oxon. OX13 5LR. Prop: B.H. Blackwell Limited. TN: (0865) 390692. TA: Books, Oxford. Telex: 83118. Est: 1879. House premises; open during normal business hours. Large stock sec. and antique. Cata: frequently. M: A.B.A., B.A., N.B.L.

BLACKWELL'S MUSIC SHOP, 38 Holywell Street, Oxford. TN: (0865) 49111. TA: Books Oxford. Est: 1953. Shop, new, and large sec. and antiq. stock. Spec: antiquarian music and books on music. Cata: antiquarian music, 1 a year. B.A. A.B.A.

THE BOOK DEPOT, The Old School, Bainton Road, Hethe, Bicester, Oxford OX6 9HA. Prop: George Depotex. TN: 086 97 672. Est: 1979. Private premises; appointment necessary. Medium stock sec. and antiq. Spec: first editions, topography, art, biography, mining. Cata: subject lists on request. Corresp: Français. B: National Girobank Account 21 874 4005. By special arrangement payment can be made to Hong Kong agent. M: P.B.F.A.

A.R. BULLOCK, 62 KELBURNE ROAD, OXFORD OX4 3SH. TN: Oxford (0865) 777951. TA: Kitab Oxford. Private premises, appointment necessary. Small sec. and antiq. stock; also English and foreign new books. Spec: Arabic, Persian and Turkish texts; all Islamica. Cata: Islamica, classical and modern Arabic, Persian, Turkish, 3–4 a year.

CHECKER BOOKS, 2 CHECKER WALK, ABINGDON, OXON OX14 3JB. Prop: O. Weir. TN: 28172. Est: 1956 (as Dene Bookshop). Stockroom; open most mornings and by appointment. Very large stock sec. and antiq. also back-numbers of journals. Cata: occasionally. Corresp: Français. B: Barclays Bank, The Square, Abingdon. Account 80948942. M: A.B.A.

E.W. CLASSEY LIMITED, P.O. BOX 93, FARINGDON, OXON. SN7 7DR. TN: (0367) 82399. TA: Bugbooks, Faringdon, Oxon. Est: 1951. Postal only. books and own publications. Spec: natural history, especially entomology. Cata: natural history, 4 a year. B.A. N.B.L.

THE CLASSICS BOOKSHOP, 43 HIGH STREET, OXFORD OX1 4AP. Prop: C.P. and A.V. Powell-Jones. TN: (0865) 726 466. Est: 1976. Shop, closed Thursday afternoons. Medium stock sec. and antiq. Spec: Latin and Greek classics, ancient history, archaeology, Oxford topography. Cata: 2 a year. Corresp: Français. M: P.B.F.A.

COURTENAY BOOKROOM, APPLEFORD, ABINGDON, OXON. OX14 4PB. Prop: G. Duffield. TN: (023 582) 319. Est: 1960. Private premises; appointment necessary. Very large stock sec. and antiq. books; also publishing and bindery for leatherbound books. Spec: history, theology, 16th and 17th century and 19th century items. Cata: 3 or 4 a year. Irregular.

F.E. COWLEY, PERRY COTTAGE, PEBBLE HILL, TOOT BALDON, OXFORD OX9 9LH. TN: Nuneham Courtenay 310. Est: 1972. Medium stock sec. and antiq. books.
Bookrooms at RICHARD KINGSTON ANTIQUES, 95 BELL STREET, HENLEY ON THAMES, OXON. and SUMMERS DAVIS & SON, HIGH STREET, WALLINGFORD, OXON.

THE DOLPHIN BOOK CO., LIMITED, 58 HURST LANE, CUMNOR, OXON. OX2 9PR. Prop: J.L. & E.H. Gili. TN: (0865) 862175. TA: Dolphin, Oxford. Private premises; appointment necessary. Medium antiq. stock. Spec: Spanish and Spanish American. Cata: occasionally. A.B.A.

TOBY ENGLISH, c/o THE GALLERY, LAMB ARCADE, WALLINGFORD, OXFORDSHIRE. Prop: Toby English. TN: (0491) 36389. Est: 1981. Postal business only, appointment necessary. Very small stock sec. and antiq. Spec: science fiction and fantasy. Cata: 2 a year. Corresp: Français. B: Barclays Bank, Wallingford, Oxfordshire. M: P.B.F.A.

GLYN EVANS BOOKS, 2 OLD POLICE STATION, FARINGDON, OXON. SN7 8AB. Prop: W.G. Evans. TN: Faringdon 20245. Est: 1977. Private premises; appointment necessary. Very small stock sec. B: Lloyds Bank, Faringdon. Account 0049747.

THE GALLERY, LAMB ARCADE, WALLINGFORD, OXFORDSHIRE. Prop: Toby English, Gresham Books. TN: (0491) 36389. Est: 1982. Shop, closed Wednesdays. Medium stock sec. and antiq. Cata: occasionally. Corresp: Français. B: Barclays Bank, Market Square, Wallingford. M: P.B.F.A.

GASTON'S ALPINE BOOKS, BROOKLANDS, UNICORN STREET, BLOXHAM, OXON. OX15 4PX. Prop: Louis C. Baume. Est: about 1947. Private premises; appointment necessary. Medium stock sec. and antiq. books; also new books. Spec: alpine, mountaineering, caving, polar. Cata: occasionally. Corresp: Français, Deutsch, Italiano, Español.

HANBOROUGH BOOKS, THE FOUNDRY, CHURCH HANBOROUGH OX7 2AB. Prop: Dennis Hall. TN: Freeland (0993) 881260. Est: 1970. Private premises, appointment necessary. Very small sec. stock. Also designer and typographer. Spec: 20th century illustrated and limited editions, typography & graphic design. Cata: on foregoing, 2 a year.

HOLDAN BOOKS LIMITED, 15 NORTH PARADE AVENUE, OXFORD OX2 6LX (AND AT 11 NORTH PARADE AVENUE). Prop: Willem A. Meeuws. TN: (0865) 57971. TA: Holdanbooks. Est: 1966. Shop, early closing Saturday. Small sec. and antiq. stock; also new books and some publishing. Spec: Foreign (French, German, Slavonic), Italian, medicine. Cata: annual miscellaneous; special subjects, about 12 a year. B.A.

GRAHAM JEFFREY LIMITED, 29 CUDDESDON ROAD, HORSPATH, OXFORD OX9 1JD. TN: (086 77) 2528. TA: Periodox, Oxford. Est: 1967. Storeroom: appointment necessary. Cata; about monthly.

JUBILEE BOOKS LIMITED, 18 HIGH STREET, BURFORD, OXON. OX8 4QE. TN: (099 382) 2209. Est: 1976. Shop, closed Wednesdays. Medium stock general sec. and antiq. books. Spec: history, literature. Cata; 3 a year. A.B.A.

JOHN A. KINNANE, 35 ASTON STREET, OXFORD OX4 1EW. TN: (0865) 243383. Est: 1978. Private premises; appointment necessary. Very small stock sec. and antiq. Spec: autographs, letters, documents. Cata: occasional. B: National Westminster Bank, Abingdon Branch, 2 Market Place, Abingdon OX14 3HH. Account 63435969. M: P.B.F.A.

E.M. LAWSON & COMPANY, KINGSHOLM, EAST HAGBOURNE, OXFORDSHIRE. Prop: W.J. & W.H. Lawson, TN: (0235) 812033. TA: Rareboke Didcot. Est: 1919. Private premises, appointment necessary. Medium sec. and antiq. stock. Spec: 17th and 18th century English literature; Africa, America, Australasia; science and medicine. Cata: general, occasionally. A.B.A.

THE LITTLE BOOKSHOP, COVERED MARKET, OXFORD. Prop: Philip Gilbert. TN: Oxford (0865) 59176, evenings. Shop. Medium stock sec. and antiq. Spec: English literature, radical, socialist, economics.

MAGNA GALLERY, 41 HIGH STREET, OXFORD. Prop: Brian Kentish. TN: (0865) 45805. Est: 1969. Shop. Very small stock sec. and antiq. Spec: antique maps and prints. Cata: occasionally. B: Lloyds Bank, South Kensington, London, S.W.3. Account 0307851. M: A.B.A.

JAMES MOLLOY LIMITED, 4 SUTTON ROAD, MILTON, ABINGDON, OXON. OX14 4ET. TN: Abingdon 831394. Est: 1974. Private premises; appointment necessary. Very small stock sec. and antiq. Spec: early English and continental books, recusant literature. Cata: occasionally on foregoing.

MARCUS R. NINER, FLAGSTONES, PARK LANE, LONG HANBOROUGH OXFORDSHIRE OX7 2JU. TN: (0993) 881339.

M. & D. REEVE, 53 CUMNOR HILL, OXFORD OX2 9EY. Prop: Margarita Reeve. TN: (0865) 862057. Private premises; appointment necessary. Small stock sec. and antiq. Spec: children's books. Cata: 4 or 5 a year. M: P.B.F.A.

A. ROSENTHAL LIMITED, 9 & 10 BROAD STREET, OXFORD OX1 3AP. TN: Oxford 243093. (STD 0865). TA: Albibooks Oxford. Est: 1936. Offices; open Monday to Friday 10.00 - 17.30 hrs. Saturday by appointment. antiq. stock. Spec: early printed books; European continental literature, autograph letters and manuscripts. Cata: on foregoing, several a year. A.B.A. B.A. N.B.L. S.L.A.M.

SANDERS OF OXFORD LIMITED, 104 HIGH STREET, OXFORD OX1 4BW. TN: Oxford (0865) 242590. Shop, early closing Saturday. Large sec. and antiq. stock; also maps, prints and drawings. Cata: general, 4 a year. A.B.A.

SOUTHMOOR BOOKS, TYTE BROOK HOUSE, SANDFORD SAINT MARTIN, OXON. OX5 4AH. Prop: R. and I. Hallett. TN: Great Tew 601. TA: (060-883) 601. Est: 1979. Private premises; appointment necessary. Small stock sec. and antiq. Spec: Africa and Near East. Cata: 2-3 a year. Corresp: Deutsch, Français. B: Barclays Bank, Little Clarendon Street, Oxford.

TALBOT BOOKS, 8 CUNLIFFE CLOSE, OXFORD, BERKSHIRE. Prop: E.R. and M.L. Roper Power. TN: (0865) 55638. Est: 1968. Private premises, appointment preferred. Small sec. and antiq. stock. Spec: French literature, architecture, typography, bindings.

. & J. TAUBENHEIM, COTSWOLD BOOKSHOP, BURFORD, OXON. OX8 4QD. TN: (099 382) 3308. Est: 1971. Shop. Stock sec. and antiq. books.

. THORNTON & SON, 11 BROAD STREET, OXFORD OX1 3AR. Prop: J.S.D. Thornton, M.A. (L.C. Oxon.). TN: Oxford (0865) 42939. TA: Hornbook Oxford. Est: 1835. Shop, closed Thursday. Very large sec. and antiq. stock, also new books, prints and maps, remainders. Spec: English literature, philosophy, theology, patristics, history, Oriental, archaeology, anthropology, and all academic subjects. Cata: on foregoing, irregularly. Corresp: Français, Deutsch, Italiano, Español. B: National Westminster Bank, High Street, Oxford. B.N.L. B.A. A.B.A.

TITLES OLD AND RARE BOOKS, 15/1 TURL STREET, OXFORD OX1 3DQ. Prop: Gillian and Ralph Stone. TN: (0865) 727928. TA: Titles, Oxford, England. Est: 1972. Shop. Medium stock sec. and antiq. Spec: travel and topography, first editions, private press and illustrated books, natural history. Cata: 2–3 a year. M: A.B.A., P.B.F.A.

TURL CASH BOOKSHOP, 3 TURL STREET, OXFORD. Prop: K.W. Swift. TN: Oxford 240241. TA: Books Oxford. Shop, no early closing. Medium sec. and antiq. stock, also rare prints and maps.

FRANCES WAKEMAN, 2 MANOR WAY, KIDLINGTON, OXFORD OX5 2BD. Prop: F. Wakeman. TN: (08 675) 78316. Est: 1967. Private premises; appointment necessary. Very small stock sec. and antiq. Spec: arts of the book, printing, papermaking. Cata: 4 a year. Corresp: Français. M: P.B.F.A.

WARRACK & PERKINS, RECTORY FARM HOUSE, CHURCH ENSTONE, OXON. OX7 4NN. TN: (060872) 572. Private premises; appointment necessary. Small sec. and antiq. stock, books and prints. Spec: 19th and turn of century; illustrated books; private presses. A.B.A.

WATERFIELD'S, 36 PARK END STREET, OXFORD OX1 1HJ. Prop: Robin Waterfield Limited. TN: (0865) 721809. TA: Sagacity, Oxford. Est: 1973. Shop. Very large stock sec. and antiq. books. Spec: 17th and 18th century English books, 20th century literature and literary autographs, academic books in the arts and humanities. Cata: regularly. M: A.B.A., P.B.F.A.

RICHARD WAY BOOKSELLER, 54B FRIDAY STREET, HENLEY-ON-THAMES, OXON. RG9 1AH. Prop: Richard Way, Diana Cook. TN: (049 12) 6663. Est: 1978. Shop, (car park at rear). Medium stock sec. and antiq. books, also old postcards. Spec: Thames Books, rowing. Cata: occasionally.

WEST BAR BOOKSHOP, 24 WEST BAR, BANBURY, OXFORDSHIRE. Prop: Marcus Niner. TN: (0295) 53090. Est: 1983. Shop: early closing Tuesdays. Small stock sec. and antiq. B: National Westminster Bank, Woodstock Branch, 16 Market Place, Woodstock, Oxford. M: P.B.F.A.

JOHN WILSON, 50 ACRE END STREET, EYNSHAM, OXFORDSHIRE OX8 1PB. TN: (0865) 880883. Cables: Documents, Oxford. Est: 1967. Appointment preferred. Large stock of autograph letters, historical documents and manuscripts only. Cata: on foregoing frequently. A.B.A.

34. BUCKINGHAMSHIRE

AYLESBURY
BUCKINGHAM
CHESHAM
HIGH WYCOMBE
IVER HEATH
MARLOW
OLNEY
PENN
SLOUGH
WENDOVER

J.A. BENNETTS, LYNBRIDGE, STOWE RISE, BUCKINGHAM MK18 1HU. TN: (0280) 812180. Est: 1975. Postal business only. Very small stock of sec. and antiq. books. Modern firsts: fine illustrated, Graham Greene. Cata: occasionally.

BUCKINGHAM BOOKS, 20 MARKET HILL, BUCKINGHAM MK18 1JK. Prop: D.H. Clegg. TN: (0280) 812800. Shop, closed Thursdays. Very small stock sec. and antiq., also new books. Appointment advisable to see antiq. stock, which is in separate part of shop. Spec: architecture. Cata: 2 a year.

PETER BULLIMORE BOOKS, THE BROADWAY, FARNHAM COMMON, SLOUGH, BUCKINGHAMSHIRE. Prop: Peter Bullimore, M.A. TN: (02814) 4979. Est: 1978. Shop; closed Monday and Wednesday afternoons. Appointments can be made. Medium stock sec. and antiq. also new books and greeting cards. Cata: occasionally. Corresp: Français. B: National Westminster Bank, 63 High St., Burnham, Slough, SL1 7JX. Account 81531850.

BUMPUS, HALDANE & MAXWELL LIMITED, COWPER HOUSE, OLNEY, BUCKINGHAMSHIRE. TN: (0234) 711529. Telex: 825547. Spec: back issues scientific periodicals.

THE COTTAGE BOOKSHOP, ELM ROAD, PENN, BUCKINGHAMSHIRE. Prop: F.H. Baddeley TN: Penn 2632. Est: 1950. Shop, closed Mondays. Very large sec. stock. M: B.A.

PETER EATON [BOOKSELLERS] LIMITED, LILIES, WEEDON, AYLESBURY, BUCKINGHAMSHIRE. TN: Aylesbury (0296) 641393. Appointment necessary. Very large sec. and antiq. stock. A.B.A.

PAUL EISLER, 54 BRYANTS ACRE, WENDOVER, BUCKINGHAMSHIRE. Prop: Paul Eisler. TN: (0296) 623709. Private premises, appointment necessary. Very small stock sec. and antiq., also large stock antique maps and prints. Spec: early maps, atlases, topography, sporting and colour plate books. Lists on request. B: Barclays Bank, 20 Aylesbury Road, Wendover, Buckinghamshire.

GOLDEN BALL BOOKS, 45 HEALEY AVENUE, HIGH WYCOMBE, BUCKINGHAMSHIRE HP13 7JR. Prop: G.R. Carlisle. TN: (0494) 442869. Est: 1979. Private premises; postal business only. Very small stock sec. and antiq. Spec: Thomas and John Bewick, local topography, illustrated books.

THE LITTLE BOOKSHOP, FARNHAM COMMON, near SLOUGH SL2 3QH. Prop: J.L. Pratt. TN: (369) 3144. Est: 1955. Shop, rear room only, no set hours. Business by mail or appointment. Small sec. and antiq. stock. Spec: domestic cats. Cata: cat books, 2 or 3 a year. M: B.A.

OLNEY BOOKS, 22 BRIDGE STREET, OLNEY MK46 4AB. Prop: M. Macdonald-Ross. Private premises; appointment necessary. Small stock sec. and antiq. Spec: natural history especially the theory of evolution and heredity. Scholarly works in science and philosophy, antiquarian chess.

OMNIPHIL LIMITED, GERMAIN'S LODGE, FULLERS HILL, CHESHAM, BUCKINGHAMSHIRE. TN: (0494) 771851. Small stock of books and prints, main stock at Stand 110, Grays Antique Market, London W1. Spec: illustrated books, colour plates and 19th century engravings.

PENDULUM BOOKS, Bull Court, Market Square, Olney, Buckinghamshire MK46 4AB. Prop: J.M. Garland. Est: 1964. Shop, open Saturdays only; appointment preferable. Very large stock sec. and antiq. also new books. Spec: children's books, history, biography, illustrated, magazines.

PENN BARN BOOKSHOP, by the Pond, Elm Road, Penn, Buckinghamshire. Prop: P.J.M. Hunnings. TN: (049 481) 5691 or 3113. TA: Hunnings, High Wycombe, Buckinghamshire. Est: 1968. Shop. Small stock sec. and antiq. books, also very large stock of old maps and prints, also mounts for engravings. Spec: illustrated, topography, cookery and wine.

POSTAPRINT, Taidswood House, Iver Heath, Buckinghamshire SL0 0PQ. (A division of Hemicon Securities Limited). TN: Denham 833720. Est: 1975. Private premises; appointment necessary. Medium stock old maps and prints. Spec: antiquarian maps and prints. Cata: frequently. Corresp: Français, Deutsch, Español. B: National Westminster Bank, 41 Lothbury, London, E.C.2. Account 00836346.

THE TUDOR GATEHOUSE BOOKSHOP [GERRARDS CROSS BOOKS], Elgiva Lane, Chesham, Buckinghamshire. Prop: Mrs. Patty Lafferty. TN: (0494) 784560. Est: 1972. Shop, also by appointment. Small stock sec. and antiq. Spec: private presses and modern first editions, collecting. B: Midland Bank, 26/28 College Road, Harrow, Middlesex. M: P.B.F.A.

WEATHERHEAD'S BOOKSHOP LIMITED, 58 Kingsbury, Aylesbury, Buckinghamshire HP20 2JG. TN: Aylesbury 23153. and 24985. Est: 1921. Shop open six days a week. New, and very large sec. and antiq. stock. Spec: Buckinghamshire history and topography. Cata: general, frequently. Free. M: A.B.A., B.A., N.B.L., P.B.F.A.

DAVID WILSON, 95 World's End Lane, Weston Turville, Aylesbury, Buckinghamshire. TN: Stoke Mandeville 2247. Est: 1969. Private premises; appointment advisable. Sec. and antiq. stock, also new books on specialist subjects. Spec: natural history, especially ornithology; topography, especially Highlands and Islands of Scotland, Hebrides, St. Kilda, Orkney, Shetland.

35. BEDFORDSHIRE

BEDFORD LUTON

COLLINS BOOKS, 58 WHITEHILL AVENUE, LUTON, BEDFORDSHIRE LU1 3SR. Prop: J.T. & S.W. Collins. TN: (0582) 23971. Est: 1983. Private premises; appointment necessary. Small stock sec. and antiq. Spec: Johnsoniana and 18th century literature. M: P.B.F.A.

JOHN GAUNT, 71 GEORGE STREET, BEDFORD MK40 3SQ. Prop: John Gaunt. TN: (0234) 217686. Est: 1983. Private premises; appointment necessary. Very small stock sec. and antiq. Spec: local topography, archaeology, numismatics. numismatics. Cata: occasionally. M: P.B.F.A.

ANDREW JOHNSON, 23 REYNES DRIVE, OAKLEY, BEDFORD MK43 7SD. Prop: A. Johnson. TN: (02302) 3873. Est: 1980. Private premises; appointment necessary. Small stock sec. and antiq. Spec: natural history and allied subjects (including gardening) only. Cata: 4 a year. B: Lloyd's Bank, All Hallows Branch, Bedford.

T.J. KELLY, 29 CLARENDON STREET, BEDFORD MK41 7SQ. Prop: T.J. Kelly. TN: (0234) 216863. Est: 1973. Private premises; appointment necessary. Medium stock sec. and antiq. Spec: private presses, natural history, bookbinding, Irish literature. Cata: 1 a year. B: Bank of Ireland, Chapel Street, Luton.

VINTAGE BOOKS, 15 SHAFTESBURY AVENUE, BEDFORD MK40 3SA. Prop: Aidan Mackey. TN: (0234) 57760. Private premises; appointment necessary. Est: 1976. Very small stock sec. and antiq. books. Spec: G.K. Chesterton, Hilaire Belloc. Cata: annually. B: Barclays Bank, 111 High Street, Bedford. Account 80920525. M: P.B.F.A.

36. HERTFORDSHIRE

ASHWELL
BARNET
BERKHAMSTED
BISHOP'S STORTFORD
CHORLEYWOOD
CODICOTE
ELSTREE
HARPENDEN
HATFIELD
HERTFORD
HITCHIN
LETCHWORTH
RICKMANSWORTH
ROYSTON
SAINT ALBANS
WALTHAM CROSS
WATFORD
WELWYN
WHEATHAMPSTEAD

ABBEY BOOKS, 36 SOPWELL LANE, SAINT ALBANS, HERTFORDSHIRE AL1 1RR. Prop: Bruce and Jill Tulloch TN: (0727) 32514. Private premises; appointment necessary. Small stock sec. and antiq. Spec: history, Hertfordshire topography. Cata: 4 a year. Corresp: Deutsch, Français, Español, Portuguese. M: P.B.F.A.

DENIS W. AMOS, 10 MILL LANE, CHESHUNT, WALTHAM CROSS, HERTFORDSHIRE EN8 0JH. Est: 1948. Postal business only. Medium stock sec. and antiq. books. Spec: tennis and all other ball games and athletic sports.

THE ANTIQUES BOOK CENTRE, 93 BRADMORE GREEN, BROOKMANS PARK, HATFIELD, HERTFORDSHIRE AL9 7QT. Prop: John and Shirley Smith. TN: (0707) 44426. Est: 1977. Shop, closed Wednesdays. Medium stock sec. and antiq. books; also large stock new books on antiques. Spec: books on antiques and collecting, architecture. Cata: on foregoing, 3 a year.

ASHWELL BOOKS, ASHWELL HOUSE, ASHWELL, HERTFORDSHIRE SG7 5NL. Prop: John de Normann, TN: (046-274) 2229. Est: 1977. Private premises; appointment necessary, Small stock sec. and antiq. Spec: natural history. Cata: frequently. Corresp: Deutsch, Français, Español, Italiano. B: Barclays Bank, High Street, Royston, Hertfordshire. Account 00122653.

THE BOOK CABIN, 379 LUTON ROAD, HARPENDEN, HERTFORDSHIRE AL5 3NF. Prop: G.W. Pearson. TN: (05827) 68581. Est: 1982. Shop, normally 9–5 but check first. Medium stock sec. and antiq. Corresp: Français, Español. B: Lloyds Bank Ltd., George Street, Luton. M: P.B.F.A.

BULCRAIG AND LEWIS, 14 MARLBOROUGH CLOSE, MARDLEY HILL, WELWYN HERTFORDSHIRE AL6 0UG. Prop: Stanley A. Lewis. TN: (043871) 4860. Est: 1983. Private premises; appointment necessary. Very small sec. and antiq. stock. Spec: physical sciences; gardening and life sciences.

CLIVE A. BURDEN LIMITED, 46 TALBOT ROAD, RICKMANSWORTH WD3 1HE. TN: Office (0923) 778097. Home (0923) 772387. Est: 1966. House premises; appointment advisable. Medium stock of sec. and antiq. books and very large stock of maps and topographical & natural history prints, county, American, Asian, Australian specialists. *Also at* 13 CECIL COURT, LONDON WC2. TN: (01) 836-2177 and P.O. Box 2792, NAPLES FL 33939, U.S.A. TN: (813) 261 1978.

JOHN T. CARR, 100 QUEENS ROAD, WATFORD, HERTFORDSHIRE. TN: Watford 38127. Est: 1920. Shop, closed Wednesdays. Very large sec. and antiq. stock. B: Midland Bank, High Street, Watford.

CASTLE BOOKSHOP, CASTLE MOAT HOUSE, CASTLE STREET, HERTFORD SG14 1HH. Prop: Mrs. Joy Checkley. TN: (0992) 56537. Est: 1976. Shop, closed Thursdays. Medium stock sec. and antiq. books. Spec: Hertfordshire. Cata: 2 a year. B: National Westminster Bank, Fore Street, Hertford. Account 07044151.

CHANDOS BOOKS, 111 PARK ROAD, NEW BARNET, HERTFORDSHIRE EN4 9QR.

CATHERINE E.M. CHELK, 24 BENSLOW LANE, HITCHIN, HERTFORDSHIRE SG4 9RE. TN: (0462) 51098. Est: 1971. Private premises; appointment preferred. Very small stock sec. and antiq. books. Spec: British, European and American rare children's books. Cata: occasionally. Corresp: Deutsch, Français.

DAVID'S BOOKSHOP, 14 EASTCHEAP, LETCHWORTH, HERTFORDSHIRE. TN: (046 26) 4631. Est: 1963. Shop. Small stock sec. and antiq., also new books. Cata: about 3 a year. B: Midland Bank, Station Place, Letchworth, Hertfordshire. M: B.A.

DEVAL & MUIR, TAKELEY, BISHOP'S STORTFORD, HERTFORDSHIRE CM22 6NA. TN: (0279) 870 312. Est: 1969. Storeroom open normal business hours, closed Saturdays. Medium sec. and antiq. stock. Spec: graphic arts, especially typography. Cata: typography, book illustration and general, about 8 a year. A.B.A., N.B.L.

MAVIS EGGLE, 11 DALKEITH ROAD, HARPENDEN, HERTFORDSHIRE. Prop: Mrs. Mavis Eggle. TN: (05827) 62603. Est: 1979. Private premises; appointment necessary. Small stock sec. and antiq. Spec: books about books. Cata: occasionally. B: Midland Bank PLC, 1 High Street, Harpenden, Hertfordshire AL5 2RS. M: P.B.F.A.

ERGO BOOKS, 65 SALISBURY ROAD, BARNET, HERTFORDSHIRE EN5 4JL. Prop: Elliott Greenfield. TN: (01) 440-0240 and (01) 202-0463. Private premises; appointment necessary. Visits can be arranged 7 days a week, including evenings. Medium stock sec. and antiq. books. Spec: detective (especially Sherlock Holmes), science fiction, children's and illustrated, art reference books. Cata: detective and science fiction, 3 a year. Corresp: Français. M: P.B.F.A.

GRESHAM BOOKS, THE OLD SWAN, AKEMAN STREET, TRING, HERTFORDSHIRE HP23 6AN. Prop: James & Margaret Hine. TN: Tring 3976. Est: 1972. Private premises; appointment necessary. Small stock sec. and antiq. Spec: art, architecture, country life, cookery, natural history and unusual subjects. Cata: occasionally. B: National Westminster Bank: 20 High Street, Tring. HP23 5AP. Account 06553206. M: A.B.A., P.B.F.A.

HAROLD GROVES, 36 GRANGE CLOSE, HITCHIN, HERTFORDSHIRE. Prop: Harold Groves. TN: (0462) 33878. Est: 1980. Private premises; postal business only. Very small stock sec. and antiq. Cata: occasional.

Corresp: Français. B: National Westminster Bank, 12 High Street, Hitchin, Herts.

ROBERT HORNUNG, 23 Meadow Way, Letchworth, Herts. SG6 3JB. Prop: Robert Hornung. TN: (046 26) 6334. Est: 1980. Private premises; postal business only. Small stock sec. and antiq. Spec: modern architecture and design. Cata: 2 or 3 a year. Corresp: Français, Deutsch. B: Lloyds Bank, 1 Finchley Lane, London NW4 1BL. Account 0030913.

LONDON BOOKS, Hall Farm, Berry Lane, Chorleywood, Hertfordshire WD3 5EX. Prop: Anthony Williams. TN: Chorleywood 4792. Est: 1983. Private premises; postal business only. Very small stock sec. and antiq. Spec: art, the classics. Cata: 4 a year. B: National Westminster Bank, Chorleywood, Hertfordshire. M: P.B.F.A.

MAGDA BOOKS, Vermont, London Road, Rickmansworth, Hertfordshire. Prop: Margaret and David May. TN: (0923) 773257. Est: 1981. Private premises; appointment necessary. Small sec. and antiq. stock. Spec: art, colour plate; topography. M: P.B.F.A.

MING BOOKS, 115 High Street, Berkhamsted, Herts. HP4 2DJ. Prop: R.W.H. and M.H.J. Richmond. TN: (04427) 2073. Est: 1983. Stockroom; appointment necessary. Small stock sec. and antiq. Spec: history, politics, horses, cricket. Corresp: Français, Deutsch. B: Williams and Glyns Bank PLC, Tottenham Court Road, London W1.

ERIC T. MOORE, 24–25 Bridge Street, Hitchin, Hertfordshire. TN: Hitchin 50497. Shop, early closing Wednesday. Large sec. and antiq. stock. Antiquarian prints and maps. Picture framing. M: A.B.A.

EIDDON MORGAN, Laburnums, Heronsgate, Rickmansworth, Hertfordshire WD3 5DB. TN: (260) 2786. Est: 1976. Private premises; appointment necessary. Very small stock sec. and antiq. books; large stock of early maps, topographical and decorative prints, some marine prints and watercolours. Spec: maps and prints. Cata: 2 a year.

H.J. MORGAN, 25 Oaklands Avenue, Brookmans Park, Hatfield, Herts. AL9 7UH. TN: (77) 52640. Spec: modern first editions.

B.A. AND C.W.M. PRATT, Orwell Grange, New Wimpole, Royston, Hertfordshire SG8 5QD. TN: (0223) 207232. Est: 1967. Private premises; appointment necessary. sec. and antiq. stock. Spec: scarce medicine and related science only.

A.J. SHEPHERDSON, 9 Wick Avenue, Wheathampstead, Hertfordshire AL4 8QD. TN: (058 283) 3218. Est: 1977. Private premises; appointment necessary. Very small stock sec. and antiq. also a few wine and brewing journals. Spec: wines and related subjects. Cata: 3-4 a year. B: Barclays Bank, Wheathampstead. Account 4079867. M: P.B.F.A.

S. SHOOP 57 Deacons Hill Road, Elstree, Hertfordshire WD6 3HZ. Prop: S. Shoop. Est: 1983. Private premises; postal business only. Medium stock sec. and antiq. Spec: science, inventions and technology, medicine, related journals and ephemera; autographs. B: National Westminster Bank, 80 Shenley Road, Borehamwood, Hertfordshire WD6 1DZ.

PETER TAYLOR, 4a Ye Corner, Aldenham Road, Watford WD1 4BS. Est: 1973. Private premises; postal business only. Small stock sec. and antiq. Spec: topography, British Isles, natural history; history of science, travel, archaeology, medicine, fine and signed editions. Cata: frequent lists.

THOMAS THORP, 9 George Street, Saint Albans, Hertfordshire AL3 4ER. TN: (0727) 65576. Very large stock sec. and antiq. Spec: English law (early), bindings. Cata: frequently. M: A.B.A.

WHELDON & WESLEY LIMITED, Lytton Lodge, Codicote, near Hitchin SG4 8TE. TN: (0438) 820 370. TA: Wheldwesley Codicote Hitchin. Est: 1843. House premises, visitors by appointment only except Saturday. New, and very large sec. and antiq. stock. Spec: natural history. Cata: natural history, 4 a year. A.B.A. B.A.

WILSON'S BOOKSHOP, 24 Castle Street, Berkhamsted, Hertfordshire. Prop: James Wilson. TN: (044 27) 73396 and 73257. Est: 1975. Shop, early closing Wednesdays. Medium stock sec. and antiq. books, also prints framing and bookbinding. B: Barclays Bank, High Street, Berkhamstead. Account 00966371.

WOODFORD BOOKSHOP, 31 Bucklersbury, Hitchin, Hertfordshire. Prop: A.A. Martin. TN: (0462) 50257. Est: 1972. Shop. Small stock sec. and antiq. Spec: warfare, military, naval and aviation and allied badges, medals etc. Cata: 4–5 a year. B: Midland Bank, Hitchin.

37. ESSEX

BILLERICAY
BENFLEET
CHELMSFORD
CLACTON ON SEA
COGGESHALL
COLCHESTER
EASTWOOD
GRAYS
INGATESTONE
LEIGH ON SEA
LOUGHTON
MALDON
ONGAR
SAFFRON WALDEN
SOUTHEND ON SEA
THAXTED
WESTCLIFF ON SEA
WOODFORD GREEN
WOODHAM FERRERS

ACRES OF BOOKS, Trinity Square, South Woodham Ferrers, Essex CM3 5JX. Prop: B.A. and H.R. Scowen. TN: (0245) 323 585. Est: 1983. Shop. Very small stock sec. and antiq. Gardening and botany only. Also new books. Cata: 4 a year. B: National Westminster, Heralds Wat, South Woodham Ferrers. M: B.A.

ALL BOOKS, 30 Mill Road, Maldon, Essex. Prop: Janet Jenkinson. TN: (0621) 55333. Est: 1981. Shop, closed Monday and Wednesday. Large stock sec. and antiq. Spec: nautical and arts subjects. B: Midland Bank, High Street, Maldon.

ALPHABETS, 13 Trinity Street, Colchester, Essex CO1 1JN. Prop: C.E. and S.M. Briggs. TN: (0206) 572751. Est: 1974. Shop, early closing Mondays and Thursdays. Medium stock sec. and antiq. books. B: Barclays Bank, Head Street, Colchester. Account 50200204.

R. ANDREWS, 138 Kingswood Chase, Leigh on Sea, Essex SS9 3BG. Prop: Bob and June Andrews. TN: (0702) 76957. Est: 1977. Private premises; appointment necessary. Medium stock sec. and antiq. Spec: crime, detective, thriller fiction. Cata: 11 a year. B: Barclays Bank, 1299–1301 London Road, Leigh on Sea. Account 40120383.

ASTRONAUTICS PUBLISHING COMPANY, 1 Herbert Road, Hornchurch, Essex RM11 3LA. Prop: G.V.E. Thompson and D.M. Thompson. TN: Hornchurch 40759. Est: 1954. Private premises, appointment necessary. Small sec. and antiq. stock, also new. Spec: astronautics and space research, Russian, mathematics, general science and technology, Chinese, reference books, pottery (crafts), music.

MICHAEL BARBER FINE BOOKS AND SEARCH SERVICE, CULVER STREET WEST, COLCHESTER, ESSEX. Prop: Michael Barber. TN: (0206) 66663. Est: 1978. Shop, closed on Thursdays. Small stock sec. and antiq. Spec: typography, music, dialect. Cata: 1 a year. Corresp: Français, Italiano, Español. B: Barclays Bank, Head Street, Colchester. Account 70631396. M: P.B.F.A.

BARSTABLE BOOKS, 28 RAVENSBOURNE DRIVE, CHELMSFORD, ESSEX CM1 2SJ. Prop: R.J. Carpenter, TN: (0245) 58649. Est: 1971. Private premises; appointment necessary. Small stock sec. and antiq. books. Spec: British topography and local history. Cata: Regional catalogues in rotation.

BILLERICAY BOOKSHOP, 7 RADFORD WAY, BILLERICAY, ESSEX. Prop: Mr. J. Walentowicz. TN: (027 74) 51423. Est: 1965. Shop, half day Thursday. Medium stock sec. and antiq. Spec: Essex, British and foreign topography, natural history, maps and prints, early photography, autographs.

THE BRAYER PRESS, ASHDON STREET, ASHDON, SAFFRON WALDEN, ESSEX CB10 2NB. Prop: R.C. Heath. TN: (079 984) 209. Est: 1949. Storeroom; appointment necessary. Medium stock sec. and antiq. books;

H. BRETT, 8 BOROUGH LANE, SAFFRON WALDON, ESSEX CB11 4AE. TN: (0799) 25778. Private premises; postal business only. Very small stock sec. and antiq.

THE BRIDGE BOOKSHOP, 27A BRIDGE STREET, COGGESHALL, COLCHESTER, CO6 1NP. Prop: Mrs. Hilda Gardner. TN: (0376) 61408. Est: 1939. Storeroom and house premises; open normal business hours. Medium stock sec. and antiq. books; also old prints and maps. Corresp: Français, Deutsch. N.B.L.

JOAN E. BURGOYNE, 34 MILL LANE, WEELEY HEATH CLACTON-ON-SEA, ESSEX CO16 9BB. TN: (0255) 830357. House premises; open during normal business hours or by appointment. Very small stock sec. and antiq. also some back numbers of journals. Spec Royalty and Royal Family only. Cata: 2 a year.

THE CASTLE BOOKSHOP, 37 NORTH HILL, COLCHESTER, ESSEX CO1 1QR. Prop: A.B. Doncaster. TN: Colchester 577520 (STD 0206). Est 1947. Shop, closed Thursday. New, and very large sec. and antiq stock. Spec: archaeology, topography of East Anglia, especially Essex Cata: general, 2 a year. B: Lloyds Bank, High St., Colchester. Account 00136352. A.B.A. B.A. N.B.L.

CLIFTON BOOKS, 34 Hamlet Court Road, Westcliffe on Sea, Essex. Prop: John R. Hodgkins. TN: home (0702) 331004. Private premises; appointment necessary. Medium stock sec. and antiq. books. Cata: frequently.

CONISTON CONNOISSEURS, 13 Avenue Terrace, Westcliff, Southend-on-Sea, Essex SS0 7PL. Prop: J.D. Roberts. TN: (0702) 41877. Est: 1966. Private premises; appointment necessary. Medium stock sec. and antiq. books; also new books. Spec: mathematics, science, philosophy (symbolic logic).

JOHN DRURY, 11 East Stockwell Street, Colchester, Essex CO1 1SS. Prop: D.R.D. Edmunds. TN: (0206) 46755. TA: Drusilla, Colchester. Est: 1971. Storeroom; appointment necessary. Small stock sec. and antiq. books. Spec: numismatics; economics. Cata: 5 a year.

BARRIE E. ELLEN, THE BOOKSHOP, 262 London Road, Westcliff-on-Sea, Essex SS0 7GJ. TN: (0702) 338763. Est: 1976. Shop, closed Wednesdays. Medium stock sec. and antiq. books; also new books. Spec: Chess books and magazines. B: National Westminster Bank, London Road, Benfleet, Essex. Account 44775911.

GAGE POSTAL BOOKS, P.O. Box 105, Westcliff-on-Sea, Essex SS0 8EQ. Prop: Laurie E. Gage B.Sc. TN: (0702) 715133. Est: 1971. Stockroom; appointment necessary. Very large stock sec. and antiq. books. Spec: full range of theology especially Methodism. Cata: 20 a year regularly. M: P.B.F.A.

R.M. GILBERT, Dunsford House, College Avenue, Grays, Essex RM17 5UW. TN: (0375) 72187. Est: 1937. Private premises; appointment necessary. Small stock sec. and antiq. books. Spec: Kent and Essex. Cata: speciality lists on request. Corresp: Français, Deutsch.

GREYFRIARS BOOKS & CRAFTS, 92B East Hill, Colchester CO1 2QN. Prop: Roy and Pauline Taylor. TN: Colchester (0206) 563138. Shop, closed Mondays. Medium sec. and antiq. stock, also craft work.

C. PAUL KNIGHT BOOKS, 100 The Broadway, Leigh on Sea, Essex SS9 1AB. Prop: Christopher Paul Knight. TN: (0702) 710474. Est: 1982. Shop, closed on Mondays. Very large stock sec. and antiq. B: Barclays Bank, High Street, Bracknell, Berkshire. M: P.B.F.A.

ALFRED D. LAMBERT, 2 Pine Drive, Ingatestone, Essex CM4 9EF. TN: (027 75) 2721. Est: 1977. Private premises; appointment necessary. Small stock sec. and antiq. Spec: English history, Kipling, Churchill, Baden-Powell.

MARJON BOOKS, 16 MANNERING GARDENS, WESTCLIFF-ON-SEA, ESSEX SS0 0BQ. Prop: R.J. Cooper. TN: (0702) 347119. Est: 1975. Private premises; appointment necessary. Very small stock sec. and antiq. books. Spec: first editions of detective mystery and thriller, crime fiction, children's books. Cata: detective fiction 4 a year.

ELKIN MATHEWS, 14A STONEHAM STREET, COGGESHALL, ESSEX CO6 1TT. Prop: Barbara and David Muir. TN: (0376) 61730. Stockroom; open any time in business hours. Medium stock sec. and antiq. also book binding. Spec: children's books, illustrated books, natural history, sociology. Cata: occasionally. Corresp: Français. B: Barclays Bank, High Street, Holt. Account 00618513.
Also at SCRIVENERS, CLAY ROAD, BLAKENEY, NORFOLK NR25 7NL Private premises; appointment necessary. TN: (0263) 740 475.

MILTON BOOKS, 9 SAINT JAMES'S AVENUE, MARDEN ASH, ONGAR, ESSEX. Prop: Anne Aylott. TN: (027 76) 4366. Est: 1976. Private premises; appointment necessary. Very small stock sec. and antiq. books. Spec: natural history.

ON THE SHELF, THE LANES, LONDON ROAD, HADLEIGH, BENFLEET ESSEX. Prop: Marion Hancock. TN: (0702) 556275. Shop, closed Wednesdays.

KEVIN PEGGS, 98 KING EDWARD'S ROAD, SOUTH WOODHAM FERRERS CHELMSFORD, ESSEX CM3 5PH. TN: (0245) 321916. Est: 1977 Private premises; postal business only. Very small stock sec. and antiq. Spec: Holy Land travel.

PILLAR-BOX BOOKS, 8 SPRINGWATER ROAD, EASTWOOD, ESSEX SS 5BJ. Prop: Leonard J. Olley. TN: (0702) 521291. Est: 1977. Private premises; postal business only. Small stock used. Spec: military biographies. Cata: Lists 2 a year. B: Trustee Savings Bank, Fleet Street, London, E.C.4. Account 079820/68.

MARGARET POLE, 19 BOLFORD STREET, THAXTED, ESSEX CM6 2PY TN: (0371) 830320. Private premises; appointment advisable. Small sec. and antiq. stock. Spec: Essex; Roman Catholic.

SAINT OSYTH BOOKS, 52 CLACTON ROAD, SAINT OSYTH CLACTON-ON-SEA, ESSEX CO16 8PA. Prop: David and Judith Butler TN: 0255 820904. Est: 1980. Private premises; appointment necessary Small stock sec. and antiq. Spec: art, theology life, books for secondary schools. Cata: 10 a year. Corresp: Français, Italiano, Español, Deutsch Hollandse. B: Barclays Bank, Spring Road, St. Osyth, Clacton, Essex Account 80169234.

TALLIS BOOKS, 44 FOREST APPROACH, WOODFORD GREEN, ESSEX IG8 9BS. Prop: Ken and Joan Haskell. TN: (01) 504-2086. Est: 1979. Private premises; postal business only. Small stock sec. and antiq. Spec: English topography, country life. Cata: occasionally. B: Barclays Bank PLC, 130 George Lane, London E18 1AZ.

D.E. TWITCHETT, LARKRISE, 14 LINKDALE, BILLERICAY, ESSEX. TN: (027 74) 4913. Private premises: appointment necessary. Very small stock sec. and antiq. books. Spec: cycles and cycling. Cata: occasionally.

WARD RARE BOOKS, 31 SEDLEY RISE, LOUGHTON, ESSEX IG10 1LS. Prop: V.J. and K.A. Ward. TN: (01) 508-0817. Est: 1963. Private premises; appointment necessary. Small stock sec. and antiq.

YOUNGS ANTIQUARIAN BOOKS, TILLINGHAM, ESSEX. Prop: P. Young. TN: (062187) 351. Est: 1970. Private premises; appointment necessary. Small stock sec. and antiq. books. Cata: occasionally. Antiquarian Booksellers to the Nobility, Landed Gentry and Clergy. Suppliers of library furniture and literary portraits.

38. AVON

BATH
BRISTOL
CHIPPING SODBURY
CLEVEDON
MARSHFIELD
THORNBURY
WESTON SUPER MARE

MRS. D. ADAMS, 25 Broad Street, Bath, Avon. Large stock sec. and antiq. books.

AMBRA BOOKS, 66 Alma Vale Road, Clifton, Bristol, Avon. Prop: Ivor Cornish & Lesley Aitchison. TN: (0272) 311962. Est: 1972. Private premises; appointment necessary. Small stock. Spec: West Country and natural history. Cata: 4 a year. P.B.F.A.

ARGOSY GALLERY AND BOOKSHOP, 2 Abbey Green, Bath, Avon BA1 1NN. Prop: Patrick and Margaret Porter. TN: (0255) 62707 Est: 1982. Shop, closed Mondays during winter months. Small stock sec. and antiq., also new books. Spec: illustrated books and private press books. Cata: approximately 2 a year. B: Midland Bank, Milson Street, Bath BA1 1DU. M: P.B.F.A.

ASPIDISTRA, 46 Saint James Parade, Bath, Avon BA1 1UG. Prop John Temple Waggoner. TN: (0225) 61948. Shop. Small stock sec and antiq. also pictures and small furniture. Spec: Mexico, India anthropology. Corresp: Français, Deutsch, Español. B: Lloyds Bank Southgate Branch, Bath. Account 0076900.

THE AVON BOOKSHOP, 6 London Street, Walcot, Bath, Avo BA1 5BU. Prop: Jane Chapman and Peter Goodden. TN: (0225 63337. Est: 1976. Shop, closed Monday, also stockroom, b appointment. Medium stock sec. and antiq. Spec: art, music. Cata irregularly, music only. B: Barclays Bank, 37 Milsom Street, Bath BA 1DW. M: P.B.F.A.

BAILEY'S BOOKS, 13 Horse Street, Chipping Sodbury, Avon BS1 6DA. Prop: Richard and Sheila Carter. TN: (0454) 313399. Est: 198 Shop, closed Monday and Wednesday. Medium stock sec. and anti Spec: cookery and theatre. Cata: 2 a year.

C.G. BAKER—FINE BOOKS, 22 Forester Road, Bath, Avon. TN (0225) 64095. Est: 1957. Postal business only. New, and medium se and antiq. stock. Spec: old and rare, first editions, private press book typography.

BEN BASS, GREYNE HOUSE, MARSHFIELD, AVON. Prop: Ben Bass. TN: (0225) 891279. Private premises; appointment necessary. Small stock sec. and antiq. Spec: modern literature and bookfinding. Cata: 4 a year. Corresp: Français, Deutsch, Español, Italiano. B: Lloyds Bank, Berkeley Square, London W1.

BATH BOOK EXCHANGE, 35 BROAD STREET, BATH, AVON BA1 5LP. Prop: L.M. Turner. TN: (0225) 5514. Est: 1959. Shop. Medium sec. stock; also stamps, postcards, records. Spec: B: Midland Bank, Milsom Street, Bath.

GEORGE BAYNTUN, MANVERS STREET, BATH, AVON. Prop: H and C. Bayntun-Coward. TN: (0225) 66000 TA: Bayntun Bath. Est: 1894. Shop and showrooms, open normal business hours, or by appointment on Saturdays. Very large sec. and antiq. stock; also bindery (incorporates the famous binding firm of Robert Riviere and Son. Est: 1829). Spec: fine bindings. Cata: occasionally. A.B.A. Bookseller to the late Queen Mary.)

JANET CLARKE, 3 WOODSIDE COTTAGES, FRESHFORD, BATH, AVON BA3 6EJ. TN: Limpley Stoke 3186. Est: 1973. Private premises, appointment necessary. Small sec. and antiq. stock. Spec: cookery, food, wine. Cata: on foregoing, 2 a year. M: A.B.A.

CLEVEDON BOOKS, 14 WOODSIDE ROAD, WALTON SAINT MARY, CLEVEDON, AVON BS21 7JY. Prop: George and Wendy Douthwaite. TN: (0272) 875862. (0272) 872304 any time. Mail order and by appointment. Gallery/Shop: small sec. and antiq. stock. Telephone call advised. Spec: antiq. maps and prints, art, plate books, atlases, history of industry, science and company histories. Cata: irregular. *Also* THE GALLERY, CINEMA BUILDINGS, OLD CHURCH STREET, CLEVEDON, AVON BS21 6NN.

EGRET BOOKS, 1 RANGERS COTTAGE, VALLEY ROAD, LEIGH WOODS, BRISTOL, AVON BS8 3PZ. Prop: P. & M. Mountford. TN: (0272) 731645. Private premises; postal business only. Catalogues. Sec. and antiq. Spec: poetry, modern first editions.

ENCHAINEMENT BOOKS, 39 ARLEY HILL, COTHAM, BRISTOL, AVON BS6 5PJ. Prop: Steve Wide. TN: (0272) 425759. Est: 1979. Private premises; appointment necessary. Small stock sec. and antiq. Spec: ballet and dance. Cata: 3 or 4 a year. Corresp: Français, Deutsch. B: National Westminster Bank, 115 Whiteladies Road, Clifton, Bristol 6. M: P.B.F.A.

FINE ART BOOKS, 22 EGERTON ROAD, BISHOPSTON, BRISTOL, AVON BS7 8HL. Prop: Roger B. Plant. TN: 47846. Est: 1977. Private premises; appointment necessary. Very small stock sec. and antiq. Spec: fine arts and Italian renaissances art and artists. Cata: yearly. B: Barclays Bank, 86 Queens Road, Clifton, Bristol. Account 90711608. M: P.B.F.A.
Also at COTHAM HILL BOOKS, 39A COTHAM HILL, BRISTOL. TN: 732344.

MICHAEL GARBETT ANTIQUARIAN BOOKS, 33 UPPER CRANBROOK ROAD, BRISTOL, AVON BS6 7UR. TN: 44843. Est: 1965. Private premises; appointment necessary. Small stock sec. and antiq. Spec: fine bindings. Cata: nineteenth century economics. M: P.B.F.A.
Also at COTHAM HILL BOOKS, 39A COTHAM HILL, BRISTOL. TN: (0272) 732344. Shop, closed Wednesdays.

WILLIAM GEORGE'S SONS LIMITED, 89, 81 & 52 PARK STREET, BRISTOL, AVON BS1 5PW. TN: Bristol 276602 (7 lines). Shop. New, and very large sec. and antiq. stock. Spec: British topography, history and travel. theology, English literature, art. Cata: A.B.A. B.A. N.B.L.

R.A. GILBERT, 4 JULIUS ROAD, BISHOPSTON, BRISTOL, AVON BS7 8EU. TN: (0272) 46936. Est: 1963. Stockroom; open by appointment. Medium stock sec. and antiq. books. Spec: occult, folklore, theology, freemasonry, nineteenth century literature. Cata: on foregoing 4 a year. M: P.B.F.A.

GOOD NEWS MEDIA, 3A FORUM BUILDING, SAINT JAMES' PARADE, BATH BA1 1UG. Prop: E. Hudson. TN: (0225) 66092. Est: 1982. Stockroom, closed Saturday. Medium stock sec. and antiq. also new books. Spec: theology, religious subjects. Cata: annual with supplements. Corresp: Français, Deutsch. B: National Westminster Bank Ltd., 39 Milsom Street, Bath.

A.R. HEATH, 62 PEMBROKE ROAD, CLIFTON, BRISTOL 8, AVON. TN: (0272) 741183. Est: 1963. Private premises; appointment necessary. Medium stock sec. and antiq. books. Spec: English antiquarian, principally 18th & 19th centuries, rare books and manuscripts. Cata: 3 or 4 a year. M: A.B.A.

HINCHLIFFE BOOKS, CLEMATIS COTTAGE, 15 CASTLE STREET, THORNBURY, BRISTOL, AVON BS12 1HA. Prop: Geoffrey Hinchliffe. TN: (0454) 415177. Est: 1972. Private premises, appointment necessary. Small stock sec. and antiq. books. Spec: topography and local studies, detective fiction. Cata: on foregoing, occasionally.

CHRISTOPHER HOLTOM, ESPERANZA, AUST, BRISTOL, AVON BS12 3AX. TN: (04545) 2557. Est: 1972. Private premises; appointment necessary. Small stock sec. and antiq. books. Spec: early children's books. Cata: on foregoing, about 4 a year.

THE KINGSLEY BOOKSHOP, 16 MARGARET'S BUILDINGS, BROCK STREET, BATH, AVON BA1 2LP. Prop: Alec N. Dakin. TN: Bath 24315. Est: 1923. Shop and storeroom. Very large sec. and antiq. stock. Corresp: Français, Deutsch.

MONTPELIER BOOKS, 32 ALMA VALE ROAD, CLIFTON, BRISTOL, AVON BS8 2HY. Prop: Michael and Margaret Buck. TN: (0272) 742690. Est: 1978. Shop, closed Mondays. Small stock sec. and antiq. Spec: theology. Cata: 3 a year. Corresp: Deutsch, Français. B: Co-operative Bank, 16 St. Stephen's Street, Bristol 1. Account 70130544. M: P.B.F.A.

ORTA BOOKS, 5 OAKWOOD AVENUE, HENLEAZE, BRISTOL, AVON BS9 4NS. Prop: Evelyn M. Mitchell. TN: (0272) 623656. Est: 1978. Private premises; appointment necessary. Small stock sec. and antiq. Spec: mountaineering, British topography and local history (particularly Welsh). Cata: 4 a year. B: National Westminster Bank PLC, 51 Henleaze Road, Bristol BS9 4JX. M: P.B.F.A.

PATTERSON AND LIDDLE, 20 CHANDOS ROAD, REDLAND, BRISTOL, AVON BS6 6PE. Prop: John D. Patterson and Stephen M. Liddle (formerly Chandos Books). TN: (0272) 731205. Est: 1980. Shop, business hours also by appointment. Small stock sec. and antiq. Spec: railways, aviation, Bristol and West Country topography. Cata: occasional. Corresp: Français. B: Barclays Bank PLC, 161 Whiteladies Road, Bristol BS8 2RJ. M: P.B.F.A., Fine Art Trade Guild.

PERIOD BINDERS, LOWER BRISTOL ROAD, TWERTON, BATH, AVON BA2 9ES. Prop: R.N. Tate. TN: (0225) 20698. Est: 1970. Shop and bindery; closed on Saturday. B: Lloyds Bank, 47 Milsom Street, Bath. Account 0222915. M: British Federation of Master Printers, Society of Book Binders and Book Restorers.

ROBERT & SUSAN PYKE, 2 BEAUFORT VILLAS, CLAREMONT ROAD, BATH, AVON BA1 6LY. Est: 1974. Private premises; appointment necessary. Small stock sec. and antiq. books. Spec: nautical and maritime. Cata: on foregoing 2 a year. P.B.F.A.

JOHN ROBERTS BOOKSHOP, 43 TRIANGLE WEST, BRISTOL, AVON BS8 1ES. Prop: John T. Roberts. TN: Bristol 28568. Est: 1955. Shop, no early closing. New and large sec. and antiq. stock, also antique prints and maps. Spec: British topography especially West Country; English literature including first editions; natural history, travel. Cata: general. occasionally. A.B.A.

LOUISE ROSS, 1 JOHN STREET, BATH BA1 2JL. Prop: Louise Ross. TN: (0225) 310332. Est: 1977. Shop, closed Mondays. Small stock sec. and antiq. Spec: fine bound sets English literature, illustrated books 1850–1935, English country maps and prints, atlases. Cata: 1 a year. B: Williams and Glyn's Bank, Quiet Street, Bath, Avon. Also Barclays Bank of New York, 15 West 50 Street, N.W., U.S.A. M: P.B.F.A., A.B.A.

GABRIELLE SIMON, 5 CHURCH STREET, ABBEY GREEN, BATH, AVON. Prop: Gabrielle and Simon Hamilton. TN: Bath 61687. Est: 1977. Shop. Medium stock sec. and antiq. B: Co-operative Bank, 4/5 Regent Circus, Swindon. Account 70073038.

S.P.C.K. 5 BLADUD BUILDINGS, BATH, AVON BA1 5LS. TN: (0225) 65402. Shop; closed on Thursday afternoons. Medium stock sec. and antiq. also new books and journals. Spec: theology, literature, history. M: B.A., N.B.L.

S.P.C.K. 8 PARK STREET, BRISTOL, AVON BS1 5HT. TN: (0272) 23461. Shop. Medium stock sec. and antiq. also new books. Spec: theology. M: B.A., N.B.L.

SPECULUM MENTIS, 15 Marlborough Buildings, Bath, Avon BA1 2LY. Prop: Piers Gascoigne. TN: (0225) 26243. Est: 1973. Postal business only. Very small stock sec. and antiq. books. Spec: English and German language, literature and criticism, philosophy. Cata: general; philosophy; occasional. Corresp: Français, Deutsch. B: Barclays Bank, 139-42 North Street, Brighton.

STERLING BOOKS, Green Lodge, 11 Cecil Road, Weston-Super-Mare, Avon BS23 2NG. Prop: David Nisbet. TN: (0934) 25056. Est: 1966. Postal business only. Small stock sec. and antiq. books. Spec: rare books, bindings, travel and topography, English literature and arts. Cata: on foregoing. A.B.A.

TWIGGERS BOOKS, 37 Copse Road, Clevedon, Avon BS21 7QN. Prop: Anne and Peter Watts. TN: (0272) 876516. Est: 1981. Shop, closed Monday. Also by appointment. Medium stock sec. and antiq. B: National Girobank, Bootle. M: P.B.F.A.

MORRIS & JULIET VENABLES, Rose Bank, 270 Henbury Road, Bristol, Avon BS10 7QR. TN: (0272) 507362. Est: 1970. Private premises; appointment necessary. Medium stock sec. and antiq. books. Spec: English literature, especially poetry, old and rare, first editions. Cata: on foregoing and general, occasionally.

DEREK AND GLENDA WALLIS, 6 Chapel Row, Queen Square, Bath, Avon BA1 1HN. TN: 24677. Est: 1980. Shop. Medium stock sec. and antiq. Spec: illustrated books, folklore and Canadiana. Cata: occasionally. B: Midland Bank, 36 Bridge Street, Swindon, Wiltshire. Account 901 669 36.

THE WISE OWL BOOKSHOP, 26 Upper Maudlin Street, Bristol, Avon BS2 8SJ. TN: (0272) 46939, after hours 514759. Shop; no early closing. Medium stock sec. and antiq. books. Spec: books on music and musicians. Cata: on foregoing. P.B.F.A.

39. WILTSHIRE

BRADFORD ON AVON
CHIPPENHAM
CALNE
CORSHAM
DEVIZES
MALMESBURY
MARLBOROUGH
MELKSHAM
MERE
SALISBURY
SWINDON
TROWBRIDGE
WESTBURY

THE ANTIQUE AND BOOK COLLECTOR, 6 Kingsbury Street, Marlborough, Wiltshire. Prop: Christopher Gange. TN: (0672) 54040. Est: 1983. Shop. Medium stock sec. and antiq. Spec: illustrated books, art and antiques, modern first editions, Africana, travel.

ARUNDELL BOOKS Arundell House, High Street, Tisbury, Salisbury, Wiltshire SP3 6QU. Prop: May and May Limited. Dir: John May, Mrs. Laurie May and Christopher May. TN: (0747) 870 353. Est: 1983. Private premises; open 9.00 a.m. to 5.00 p.m. Wednesdays and Saturdays; other days strictly by appointment. Small stock of sec. and antiq. books on Wiltshire and Cranborne Chase. Cata: on foregoing, 2 or 3 per year.

A. & B. BANCROFT, Springfields, Ogbourne, Colerne, Near Chippenham, Wiltshire SN14 8DJ. Prop: A. and Brenda Bancroft. TN: (0225) 742156. Est: 1979. Private premises; appointment necessary. Very small stock sec. and antiq. Spec: country matters. Cata: 4 a year. B: Giro.

BATSTONE BOOKS, 24 Gloucester Street, Malmesbury, Wiltshire SN16 0AA. TN: (06662) 3072.

D.M. BEACH, 52 High Street, Salisbury, Wiltshire. Prop: Anthony Pearce. TN: Salisbury 3801. Est: 1933. Shop, 9-5.30 Monday to Saturday. Large sec. and antiq. stock. Spec: atlases, colourplate, travel & topography children's, bindings. Corresp: Deutsch, Niederlandse. B: Barclays Bank, 1 Castle Street, Salisbury. Account 10694657. A.B.A., B.A.

PHILIP R. BOULTON, 50a The Butts, Westbury, Wiltshire BA13 3EX. TN: 822638. Est: 1940 (31 years at 8 Fore Street, Westbury) Private premises; postal business only (semi-retired).

R.L. COOK, Belmont House, Little Horton, Devizes, Wiltshire SN10 3LJ. TN: Cannings 214. Est: 1950. Private premises appointment necessary. Small sec. and antiq. stock. Spec: fine bindings, rare books. Cata: general, 1/2 a year. A.B.A.

D'ARCY BOOKS, THE CHEQUERS, HIGH STREET, DEVIZES, WILTSHIRE SN10 1AT. Prop: Mr. & Mrs. C.G.O. MacGregor. TN: (0380) 6922, after hours Bromham (0380) 850319. Est: 1974. Shop, early closing Wednesdays. Very large stock sec. & antiq. books, also some local prints and maps. B: National Westminster Bank, Market Place, Devizes, Wiltshire. Account 04626192. M: P.B.F.A.

G.M. & R.C. DAVIS, 6 CHAPEL RISE, ATWORTH, NEAR MELKSHAM, WILTSHIRE SN12 8JZ. TN: (0225) 702518, Est: 1976. Private premises; appointment essential. Small stock sec. and antiq. books. Spec: Richard Jefferies, John Clare, Edward Thomas, H.E. Bates, Alison Uttley, windmill and watermills. Cata: 4 a year. M: P.B.F.A.

MRS. ASSIA DOYLE, TEFFONT, SALISBURY, WILTSHIRE, SP3 5QP. Medium general sec. and antiq. stock. Spec: agriculture, biography, history, natural history, travel & topography. Cata: 4 a year. Corresp: Français. B: National Westminster Bank, Minster Street, Salisbury. Account 68518978.

SOPHIE DUPRE, 14 THE GREEN, CALNE, WILTSHIRE SN11 8DQ. TN: (0249) 816793. Private premises; appointment necessary. Medium stock of autograph letters, historical documents, manuscripts, signed books and signed photos, some ephemera. Cata: on foregoing.

DAVID EVANS FINE BIRD BOOKS, WARREN COURT FARMHOUSE, WEST TYTHERLEY, NEAR SALISBURY, WILTSHIRE SP5 1LU. Prop: David Evans. TN: (0980) 862366. Est: 1968. Private premises appointment necessary. Small stock sec. and antiq. Spec: ornithology B: National Westminster Bank Ltd., 27 High Street, Fordingbridge Hampshire.

EVERYMAN BOOKSHOP, 5 BRIDGE STREET, SALISBURY, WILTSHIRE SP1 2ND. Prop: Tony Martin. Salisbury 3531. Est: 1975. Shop. Small stock sec. and antiq. also new books. Corresp: Français. B: Barclays Bank, High Street, Salisbury. Account 80362077.

FRANK & MAUREEN FOX, 1 Ashley Villas, Box, Corsham, Wiltshire SN14 9AD. TN: BOX 742775. Est: 1972. Private premises; appointment necessary. Medium stock sec. and antiq. books. Spec: India; the sea; travel. P.B.F.A.

RICHARD HATCHWELL, The Old Rectory, Little Somerford, Chippenham, Wiltshire. TN: Malmesbury 3261. Est: 1952. Private premises, appointment necessary. Medium sec. and antiq. stock. Spec: English and French books before 1800; Wiltshire topography. Cata: on foregoing, occasionally.

JOHN & JUDITH HEAD, The Barn Book Supply, 88 Crane Street, Salisbury, Wiltshire. TN: Salisbury 27767. Est: 1958. Office and showroom, appointment preferred. Medium sec. and antiq. stock. Spec: angling and field sports. Cata: angling, field sports, the horse, 6 a year. A.B.A.

HERALDRY TODAY, Parliament Piece, Ramsbury, Nr. Marlborough, Wiltshire. Prop: Mrs. Rosemary Pinches. TN: Marlborough 20617. Est: 1954. Coachhouse, open during normal business hours. Very large stock sec. and antiq. also back numbers of journals and new books and periodicals. Heraldic and genealogical research. Spec: heraldry, genealogy and topography in all languages. Cata: 3 times a year. Corresp: Français. M: A.B.A.

JOHNSON ARCHITECTURAL BOOKS, Tynings House, Sherston, Malmesbury, Wiltshire. Prop: Mrs. V. Johnson. TN: (0948) 840404. Est: 1979. Private premises; appointment necessary. Very small stock sec. and antiq. Spec: architecture, building construction, fine and decorative arts. Cata: 2 a year. Corresp: Deutsch. B: Barclays Bank, High Street, Malmesbury, Wiltshire. M: P.B.F.A.

BERIC JONES, 277a The Gravel, Holt, Trowbridge, Wiltshire BA14 6RA. TN: North Trowbridge (0225) 782421. Est: 1978. Private premises; appointment necessary. Small stock sec. and antiq. and some new. Spec: books relating to Wales and Wiltshire. B: Midland Bank, 45 Milstom Street, Bath, BA1 1DU. Account 21091352. M: P.B.F.A.

RONALD LEES, 32 Saint John's Street, Devizes, Wiltshire SN10 5LT. TN: Devizes 2774. Est: 1972. Shop, early closing Wednesday. Medium sec. and antiq. stock. Corresp: Français, Deutsch. B: Lloyds Bank, Market Place, Devizes. Account 0475263.

ERIC MACRO, The Bowehous, Chitterne, Warminster, Wiltshire. TN: Warminster 50551.

THE MARLBOROUGH BOOKSHOP, THE PARADE, MARLBOROUGH, WILTSHIRE. Prop: R. Collens. TN: (0672) 54074. Est: 1977. Shop and stockroom, open weekdays, also Sundays by appointment. Large stock sec. and antiq. also new books. Spec: art books, modern first editions and private presses. Cata: occasional. Corresp: Français, Deutsch, Español, Italiano, Arabic. B: Barclays Bank, Main Street, Marlborough, Wilts.

MAY & MAY LIMITED, ARUNDELL HOUSE, HIGH STREET, TISBURY, SALISBURY, WILTSHIRE SP3 6QU. Dir: John May, Mrs. Laurie May and Christopher May. TN: 0747-870 353. Est: in London as a partnership in 1963: incorporated and moved to new premises in Wiltshire in 1983. Private premises; open 9.00 a.m. to 5.00 p.m. Wednesdays and Saturdays, other days strictly by appointment. Medium stock of sec. and antiq. books on music and printed music. Also some new books. Cata: foregoing, 10 per year.

R. & S. OTWAY, DUTCH BARTON COTTAGE, CHURCH STREET, BRADFORD-ON-AVON, WILTSHIRE BA15 1LN. TN: (022 16) 3885. Est: 1973. Shop; closed Wednesdays. Small stock sec. and antiq. books; also new books. Spec: English literature; natural history; topography. Corresp: Français, Deutsch, Español, Italiano. M: A.B.A., P.B.F.A. B: Lloyds Bank, Church Street, Bradford-on-Avon. Account 0243179.

CYRIL SCOTT, 1 CHURCH STREET, MERE, WILTSHIRE BA12 6DS. TN: (747) 860 297. Est: 1977. Private premises; postal business only. Small stock sec. and antiq. Spec: history of science. Cata: occasionally. Corresp: Français. B: Lloyds Bank, 6 Pall Mall, London, SW1Y 5NH. Account 6133924. M: P.B.F.A.

VICTORIA BOOKSHOP, 30 WOOD STREET, OLD TOWN, SWINDON, WILTSHIRE SN1 4AB. Prop: S. Austin. TN: (0793) 27364. Est: 1966. Shop. Very large stock sec. and antiq. books; also new books. Spec: topography; railways. B.A.

VIRGO BOOKS, "LITTLE COURT", SOUTH WRAXALL, BRADFORD-ON-AVON, WILTSHIRE BA15 2SE. Prop: Mrs. Q.V. Mason. TN: (02216) 2040. Est: 1979. Private premises; appointment necessary. Very small stock sec. and antiq. Spec: modern first editions, letters and diaries of literary personalities, biography. Corresp: Deutsch, Français. B: Lloyds Bank, Bradford-on-Avon, Wiltshire. Account 0208519.

WHITE HORSE BOOKSHOP, 136 HIGH STREET, MARLBOROUGH, WILTSHIRE. TN: (06725) 2071. Est: 1947. Shop, early closing Wednesdays. Small sec. and antiq. stock; also new books, stationery and art materials, greetings cards. B.A. N.B.L.

WINSTANLEY-SALISBURY BOOKBINDER, 213 DEVIZES ROAD, SALISBURY, WILTSHIRE SP2 9LT. Prop: Alan Winstanley. TN: (0722) 4998. Est: 1960. Workshop and stockroom, closed on Saturdays. Very small stock sec. and antiq. Spec: illustrated books; craft bookbinding and restoring. B: Barclays Bank, High Street, Salisbury. Account 60973513.

40. BERKSHIRE

BRACKNELL
COOKHAM
HERMITAGE
HUNGERFORD
HURST
KINTBURY
MAIDENHEAD
NEWBURY
READING
THATCHAM
TILEHURST
WINDSOR
WOODCOTE

ANYTHING NOSTALGIC, 35 Northcourt Avenue, Reading, Berkshire RG2 7HE. Prop: W.A. and P.M. Gulliver. TN: (0734) 871479. Est: 1982. Private premises; appointment advisable. Small stock sec. and antiq. B: Midland Bank, 24 Broad Street, Reading.

P.N. BARNARD, Bag End, Hurley, Maidenhead, Berkshire SL6 5NB. Prop: P.N. Barnard. TN: (062 882) 4337. Est: 1960. Private premises, appointment essential. Small sec. and antiq. stock. Spec: children's, illustrated, Irish.

BLAKEWAY BOOKS, 13 Bridge Street, Hungerford, Berkshire RG17 0EH. Prop: M.G. Blakeway. TN: (0488) 83581. Est: 1977. Shop, open Fridays and Saturdays. Small stock sec. and antiq. also bookbinding. Spec: history, biography, children's. B: Barclays Bank, High Street, Hungerford. Account 60188646.

CHARLES BREWIN, 15 Dorset Road, Windsor, Berkshire SL4 3BA. TN: (95) 69979. Est: 1973. Private premises; appointment necessary. Very small stock sec. and antiq. books. Spec: Berkshire; Windsor; Nigeria; French illustrated. Cata: Windsor, Berkshire, French Illustrated, 1 a year.

D.F. BROOKE-HITCHING LIMITED, Osmington House, Kintbury, Berkshire RG15 0TL. Prop: D.F. Brooke-Hitching. TN: (0488) 58750. Telex: 848507. Est: 1972. Private premises; appointment necessary. Small stock old and rare books before ca. 1860.

COOKHAM BOOKSHOP, High Street, Cookham, Berkshire SL6 9SJ Prop: Jean Hedger. TN: Bournend 28217. Est: 1979. Shop, closed on Wednesday afternoons. Small stock sec. and antiq. Spec: children's and illustrated and Thames books. Corresp: Français. B: National Westminster Bank, Havant. Account 8891073.

I.J. DORAN, 15 Tawfield, Bracknell, Berkshire. TN: Bracknell 29409. Est: 1977. Private premises; postal business only. Very small stock sec. and antiq. Spec: horse racing and breeding, betting, gambling, bookmaking, anything on the turf. Cata: 4–6 a year.

ETON ANTIQUE BOOKSHOP, 88 High Street, Eton, Windsor, Berkshire. Prop: D. Kernec. TN: (07535) 55534. Shop. Stock of sec. and antiq. books and prints.

H.W. EDWARDS, Ashmore Green, Newbury, Berkshire. TN: (0635) 62105. TA: Dryasdust Newbury. Est: 1917. Postal business only. Medium sec. and antiq. stock. Spec: books before 1840. A.B.A.

FOOTBALLANA, 275 Overdown Road, Tilehurst, Reading RG3 6NX. Prop: Bryan Horsnell. Private premises; postal business only. Very small stock sec. and antiq. books; programmes; curios especially pre-war items purchased. Spec: Association Football. Cata: occasionally.

GABY GOLDSCHEIDER, 29 Temple Road, Windsor, Berkshire SL4 1HP. TN: (95) 61517. Est: 1971. Private premises; appointment necessary. Medium stock sec. and antiq. also a few new books and prints, and antiquarian toys. Spec: Children's and illustrated books; literature (English and American); theatre; collectors' items, Sherlock Holmes, Conan Doyle. Cata: about 4 a year (by subject). Corresp: Deutsch, Français, Espanñol, Italiano, Nederlandse. B: Barclays Bank, 49 Saint Leonards Road, Windsor. Account 80418838.

INVICTA BOOKSHOP, 8 Cromwell Place, Northbrook Street, Newbury, Berkshire. Prop: Dorothy Hall. TN: (0635) 31176. Est: 1969. Shop, closed Monday and Wednesday. Medium sec. and antiq. stock.

MALLORN BOOKS, 58 Waldeck Street, Reading, Berkshire. Prop: Lyndon and Izzy Green. TN: (0734) 863525. Est: 1982. Private premises; appointment necessary. Very small stock sec. and antiq. B: Williams and Glyn's Bank, 4 Market Place, Reading, Berkshire.

MARBECK BOOKS, 2 Marbeck Close, Windsor, Berkshire. Prop: D.C. and B. Hedges. TN: (95) 64354. Private premises; appointment necessary. Small stock sec. and antiq. Spec: topography, especially River Thames, and Berkshire. Corresp: Français. B: Lloyds Bank Ltd., Thames Street, Windsor, Berkshire. M: P.B.F.A.

VERONICA MAYHEW, Trewena, Behoes Lane, Woodcote, Near Reading, Berkshire RG8 0PP. TN: (0491) 680743. Est: 1972. Private premises; appointment necessary. Very small stock sec. and antiq. books; also new books. Spec: domesticated birds and animals. Cata: Poultry; pigeons; cagebirds; farm livestock; dogs and cats; rabbits etc. about 1 a year on each subject.

SHEILA PAYNE, Lawford, Wokingham Road, Hurst, Berkshire. Private premises: postal business only: small sec. and antiq. stock: also binding and restoration.

RAILWAY BOOK AND MAGAZINE SEARCH, Brambles End, Orchard Close, Hermitage, Berkshire RG16 9RU. Prop: Mr. N.J. Bridger. TN: (0635) 200507. Est: 1982. Private premises; appointment necessary. Very small stock sec. and antiq. Spec: railways.

THE RED PALE, The Little Dutch House, 11 Horton Road, Datchet, Berkshire.

EDWARD SANDERSON, 60A Upton Park, Slough SL1 2DE. TN: Slough (0753) 26601. Est: 1975. Private premises; postal business only. Very large stock sec. and antiq. Spec: Scottish, medical, psychology, social science, angling, photography. Cata. M: P.B.F.A.

WILLIAM SMITH [BOOKSELLERS] LIMITED, 35–39 London Street, Reading, Berkshire RG1 4PU. TN: Reading 595555. TA: Bibliostat Reading. Est: 1832. Shop, no early closing. New, and medium sec. and antiq. stock. Cata: general, 3 a year. B: Barclays Bank, King Street, Reading. Account 50851655. A.B.A. B.A. N.B.L.

WATERLOO FINE ARTS LIMITED, PENTHOUSE, CALCOT GRANGE, MILL LANE, READING, BERKSHIRE RG3 5RS. Prop: Paul and Mona Nicholas. TN: (0734) 411706. Telex No. 296500 Ref Fl. Est: 1977. *Also at* 1 CECIL COURT, LONDON WC2. Shop, also by appointment. Very small stock sec. and antiq. Spec: antiq. maps and prints. Cata: monthly. B: Midland Bank, 6 Fore Street, Okehampton, Devon.

WYSEBY HOUSE BOOKS, SIVER BIRCHES, OXDROVE, BURGHCLERE, NEWBURY, BERKSHIRE RG15 9JS. Prop: Dr. Tim Oldham. TN: (063) 527 232. Est: 1978. Private premises, also stockroom; appointment necessary. Spec: natural history, gardening, travel. Small stock sec. and antiq., also new books. Cata: 4 or 5 a year. Corresp: Français. B: Midland Bank, Mansion House Street, Newbury, Berkshire. M: P.B.F.A.

41. LONDON (EAST POSTAL DISTRICTS)

ALBION VILLAGE BOOKS, Albion Drive, London E8 4ET. Prop: Iain Sinclair. TN: (01) 254 8571. Est: 1975. Private premises; appointment necessary. Small stock sec. and antiq. Spec: modern first editions, literature. Cata: occasionally. Small stock sec. and antiq. Spec: modern first editions, poetry. Cata: 4 a year.

DALIAN BOOKS, 81 Albion Drive, London Fields, London E8 4LT. Prop: David P. Williams. TN: (01) 249-1587. Private premises; appointment necessary. Small stock sec. and antiq. books. Spec: modern first editions, detective, science fiction, fantasy. Cata: 2 or 3 a year.

DAWSON, MASSON ASSOCIATES, B-2 Metropolitan Wharf, Wapping Wall, London E1. TN: (01) 481-1974. Est: 1976. Stockroom and Gallery; gallery closed Mondays. Stockroom for books by appointment. Small stock sec. and antiq. Spec: photography 19th and 20th century, avant-garde art design and architecture books. Also rare periodicals, graphics posters and (very selective) new books stocked. Cata: 6 to 12 a year. Corresp: Deutsch, Français, Italiano, Español.

I.D. EDRICH, 17 Selsdon Road, Wanstead, London E11 2QF. Prop: I.D. and S. Edrich. TN: (01) 989-9541. Est: 1965. Private premises; appointment necessary. Large stock sec. and antiq. books. Spec: literature (modern first editions, poetry, literary periodicals and related items). Cata: 3 or 4 a year and lists. Corresp: Français. B: Barclays Bank 55–57 High Street, Wanstead, London E11 2AD and National Giro Account 583 8355.

L.S. ELLIOTT, 17 Langdon Crescent, London E6 2PW. TN: (01) 472-6310. Est: 1956. Private premises, appointment necessary. New, and medium sec. and antiq. stock. Spec: historical (including some fiction); juvenile, Old Boy's Books 1840–1940. fantasy & science fiction, U.S.A. & British; detective & associated subjects.

S. DAS GUPTA, 6 Lake House Road, Wanstead, London E11. Prop: S. Das Gupta and Clotilde Das Gupta. TN: (01) 989-6101. Est: 1935. Private premises; postal business only. Large stock sec. and antiq. Spec: South Asia, S.E. Asia, Middle East, Far East, Africa south of the Sahara, Spain, Latin America, U.S.A. Corresp: Español. B: National Westminster Bank, High Street, Wanstead, London, E.11. Account 29256380.

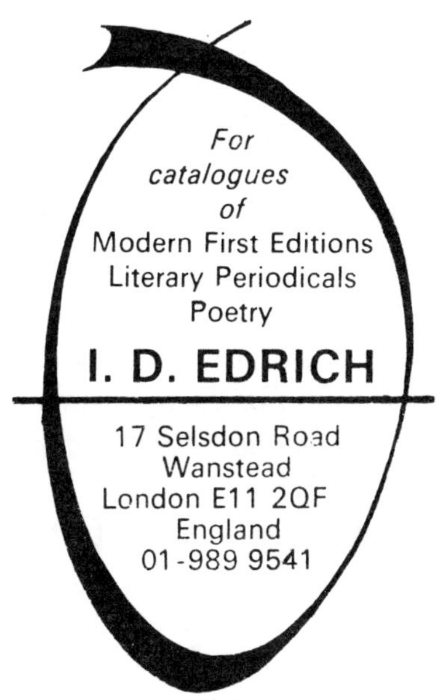

NORMAN LORD, Antique City, 98 Wood Street, London E17. Prop: Norman Lord. TN: (01) 520 4032. Shop; closed on Wednesdays and Thursdays. Small stock sec. and antiq. Spec: literature, 18th century to date, biography, travel, topography, illustrated books, performing arts, private presses. Cata: occasionally.

IAIN SINCLAIR, BOOKS, 28 Albion Drive, London E8 4ET. TN: (01) 254-8571. Est: 1975. Storeroom and private premises; appointment necessary. Small stock sec. and antiq. Spec: modern first editions, especially poetry.

BRIAN TROATH BOOKS, 106 Graham Road, London E8 1BX. TN: (01) 254-2912. Est: 1970. Private premises; appointment necessary. Medium stock sec. and antiq. Spec: modern literature and periodicals, signed and some special editions. B: Barclays Bank, 1 Kingsland High Street, London E8 2JT.

42. LONDON (EAST CENTRAL POSTAL DISTRICTS)

J. ASH [RARE BOOKS], 25 Royal Exchange, London EC3. Prop: Laurence Worms. TN: (01) 626-2665. Est: 1946. Shop, closed Saturdays. Medium stock sec. and antiq. books; also prints and maps, picture framing and mounting. Spec: first editions; London; plate-books atlases; rare and fine books. Cata: occasionally.

STUART BENNETT RARE BOOKS, 35 Breakspears Road, London SE4 1YR. TN: (01) 691-8805 Est: 1980. Private premises; appointment necessary. Small stock sec. and antiq. Spec: English literature before 1850, especially poetry, philosophy, fiction, satire and criticism. Cata: 2 a year.

ROY BLOOM LIMITED, 81 Goswell Road, London EC1. TN: (01) 251-4345. Telex: 24224 (Ref 2121). Remainder Dealer.

J. CLARKE-HALL LIMITED, Bride Court, Fleet Street, London EC4 8DU. TN: (01) 353-4116. Shop, closed Saturday. Large sec. and antiq. stock, prints and maps. A.B.A.
[*Also at S22 Bride Lane,* for prints and maps. TN: (01) 353-5483].

PAGODA BOOKS, Charterhouse Chambers, Charterhouse Square, London EC1M 6AH. Prop: Julie Speedie TN: (01) 250-3269. Est: 1982. Office premises; postal business only. Very small stock sec. and antiq. Spec: the 1890's. Cata: 2 a year. B: Midland Bank, 96 Old Broad Street, London EC2N 1BA.

43. LONDON (NORTH POSTAL DISTRICTS) AND NORTH MIDDLESEX

A LA MODE, 1 Oakwood Park Road, London N14. Prop: R.C.H. Witt. (01) 785-6911. Small stock sec. and antiq. Spec: fashion, dress, folk costume, history and topography of Greece, Albania and the Balkans. Cata: 3 a year.

ALPHA BOOKS, 60 Langdon Park Road, London N6 5QG. Prop: Tony Maddock. TN: (01) 348-2831. Est: 1983. Private premises; appointment necessary. Medium stock sec. and antiq. Spec: occult, folklore, The Orient, travel, modern literature. Cata: about 4 a year. M: P.B.F.A.

BONAVENTURE, 259 Archway Road, Highgate, London N6. Prop: R. O'Farrell, B.A. TN: (01) 341-2345. Est: 1968. Shop; closed Mondays and Thursdays. Medium stock sec. and antiq. books; also old maps and prints. Spec: travel, world-wide but especially the Americas. Corresp: Français, Español, Italiano, Deutsch. B: Barclays Bank, 345 Archway Road, London, N.6. Account 506756695.

G.W. ANDRON, 162a Brunswick Park Road, London N11. TN: (01) 361-2409. Est: 1972. Postal business only. Small stock sec. and antiq. books. Spec: British topography; natural history. Cata: 2 or 3 a year.

ARMS AND MILITARIA BOOKSHOP, 34–36 High Street, Southgate, London N14 6EE. Prop: J.E. Luck. TN: 01-886 0334. Est: 1967. Shop, closed Tuesdays and Thursdays. Very small sec. and antiq. books, also new. Spec: books on weapons (antique and modern), military equipment, uniforms, model soldiers, medals, badges; some regimental and military history.

BANNATYNE BOOKS LIMITED, 6 Bedford Road, London N8. Prop: Mr. and Mrs. Court. TN: (01) 340-1953. Est: 1980. Private premises; appointment necessary. Very small stock sec. and antiq. Spec: books by and about John Buchan. Cata: 2 a year. B: Midland Bank, 138 Tottenham Court Road, London W1P 0AY.

BARN BOOKS, 1a Highbury Park, Islington, London N5. Prop: L. Freeman Shop, closed Thursdays.

PAUL BENTLEY, 8 Baxendale, London N20 0EG. TN: (01) 445-9791. Est: 1969. Postal business only. Very small sec. and antiq. stock. Spec: British and foreign illustrated topography and travel; maps, plans and panoramas, especially of London; early atlases; fine colourplate books before 1860.

BOOKFINDERS, 19 OXFORD GARDENS, LONDON N20 9AG. Prop: R.H. Lewis. TN: (01) 446-0946. Postal Business only. Very small sec. and antiq. stock.

BOOKMASTERS, JUPITER BOOKS LONDON LIMITED , 167 HERMITAGE ROAD, LONDON N4 1LZ. Prop: The Rare Book Company Limited. TN: (01) 800-6601. Telex: 8954665 GITS-G Bookmasters. Est: 1972. Showroom and warehouse; appointment necessary (not on Saturdays). Very large stock of new remainders only. Cata: twice a year. B: Barclays Bank, 53 Maida Vale, London, W9 1SL and Barclays Bank of New York 9, W.57th Street, New York, NY 10019, U.S.A.

THE BOOK SHOP, 36 GORDON ROAD, ENFIELD, MIDDLESEX. Prop: J.E. Luck. Est: 1982. Shop and stockroom, open only Thursday afternoon and Saturday 10.30–3.30 p.m. Also by appointment. Medium stock sec. and antiq. Spec: some doll and toy books. M: P.B.F.A.

JOHN BUNTING, 17 NORTHVIEW, TUFNELL PARK ROAD, LONDON N7. TN: (01) 609-4284. Private premises; appointment necessary. Medium stock sec. and antiq. books. Spec: English literature; history; applied arts.

J. BURKE, 6 WOODBERRY DOWN, LONDON N4 2TG. TN: (01) 800-5161. TA: Bouquins London N.4. Mail order, export only. Medium sec. and antiq. stock. Spec: voyages and travels, ethnography and similar. Cata: travel, 3–4 a year. A.B.A.

THE CAMBERWELL BOOKSHOP, 28A CAMBERWELL GROVE, LONDON SE5. Prop: Nicholas McConnell and Mark Ransom. TN: (01) 701-1839. Shop. Medium stock sec. and antiq. books, also prints and binding equipment.

CAMDEN PASSAGE SITES LIMITED, PHELPS COTTAGE, 357 UPPER STREET, ISLINGTON, LONDON N1 0PD. Prop: John Friend. TN: (01) 359-0190. Open air book market in Camden Passage, open every Thursday and Friday, 09.00 to 16.00 hrs. Medium stock sec. and antiq. books offered by ten to twenty dealers in the market.

CHAPTER ONE, PIERREPONT ROW, CAMDEN PASSAGE, ISLINGTON, LONDON N1. Prop: Lady Wolfson. TN: (01) 359-1185. Est: 1981. Shop, open Wednesdays and Saturdays 10–4.30 pm, also by appointment. Very small stock sec. and antiq. Spec: fine leather bindings. B: Barclays Bank, 251 Regent Street, London W1.

CROUCH END BOOKSHOP, 60 Crouch End Hill, London N8 8AG. Prop: Marsha Carters. TN: (01) 348-8966. Est: 1973. Shop. New and small sec. and antiq. stock.

DECOR BOOKS, 57 Cholmeley Crescent, Highgate, London N6 5EX. Prop: Mrs. S. Forsling. TN: (01) 340-7041. Est: 1975. Private premises; appointment necessary. Small sec. and antiq. stock. Spec: the arts. Cata: the arts, 4 a year.

DUPONT ET FILS, 68 Lincoln Road, East Finchley, London N2. TN: (01) 883-7852. Est: 1910. Storeroom and office, trade only seen by appointment. Antiq. stock. Spec: geography, old travel, colour-plate, views, Greece, Malta, Cyprus, South America, Turkey, Spain, Portugal, France, Belgium, Germany, Switzerland, Italy, Scandinavia, Palestine, Egypt, Arab World. costumes. Cata: lists on foregoing. A.B.A.

THE FINCHLEY BOOKSHOP, 13 Long Lane, London N3 2PR. Prop: Martin Keene. TN: (01) 349-2597. Est: 1975. Shop, closed on Mondays. Medium stock sec. and antiq. books; also picture framing. Spec: humour. Cata: occasionally.

FISHER & SPERR, 46 Highgate High Street, London N6. Prop: J.R. Sperr. TN: (01) 340-7244. Est: 1940. Shop, four floors. Very large general sec. and antiq. stock. Spec: art, philosophy, topography, sets, literary criticism. Cata: art and general, 1 a year. A.B.A. B.A. Corresp: Français, Deutsch. B: Barclays Bank, 54 Highgate High St., London, N6 5JB.

W. FORSTER, 83a Stamford Hill, London N16. TN: (01) 800-3919. Private premises, appointment necessary. Sec. and antiq. stock. Spec: bibliography. Cata: on foregoing and general, 10 a year. A.B.A.

WALTER H. GARDNER LIMITED, 74–80 Stamford Hill, London N16 6XS. Prop: W.H. Gardner. TN: (01) 806-1981. Est: 1978. Stockroom; appointment necessary. Small stock sec. and antiq. and back numbers of journals. Spec: learned, scientific and art illustrated periodicals and reference books, also remainders. Corresp: Deutsch. B: Barclays Bank, Hampstead Garden Suburb Branch, 1–3 Lyttelton Road, London N2 0DP. Account 30914649.

'HAMAKRIK' BOOK & BINDING COMPANY, 45 Craven Walk, London N16. TN: (01) 800-5655. Storeroom appointment necessary. Large sec. and antiq. stock. Spec: early Hebrew books, incunabula.

PETER MURRAY HILL [RARE BOOKS] LIMITED, 35 NORTH HILL, HIGHGATE, LONDON N6. Prop: Martin Hamlyn. TN: (01) 340-6959. TA: Hilliber, London-N6. Est: 1939 reconstituted 1965. Private premises; appointment necessary. Medium stock sec. and antiq. books. Spec: English literature before 1850, especially verse, novels, theatre, philosophy, educational and social history. Cata: on foregoing, about 5 a year. A.B.A., N.B.L. Corresp: Français, Deutsch. B: National Westminster Bank, 349 Archway Road, London, N.6. Account 38231816.

W.E. HERSANT LIMITED, THE CHOLMELEY BOOKSHOP, 228 ARCHWAY ROAD, HIGHGATE, LONDON N6 5AZ. TN: (01) 340-3869. Shop, closed Thursday. Large sec. stock, also new. Spec: aeronautics, military history. Cata. A.B.A. B.A. N.B.L.

B. HIRSCHLER, 62 PORTLAND AVENUE, LONDON N16 AND AT 71 DUNSMURE ROAD, LONDON N16. TN: (01) 800-6395. Est: 1943. Storeroom, appointment necessary. New, and large sec. and antiq. stock. Spec: Hebraica and Judaica. Cata: on foregoing, 3 a year.

THE HISTORY BOOKSHOP, 2 THE BROADWAY, FRIERN BARNET ROAD, LONDON N11 1ER. Prop: M. Gladman and J.W. Prickett. TN: (01) 368-8568. TA: Histybooks. Est: 1963. Large shop open between 9.30 am and 5.30 pm Wednesday-Saturday. Very large stock used. Spec: social and economic history, English local history, architecture, transport, aviation, naval and military, bibliography. Back numbers of some journals stocked. Cata: 6 per year. Corresp: all major European languages. B: Barclays Bank, 233 Woodhouse Road, London N12 2BH. Account 20797901. M: P.B.F.A., B.A.

HOUSMANS BOOKSHOP LIMITED, 5 CALEDONIAN ROAD, KING'S CROSS, LONDON N1. TN: (01) 837-4473. Shop, no early closing. New and small sec. stock, specialising in pacifism and radical issues. Cata: lists. B.A., N.B.L.

INTERCOL LONDON, 1A CAMDEN WALK, ISLINGTON GREEN, LONDON N1 8DY. Prop: Yasha Beresiner. TN: (01) 354-2599. Est: 1981. Shop. Very small stock sec. and antiq. also new books. Spec: playing cards, banknotes, numismatics, maps. Cata: 4 a year. M: Fellow of the Royal Numismatic Society.

KĀMILIYA BOOKS, PRIORY COTTAGE, 102 SAINT PAUL'S ROAD, CANONBURY, LONDON N1 2LR. Prop: Mr. Farid Kioumgi. TN: (01) 226-5240. CA: Kamiliya Books, London N1. Est: 1983. Private premises; appointment necessary. Very small stock sec. and antiq. also new books. Spec: Middle East, Islamic books.

BEN KANE BOOK SERVICE, 33 KENVER AVENUE, LONDON N12 0PG. TN: (01) 445-5623. Est: 1968. Private premises. Medium sec. and antiq. stock. Spec: modern literature and the social sciences.

IAN McKELVIE, 45 HERTFORD ROAD, LONDON N2 9BX. Est: 1969. Private premises, appointment necessary. Medium sec. and antiq. stock. Spec: modern first editions, English and American literature. Cata: on foregoing, 4 a year.

BARRIE MARKS LIMITED, 5 PRINCES AVENUE, MUSWELL HILL, LONDON N10 3LS. TN: (01) 883-1593. Private premises; appointment necessary. Very small sec. and antiq. stock, also a few new books. Spec: fine, modern illustrated, private press, limited editions. M: P.B.F.A., A.B.A.

NICOLAS BOOKS, 57 Fallowcourt Avenue, Finchley, London N12 0BE. Prop: A. Nicolas. TN: (01) 445-9835. Est: 1969. Private premises; appointment necessary. Small stock sec. and antiq. Spec: Central and Eastern Mediterranean, Greece, Cyprus, Malta, Palestine, general illustrated books and atlases, maps and prints. Corresp: Greek. B: National Westminster Bank, 12 Station Parade, London NW2 4NN. M: P.B.F.A.

STANLEY NOBLE, 24 Gladwell Road, London N8 9AB. TN: (01) 340-2831. Est: 1958. Storeroom and house premises; appointment necessary. Medium stock sec. and antiq. books. Spec: modern first editions, literary criticism; history; economics; philosophy; world politics. Cata: 2 a year. A.B.A.

PRINTING SERVICES, Croyde, Church Crescent, Finchley, London N3 1BE. Prop: Norman F. Bell. TN: (01) 346-3618. Est: 1965. Private premises; appointment necessary. Very small stock sec. and antiq. Spec: books of Irish interest.

RAMBORO ENTERPRISES LIMITED, 64 Pentonville Road, London N1. Prop: Donald Murray. TN: (01) 609-3091. TA: Donsbar, London, N.5. Very large stock of publisher's remainders at showroom, 81 Goswell Road, London, E.C.1. Cata: 4 a year. B: Barclays Bank, 103 Cannon Street, London, E.C.1. Account 20825131.

C.H. & J.S. SANDERS, 59 Stanhope Gardens, London N4 1HY. Est: 1957. Postal business only. Medium sec. and antiq. stock. Spec: history, politics, economics, literature and art. Cata: frequent.

ANTHONY J. SIMMONDS, 214 Archway Road, Highgate, London N6 5AX. TN: (01) 341-2934. Private premises; appointment necessary. Small stock sec. and antiq. books; also new books. Spec: naval, maritime, ships and sea and reprints on same subjects. Cata: on foregoing, 2 a year. B: Barclays Bank, 54 Highgate High St., London, N6 5JD. Account 50801771. M: P.B.F.A.

S. SIMPSON, 1a Granville Road, North Finchley, London N12 0HJ. TN: (01) 445-6723. Private premises; appointment necessary. Very small stock sec. and antiq. Cata: occasionally. B: National Westminster Bank, 48 Ballards Lane, London, N3. Account 37556010

ELIZABETH SPINDEL, 12 CANONBURY GROVE, LONDON N1 2HP. TN: (01) 359-4040. Est: 1979. Private premises; appointment necessary. Small stock sec. and antiq. Spec: modern first editions juveniles since 1900. M: P.B.F.A., N.B.L.

M.A. STROH, 485 SEVEN SISTERS ROAD, TOTTENHAM, LONDON N15 6EP. TN: (01) 802-4635, 802-9721 or 800-0613. Est: 1956. Office premises; postal business only. Very large stock sec. and antiq. books. Spec: history of science. Cata: occasionally. Corresp: Français.

ROBERT TEMPLE, 65 MILDMAY ROAD, LONDON N1 4PU. Prop: P.J. Allen. TN: (01) 254-3674. Est: 1977. Private premises; appointment necessary. Small stock sec. and antiq. Spec: English and American literary first editions. Cata: 7 a year. Corresp: Français, Turkish, Russian. B: Barclays Bank PLC, 40–41 Newington Green, London N16 9PS. Account 50115827.

JOHN TROTTER, 11 LAUREL WAY, LONDON N20. TN: 445 4293. Est: 1973. Private premises; appointment necessary. Medium stock sec. and antiq. books, also prints and maps. Spec: Middle East travel, archaeology, Judaica, Hebraica; Arabia and Islam. Cata: on foregoing, 6 a year. *Shop at* 80 East End Road, London N3. TN: 346 2288. Stocks also new books. Closed Saturdays.

RAY UPTON, 143 QUEEN'S DRIVE, LONDON N4 2BB. Est: 1955. Private premises; appointment necessary. Medium stock sec. and antiq. books; also antiques and fine printing by letterpress. (Collection of historical typefaces.) Spec: London, collecting, travel. Cata: occasionally.

G.W. WALFORD, 186 UPPER STREET, LONDON N1 1RH. TN: (01) 226-5682. Telex: 8813271 (GECOMS G WALFORD). Shop. Large sec. and antiq. stock. Spec: illustrated natural history, travel, science, medicine, social history and economics, fine antiquarian books and sets, topography. Cata: regularly. M: A.B.A.

TIM AND RIKKI WATSON, 134 STOKE NEWINGTON CHURCH STREET, LONDON N16. Prop: T. and R. Watson. TN: (01) 249-8067. Est: 1982. Shop, irregular opening hours, please telephone before coming. Small stock sec. and antiq. B: Midland Bank, Cambridge Circuis, London WC2.

DONALD WEEKS, 106A SHEPHERDESS WALK, LONDON N1. Prop: Donald Weeks. Est: 1975. Private premises; postal only. Very small stock sec. and antiq. B: Detroit Bank and Trust Company, 9-12 Basinghall Street, London, EC2.

GRAHAM WEINER, 78 Rosebery Road, London N10 2LA. TN: (01) 883-8424. Est: 1973. Private premises; appointment necessary. Medium stock sec. and antiq. books. Spec: history and philosophy of science, technology and medicine. Cata: on foregoing, 4 a year. M: A.B.A.

WHETSTONE BOOKS, 368 Oakleigh Road North, Whetstone, London N20. Prop: T.J. Carty. TN: (01) 368-8338. Est: 1977. Shop, closed on Mondays and Thursdays. Small stock sec. and antiq. Corresp: Français. B: National Girobank, Bootle, Merseyside. Account 570514002.

EDNA WHITESON LIMITED, 343 Bowes Road, London N11. Prop: Edna and Maurice Whiteson. TN: (01) 361-1105. Est: 1962. Shop, closed Wednesdays. Large stock sec. and antiq. books. Spec: modern first editions, English literature, travel and topography, early maps and prints. Cata: 3 or 4 a year. B: National Provincial Bank, 98 Cockfosters Road, Cockfosters, Herts. Account 44691661. A.B.A., P.B.F.A.

WORM BOOKS, 36 Conway Road, London N14 7BE. Prop: Mrs. Joyce L. Clark. TN: (01) 886-5799. Est: 1981. Bookfinding service; no stock. B: Co-operative Bank PLC, 1 Islington High Street, London N1 9TR.

44. LONDON (NORTH WEST POSTAL DISTRICTS) AND WEST MIDDLESEX

EDGWARE
HAMPTON
HARROW
HOUNSLOW
LONDON NW
NORTHWOOD
PINNER
STAINES
TEDDINGTON
TWICKENHAM
UXBRIDGE
WEMBLEY

ANTIQUARIAN BOOK COMPANY, 95 Bell Street, London NW1 6TB. Prop: P.J. Cassidy. TN: (01) 262-7661 and 724-0876. Est: 1975. Shop, closed Mondays. Medium stock sec. and antiq. books, also prints.

ALBION BOOKS, 72B Fellows Road, London NW3 3LJ. Prop: Richard Lucas. TN: (01) 722-4738 and (01) 722-6708. Est: 1975. Private premises; appointment necessary. Medium stock sec. and antiq. Cata: lists occasionally. B: Barclays Bank, England's Lane, Haverstock Hill, London, NW3 4YE. Account 40604655. M: P.B.F.A.

ARCHIVE BOOKSTORES, 83 Bell Street, Marylebone, London NW1 6TB. Prop: Tim Meaker. TN: (01) 402-8212. Est: 1973. Shop. Medium stock sec. and antiq. Spec: music. Cata: occasionally. Collections purchased or assessed.

'HE ATTIC GALLERY, 6 Park Road, Teddington, Middlesex. Prop: Graphic Allegra Limited. Est: 1974. Stockroom; appointment necessary. Very small stock sec. and antiq. Also dealers in antiquarian prints and engravings. B: Williams and Glyn's Bank, 21–23 Victoria Street, London SW1H 0HA.

ARAH BADDIEL, 43 Kendal Road, Gladstone Park, London NW10 TN: (01) 452-7243. Est: 1972. Private premises; appointment necessary (08.30 to 20.30 Monday to Saturday). Very small stock sec. and antiq. books, and golfiana. Spec: juvenile and illustrated books. Cata: juvenile and illustrated books, golfiana, motoring, 3 a year. B: Midland Bank, 75 Broadway, London NW7 3BX. Account 91032801. *Also at* Book Gallery, 127 Gray's Antique Market, 58 Davies Street, London W1 Monday to Friday.

. BARON, 136 Chatsworth Road, London NW2 5QU. TN: (01) 459-2035. TA: Musicbaron, London NW2. Est: 1949. Private premises; appointment necessary. Large sec. and antiq. stock of music and books on music only, also musical autographs and letters, portraits and iconography.

BEAGLE BOOKS, 21 Derwent Avenue, Ickenham, Uxbridge, Middlesex. Prop: A.F. and G.B.A. Blakeley. TN: (71) 39189. Est: 1979. Private premises; appointment necessary. Small stock sec. and antiq. Spec: natural history, country life, gardening, modern first editions. Cata: 2 a year. B: Barclays Bank PLC, Swakeleys Road, Ickenham, Middlesex. M: P.B.F.A.

BIBLIAGORA, P.O. Box 7, Hounslow, Middlesex TW3 2LA. Prop: David Rex-Taylor. TN: (01) 894-6262 and (01) 898-1234. Est: 1973. Storerooms; appointment necessary. Large stock sec. and antiq, also new books. Spec: contract bridge; games of skill and chance; conjuring; Bertrand Russell. Cata: occasionally.

BIBLIOPOLA, The Antique Market, 13–25 Church Street, Marylebone, London NW8. Prop: Joseph del Grosso. TN: (01) 723-0429. Shop, closed Mondays. M: A.B.A.

BLACK BIRD BOOKS, 24 Grampian Gardens, London NW2. Prop: James Lay. TN: (01) 455-3069. Est: 1982. Private premises; appointment necessary. Very small stock sec. and antiq. Spec: crime and mysteries. Cata: periodically. B: Co-operative Bank, 78/80 Cornhill, London EC3V 3NJ. M: P.B.F.A.

MR. MICK BODDY [LILY BOOK DEALER], 21A LOWFIELD ROAD, WEST HAMPSTEAD, LONDON NW6 2PP. Prop: Mr. Mick Boddy. Est: 1980. House premises; any time in business hours, and by appointment. Very small stock sec. and antiq. Spec: books, manuscripts, theses, periodicals, articles, anything on lilies (true lilium species and hybrids) only. B: Lloyds Bank, 325 Kilburn High Road, London NW6 7PX.

PAUL BREMAN LIMITED, 1 ROSSLYN HILL, LONDON NW3 5UL. TN: (01) 435-7730. Est: 1961. Private premises, appointment necessary. Very small stock antiq. Spec: architecture, European, military, garden, perspective. Cata: 2 a year. Corresp: Niederlandse, Français, Deutsch. B: National Westminster Bank, 36 St. James's Street, London SW1A 1JF. Account 23108096. M: A.B.A.

D.I. BROWN, 73 PATSHULL ROAD, KENTISH TOWN, LONDON NW5 2LE. TN: (01) 485-2281. Est: 1965. Private premises; appointment necessary. Small stock sec. and antiq. also new books. Cata: 1 a year.

CHANCERY HOUSE BOOKS, 104–106 HARMOOD STREET, CHALK FARM, LONDON NW1. Prop: John Welsh. TN: (01) 485-9331. Est: 1957. Shop, closed Saturday. Very large sec. and antiq. stock. Spec: academic books in all fields, including fine art, history, literature, music, drama, the humanities. Cata: on foregoing, 12 a year. B.A.

MARY CHAPMAN BOOKS, 83 CAMBRIDGE ROAD, NORTH HARROW, MIDDLESEX HA2 7LB. Prop: Mary Chapman. TN: (01) 866-5195. Est: 1975. Private premises; appointment necessary. Small stock sec. and antiq. books. General lists 3 or 4 a year.

COLLEY CIBBER MUSIC SHOP, 63 MAY ROAD, TWICKENHAM, MIDDLESEX TW2 6RJ. Prop: Joanne M. Talbot. TN: (01) 898-9268. Private premises; appointment necessary. Stock of sec. and antiq. music, books and scores. Spec: Americana.

. CSELIK, 26 RISINGHOLME ROAD, HARROW, MIDDLESEX HA3 7ER. Est: 1970. Postal business only. Very small stock sec. and antiq. books. Spec: Hungary and Hungarian people (non-fiction pre-1945).

.G. de LOTZ BOOKS, 20 DOWNSIDE CRESCENT, BELSIZE PARK, LONDON NW3 2AP. TN: (01) 794-5709. TA: Delotzbooks. Est: 1968. Private premises; appointment necessary. Medium stock sec. and antiq. books. Spec: History of warfare, military, naval, aviation. Cata: military, naval, aviation, 1 a year. A.B.A.

LEON DRUCKER, 25 Dicey Avenue, London NW2 6AS. TN: (01) 452-1581. Est: 1957. Private premises; appointment necessary. Medium stock sec. and antiq. books; also new books. Spec: first editions; manuscripts; cinema; modern Prime Ministers. N.B.L.

D.J. DUNBAR, 31 Llanvanor Road, London NW2. TN: (01) 455-9612. Est: 1966. Postal business only. Very small stock sec. and antiq. books. Spec: books about butterflies and moths, topography and plate books.

E.M.S. BOOKS, 223 Salmon Street, London NW9 8ND. Prop: Mrs. E.M. Schiff. TN: (01) 205-2905. Est: 1977. Private premises; appointment necessary. Small stock sec. and antiq. books. Spec: Judaica, Palestine, Middle East, German books. Cata: Jewish books. 2 a year.

FAUNA FLORA BOOKS, 6 The Park, London NW11 7SU. Prop: G.L. Nicol. TN: (01) 455-4295. Est: 1974. Private premises; appointment necessary. Very small stock sec. books. Spec: nutrition and foods, vitamins, health. B: National Westminster Bank, 185 Haverstock Hill, London NW3 4QH.

THE FLASK BOOKSHOP, 6 Flask Walk, Hampstead, London NW3. Prop: Joseph Connolly. TN: (01) 435-2693. Shop. Medium stock sec. and antiq. books. Spec: art, literature, modern first editions P.G. Wodehouse. A.B.A. N.B.L.

FITZJOHNS BOOKS, Northways Parade, College Crescent, Swiss Cottage, London NW3. Prop: Kenneth Smith. TN: (01) 722-9864. Est: 1982. Shop. Medium stock sec. and antiq. B: Barclays Bank, 13 Bournemouth Road, Parkstone, Poole, Dorset. M: P.B.F.A., B.A.

THE FOUR PAGES, 34 Woodhall Drive, Pinner, Middlesex HA5 4TQ. Prop: Christopher and Tessa Davis. TN: (01) 428-7868. Est: 1975. Private premises; appointment necessary. Very small stock sec. and antiq. books. P.B.F.A.

FOSTER-CHERRINGTON, 39 Clarence Gate Gardens, Glentworth Street, London NW1 6BA. Prop: Joan Dyson and Eva Salter. TN: (01) 262-7201. Est: 1978, Private premises; appointment necessary Small stock sec. and antiq. Spec: Central and South America and the West Indies. Cata: 3 or 4 a year.

GUILDHALL BOOKSHOP, 25 York Street, Twickenham, Middlesex TW1 3JZ. TN: (01) 892-0331. Prop: A.F. Wallis, Ltd. Est: 1956 Shop, no early closing. Very large sec. and antiq. stock. A.B.A.
Also at: 8 Victoria Road, Surbiton, Surrey KT6 4JU. Warehouse

appointment necessary. TN: (01) 390-2552. Both premises SW London, 16–20 mins from Waterloo St.

OTTO HAAS, 49 Belsize Park Gardens, London NW3 4JL. Prop: A. & M. Rosenthal. TN: (01) 722-1488. TA: Solmifa London NW3. Est: 1866. House and storeroom, early closing Saturday. Large sec. and antiq. stock. Spec: music, musical literature and autographs. A.B.A., N.B.L.

ANTHONY C. HALL, 30 Staines Road, Twickenham, Middlesex TW2 5AH. TN: (01) 898-2638. TA: Chall, Twickenham. Est: 1966. Shop, and storerooms; early closing Wednesdays & all day Saturday. Small general and very large sec. and antiq. specialist stock. Spec: Russia and Eastern Europe, Middle East, Africa, Asian and European history, industrial history. Cata: on foregoing, occasionally. M: A.B.A., P.B.F.A.

LIONEL HALTER, 7 Hale Lane, Mill Hill, London NW7 3NU. TN: (01) 959-2936. Est: 1975. Shop, closed on Saturdays, open Sunday mornings. Small stock sec. and antiq. books, also printing to the trade. Spec: boxing, signed and limited editions, illustrated books. M: P.B.F.A.

HARROW BOOK SHOP, 14 Clarendon Road, Harrow, Middlesex. Prop: Mrs. H.M. Howard and Mr. K.A. Palfrey. TN: (01) 861-1268. Est: 1980. Shop, closed Tuesdays. Medium stock sec. and antiq. Cata: occasionally. Corresp: Français. B: National Westminster Bank, Saint Annes Road, Harrow, Middlesex.

R.A. HARTLEY, 542 Kings Drive, Wembley, Middlesex HA9 9JD. TN: (01) 904-6413. Private premises; appointment necessary. Very small stock sec. and antiq. books. Spec: boxing (historical & biographical).

THE HAYES BOOKSHOP, 6 GLEBE AVENUE, ICKENHAM, NEAR UXBRIDGE, MIDDLESEX. Prop: Charles and Betty Glover. TN: (01) 573-2813 and (71) 37725. Est: 1948. Shop. Medium stock sec. and antiq. books; also new books.

B. HEYMAN, 45 ROYSTON PARK ROAD, HATCH END, PINNER, MIDDLESEX. Postal business only. Small sec. and antiq. stock. Spec: theatre and drama. occasional lists.

CHARLES HIGHAM (S.P.C.K.), HOLY TRINITY CHURCH, MARYLEBONE ROAD, LONDON NW1 4DU. TN: (01) 387-5282. Shop, closed all day on Saturdays. Very large stock sec. and antiq. theology, also back numbers of journals and new books and periodicals. Spec: theology. Cata: 2–3 a year. M: B.A., N.B.L.

INDIVIDUAL BOOKS, 9 HAMMERS LANE, MILL HILL, LONDON NW7 4BY. Prop: Miss Diana Daniels. TN: (01) 959-1089. Est: 1971. Private premises; appointment necessary. Very small stock sec. and antiq. books; also a few new. Spec: animals and birds. Cata: 3 or 4 a year.

INQUOT LIMITED. 1 HOLMES ROAD, KENTISH TOWN, LONDON NW5 3AA. Prop: Alick and Sheila Elithorn TN: (01) 485-2188. Est: 1976. Shop and store, closed Mondays. Small stock sec. and antiq. and some new books. Spec: Chess and other games: cookery: Childrens' Books B.A.

JOHN IVES ANTIQUARIAN BOOKS, 5 NORMANHURST DRIVE, SAINT MARGARETS, TWICKENHAM, MIDDLESEX TW1 1NA. Prop: John Ives. TN: (01) 892-6265 after 17.00 hours. Est: 1978. Private premises; appointment necessary. Small stock sec. and antiq. Spec: antiques and collecting. Cata: 3 a year. Corresp: Français, Deutsch. B: Barclays Bank PLC, 1 The Causeway, Teddington, Middlesex.

E. JENKINS, 13 MURRAY STREET, LONDON NW1. TN: (01) 485-3690.

PLEASE MENTION THIS DIRECTORY WHEN QUOTING!

CLIFFORD E. KING, 2 Saint John's Lodge, Harley Road, London NW3 3BY. TN: (01) 722-8067. TA: Bellibro London NW3. Private premises, appointment necessary. Antiq. stock. Spec: rare books, Continental early editions, 16th century Italian books. Cata: 1–2 a year. A.B.A.

M.E. KORN, 51 Lady Margaret Road, London NW5 2NH. TN: (01) 267-2936 or (Home) 267-5035. Est: 1969. Private premises, appointment necessary. Medium sec. and antiq. stock. Spec: history of science, natural history, modern first editions, antiquarian. Cata: on foregoing and general, sporadically. A.B.A. P.B.F.A.

HAROLD A. LANDRY, 19 Tanza Road, London NW3 2UA. TN: (01) 435-6167 and (01) 435-8354. Est: 1964. Private premises; appointment necessary. Medium stock sec. and antiq. books. Spec: 19th and 20th century literary and art periodicals. Cata: periodicals. 2 a year.

MARIC BOOKS, Hampstead House, 5b Dene Road, Northwood, Middlesex HA6 2AE. Prop: M.M. & E.S. Snell. TN: (65) 21337. Est: 1977. Private premises; appointment necessary. Very small stock sec. and antiq. also new books. Spec: British fine art, especially watercolourists and etchers. Cata: 2 a year. B: National Westminster, 37 Green Lane, Northwood, Middlesex HA6 3AF.

METROPOLIS (ANTIQUARIAN BOOKS) LTD., 115 Cholmley Gardens, Fortune Green Road, London NW6 1UP. Prop: E.T. and R. Brueck. TN: (01) 435-2753. Est: 1978. Private premises; appointment necessary. Medium stock sec. and antiq. Spec: German books, Judaica, modern first editions especially modern European literature, history and politics. Cata: occasionally. Corresp: Duetsch, Français. B: National Westminster Bank, 280 Finchley Road, London NW3. Account 38152568.

MINERVA RARE BOOKS, Flat 3, 18 East Heath Drive, Hampstead, London NW3. Prop: Paul Rassam. Private premises; appointment necessary. Small stock sec. and antiq. Spec: modern first editions, detective and fantasy fiction, literary periodicals. Cata: 2 or 3 a year. Corresp: Français, Deutsch. B: European American Bank, 10 Columbus Circle, New York 10020, U.S.A. M: P.B.F.A.

GEORGE AND VERA NADOR, 63 Cranbourne Road, Northwood Middlesex. TN: (65) 21152. TA: Nadorbooks, Northwood. Private premises; appointment necessary. Small stock sec. and antiq. Spec: philosophy, logic, Judaica, German, illustrated. Cata: 2 or 3 a year. Corresp: Deutsch. M: P.B.F.A. N.B.L.

AVRIL NOBLE, ABERDARE LODGE, 64 ABERDARE GARDENS, LONDON NW6. Est: 1973. Private premises, but books exhibited at Provincial Booksellers Fairs in London and maps and engravings at shop at 177/8 at Grays, 58 Davies Street, London W1 and at the Panton Gallery, W11 on Saturdays only. Very small stock sec. and antiq. books, also large selection antique maps and engravings. Spec: early topography. P.B.F.A.

OFFSTAGE THEATRE SHOP AND GALLERY, 37 CHALK FARM ROAD, LONDON NW1 8AJ. Prop: B. Dalton. TN: (01) 485-4996. Est: 1982. Shop, closed Mondays, open Sundays. Small stock sec. and antiq., also new books. Spec: the performing arts, particularly theatre. B: National Westminster Bank, 25 Hampstead High Street, London NW3. M: P.B.F.A.

THE OLD BAKEHOUSE BOOKSHOP, 16 THE GREEN, WEST DRAYTON, MIDDLESEX. Prop: Mrs G.M. Deith. TN: (0895) 440516. Est: 1983. Shop, closed Wednesdays. Small stock sec. and antiq. Spec: cookery, wine, gastronomy, gypsies. Cata: 2 a year.

OLD CRICKET, 6 BUCKINGHAM ROAD, HAMPTON, MIDDLESEX TW12 3J. Prop: Deryk Brown. TN: (01) 941-6150. Est: 1982. Private premises; appointment necessary. Very small stock sec. and antiq. Spec: Wisden Cricketers' Almanack, also new books. Cata: occasionally. B: Barclays Bank, 7 High Street, Hampton, Middlesex TW12 2SD.

PHILIPS ANTIQUARIAN BOOKS, 151 BROAD LANE, HAMPTON, MIDDLESEX. Prop: David and Fiona Philips. TN: (01) 979-2453. Est: 1980. Private premises; appointment necessary. very small stock sec. and antiq. Spec: children's, illustrated, miniature, 18th century and early 19th century literature. Cata: 3 a year. B: Lloyds Bank, Hampton, Middlesex.

MARION PITMAN, 29 HAMPTON ROAD, TWICKENHAM, MIDDLESEX. TN: (01) 898 7165. Shop, closed Mondays and Wednesdays.

H. PORDES, 529B FINCHLEY ROAD, LONDON NW3 7BH. TN: (01) 485-9878 and 9879. Shop and storeroom, early closing Saturday. New and large sec. and antiq. stock; also publishers and wholesale booksellers. Spec: bibliography, reprints, antiquarian, learned, scientific and technical periodicals; dictionaries; modern Judaica; remainders. Cata: all subjects, occasionally.

PRIMROSE HILL BOOKS, 134 REGENTS PARK ROAD, LONDON NW1. Prop: R.C. Frew and J.F. Mackenzie. TN: (01) 586-2022. Est: 1977. Shop. Medium stock sec. and antiq. also new books. Spec: art, literature, illustrated, travel. Corresp: Français, Español. B: National Westminster Bank, 508 Edgware Road, London W2 1EN. Account 43971254. M: P.B.F.A., B.A.
Also at 12 AND 13 LIPKA'S ARCADE, 284 WESTBOURNE GROVE, LONDON W11.

MARY E. ROBERTS, 28 SOUTHVIEW AVENUE, NEASDEN, LONDON NW10 1RL. Est: 1968. Private premises, appointment necessary. Small antiq. stock. Spec: topography, colour plate books, fine illustrated books, art. TN: (01) 450-5323.

SCIENTIFIC CIRCULATIONS LIMITED, HORTON ROAD, STANWELL MOOR, STAINES, MIDDLESEX. TN: Colnbrook (028 12) 2266. TA: Halechemic Staines. Est: 1946. Postal business only. Spec: serial periodicals. Monthly lists.

T.F.S. SCOTT, FLAT 3, 32 ETON AVENUE, LONDON NW3 3HL. TN: (01) 794-6640. Est: 1979. Private premises; appointment necessary. Medium stock of antiquarian books. Spec: English literature, Asian and European travel and British topography. M: P.B.F.A.

R.S. AND P.A. SCOWEN, 9 BIRCHWOOD GROVE, HAMPTON, MIDDLESEX TW12 3DU. TN: (01) 979-7429. Est: 1978. Private premises; appointment necessary. Very small stock sec. and antiq. Spec: chess, games. History of computing. Back numbers of journals stocked. Cata: occasionally. Corresp: Français. B: Post Office Giro. Account 32 947 2003.

SEVIN SEYDI, 80 MARQUIS ROAD, LONDON NW1 9UB. Prop: S. Seydi and M. Whitby. TN: (01) 485-9801. Est: 1970. Private premises: appointment necessary. Medium stock sec. and antiq. also back numbers of journals. Spec: classical antiquity, early continental. Back numbers of journals. Cata: occasionally. Corresp: Français. B:

National Westminster Bank, 300 King's Road, SW3. Account 30060184.

RITA SHENTON, 148 Percy Road, Twickenham, Middlesex TW2 6JG. TN: (01) 894-6888. Est: 1974. Private premises; stock available any day but telephone first. Small stock sec. and antiq. also new. Books and periodicals on horology only. Cata: available.

IAN SHERIDAN'S BOOKSHOP AT HAMPTON, 34 Thames Street, Hampton, Middlesex. Prop: Ian Sheridan. TN: (01) 979-1704. Est: 1960. Shop, stockroom and private premises; open till 7 p.m., 7 days a week. Large stock sec. and antiq. Corresp: Français, Deutsch.

STANLEY SMITH AND KEITH FAWKES BOOKSHOP, 1–3 Flask Walk, Hampstead, London NW3. TN: (01) 435-0614. Est: 1977. Shop. Very large stock sec. and antiq. books. Spec: art, literature, music, sciences, illustrated, rare book department. A.B.A.

THE SOCIAL SCIENCES BOOKSHOP LIMITED, 74 Park Chase, Wembley, Middlesex HA9 8EH. Directors: Norma Feather and Raymond Feather, LL.B., Dip.Soc. TN: (01) 902-3659. Est: 1968. Private premises; appointment necessary. (Nearest Underground Railway station, Wembley Park, (Metropolitan Line). Stock of 25,000 books and 100,000 pamphlets, reports and runs of journals in the social and behavioural sciences. Spec: criminology and penal reform, housing and town planning, history and methodology of education, psychology and psychiatry, sociology, social services and local government; economics. Cata: on foregoing, occasionally. Corresp: Deutsch, Yiddish, Hebrew. B: Midland Bank, Wembley Park, Wembley.

M. SOLOMONS, 16 Waltham Avenue, Kingsbury, London NW9 9SJ. TN: (01) 204-6094. Est: 1975. Postal business only. Very small stock sec. and antiq. books. Spec: law, books about books. Cata: 2 a year.

ERIC & JOAN STEVENS, 74 FORTUNE GREEN ROAD, LONDON NW6 1DS. TN: (01) 435-7545. Est: 1961. Shop, offices and storeroom, open Saturdays only or by appointment. Medium sec. and antiq. stock. Spec: scholarly, poetry, literature and art of 19th and 20th centuries, feminism, Powys family, Edward Thomas. Cata: 4 a year. Corresp: Français, Deutsch. A.B.A.

MYRIL STEVENSON, 40 THE HIGHLANDS, EDGWARE, MIDDLESEX HA8 5HL. TN: (01) 952-6362. Est: 1971. Private premises, appointment necessary. Small stock sec. and antiq. books. Spec: English literature, art and illustrated books, Old English country customs, crafts, gardening. Cata: on foregoing, 4 a year.

BARBARA STONE, ALFIE'S ANTIQUE MARKET, 13 CHURCH STREET, LONDON NW8 6EE. Prop: Barbara Stone. TN: (01) 723-2829. Est: 1975. Shop, closed Mondays. Small stock sec. and antiq. Spec: early children's books, illustrated books, books on the arts. Cata: 4 a year. Corresp: Français, Español. B: National Westminster Bank, 16 Finchley Road, London NW8 6EE. M: P.B.F.A.

UNICORN BOOKS, 10 Faber Gardens, Hendon, London NW4 4NR. Prop: Mrs. Sheila Feller. TN: (01) 202-6342. Est: 1969. Private premises; appointment necessary. Very small stock sec. and antiq. Spec: children's books, illustrated books, bibliography. Cata: about 6 a year. Corresp: Français, Italiano. B: Lloyds Bank, 1/3 Finchley Lane, Hendon, London NW4. M: P.B.F.A.

VILLAGE BOOKSHOP, 46 Belsize Lane, Belsize Village, London NW3. Prop: D.M. Smith and B. Harrison. TN: (01) 794-3180. Est: 1967. Shop. Medium stock. Spec: 19th century sec. and antiq. and pre-war German books.

JEANETTE WHITE, c/o 61 Park Road, London NW1 6XG. (late of Richmond Antiquary, Richmond, Surrey). Postal business only. Spec: juveniles. Cata: 3 or 4 a year. B: National Westminster Bank, Baker Street Station Branch, London W1. Account 12189782.

45. LONDON (SOUTH EAST POSTAL DISTRICTS)

STUART BENNETT, 35 Breakspear's Road, London SE4 1XR. TN: (01) 691-8805. Private premises; appointment necessary.

BOOKS OF BLACKHEATH, 11 Tranquil Vale, London SE3 0BU. Prop: A. Irving. TN: (01) 852-8185. Est: 1970. Shop, first floor, open Fridays and Saturdays. Medium stock sec. and antiq. books; also new books. (New book department open every weekday.)

BOOKSHOP BLACKHEATH LIMITED, 74 TRANQUIL VALE, BLACKHEATH, LONDON SE3 0BN. Prop: L. Leff. TN: (01) 852-4786. Est: 1949. Shop, closed Thursday. Large sec. and antiq. stock, some new. Spec: Kent, London, general travel. Cata: general, 2 a year. A.B.A. N.B.L.

THE BOOKSHOP, CRYSTAL PALACE, 89 CHURCH ROAD, UPPER NORWOOD, LONDON SE19. Prop: J.S.H. Collins. TN: (01) 771-9719. Est: 1967. Shop, no early closing. Medium sec. and antiq. stock.

FIONA CAMPBELL, 158 LAMBETH ROAD, LONDON SE1. TN: (01) 928-1633. Est: 1970. Private premises; appointment necessary. Small stock sec. and antiq. books, also bookbinding. Spec: books on Italy, travel; Victoriana. Cata: occasionally. A.B.A. N.B.L.

CHECK BOOKS, 14 CAMDEN ROW, BLACKHEATH, LONDON SE3 0XY. Prop: Gabriel Beaumont. TN: (01) 852-5888 & 318-0460. Est: 1979. Private premises; appointment necessary. Small stock sec. and antiq.

Spec: foreign topography, history, anthropology, art. Cata: 5 a year. Corresp: Français, Deutsch. B: Lloyds Bank, Blackheath, London SE3. M: P.B.F.A.

CHILDHOOD BOOKS, 132 Macoma Road, London SE18 2QZ. Prop: Michael and Nicole Gill. TN: (01) 854-1963. Est: 1981. Private premises; appointment necessary. Small stock sec. and antiq. Spec: juvenile fiction, some adult fantasy, illustrated books. Cata: 6 a year. B: Barclays Bank, Plumstead Common Road Branch, 69 Plumstead Common Road, London SE18 3AR.

J.W. DANIELS, 98 Foxberry Road, London SE4. TN: (01) 274-4728. Shop, open first two Saturdays of each month or by appointment. Very small stock sec. and antiq. books. Spec: football.

DONALD FRASER, 48 Dalkeith Road, West Dulwich, London SE21. TN: (01) 670-3274. House premises; appointment necessary. Sec. and antiq. stock.

THE GALLERY BOOKSHOP, 1 Carlton Terrace, Dulwich Village, London SE21 7DE. Prop: R.W. Collins. TN: (01) 693-2808. Shop. Small stock sec. and antiq., also new books. M: B.A.

JANE GIBBERD, 20 Lower Marsh, London SE1 7RJ. TN: (01) 633-9562. Est: 1968. Shop, closed Monday, Tuesday & Saturday. Small sec. stock.

GILHAM BOOKS, 4 Saint Austell Road, London SE13. Prop: Margaret Mendel M.A., B.Mus. TN: (01) 852-1905. Est: 1983. Private premises; appointment necessary. Very Very small stock sec. and antiq. Spec: music.

HILLYERS, 301 Sydenham Road, London SE26. Prop: T.A. Hillyer. TN: (01) 778-6361 and (01) 777-2506 (Home). Est: 1953. Shop, closed Wednesdays. Small sec. and antiq. stock, also antiques, furniture, china and glass.

SIMON JUDD, 177 Peckham Rye, London SE15 3HZ. TN: (01) 639-4486.

PAUL KEANE, 93 Camberwell Grove, London SE5 8JH. TN: (01) 701-3450. Private premises, appointment necessary. Very small sec. and antiq. stock. Spec: decorative arts 1880-1940, decorative and commercial art periodicals, advertising annuals.

MARCET BOOKS, 4a Nelson Road, Greenwich, London SE10. Prop: Martin Kemp. TN: (01) 853-5408. Est: 1981. Shop. Small stock sec. and antiq. B: Lloyds Bank, Greenwich. M: P.B.F.A.

MAYOW BOOKS, 46 Bishopsthorpe Road, London SE26 4PA. Prop: H.L. Spilstead. TN: (01) 778-2128. Est: 1970. Private premises; appointment necessary. Small stock sec. and antiq. Spec: 1890's, art, music, illustrated, English literature. B: Midland Bank, 14 Sydenham Road, London, SE26 4PA. Account 61022873. M: Private Libraries Association. P.B.F.A.

PHANTASMAGORIA BOOKS, 8 Colwell Road, London SE22. Prop: John Eggeling. TN: (01) 693-1938. Est: 1971. Office and showroom, open Monday to Friday, but appointment advisable. Small stock sec. and antiq. books; also selected new books. Spec: science fiction, fantasy, weird; pre-war fiction magazines. Cata: on foregoing, 8 a year. The Ephemera Society.

NIGEL PHILLIPS, 26 Radcliffe Square, Putney Hill, London SW15. Prop: Nigel Phillips. TN: (01) 788-2664 (24 hours). TA: INPRINCIPIO London SW15. Telex: 28604 Ref 589. Est: 1981. Private premises appointment necessary. Spec: history of medicine, science and technology, history of ideas. Cata: 2 a year. Corresp: Français, Deutsch.

M.C.D. RANSON, 215 Stanstead Road, London SE23 1HU. Est: 1975. Postal business only. Small stock sec. and antiq. books, also selected new books. Spec: art (fine and decorative), antiques, numismatics. Cata: occasionally.

ROGERS TURNER BOOKS LIMITED, 22 Nelson Road, London SE10. TN: (01) 853-5271. Shop, early closing Thursdays. Medium stock sec. and antiq. Spec: German, horology, science, academic history, linguistics. Cata: 6 or 8 a year. Corresp: English, French, German, Spanish.
Paris Office: 24 rue du Buisson Richard, F-78600 Le Mesnil-le-Roi, France. TN: 3 912 11 91.

AUDREY SALKELD, Flat 5, 21 Dartmouth Row, London SE10. Est: 1968. Private premises, appointment necessary. Very small sec. and antiq. stock, also new books. Spec: mountaineering, mountain topography and travel, polar, caving, countryside. Cata: on foregoing, 4-5 a year.

NORMAN SHAW, 84 Belvedere Road, London SE19 2HZ. TN: (01) 771-9857. Private premises, appointment necessary. Large sec. and antiq. Private premises; appointment necessary. Large sec. and antiq. stock. Spec: old boys' books, journals, juvenile.

SPREAD EAGLE BOOKSHOP, 8 Nevada Street, Greenwich, London SE10. Prop: Richard F. Moy. TN: (01) 692-1618. Est: 1960. Shop. Medium stock sec. and antiq. Spec: travel and topography, the arts, theatre and cinema, modern history, children's books, bindings. Corresp: Français, Deutsch. B: Barclays Bank, Blackheath Village, London SE3.

STONE TROUGH BOOKS, 59 Camberwell Grove, London SE5 8JA. Prop: George Ramsden. TN: (01) 708 0612. Shop; open 10.00 to 18.00 hrs, closed Mondays. Medium stock sec. and antiq. Spec: modern first editions.

ROMAN UMAISTOWSKI, 1 Fountain Drive, London SE19. Private premises, appointment necessary. Spec: atlases, maps. Large collection of American maps. Views of Italy, Poland, Germany, Scandinavia, Africa and Australia; world maps 15th to 17th centuries.

WARWICK LEADLAY GALLERY, 5 Nelson Road, Greenwich, London SE10 9JB. Prop: Warwick Leadlay. TN: (01) 858-0317. Est: 1974. Shop, also by appointment. Very small stock sec. and antiq. Spec: illustrated books, maps and prints, especially South East London and North West Kent material. Cata: prints and maps occasionally. B: National Westminster Bank PLC, Blackheath Village Branch, London SE3 9RH.

WELL READ BOOKSHOP, 61 Roupell Street, London SE1. Prop: Kathleen P. Collins. TN: (01) 928-1828. Est: 1980. Shop; closed on Mondays and Saturdays. Large stock sec. and antiq. also prints. B: Barclays Bank, British Museum Branch, 2 Bloomsbury Way, WC1A 2TF. Account 10132101.

.E. WHITEHART, 40 Priestfield Road, Forest Hill, London SE23 2RS. TN: (01) 699-3225. Est: 1952. Private premises, but open normal business hours (early closing Wednesdays) and by appointment. Medium stock sec. and antiq. books and a few specialist new. Medicine, science and technology only, no general stock. Cata: 4 a year. M: A.B.A., P.B.F.A.

46. LONDON (SOUTH WEST POSTAL DISTRICTS)

J.A. ALLEN & CO. [THE HORSEMAN'S BOOKSHOP] LIMITED, 1 Lower Grosvenor Place, Buckingham Palace Road, London SW1W 0EL. TN: (01) 828-8855 and (01) 834-5606. Est: 1910. Shop and storerooms. New, sec. and antiq. stock. Spec: horses, horseriding, racing, breeding, driving, polo and other horse sports only; no general stock. Cata: (a) current new books, (b) antiquarian books. A.B.A. B.A. N.B.L.

ANTIQUICO LIMITED, 22 Thurloe Street, London SW7 2LT. Prop: F. Pulteney. TN: (01) 589-0522. Est: 1950. Shop, early closing Saturdays; appointment necessary. Small stock sec. and antiq. books; also new. B.A.

CHARMIAN APPS, 112 Brompton Road, London SW7. Private premises; appointment necessary. Small sec. and antiq. stock. Spec: perfumery, cosmetics, coiffure (history and technology). Cata: general, occasionally.

M. & M. BALDWIN, 98 Kenyon Street, London SW6 6LB. Prop: M. & M. Baldwin. TN: (01) 385-2036. Est: 1978. Private premises; appointment necessary. Small stock sec. and antiq. and back numbers of journals. Spec: transport and industrial history, particularly canals. Cata: 3–4 per year. Corresp: Français. B: National Westminster Bank, 322 Lillie Road, London SW6 7PR. Account 03901726.

WILLIAM BARNES, 86 Saint Dion's Road, Parson's Green, London SW6. TN: (01) 736-5860. Private premises; appointment necessary. Very small stock sec. and antiq. books. Early cinema and Victorian photography only.

ROBIN DE BEAUMONT, 25 Park Walk, Chelsea, London SW10 0AJ TN: (01) 352-3440. Est: 1980. Private premises; appointment necessary. Very small stock sec. and antiq. Spec: Victorian colour printing, Victorian illustrated, art, architecture, fine bindings. Cata occasionally. Corresp: Français. M: A.B.A.

JOANNA BOOTH, 247 Kings Road, London SW3. TN: (01) 352-8998 Est: 1965. Shop. Medium stock antiq. books; also antiques. Spec French, history and literature 17th, 18th and 19th centuries. Cata: 2 year. M: A.B.A.

D. M&CDONALD-BOOTH, 45 Melton Court, Old Brompton Road London SW7. TN: (01) 589-4068.

R. CAMERON, 37b Redcliffe Gardens, London SW10. TN: (01 352-0029. Est: 1962. Private premises; appointment necessary. Ver small stock sec. and antiq. books. Spec: Persia and Persian art. B: Barclays Bank, 30 Sloane Square, London, S.W.1.

CAVENDISH RARE BOOKS, 2–4 PRINCES ARCADE, PICCADILLY, LONDON SW1Y 6DS. Prop: Barbara Gigor-Taylor. TN: (01) 734 3840. Est: 1974. Shop. Large stock sec. and antiq. books. Spec: travel and voyages, maritime history. mountaineering, polar, English literature, sets, printed ephemera. M: N.B.L., A.B.A.

CHELSEA RARE BOOKS, 313 KINGS ROAD, LONDON SW3 5EP. Prop: L.S. Bernard. TN: (01) 351-0950. TA: Bookmark London SW3. Shop. Medium stock sec. and antiq. books. Spec: English literature; illustrated books; travel, antique maps and prints. Cata: literature and travel, 3 a year. M: A.B.A.

L. CHRISTIE, 129 FRANCISCAN ROAD, TOOTING, LONDON SW17 8DZ. TN: (01) 672-4024. Est: 1957 (formerly at Streatham). Private premises; appointment necessary. Small stock sec. and antiq. Spec: entomology, miniature books. Some new books also stocked.

COBB & WEBB, 21 LACY ROAD, PUTNEY, LONDON SW15. Prop: John Willson. TN: (01) 789-8840. Est: 1971. Shop. Medium sec. and antiq. stock; also new books.

THE CONSTANT READER, 627 FULHAM ROAD, LONDON SW6. Prop: Geoffrey and Anna Mullett. TN: (01) 731-0218. Est: 1982. Shop. Medium stock sec. and antiq. Spec: Oriental, general travel. Corresp: Français. B: Lloyds Bank, 118 High Street, Hungerford, Berkshire.

COSTUME AND FASHION BOOKSHOP, QUEEN'S ELM PARADE, OLD CHURCH STREET, CHELSEA, LONDON SW3 6EJ. Prop: Lesley Hodges. TN: (01) 352-1176. Est: 1979. Shop, closed Saturdays. Small stock sec. and antiq. also back-numbers of journals stocked and new books. Spec: costume and fashion. Cata: 2 a year. Corresp: Deutsch, Français. B: National Westminster Bank, Old Church Street Branch, 243 Fulham Road, SW3. Account 05937868.

GARY DE VERE, 33 HELIX GARDENS, LONDON SW2 2JI. TN: (01) 674-4511. Est: 1966. Private premises; a postal business only. Very large stock sec. and antiq. Spec: Australasian; minor 19th century novels; feminism.

JOHN FAUSTUS, 94 JERMYN STREET, LONDON SW1Y 6JE. Prop: Faustus Bibliographics Ltd. TN: (01) 839-3388. Est: 1970. Shop, closed Saturdays. Small stock sec. and antiq. books. Spec: fine bindings. Cata: occasionally.

FERRET FANTASY, 27 BEECHCROFT ROAD, UPPER TOOTING, LONDON SW17 7BX. Prop: G.W. and R.M. Locke. TN: (01) 767-0029. Est: 1971. Private premises; appointment necessary. Medium stock sec. and antiq. also new books and publishing. Spec: Fiction (science, detective, Victorian, Sherlockiana, modern firsts), proof copies. Cata: on foregoing 5 or 6 a year. M: P.B.F.A., A.B.A.
Also at: 30 SACKVILLE STREET (BASEMENT) LONDON W1X 1DB Shop.

FOLLIES, STAND M7, ANTIQUARIUS, 135 KINGS ROAD, LONDON SW3. Prop: Mr. & Mrs. H. Carlton. TN: (01) 352-1129. Est: 1974. Shop. Very small stock sec. and antiq. books; also postcards and ephemera. Spec: children's illustrated, performing arts.

PETER C. FORREST, 14 WARRINER GARDENS, LONDON SW11. TN: (01) 622-9635. Est: 1960. Private premises, appointment necessary. Medium sec. and antiq. stock. Spec: Americana, travel.

GLOUCESTER ROAD BOOKSHOP, 123 GLOUCESTER ROAD, LONDON SW7. Prop: Nick Dennys. TN: (01) 370-3503. Est: 1983. Shop. Medium stock sec. and antiq. Cata: occasionally. Corresp: Deutsch. B: National Westminster Bank, 88 Cromwell Road, London SW7. M: B.A.

DAVID GODFREY'S OLD NEWSPAPER SHOP, 37 KINNERTON STREET, LONDON SW1X 8ED. Prop: David Godfrey. TN: (01) 235-7788. Est: 1972. Shop, open 11.30–3.30, also by appointment. Closed Saturdays. Medium stock antiq. and 20th century newspapers; no books. Newspapers classified according to most interesting contents.

E.P. GOLDSCHMIDT & COMPANY, LTD., 64 DRAYTON GARDENS, SOUTH KENSINGTON, LONDON SW10 9SB. Prop: J.L. Vellekoop. TN: (01) 373-2266. TA: Playbook London. Est: 1923. Private premises, appointment necessary. Medium antiq. stock. Spec: books of the 16th and 17th centuries. Cata: on foregoing, 3 a year. ABA. ILAB.

GREENWAY BOOKS, 56 TELFORD AVENUE, LONDON SW2 4XF. Prop: Guy Abel. TN: (01) 674-3930. Est: 1981. Private premises; postal business only. Very small stock sec. and antiq. Spec: Penguins. Cata: 2 a year. B: Lloyds Bank PLC, 39 Piccadilly, London W1.

ROBIN GREER, 30 SLOANE COURT WEST, LONDON SW3. TN: (01) 736-5438 (Mon-Fri.10.00 to 16.00) (01) 730-7392 (Other times). TA: Rarities, London SW3. Est: 1966. Private premises; appointment necessary. Small stock sec. and antiq. books. Spec: children's; illustrated; travel. Cata: illustrated and travel, 5 a year. A.B.A.

GREY HOUSE BOOKS, 12A LAWRENCE STREET, CHELSEA, LONDON SW3 5NE. Prop: Mrs. Camille Wolff. TN: (01) 352-7725. Est: 1972. Private premises; appointment necessary (any day, including Sundays).

Small stock sec. and antiq. books. Spec: only detective fiction, criminology, notable British trials. Cata: on foregoing, occasionally. P.B.F.A.

VICTOR HALL, 44 HARCOURT TERRACE, LONDON SW10 9JR.

HAN-SHAN TANG LIMITED, 717 FULHAM ROAD, LONDON SW6 5HL. Prop: Ch. Von der Burg. (01) 731-2447. TA: Hanshanbooks. Est: 1972 (Stockholm), 1978 (London). Shop; closed on Saturdays, unless by appointment, on other days appointment preferable. Large stock sec. and antiq. and back numbers of journals and new books also publishing in related fields. Spec: art and culture of the Far East, publications in oriental languages. Cata: 8 per year. Corresp: Français, Deutsch, Italiano, Swedish and Japanese. B: Midland Bank, 196a Piccadilly, W.1. Account 81046837. European Bank & Trust Company, 10 Hanover Square, New York, NY10079. Account 1112817190. M: A.B.A.

HAMMERSMITH BOOKS, LIFFORD'S PLACE, BARNES HIGH STREET, LONDON SW13. Prop: The Hammersmith Bookshop Ltd. TN: (01) 876-7254. TA: Hamboox London S.W.13. Est: 1948. Warehouse. Specialist mail order bookseller. Over 100,000 titles on Economics, World Politics and Social History. Special areas: Afro-Asian-Soviet Affairs; Russia, old and new; Socialism, Communism, Anarchism, Suffragettes, Trade Unions; War, Revolution, Peace; Resistance and Guerrillas; Spanish Civil War; African-Negro-West Indian writers; Russian authors.

HARRINGTON BROTHERS, CHELSEA ANTIQUE MARKET, 253 KINGS ROAD, LONDON SW3. TN: (01) 352-5689. Est: 1968. Shop. Large stock strictly antiquarian books. Spec: illustrated, natural history, voyages and travel, Europe and Middle East, children's illustrated and bound sets, also good general stock including maps.

THOMAS HENEAGE & CO. LIMITED, 26 CHELSHAM ROAD, LONDON SW4 6NP. Prop: Thomas Heneage. TN: (01) 720-1503. Telex: 893359. Est: 1977. Private premises; appointment necessary. Small stock sec. and antiq. Spec: fine and applied art, archaeology. Corresp: Français. Cata: 2 or 3 a year. B: Barclays Bank, 12a Curzon Street, London. Also Barclays Bank of New York, 9 West 57th Street, N.Y.

HERALDRY TODAY, 10 BEAUCHAMP PLACE, LONDON SW3. Prop: Mrs. R. Pinches. TN: (01) 584-1656. Est: 1954. Shop, closed Thursday, Friday and Saturday. Medium sec. and antiq. stock, also new books. Spec: heraldry, genealogy, topography. Cata: 3 a year.

HOLLYWOOD ROAD BOOKSHOP, 8 Hollywood Road, London SW10.

STEPHANIE HOPPEN LIMITED, The Studio, 17 Walton Street, London SW3. Prop: Stephanie Hoppen. TN: (01) 589-3678. Est: 1966. Shop, closed Mondays. Small stock sec. and antiq. Spec: atlases, voyages, maps, 16th century illustrated books, gastronomy, antique prints of flowers and fruits, shells, caricatures, curiosities. Cata: 3 a year. Corresp: Deutsch, Français, Italiano. B: Williams & Glyn's Bank, 24 Grosvenor Place, SW1. Account 10086205. M: A.B.A.

ISLAND BOOKS, 1A Pinfold Road, Streatham, London SW16 2SL. Prop: S.F.J. Westall. TN: (01) 769-5396. Est: 1973. House premises; stock can be seen during normal business hours. Small stock sec. and antiq. books. Spec: bibliography and palaeography, British topography and local history. Cata: 4 a year. Corresp: Français. B: National Westminster Bank, 266 Streatham High Road, London, S.W.16. Account 23488530.

JENNINGS BOOKSHOP, 556 Streatham High Road, Streatham, London SW16 3QG. Prop: A.H. Jennings. TN: (01) 764-8135. Est: 1909. Shop, open Thursday, Friday & Saturday. Medium stock sec. and antiq. also new books.

H.D. LYON, 18 Selwood Terrace, London SW7. TN: (01) 373-2709. Private premises, appointment necessary. Antiq. stock. A.B.A.

JUDITH MANSFIELD, 60A Dornton Road, London SW12. Prop: Judith Mansfield. TN: (01) 673-6635. Est: 1981. Private premises; appointment necessary. Very small stock sec. and antiq. Spec: embroidery, lace, textiles and related subjects. Cata: approximately 2 a year. B: Midland Bank, Upper Tooting, London SW17.

THE MAP HOUSE, 54 Beauchamp Place, Knightsbridge, London SW3 1NY. Prop: The Earl of Mexborough and the Hon. C.A. Savile. TN: (01) 589-4325 and (01) 589-9821. TA: Mappamundi. Est: 1907. Shop. Small stock antiq. books and large stock antique maps and atlases and engravings, also new guide books and maps. Cata: antique maps, occasionally. B.A.

FRANCIS MARSDEN, c/o 140–142 King's Road, Chelsea, London SW3 4UX. TN: (01) 735-8570. Est: 1946. Private premises; mail order only. New, sec. and antiq. stock. Spec: British art and architecture. A.B.A. B.A. N.B.L.

NICHOLAS MEINERTZHAGEN, 82 RITHERDON ROAD, LONDON SW17 8QG. TN: (01) 672-2288. Private premises; appointment necessary. Small stock sec. and antiq. books. Spec: old and rare, French and German, philosophy and economics, science and medicine.

HAROLD MORTLAKE AND CO., 28 FERRY ROAD, BARNES, LONDON SW13 9PR. TN: (01) 748-9675. Private premises; appointment necessary. A.B.A.

ORBIS BOOKS (LONDON) LTD., 66 KENWAY ROAD, LONDON SW5 0RD. Prop: Aleksandra Kulczcka. TN: (01) 370-2210. Est: 1972. Shop. Small stock sec. and antiq. also new books. Spec: Polish books, all subjects, but mainly history and literature. Cata: 3 a year. Corresp: Français, Deutsch, Polish, Russian. B: Midland Bank PLC, 95 Gloucester Road, London SW7 4SX. M: B.A.

MIKE PARK, 119 SOUTH PARK ROAD, WIMBLEDON, LONDON SW9 8RX. Prop: Mike Park and Ian Smith. TN: (01) 542-8390. Est: 1974. Private premises; appointment necessary. Small stock sec. and antiq. Spec: gardening, botany and natural history. Cata: 6 a year. B: National Westminster Bank, 8 Station Parade, Kew, Richmond, Surrey. Account 38976226.

MICHAEL PHELPS, 19 CHELVERTON ROAD, PUTNEY, LONDON SW15 1RN. TN: (01) 785-6766. Est: 1974. Private premises; appointment necessary. Medium stock sec. and antiq. books; a few new. Spec: history of medicine, natural, pure and applied science. Cata: on foregoing, 4 a year.

PICKERING & CHATTO LIMITED, 16 AND 17 PALL MALL, LONDON SW1Y 5NB. Chairman: Sir William Rees-Mogg. TN: (01) 930-2515. TA: Lycious, London SW1. Est: 1809. Shop. Medium sec. and antiq. stock. Spec: English literature and history, science and medicine, economics, politics and philosophy, autographs and manuscripts, music, travel. Cata: regularly.

THE PORTMAN BOOKSTORE, PORTMAN HOUSE, 17 BRODRICK ROAD, LONDON SW17 7DZ. Prop: Mary Camidge. TN: (01) 672-1022. Est: 1977. Private premises; appointment necessary. Large stock sec. and antiq. Spec: juvenile fiction illustrated, annuals, comics and cinema. Cata: 2-3 a year. B: Barclays Bank, Wandsworth Common. Account 40872520.

JOHN RANDALL [BOOKS OF ASIA], 717 FULHAM ROAD, LONDON SW6 5UL. Prop: John Randall. TN: (01) 736-9424. Est: 1979. Shop. Medium stock sec. and antiq. also new books. Spec: Asian and Pacific arts and culture. Corresp: Français, Malay. B: Lloyds Bank, 39 Old Bond Street, London W1. M: P.B.F.A.

WILLIAM REEVES BOOKSELLER LIMITED, 1A NORBURY CRESCENT, LONDON SW16 4JR. TN: (01) 764-2108. Est: 1871. Storeroom, appointment essential; early closing Saturday. New, and medium sec. and antiq. stock. Spec: music and music books. Cata: occasionally. A.B.A.

SAINT GEORGE'S GALLERY BOOKS LIMITED, 8 DUKE STREET, SAINT JAMES'S, LONDON SW1. TN: (01) 930-0935. Shop, early closing Saturday. New, and small sec. and antiq. stock. Spec: fine art. Cata: fine art, monthly. B.A.

THOMAS E. SCHUSTER, 9 GILLINGHAM ROAD, LONDON SW1. TN: (01) 828-7963. Est: 1973. Shop, closed Saturday. Also by appointment. Medium stock antiq. books, very large stock antiq. maps and prints. Spec: natural history, botany, topography, atlases, maps and prints by David Roberts and Audubon. Cata: 1 a year. Corresp: Deutsch. B: Barclays Bank, New York, U.S.A. M: A.B.A., P.B.F.A.

TIMOTHY SHAW, 1 LANARK PLACE, LONDON W9 1BT. TN: (01) 289-1200. Est: 1975. Shop. Small stock antiq. books. Cata: occasionally.

SIMS, REED AND FOGG LIMITED, 58 Jermyn Street, London SW1Y 6LX. TN: (01) 493-5660 and (01) 493-0952. Est: 1976. Office. Medium stock sec. and antiq. books. Spec: art reference; decorative arts; architecture; illustrated books. Cata: fine and applied art, 8 a year.

SNOWDEN SMITH BOOKS, 41 Godfrey Street, London SW3 3SX. TN: (01) 352-6756. TA: Snosmith, London SW3. Est: 1974. Private premises; appointment necessary. Very small stock sec. and antiq. books. Spec: travel; anthropology, Middle East, Asia, Africa and Australia. Cata: 2 or 3 a year.

SPINK & SON LIMITED, 5–7 King Street, Saint James's, London SW1Y 6QR. TN: (01) 930-7888. Telex: 916711 (Spink). TA: Spink London S.W.1. Est: 1666. Shop, closed Saturday. Spec: numismatics. Cata: coin and medal collecting and books. 'The Numismatic Circular', 10 issues a year. 5.

VICTOR SUTCLIFFE, 36 Parklands Road, London SW16 6TE. TN: (01) 769-8345. Est: 1969. Private premises; appointment necessary. Very small stock sec. and antiq. Spec: military history before 1914. Cata: 12 a year.

TROCCHI RARE BOOKS, Antiquarius, Stands L8 and L9, 15 Flood Street, Kings Road, London SW3 4PW. Prop: Alexander Trocchi. TN: (01) 351-3820. Est: 1970. Shop. Small stock sec. and antiq. Spec: travel, art, natural history, literature, illustrated books. A few back numbers of journals stocked. Cata: occasionally. Corresp: Français. B: Royal Bank of Scotland, Imperial House, 15 Kingsway, WC2. Account 270303.

VANDELEUR ANTIQUARIAN BOOKS, 69 Sheen Lane, London SW14. TN: (01) 878-6837 and (01) 393 7752. TA: Brybec, Epsom. Est: 1971. Shop, but prior telephone call advised. Medium stock sec. and antiq. books. Spec: travel and exploration, big game hunting, natural history. Cata: irregularly. M: P.B.F.A.

RICHARD VON HÜNERSDORFF, 57 Drayton Gardens, London SW10. TN: (01) 373-3899. TA: Nacatenus London, S.W.10. Est: 1969. Private premises, appointment necessary. Medium antiq. stock. Spec: rare and important continental books of 15th to 19th centuries, history of medicine & science, military science, Latin America. Cata: 1 a year. A.B.A. V.D.A.

ROWLAND WARD'S OF KNIGHTSBRIDGE LIMITED, 25 Lowndes Street, London SW1X 9JF. TN: (01) 235-4844. TA: Jumboglas London SW1. Est: over 100 years. Shop, closed Saturdays and Sundays. Very small stock sec. and antiq. books; also new books and engraved glass. Spec: big game, natural history, ornithology, field sports; Africana. Cata: on foregoing, 2 a year. B.A.

JEREMY F. WEST, 34 Fullerton Road, Wandsworth, London SW18. TN: (01) 870-7555. Spec: topography.

BAYNTON-WILLIAMS, 18 Lowndes Street, Belgravia, London SW1X 9EY. Prop: R.H. Baynton-Williams. TN: (01) 235-6595. Est: 1946. Shop, early closing Saturday. Very large stock antique maps and prints, very small antiq. books stock. Spec: antique maps and prints. Cata: occasionally. A.B.A. B.A.D.A.

N.E.I. WOOD, 12 Wetherby Gardens, London S.W.5. TN: (01) 373-7206. Est: 1968. Private premises, appointment necessary. Very small sec. and antiq. stock. Spec: Greece, Middle East, Turkey and Cyprus. Cata: occasionally.

WOODRUFF RARE BOOKS, 26 Yeoman's Row, Knightsbridge, London SW3. Prop: Charles Woodruff. TN: (01) 584-0370. Private premises; appointment necessary. Very small stock sec. and antiq. Spec: British topography, architecture, applied art. Cata: 4 a year. Corresp: Français. B: Coutts & Co., 188 Fleet Street, London EC4A 2HT.

HARRIET WYNTER LIMITED, 50 Redcliffe Road, London SW10 9NJ. TN: (01) 352-6494. Telex 21879. ATT: Harriet. Est: 1956. Private premises; telephone for appointment. Small stock sec. and antiq. books; also new books and antique scientific instruments. Spec: history of science and technology. Cata: on foregoing, occasionally. B: Barclays Bank 20-63-41. Account 90434698. M: British Antique Dealers Association.

47. LONDON (WEST POSTAL DISTRICTS)

ANY AMOUNT OF BOOKS, 103 Hammersmith Road, London W14. Prop: N. Burwood. TN: (01) 603-9232. Est: 1976. Shop, open 11.00 to 19.00 hrs. closed Mondays. Medium stock sec. and antiq. books. Spec: art, modern bookplates. Corresp: Deutsch, Français, Español.

AUSTRALIANA, Stand A30, Grays Antiques, Davies Mews, London W1. Prop: Pam Fisher. TN: (01) 629-2813 or (0491) 35077 (home). Est: 1979. Stand open every Wednesday or by appointment. Small stock books, maps, prints on Australia, mostly 19th century or earlier. Cata: occasionally. M: P.B.F.A.

BRIAN L. BAILEY, Westbourne Antique Arcade, 113 Portobello Road, London, W11. TN: (01) 229-1692. Est: 1973. Stand on Saturdays only between 09.00 and 16.00 hrs. Medium stock sec. and antiq. Spec: topography and illustrated books. B: Barclays Bank, 35 Notting Hill Gate, W11 3JR. Account 20141518.

DAVID BATTERHAM, 36 Alexander Street, London W2. TN: (01) 229-3845. Est: 1966. Shop, appointment necessary. Small stock sec. and antiq. books. Spec: art; applied arts; fashion; caricature. Cata: applied art; advertising, 5 or 6 a year.

BOOKS & THINGS, Dolphin Arcade, 157 Portobello Road, London W11. Prop: M.M. Steenson. TN: (01) 370-5593. Est: 1972. Shop, open Saturdays only. Small stock sec. and antiq. books. Spec: children's and 20th century illustrated, first editions, decorative art, original illustrations and posters. Cata: on foregoing, 2 a year. B: Barclays Bank, 11 Bruton Street, London W1X 8DN. Account 70843547. M: P.B.F.A., A.B.A.

THE BOOKSMITH, 201 KENSINGTON HIGH STREET, LONDON W6 6BA. Prop: Bill Smith and Fred Bass. TN: (01) 937-5002. Mainly publishers' remainders; also new books. B.A.

JOHN BURKE & PARTNERS, 20 PEMBRIDGE ROAD, KENSINGTON, LONDON, W11 3HL. TN: (01) 229-0862. Est: 1959. Shop, closed Thursdays. Medium sec. and antiq. stock, also antiques. Spec: travel, fine bindings, literature.

GABRIEL L. BYRNE AND DENISE FRANCIS, WESTBOURNE GROVE ANTIQUE ARCADE, WESTBOURNE GROVE, LONDON W11. TN: (01) 727-6054 (Answerphone). Est: 1966. Stand, open Saturdays only. Small stock sec. and antiq. books. Spec: topography, travel, illustrated. Cata: occasionally.

JOHN CUMMING, 22 CONWAY STREET, LONDON, W1P 5HP. TN: (01) 388-3029. Est: 1978. Private premises; appointment necessary. Very small stock sec. and antiq. Spec: illustrated books to 1850 including natural history, travel, topography, atlases, historical documents and printed ephemera. Corresp: Deutsch, Français.

DEMETZY BOOKS, 113 PORTOBELLO ROAD, LONDON, W11. Prop: A.P. and M. Hutchinson. TN: (0993) 2209. Est: 1971. Shop; open on Saturdays only, 09.00 to 15.30 hrs. Medium stock sec. and antiq. Spec: leather bound books, cookery, natural history, medicine, architecture and miniature books. Corresp: Deutsch, Français. B: Barclays Bank, High Street, Witney, Oxon. Account 70507946. M: A.B.A., P.B.F.A. Correspondence to: Manor House, Ducklington, Witney, Oxfordshire OX8 7UX.

MAGGIE DOBSON BOOKS, 70 BLACK LION LANE, LONDON W6. TN: (01) 748-1943. Est: 1974. Postal business only. Very small stock sec. and antiq. books; also some new. Spec: 20th century art.

R. DRUMMOND, 30 HART GROVE, EALING COMMON, LONDON, W5 3NB. TN: (01) 992-1974. Private premises, appointment necessary. New, and small sec. and antiq. stock. Spec: all crafts only. Cata: art and craft (one for each craft), frequently. Corresp: Français. B: National Westminster Bank, Ealing Common, London W5. B.A.

PETER EATON, 80 HOLLAND PARK AVENUE, LONDON W11 3RE. TN: (01) 727-5211. TA: Peatenboox London W.11. Est: 1938. Shop. Very large sec. and antiq. stock. A.B.A. B.A. N.B.L.

ANDREW EDMUNDS, 44 Lexington Street, London W1R 3LH. TN: (01) 437-8594 and (01) 439-8066. TA: Satire London-W1. Shop, closed Saturdays. Very small antiq. stock, also large stock of prints and some drawings. Spec: prints, illustrated books, caricature.

FRANCIS EDWARDS LIMITED, 83 Marylebone High Street, London W1M 4AL. TN: (01) 935-9221. TA: Finality London W.1. Est: 1855. Shop, closed Saturday. Very large antiq. stock. Spec: Africa, Australia, America, Far East, Atlases, Military, Naval, Mountaineering, natural history; general literature; history, early English literature; incunabula, bibliography; topography. Cata: general and specialized, about 12 a year. A.B.A. N.B.L.

DEREK EVANS, 35 Pembridge Square, London W2 4DT. TN: (01) 221-3603. Business by post only. Small stock sec. and antiq. Spec: European literature in English translation

EXPRESS BOOK SERVICE, 13 Beryl Road, London W6 8JS. Prop: G.G. Stevens. Est: 1948. Spec: Polish, Russian Antiquarian Books. Cata: 4–6 a year.

FERRET FIRST EDITIONS, 30 Sackville Street (Basement) London W1X 1DB. Shop, open Tuesdays to Fridays 12.00 to 18.00 hrs. Sec. and antiq. stock. Spec: fantasy and detective fiction, modern firsts, Victorian fiction. P.B.F.A.

RICHARD FORD, 70 Chaucer Road, London W3 6DP. Prop: Richard Ford. TN: (01) 993-1235. Est: 1982. Private premises; appointment necessary. Small stock sec. and antiq. Spec: autographs, historical documents. Cata: 2 a year. Corresp: Français, Italiano. M: P.B.F.A.

W.A. FOSTER, 134 AND 183 CHISWICK HIGH ROAD, LONDON W4. TN: (01) 995-2768 and 994-1610. Est: 1968. Shop, closed Thursday. Large sec. and antiq. stock, prints. Watercolours only at 183. illustrated books 1830-1930, fine bindings.

FULLER D'ARCH SMITH, 37B NEW CAVENDISH STREET, LONDON W1M 8JR. Prop: Jean Overton Fuller and Timothy D'Arch Smith. TN: (01) 722-0063. Est: 1969. Private premises; appointment necessary. Very small stock sec. and antiq. also new books to order. Cata: occasionally. Corresp: Deutsch, Français, Italiano, Russian. B: Lloyds Bank, Cox and King's Branch, 6 Pall Mall, London SW1Y 5NH.

M. & R. GLENDALE, 9A NEW CAVENDISH STREET, LONDON W1. Prop: R. Sands and M. Sears. TN: (01) 487-5348. Est: 1970. Shop closed on Saturdays. Open other days between 10.00 and 18.00 hrs. Small stock sec. and antiq. Spec: juvenilia, illustrated books, social history, ephemera, games. Corresp: Italiano, Français, Deutsch, Polish. Cata 2-3 yearly. B: Barclays Bank, 135 Finchley Road, London, NW3 6JA Account 80390410. M: A.B.A.

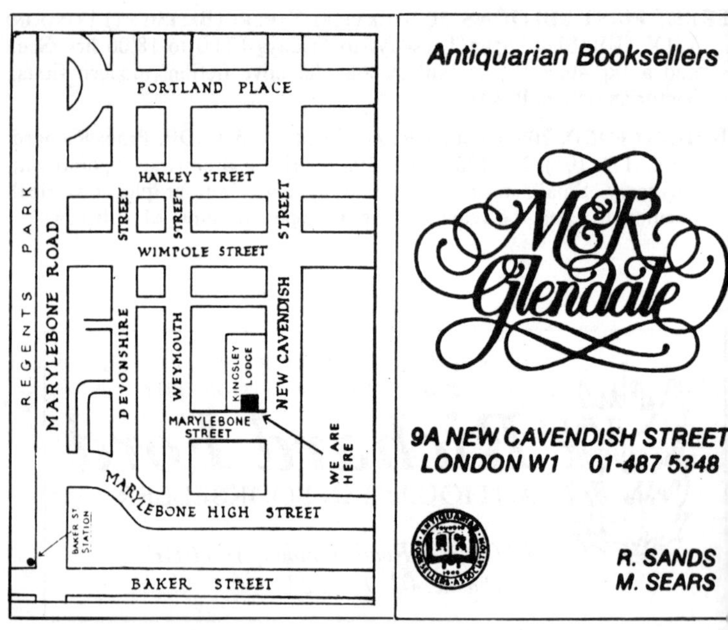

G.L. GREEN, 104 Pitshanger Lane, Ealing, London W5 1QX. TN: (01) 997-6454. Est: 1974. Shop, open Wednesdays to Saturdays. Medium stock sec. and antiq. books; also new books. Spec: naval and maritime. Cata: naval and maritime, 12 a year. B: National Girobank. Account 501224009.

R.D. GURNEY LIMITED, 23 Campden Street, Kensington Church Street, London W.8. TN: (01) 727-6644. Private premises, appointment necessary, early closing Saturday. Small antiq. stock. Spec: medicine and science. Cata: on foregoing, 3 a year. A.B.A.

HAB BOOKS, 35 Wellington Road, Ealing, London W5 4UJ. Prop: T. Habraszewski. Est: 1981. Private premises; postal service only. Small stock sec. and antiq. Spec: biography, theology, politics, Eastern Europe, books in Polish. Cata: occasional lists. Corresp: Polish. B: National Westminster Bank, London.

HATCHARDS, 187 Piccadilly, London W1V 9DA. TN: (01) 439-9921. Est: 1797. Shop, early closing Saturday. Small sec. and antiq. stock also new books. Catalogues. Spec: fine bindings, travel, illustrated books, childrens books, English literature. Cata: 1 a year. Corresp: Français, Deutsch. B: Clydesdale Bank, Piccadilly Circus, London, W.1. Account 70000220. A.B.A. B.A. N.B.L.

G. HEYWOOD HILL LIMITED, 10 Curzon Street, London W1Y 7FJ. TN: (01) 629-0647. A.B.A.

ROBERT HUMM, 6 Fairlawn Grove, London W4 5EH. Prop: Robert and Clare Humm. TN: (01) 995-5005. Est: 1974. Private premises; appointment necessary. Small stock sec. and antiq. Spec: railways and transport, industrial history. Cata: 2 or 3 a year. B: National Westminster Bank, 61 Victoria Street, London SW1.

IRENE EDITIONS, 5c Shepherd Street, Mayfair, London W1Y 7LD. Prop: Barry Phelps. TN: (01) 499-9800. Est: 1977. Private premises; postal business only. Very small stock sec. and antiq. and some back numbers of journals and new books. Spec: P.G. Wodehouse, modern firsts. Cata: 4 a year. B: Coutts & Company, Lombard Street, London EC3.

E. JOSEPH, 1 Vere Street, London W1M 9HQ. TN: (01) 493-8353. Telex: 893231 (joseph g.) Cables: Bookjos-London W1. Est: 1876 (formerly in Charing Cross Road).

JOTHCO BOOKS, 38 HORNTON STREET, LONDON, W8 4NT. Prop: Jonathon Schrire. TN: (01) 937-6195. Est: 1979. Private premises; appointment necessary. Very small stock sec. and antiq. Spec: hand coloured plate books on natural history, travel and illustrated private press books. M: P.B.F.A.

M. KEMP, 14–15 LONDON MEWS, LONDON STREET, LONDON W.2. TN: (01) 723-0487. Office and warehouse; postal business only. Small sec. and antiq. stock. Spec: topography, detective fiction, food and drink.

PETER LOVEDAY PRINTS, 46 NORLAND SQUARE, LONDON W11 4PZ. Prop: Peter Loveday. TN: (01) 221-4479. Est: 1976. Private premises; appointment necessary. Very small stock sec. and antiq. also new books. Spec: sporting art and animals, prints. M: L.A.P.A.D.A.

MAGGS BROTHERS LIMITED, 50 BERKELEY SQUARE, LONDON W1X 6EL. TN: (01) 499-2007 and 499-2051. TA: Bibliolite London W.1. Shop and storerooms. Antiq. stock. Spec: rare books, illuminated manuscripts, autograph letters. Cata: all subjects, sometimes charged. A.B.A. B.A. N.B.L. B.A.D.A.

MARLBOROUGH RARE BOOKS LIMITED, 35 OLD BOND STREET, LONDON W1X 4PT. TN: (01) 493-6993. TA: Bondlibro London W.1. Shop, closed Saturday. Small sec. and antiq. stock. Spec: illustrated books, fine arts, architecture, bibliography. Cata: 4 a year. M: A.B.A.

D. MELLOR AND A.L. BAXTER, 121A KENSINGTON CHURCH STREET, LONDON W8 7LP. Prop: D. Mellor and A.L. Baxter. TN: (01) 229-2033. Est: 1968. Shop. Medium stock sec. and antiq. Spec: sciences, travel, rare books. Cata: 1 or 2 a year. Regular short lists. B: Midland Bank, 1 Sydney Place, London SW7. M: L.A.P.A.D.A.

CHRISTOPHER MENDEZ, 51 LEXINGTON STREET, LONDON W1R 4HL. TN: (01) 734-2385. Est: 1966. Shop, closed Saturdays. Very small stock sec. and antiq. books. Spec: old Master and English 18th century prints. Cata: on foregoing, 3 a year. A.B.A.

W.T. MORRELL & COMPANY LIMITED, 2, 3 4 AND 5 SACKVILLE STREET, PICCADILLY, LONDON W1X 2DP. TN: (01) 734-0308. Est: circa 1860. Very small new and sec. stock in fine bindings, general and fine.

NIBRIS BOOKS, FLAT 2, 76 WESTBOURNE TERRACE, LONDON W2 60A Prop: Nigel Israel. TN: (01) 402 5984. Est. 1980. Private premises; appointment necessary. Very small stock sec. and antiq. Spec: Gemstones and jewellery. Cata: occasionally. B: Midland Bank, 64 Finsbury Pavement, London EC2A 1ND.

THE PARKER GALLERY, 2 ALBERMARLE STREET, PICCADILLY, LONDON W1X 3HF. TN: (01) 499-5906. Prop: Thomas H. Parker, Ltd. TA: Taychpee London W.1. Gallery, open to public and trade. Old historical prints and paintings; no books. Also relics and ships' models. Spec: marine, military, sporting and topographical prints. Cata: on foregoing, annually. N.B.L. B.A.D.A. Soc. of London Art Dealers

PICCADILLY RARE BOOKS LIMITED, (INCORPORATING THE WORLD OF BOOKS). 30 SACKVILLE STREET, LONDON W1X 1DB. Prop: Paul Minet. TN: (01) 437-2135. Est: 1974. Shop open seven days a week from 10.00 to 18.00 hrs. Very large stock sec. and antiq. Spec: travel, history, biography and cookery, also remainder dealers. Cata: 4 a year. M: A.B.A., P.B.F.A.

WILLIAM POOLE, 97 NEW BOND STREET, LONDON W1Y 9LF. TN: (01) 629-8738. Est: 1979. Private premises; appointment necessary. Small stock sec. and antiq. Spec: books prior to 1800, English and continental literature, Greek and Latin classics, humanism, early science, Foulis Press. Cata: 2 a year.

JONATHAN POTTER LTD., 1 GRAFTON STREET, LONDON W1X 3LB. Prop: Jonathan Potter. TN: (01) 491-3520. Est: 1975. Shop: Open Mon-Fri, also Saturday 9.30-11.30 only. Large stock sec. and antiq. maps and atlases; also reference books on the history of cartography. Cata: 1 a year. Lists occasionally. M: A.B.A.

PUBLISHING & DISTRIBUTING COMPANY LIMITED, 177 REGENT STREET, LONDON W1. TN: (01) 734-6534. TA: Pubdisco London W.1. Overseas and United Kingdom trade directories. Cata: of directories. 1.50, of overseas newspapers and periodicals, 2 volumes, 4.00.

BERNARD QUARITCH LIMITED, 5–8 LOWER JOHN STREET, GOLDEN SQUARE, LONDON W1R 4AU. TN: (01) 734-2983. Telex: 8955509. TA: Quaritch London W.1. Est: 1847. Shop. Rare books and manuscripts. Spec: incunabula, early printed, 18th, 19th and 20th century literature, natural history, old science and medicine, travel, bibliography, Orientalia, politics, philosophy, economics and autograph letters, signed, from all periods. A.B.A.

LESLIE ROBERT, 74 DEVONPORT, SUSSEX GARDENS, LONDON. Prop: Leslie Robert. TN: (01) 402-9567. Est: 1978. Private premises; appointment necessary. Very small stock sec. and antiq. Spec: psychology, sociology, medical. B: Barclays Bank, 19/21 Brook Street, London W1.

CHARLOTTE ROBINSON, 35 GREAT PULTENEY STREET, LONDON W1. TN: (01) 437-3683. Shop, open 11–6 p.m. Spec: modern first editions, children's illustrated, World War I, Henry Williamson. Catalogues issued.

ROBERT G. SAWERS, P.O. BOX 40A, LONDON W1A 4QA. TN: (01) 267-3316. Est: 1971. Private premises, appointment necessary. Very small sec. and antiq. stock, also Japanese prints and Japanese and Chinese painting. Spec: Oriental. M: A.B.A.

CHAS. J. SAWYER, NO. 1, GRAFTON STREET, BOND STREET, LONDON W1X 3LB. TN: (01) 493-3810. TA: Vespucci London W.1. Est: 1894. Shop, early closing Saturday. Large antiq. stock. Spec: rare and fine books, bindings, manuscripts, illustrated books and original works of book illustrators, Africana, etc. Cata: on foregoing, 6 a year, charged.

SEAL BOOKS, 2 CONINGSBY ROAD, LONDON W5 4HR. Prop: E.A. Lewisohn. TN: (01) 567-7198. Est: 1970. Shop, closed Monday and Tuesday. Large sec. and antiq. stock. Spec: English literature, History, topography, natural Hist. Also nearby Bookroom (by appt.) 567 8452.

A.F. SEPHTON, 16 BLOEMFONTEIN AVENUE, SHEPHERDS BUSH, LONDON W12 7BL. TN: (01) 749-1454. Est: 1966. Private premises, appointment necessary. Very small sec. and antiq. stock. Spec: plate books and 18th century engravings by William Hogarth.

BERNARD J. SHAPERO, GRAY'S ANTIQUE MARKET, 58 DAVIES STREET, LONDON, W.1. TN: (01) 449-4340. Est: 1978. Shop. Small stock sec. and antiq. Spec: Baedeker travel guides, plate books, sporting. Cata: 1 a year. Corresp: Deutsch, Français, Italiano. B: Lloyds Bank, Baker Street, London, W1. Account 0244509. M: P.B.F.A.

JAMES SMITH, 94 GRAYS INN ROAD, LONDON W1X 8AA. TN: (01) 405-5697. New, and very small sec. stock.

HENRY SOTHERAN LIMITED, 2, 3, 4 AND 5 SACKVILLE STREET, PICCADILLY, LONDON, W1X 2DP. Managing Director: R.D. Kirkman. TN: (01) 734-1150 and 734-0308. TA: Bookmen London-W1. Est: 1761 in York, 1815 in London. Shop, closed Saturdays. Very large stock sec. and antiq. and new books; also autographs, prints and bookbinding. Spec: natural history; fine bindings. Cata: fine books, general, occasionally. B: Lloyds Bank, Piccadilly, London, W.1. Account 0287713. M: B.A., A.B.A., N.B.L. Fine Art Trade Guild.

STRAND BOOKS, 166 THAMES ROAD, STRAND ON THE GREEEN, LONDON W4. Prop: J.R. Compston. TN: (01) 994-1912. Est: 1978. Shop, closed Mondays, open Sundays. Small stock sec. and antiq. and some back-numbers of journals, also antiques. Cata: occasionally. B: Lloyds Bank, Ryde, Isle of Wight. Account 0065063.

MELVIN TENNER, 76 LADBROKE GROVE, LONDON W11 2HE. Prop: Melvin Tenner and Eva Callomon. TN: (01) 229-7794. TA: Politikos London W11. Est: 1980. Private premises; appointment necessary. Small sec. stock; some new. Spec: politics, international affairs, strategic studies. Cata: on foregoing, 2 a year.

TRADITION, 5A AND 5B SHEPHERD STREET, MAYFAIR, LONDON W1Y 7LD. TN: (01) 493-7452. Est: 1947. Shop, early closing Saturdays Small sec. and antiq. stock of military items only also new books.

THE TRAVEL BOOKSHOP LIMITED, 13 BLENHEIM CRESCENT LONDON W11 2EE. Prop: Sarah Anderson. TN: (01) 229-5260. Est 1980. Shop; closed on Mondays. Medium stock sec. and antiq. Spec travel books and all related subjects. Back numbers of journals stocked and new books and periodicals. B: Drummonds Bank, 49 Charing Cross, S.W.1. Account 00272660. M: B.A.

WELBECK GALLERY, 18 THAYER STREET, LONDON W1M 5LD. Prop Mr. & Mrs. Spellman. TN: (01) 935-4825. Est: 1975. Shop, early closing Saturdays. Spec: prints. B: National Provincial Bank Marylebone High Street, London, W.1. Account 04527496.

MRS. TERESA WHITE, Flat 9, 47 Bassett Road, London W10 6JX. Postal business only.

WHOLEFOOD BOOKS, 24 PADDINGTON STREET, LONDON W1M 4DR. TN: (01) 935-3924. Est: 1960. Shop, early closing Saturdays. Very small stock sec. and antiq. books; also new books and organically grown produce and restaurant. Spec: organic husbandry, ecology, natural health. Corresp: Français.

WORLD OF BOOKS, 30 SACKVILLE STREET, LONDON W1X 1DB. See: Piccadilly Rare Books Ltd. TN: (01) 437-2135.

48. LONDON (WEST CENTRAL POSTAL DISTRICTS)

THE ALTERNATIVE BOOKSHOP, 3 Langley Court, Covent Garden, London WC2E 9JY. TN: (01) 240-1804. Est: 1980. Shop. Very small stock sec. and antiq. also new books. Spec: Libertarian books all subjects.

ANGLEBOOKS LIMITED, 2 Cecil Court, London WC2. Prop: M. Holman. TN: (01) 836-2922. Est: 1968. Shop, closed Saturdays. Medium stock sec. and antiq. books. Spec: English local history and topography; angling. Cata: on foregoing, 4 a year. A.B.A.

ATLANTIS BOOKSHOP, 49a Museum Street, London WC1A 1LY. Prop: Mrs. K.P. Collins. TN: (01) 405-2120. Shop. Medium stock sec. and antiq. books; also new books. Spec: occult, astrology, palmistry, magic, myth, legend, tarot, Yoga, E.S.P., I-Ching, Qabbalah, Works of Crowley; microscopy. Cata: Crowley, Qabbalah, I-Ching, Tarot, occasionally.

BELL, BOOK & RADMALL LIMITED, 4 CECIL COURT, LONDON WC2N 4HE. Directors: C.T.A. Radmall and J.G.R. Bell. TN: (01) 240-2161 and (01) 836-5888. Est: 1975. Shop, closed Saturdays. Large stock sec. and antiq. books. Spec: first editions of English and American literature, detective, science and fantasy fiction, first editions etc. Cata: 6 a year. M: A.B.A.

ANDREW BLOCK, 20 BARTER STREET, LONDON WC1. TN: (01) 405-9660. Est: 1911. Shop and storeroom, no early closing. Large sec. and antiq. stock. Spec: drama and entertainment; also ephemera. B: Midland Bank, 52 Oxford Street, London W1. Account 400517. Member of the Bibliographical Society. ABA Private Libraries Association, Ephemera Society.

BLOOMSBURY BOOKSHOP, 31–35 GREAT ORMOND STREET, LONDON WC1N 3HZ. Prop: Teresa Chilton. TN: (01) 242-6780. Est: 1967. Shop, closed Saturdays. Small stock sec. and antiq. books; new books on Jazz. Spec: Jazz; Bloomsbury group of writers.

LOUIS W. BONDY, 16 LITTLE RUSSELL STREET, LONDON WC1A 2HN. TN: (01) 405-2733. Est: 1946. Shop. Medium sec. and antiq. stock. Spec: the 16th century; rare, old and modern illustrated books, early juvenile and education, miniature books. Cata: general, 1 a year. M: A.B.A.

THE BOOKSMITH, 33 MAIDEN LANE, LONDON WC2E 7JS. Prop: Bill Smith and Fred Bass. TN: (01) 836-3341. Est: 1965. Shops. Some sec. and antiq. and new paperbacks, publishers' remainders. Cata: general, 4 or 5 a year. B.A.
Also at 148 CHARING CROSS ROAD, LONDON WC2H 0LB. TN: (01) 836-3032. *and at* 36 SAINT MARTIN'S LANE, LONDON WC2N 4ER. TN: (01) 836-5110. *and at* 33 MAIDEN LANE, LONDON WC2E 7JS *and at* BRIGHTON, Q.V.

BOSWELL BOOKS AND PRINTS, 44 GREAT RUSSELL STREET, LONDON WC1B 3PA. Prop: Christopher Busby and John Rose. TN: (01) 580-7200. Est: 1981. Shop. Small stock sec. and antiq. Spec: Japanese woodblock prints; Japan, China; 18th and 19th century natural history; English literature. Corresp: Français, Deutsch, Italiano, Español, Slav Languages, Chinese. B: Barclays Bank PLC, 2 Bloomsbury Way, London WC1A 2TF.

ALAN BRETT LIMITED, 24 CECIL COURT, CHARING CROSS, LONDON WC2N 4HE. TN: (01) 856-8222. TA: Brettbooks Ldn-WC2. Telex: 268048 (Ext. Ldn G). Shop and storeroom. Very small stock sec. and antiq. Spec: topographical, maps and prints, foreign and continental, plate books, maps from 1540. B: Lloyds Bank, Camden Town, London, N.W.

CLIVE BURDEN, 13 CECIL COURT, CHARING CROSS ROAD, LONDON WC2. TN: (01) 836-2177. Shop, closed Saturdays. Medium sec. and antiq. stock. Spec: natural history, antique maps, prints etc. A.B.A.

BURNETT & SIMEONE LIMITED, c/o THE BOOKSHOP, 29 MUSEUM STREET, LONDON WC1A 1LH. TN: (01) 637-5862. Est: 1979. Shop. Large stock antiq. music and music books. Cata: 3 a year.

MARY CAMPBELL [IRISH BOOKS] LONDON, 37 WHARTON STREET, LONDON WC1. TN: (01) 837-2978. Est: 1978. Private premises; appointment necessary. Small stock sec. and antiq. Spec: Irish interest. Small stock of back numbers of journals stocked. Cata: specialist lists on request.

FRANK CASS [BOOKS] LIMITED, 10 WOBURN WALK, LONDON WC1. TN: (01) 387-7340. Telex: 897 719. TA: Simfay London WC1. Est: 1952. Shop, closed Saturday. Medium sec. and antiq. stock. Spec: Africana, Oriental, history, economics, medicine, science, travel, parliamentary papers.

CENTRAL BOOKS, 37 GRAYS INN ROAD, LONDON WC1X 8PS. TN: (01) 242-6166. TA: Cenbooks, London WC1X 8PS. Est: circa 1940. Shop. Small stock sec. and antiq. also new books. Spec: Marxism, Socialism. Cata: 3 a year. Corresp: Français, Deutsch. B: National Westminster Bank, Borough Branch, 34 Borough High Street, London SE1. M: B.A.

CHANCERY LANE BOOKSHOP, 6 CHICHESTER RENTS, CHANCERY LANE, LONDON WC2A 1EJ. Prop: E.C. Nolan. TN: (01) 405-0635. Est: 1971. Shop, closed Saturday. Large sec. and antiq. stock. Spec: Irish books, travel, London and suburbs. Cata: general, 5 a year.

THE CINEMA BOOKSHOP, 13–14 GREAT RUSSELL STREET, LONDON WC1B 3NH. Prop: Fred Zentner. TN: (01) 637-0206. Est: 1969. Shop, no early closing. Large sec. and antiq. stock and new books exclusively on cinema.

COLLINS & GRAY, 49A MUSEUM STREET, LONDON WC1A 1LY. Prop: Mrs. K.P. Collins, TN: (01) 405-2120. Shop. Medium stock sec. and antiq. books; also new books. Spec: natural history; microscopy.

DANCE BOOKS LTD. 9 CECIL COURT, CHARING CROSS ROAD, LONDON WC2N 4EZ. Prop: John O'Brien and David Leonard. TN: (01) 836-2314. Est: 1961. Shop and storeroom, no early closing. Small sec. and antiq. stock, also new books. Spec: ballet and dance. Cata: new books. B.A.

LEWIS DAVENPORT, 51 GREAT RUSSELL STREET, LONDON WC1. TN: (01) 405-8524. Est: 1898. Shop, early closing Saturdays. Small stock sec. and antiq. also tricks, jokes and puzzles. Spec: conjuring, ventriloquism, games and recreation, puzzles, white magic.

DICKENS' OLD CURIOSITY SHOP, 13 & 14 PORTSMOUTH STREET, KINGSWAY, LONDON WC2. TN: (01) 405-9891. Shop, no early closing. New, and very small sec. and antiq. stock.

DILLONS UNIVERSITY BOOKSHOP LIMITED, 1 MALET STREET, LONDON WC1E 7JB. TN: (01) 636-1577 (15 lines). Est: 1938. Shop and storeroom, early closing Saturday. Very large sec. and antiq. stock, and very large stock new books. Spec: academic and rare, industrial history. M: A.B.A., B.A., N.B.L.

ROBERT DOUWMA LIMITED, 4 HENRIETTA STREET, LONDON WC2E 8QU. TN: (01) 636-4895. TA: Wedou London. Shop. Large stock of maps, and of topographical and decorative prints. Spec: topography, (British and foreign), prints and maps. Cata: selected subjects. M: A.B.A., N.B.L.

THE ECONOMISTS' BOOKSHOP LIMITED, CLARE MARKET, PORTUGAL STREET, LONDON WC2. Prop: The Economist and The London School of Economics. TN: (01) 405-5531. Est: 1947. Shop, closed Saturday. Medium sec. stock. Spec: economics, statistics, history, politics, geography, antropology, psychology, sociology, business. Cata: on foregoing and the social sciences generally, 3–4 a year. B.A. N.B.L.

THE ECONOMISTS BOOKSHOP, ['SHOP ACROSS THE STREET'], PORTUGAL STREET, LONDON WC2. TN: (01) 405-5532. Est: 1966. Shop, closed Saturdays. Large stock sec. and antiq. books. and new periodicals. Spec: social science, history, philosophy. B.A., N.B.L.

FINE BOOKS ORIENTAL LIMITED, EMPIRE HOUSE, 34–35 HIGH HOLBORN, LONDON WC1. Prop: Jeffrey Somers. TN: (01) 405-0676 (0650 24 hours). TA: Orientome, London WC1. Est: 1977. Shop, closed Saturdays. Small stock sec. and antiq. Spec: Japan, The Far East, The Middle East. Cata: monthly. Corresp: Français, Japanese. B: Barclays Bank, 9 Gracechurch Street, London EC3. Account 50372153. M: P.B.F.A.

H.M. FLETCHER, 27 CECIL COURT, CHARING CROSS ROAD, LONDON WC2N 4EZ. Prop: W.R., I.M. and K.R. Fletcher. TN: (01) 836-2865. Telex: 28905 Ref: 2865. TA: Achemeff London WC2. Est: 1906. Shop, closed Saturdays. Large sec. and antiq. stock. A.B.A. (Past President). N.B.L.

W. & G. FOYLE LIMITED, 119 CHARING CROSS ROAD, LONDON WC2. TN: (01) 437-5660. TA: Foylibra London W.C.2. Shops, no early closing. New, and large antiq. stock. Cata: general. M: A.B.A., B.A., N.B.L.

FROGNAL RARE BOOKS, 18 CECIL COURT, LONDON WC2N 4HE. Prop: The Frognal Bookshop Ltd. TN: (01) 240-2815. TA: Finresbook, London, W.C.2. Est: 1955. Shop. Large sec. and antiq. stock. Spec: Law (Before 1850), history, economics, sociology. Cata: 3-4 a year. Corresp: Français, Deutsch, Italiano. B: Barclays Bank, 171 Broadway. Cricklewood, London, NW2 3JB.

GAY'S-THE-WORD BOOKSHOP, 66 MARCHMONT STREET, LONDON WC1. TN: (01) 278-7654. Shop and Café. Small sec. stock; also new books. Spec: homosexual and feminist.

GOLFIANA MISCELLANEA LIMITED, HAMPDEN HOUSE, 84 KINGSWAY, LONDON WC2. Prop: David White. TN: (01) 405-5323. Est: 1973. Showroom, appointment necessary. Small stock sec. and antiq. books on golf only. M: N.B.L.

GREEN KNIGHT BOOKSHOP, 34 SAINT MARTIN'S COURT, LONDON WC2. TN: (01) 836-3800. Shop. Small stock sec. and antiq. Spec: literature and the Arts. Prop: Keith Nicholson, Peter Freeman.

HELLENIC BOOKSERVICE, 122 CHARING CROSS ROAD, LONDON WC2H 0JR. Props: Mrs. P. Constantinou and Mrs. M. Stoddart. TN: (01) 836-7071. Est: 1966. Shop, no early closing. Medium size sec. and antiq. stock also new books. Spec: Greece, Cyprus, Crete, Greek Islands, Turkey, Balkans; religion, prints, Byzantium, classics, art, architecture, books in Greek: Cata: on foregoing, 1 a year. B.A.

HOLBORN BOOKS, 14 CHARING CROSS ROAD, LEICESTER SQUARE, LONDON WC2. Prop: John Adrian. TN: (01) 240-2337. Est: 1970. Shop, open seven days a week. Large stock sec. and antiq. Cata: 1 a year. B: Overseas Trust Bank of Hong Kong, 30 Old Compton Street, London WC. Chinese and Oriental Booksellers Association, Hong Kong.

DON HOLDER, THE MARCHMONT BOOKSHOP, 39 BURTON STREET, LONDON WC1. Shop.

IMAGES, 16 CECIL COURT, CHARING CROSS ROAD, LONDON WC2N 4HE. Prop: Peter Stockham. TN: (01) 836-8661. Shop. Large stock sec. and antiq. books. Backnumbers of children's journals, ephemera, also Book Trade Consultancy. Spec: art and illustrated books, children's books and toys, reference books, scholarly monographs. Cata: 3 a year. B: National Westminster Bank, Tavistock Square, London, W.C.1. Account 36390186. B.A., N.B.L., P.B.F.A.

JARNDYCE ANTIQUARIAN BOOKSELLERS, 68 NEAL STREET, COVENT GARDEN, LONDON WC2H 9PA. Prop: Brian Lake and Janet Nassau. TN: (01) 836-9182 and (01) 267-2307. Est: 1969. Office and storeroom; appointment preferred. Medium stock of antiquarian books. Spec: fine, rare and interesting books before 1900; (especially first editions of English literature, social, economic & political history) Dickens first editions and Dickensiana, autograph letters and manuscripts. Cata: selections from stock, 3 or 4 a year.

JENNER, 19 GREAT ORMOND STREET, LONDON WC1N 3JB. Prop: Dr. N Dewey. TN: (01) 404-4415. Est: 1975. Medium stock, old and rare medical books, some history of science, prints and anatomical drawings. Cata: 3 or 4 a year. M: P.B.F.A.

ALFRED KOFFLER, 28 Museum Street, London WC1A 1LH. TN: (01) 636-4205. TA: Volumina London WC1. Spec: rare books, bibliography, periodicals.

H.K. LEWIS & COMPANY LIMITED, 136 Gower Street, London WC1E 6BS. TN: (01) 387-4282. TA: Publicavit London WC1. Shop and showroom, early closing Saturday. New, and large sec. stock. Spec: medicine, science, technology. Cata: on foregoing, occasionally. B.A. N.B.L. P.A.

S. LINDEN, 33 Craven Street, Strand, London WC2N 5NP TN: (01) 930-3659. Storeroom, appointment recommended. Large sec. and antiq. stock. Spec: history, Literature, philosophy, Science. Cata: on foregoing.

LUZAC & COMPANY LIMITED, P.O. Box 157, 46 Great Russell Street, London WC1. TN: (01) 636-1462. TA: Obfirmate London WC1. Est: 1740. Shop. New, sec. and antiq. stock; also art. Spec: topography and languages of the Near and Far East. No fiction. Cata: occasionally. A.B.A. B.A. N.B.L.

R.W. MALYNOWSKY, 18 Doughty Street, London WC1. Business by post only. Large sec. stock. Spec: history, economics, literature (English and Foreign in English translation), drama, public library fiction. Cata 2-3 a year. B: Barclays Bank, 478 Harrow Road, London, W.9.

MUSEUM BOOKSHOP, 36 Great Russell Street, London WC1B 3PP. Prop: Ashley Jones and David Mezzetti. TN: (01) 580-4086. Est: 1979. Shop. Medium stock sec. and antiq. Spec: classics, archaeology, history, egyptology, Middle East. Few back numbers of journals stocked and new books. Cata: 4 a year. Corresp: Français, Italiano. B: Barclays Bank, 147 Holborn, EC1N 2NU. Account 90676667.

WINIFRED A. MYERS [AUTOGRAPHS] LIMITED, SUITE 52, 91 SAINT MARTIN'S LANE, LONDON WC2. Directors: Winifred A. Myers and Ruth Shepherd. TN: (01) 836-1940. TA: Myersliber London WC2. Est: 1889. Autograph letters and documents, manuscripts and inscribed books. Cata: autograph letters, occasionally, A.B.A.

ARTHUR PAGE, THE BOOKSHOP, 29 MUSEUM STREET, LONDON WC1A 1LH. TN: (01) 636-8206. Est: 1972. Shop; open 7 days a week. Medium stock sec. and antiq. Spec: music books, Lewis Carroll, 17th century English. Corresp: French. Cata: occasionally. B: Williams & Glyn's Bank, Camden Town, London, N.W.1. Account (16-00-23) 12995088.

PLEASURES OF PAST TIMES, 11 CECIL COURT, CHARING CROSS ROAD, LONDON WC2N 4EZ. Prop: David Drummond. TN: (01) 836-1142. Est: 1963. Shop, early closing Saturday except the first in the month; other days 11 a.m. to 2.30 p.m. and 3 p.m. to 6 p.m. Small sec. and antiq. stock, very large stock early postcards. Spec: theatre and relevant data—paybills, posters, etc; juvenile books, games, toys. B: Barclays Bank, Dulwich Village, London, SE21. Account 00329452. N.B.L.

ARTHUR PROBSTHAIN, 41 GREAT RUSSELL STREET, LONDON WC1B 3PH. Prop: Walter Sheringham. TN: (01) 636-1096. Est: 1902. Shop, early closing Saturdays. Large stock sec. and antiq. books; also new books. Spec: oriental. Cata: oriental, 3 a year. A.B.A.

QUEVEDO BOOKSHOP, 25 CECIL COURT, LONDON WC2N 4EZ. Prop: J.F.T. Rodgers. TN: (01) 836-9132. Est: 1977. Shop, closed Saturdays. Medium stock sec. and antiq. books. Spec: rare Continental and English books before 1840, Spanish books. A.B.A.

READ'S, 48A CHARING CROSS ROAD, LONDON WC2H 0BB. Prop: Cagebrown Limited. TN: (01) 379-7669. Est: 1982. Shop, also open Sundays 2–7 pm. Very large stock sec. and antiq. Spec: travel and topography, performing arts. Cata: 2 a year. Corresp: Français, Deutsch. B: Royal Bank of Scotland PLC, 48 Haymarket, London SW1Y 4SE. M: P.B.F.A.

Also at 13 GREAT NEWPORT STREET, LONDON WC2.

REG AND PHILIP REMINGTON, 14 CECIL COURT, LONDON WC2N 4HE. Prop: Reg and Philip Remington. TN: (01) 836-9771. Est: 1979. Shop. Small stock sec. and antiq. Spec: voyages and travel. Corresp: Français, Español. B: National Westminster Bank, 9 Marylebone High Street, London W1. M: A.B.A., P.B.F.A.

ROBINSON & WATKINS, 19–21 CECIL COURT, CHARING CROSS ROAD, LONDON WC2N 4HB. Prop: Robinson and Watkins Limited (Richard Robinson). TN: (01) 836-2182. TA: Mystibuks London WC2. Shop. Very small stock sec. and antiq. books, also new books and publishing. Spec: comparative and oriental religions, mysticism, crafts, self-sufficiency. Cata: on foregoing, 2 a year. M: B.A.

C.G. ROSENBERG & COMPANY LIMITED, 92 GREAT RUSSELL STREET, LONDON WC1. TN: (01) 636-0639. Est: 1936. Appointment necessary, closed Saturday. New and medium antiq. stock. Spec: fine arts. M: A.B.A., B.A.

BERTRAM ROTA LIMITED, 30 & 31 LONG ACRE, LONDON WC2E 9LT. TN: (01) 836-0723 TA: Rotabook London-WC2. Est: 1923. Shop, closed Saturdays. New, and medium sec. and antiq. stock. Spec: modern first editions, private press books. English literature; literary autographs. Cata: on foregoing irregularly. A.B.A. B.A. N.B.L.

IAN SHIPLEY [BOOKS] LIMITED, 34 FLORAL STREET, COVENT GARDEN, LONDON WC2 9DJ. Manager: W.R. Barnes. TN: (01) 836-4872. Est: 1977. Shop. Very small stock sec. and antiq. also new books. Spec: art (architecture, design, photography, fashion, printing, sculpture). Cata: 3 a year. B: Coutts & Co., Trafalgar Branch, 440 Strand, London, W.C.2.

SKOOB BOOKS LIMITED, 15 SICILIAN AVENUE, SOUTHAMPTON ROW, LONDON WC1A 2QH. Prop: Managing Director: Ike Ong. TN: (01) 404-3063. Est: 1979. Shop and Basement in pedestrian arcade. Open Monday to Saturday from 10.30 to 18.30 hrs. Very large stock sec. and antiq. Spec: literature and literary criticism, Penguins, esoterica, politics, history, scientific & technical subjects for higher education. Corresp: Français, Deutsch, Chinese and Malay. Cata: 1 a year. B: Williams & Glyn Bank, High Holborn, London WC1. M: P.B.F.A.

STAGE DOOR PRINTS, CECIL COURT, LONDON WC2. Prop: A.L. Reynold. TN: (01) 240 1683. Est: 1982. Medium sec. and antiq. stock, mainly prints and ephemera. Spec: ballet, opera, music.

HAROLD T. STOREY, 3 CECIL COURT, CHARING CROSS ROAD, LONDON WC2N 4EZ. Prop: Norman T. Storey. TN: (01) 836-3777. TA: Storybook London WC2. Est: 1928. Shop, early closing Saturday. Large sec. and antiq. stock. Spec: finely bound and illustrated books. A.B.A.

TRAVIS & EMERY, 17 CECIL COURT, CHARING CROSS ROAD, LONDON WC2N 4EZ. TN: (01) 240-2129. Prop: Valérie Emery. Est: 1960. Shop, early closing Saturday. New, and large sec. and antiq. stock. Spec: music and books on music. Cata: on foregoing. A.B.A.

THE VADE-MECUM PRESS LIMITED (PUBLISHERS & BOOKSELLERS), BCM BOX 6420, LONDON WC1N 3XX. Prop: Robert Connelly. Est: 1983. Stockroom; postal business only. Small stock sec. and antiq. also new books. Spec: medicine, science, bibliography, local history, horology, anthropology, psychology. Cata: 4 a year. B: National Westminster Bank Ltd., 149 Church Road, London SW13 9HS. Account 35639865. M: P.B.F.A.

VINTAGE MAGAZINE SHOP LIMITED, VINTAGE HOUSE, GREAT WINDMILL STREET, LONDON WC2. (CORNER OF 39–41 BREWER STREET). Prop: Danny Posner. TN: (01) 439-8525. Est: 1974. Shop; open every weekday between 10.00 and 23.00 hrs. Very large stock. Magazines only. Spec: film, theatre, sport, fashion, transport, news, science fiction, pop, rock, comics, newspapers. Cata: occasionally.

B. WEINREB ARCHITECTURAL BOOKS LIMITED, 48 GREAT RUSSELL STREET, LONDON WC1B 3QL. TN: (01) 636-4895. Offices, appointment preferred, closed Saturday. Very large sec. and antiq. stock, some new. Spec: architecture, civil engineering and related subjects. Cata: on foregoing. A.B.A. N.B.L.

WILDY & SONS LIMITED, LINCOLN'S INN ARCHWAY, CAREY STREET, LONDON WC2A 2JD. Prop: W.E. Sinkins. TN: (01) 242-5778. Est: 1830. Two shops and three storerooms, New, and very large sec. and antiq. stock. Spec: law. A.B.A. B.A. N.B.L.

ZENO, 6 DENMARK STREET, LONDON WC2H 8LP. Prop: M.P. Zographos. TN: (01) 836-2522. TA: Zengreek London WC2. Est: 1944. Shop and storeroom, no early closing. New, and large sec. and antiq. stock. Spec: Greek books; books about Greece, Turkey, Ionian and Aegean Islands, Crete, Cyprus, Balkans, Middle East. Cata: on foregoing, 2–3 a year. M: B.A.

A. ZWEMMER LIMITED, LITCHFIELD STREET, LONDON WC2. TN: (01) 836-4710. TA: Zwemmera London WC2. Est: 1924. Shops, no early closing. New, and very large sec. and antiq. stock; also original works of art, especially modern paintings, drawings, etc. Spec: fine art. Cata: on foregoing and applied arts. A.B.A. B.A. N.B.L. P.A.

49. SOMERSET

AXBRIDGE
BRIDGWATER
BRUTON
BURROWBRIDGE
CASTLE CARY
DULVERTON
FROME
GLASTONBURY
LANGPORT
MARTOCK
MINEHEAD
TAUNTON
WEDMORE
WELLINGTON
WELLS

ALCOMBE BOOKS, 26 ALCOMBE ROAD, MINEHEAD, SOMERSET TA24 6AZ. Prop: N.V. Allen & C.J. Giddens. TN: Minehead 3425. Est: 1970. Shop, early closing Wednesday and Saturday. Medium sec. and antiq. stock, also new books on topography and ornithology. Spec: Exmoor, Somerset, Red Deer

ANSFORD BOOKS, AIRLIE HOUSE, LOWER ANSFORD, CASTLE CARY, SOMERSET. Prop: N.J., B.M. and Dr. M.A. Ogilvie. TN: Castle Cary 50512. Est: 1966. Storeroom, open normal business hours. Medium sec. and antiq. stock. Spec: natural history, especially ornithology; West Country and Somerset topography. Cata: on foregoing, occasionally. N.B.L.

TONY APPLETON, THE OLD SCHOOL, BUCKLAND DINHAM, FROME, SOMERSET BA11 2QR. TN: (0373) 62929. Est: 1967. Private premises; appointment essential. Small sec. and antiq. stock. Spec: typography, printing history, bookbinding, papermaking, press books, etc. Cata: on foregoing occasionally. M: A.B.A.

BAILEY HILL BOOKSHOP, FORE STREET, CASTLE CARY, SOMERSET BA7 7BG. Prop: N.P. Purcell. TN: (0963) 50917. Est: 1980. Shop. Medium stock sec. and antiq. also new books. Corresp: Français. M: B.A.

EDDIE BAXTER-BOOKS, 88 BENEDICT STREET, GLASTONBURY, SOMERSET BA6 9EZ. Prop: Eddie Baxter. TN: (0458) 31662. Est: 1956. Private premises; postal business only. Small stock sec. and antiq. Spec: dance band, nostalgia, Jazz. Cata: 3 or 4 a year. B: Midland Bank, 13 High Street, Glastonbury, Somerset BA6 9DP.

BEE BOOKS NEW AND OLD, TAPPING WALL FARM, STATHE ROAD, BURROWBRIDGE, SOMERSET TA7 0RY. Prop: J.S. Kinross. TN: Burrowbridge 781. Est: 1971. Private premises; appointment necessary. Very small stock sec. and antiq. also some back-numbers of journals and new books. Spec: beekeeping; home made wine. Cata: 4 a year. Corresp: Français. B: Barclays Bank, North Street, Taunton. Account 90158100. National Giro, Account 279 7151.

BLACKDOWN BOOKS CHARNWOOD, HIGHER NYNEHEAN, NEAR WELLINGTON, SOMERSET. Prop: Richard Emery. TN: (082 347) 3362. Private premises; appointment necessary.

BOOKS FOR NATURALISTS, 81 ROCKWELL GREEN, WELLINGTON, SOMERSET TA21 9BX. Prop: Dr. Anthony Eve and Julia C. Fisher. TN: Wellington 7234. Est: 1969. Private premises, appointment necessary. New, and medium sec. and antiq. stock. Spec: natural history, zoology, botany, geology, ecology, conservation. Cata: on foregoing, about 3 a year.

THE BOOKSHOP, 37 SAINT THOMAS STREET, WELLS, SOMERSET. Prop: Marian Morris. TN: Wells 73556. Est: 1978. Shop, early closing Wednesdays. Small stock sec. and antiq. books.

BROOK HOUSE BOOKS, BROOK HOUSE, 13 FRIARN STREET, BRIDGWATER, SOMERSET TA6 3LH. Prop: C.B. and C.M. Arden. TN: (0278) 422282. Private premises; appointment necessary.

CIDERPRESS BOOKS, THE COTTAGE, KINGSBURY EPISCOPI, MARTOCK, SOMERSET TA12 6AU. Prop: Peter and Naomi Bickford. TN: Martock 823326. Est: 1974. Private premises; appointment necessary. Small sec. and antiq. stock. Spec: Russia and Eastern Europe; Asia; Africa; Big Game; natural history, gardening. Cata: on foregoing, 8 a year. Corresp: Français. B: National Westminster Bank, Langport. Account 55647792.

P.T. CLARKE, JORDANS, PITNEY, LANGPORT, SOMERSET TA10 9AE. TN: (0458) 250610. Est: 1969. Private premises; appointment necessary. Small stock sec. and antiq. books. Cata: general, 8 a year.

C.R. EASTWOOD, 32 RIVERTON ROAD, PURITON, BRIDGWATER, SOMERSET. TN: 683894. Est: 1978. Private premises; appointment necessary. Medium stock sec. and antiq. Spec: Somerset and Dorset topography, 19th century fiction, fiction generally, literature, history. Cata: 4-6 a year. Corresp: Deutsch. B: National Westminster Bank, Bridgwater. Account 53219759. M: P.B.F.A. Library Association.

EPISCOPI BOOKS, MANOR HOUSE, KINGSBURY EPISCOPI, NEAR MARTOCK, SOMERSET TA12 6AT. Prop: S.R.T. Wicks. Est: 1960. Private premises; postal business only. Very large stock sec. and antiq. books. Spec: theology, gardening, biography, out of print fiction.

GILBERT'S, LANGFORD MANOR, LOWER SWELL, FIVEHEAD, TAUNTON, SOMERSET TA3 6PH. Prop: J.R. Gilbert. TN: (046 08) 457. Est: 1971. Appointment necessary. Small stock sec. and antiq. Spec: prints and maps, also illustrated material.

HADDAN'S BOOKSHOP, 30 BENEDICT STREET, GLASTONBURY BA6 9EX. Prop: Mrs. D.L.A. Thomas. TN: Glastonbury 31753. Est: 1978. Shop. Medium stock sec. and antiq. Corresp: Français. B: National Westminster Bank, 5 Market Place, Glastonbury BA6 9HB. Account 54439106. M: P.B.F.A.

HELIOS BOOKS, 2 HIGH STREET, GLASTONBURY, SOMERSET BA6 9DU. Prop: Helene Koppejan. TN: (0458) 34184. Est: 1963. Shop, stock sec. and antiq. also new books. Spec: religion, spiritual, new age. Cata: monthly. (New books cata. annually). B: Midland Bank, Glastonbury.

INLAND POOL BOOK SERVICE, 5 CORNHILL, WELLINGTON, SOMERSET. Prop: T.E. and A.R. Coxe. TN: (0823 47) 2650. Est: 1980. Shop. Medium stock sec. and antiq. Cata: monthly to the trade. Corresp: Français, Deutsch, Italiano. B: National Westminster Bank, 12 Fore Street, Wellington, Somerset TA21 8AL.

A.A. JOHNSTON, OLD LION CHAPEL, SUTTON ROAD, SOMERTON. TN: Somerton 72713. Est: 1962. Storeroom, open normal business hours or by appointment. New, sec. and antiq. stock. Spec: military. Cata: military books and prints, 6 a year.

MICHAEL LEWIS GALLERY AND THE ASHLEY BINDERY, 17 HIGH STREET, BRUTON, SOMERSET. TN: (0749 81) 3557. Shop. Large stock of antiquarian and scholarly books in fields of literature, history, economics, illustrated, typography, original and antiquarian bindings. Also maps and prints, some watercolours.

MAX GATE BOOKS, MAX GATE, THEALE, WEDMORE, SOMERSET. Prop: Mrs. J.M. Dupont. TN: (0934) 712267. Est: 1983. Private premises; appointment necessary. Small stock sec. and antiq.

OLD CURIOSITY SHOP, 15 CATHERINE HILL, FROME, SOMERSET BA11 1BZ. Prop: R.P. and B.L. Hackett. TN: (0373) 4482. Est: 1969. Shop, early closing Thursdays; normal business hours or other times by appointment. Large stock sec. and antiq. books. Spec: children's; illustrated. Cata: one subject each month. P.B.F.A.

ORCHARD BOOKS, ORCHARD NEVILLE HOUSE, BALTONSBOROUGH, GLASTONBURY, SOMERSET. Prop: Chris and Jean Saunders. TN: (0458) 50443. Est: 1981. Private premises; appointment necessary. Medium stock sec. and antiq. Spec: children's books. Cata: infrequently. M: P.B.F.A.

ORIENT BOOKS, LITTLE BLAKES, HALSE, TAUNTON, SOMERSET TA4 3AG. Prop: C.E. Rusbridge. TN: (0823) 432466. Est: 1969. Private premises; appointment necessary. Small stock sec. and antiq. books. Spec: Asia and Africa, fringe areas of Europe and Pacific. Cata: on foregoing, 2 a year. M: P.B.F.A.

SHEILA PAYNE, THE AXBRIDGE BOOKSHOP AND TEA ROOMS, 18 HIGH STREET, AXBRIDGE, SOMERSET. Prop: Sheila Payne. TN: (0934) 73281. Est: 1982. Shop, closed Monday all day, and Saturday afternoons. Spec: English literature, local history and topography of Somerset. Corresp: Français. B: National Giro.

ROTHWELL AND DUNWORTH, 15 PAUL STREET, TAUNTON, SOMERSET, TA1 3PF. Prop: M. Dunworth and C. Rothwell. TN: Taunton 82476. Est: 1979. Shop. Large stock sec. and antiq. Spec: history and literature, natural history, sporting. M: P.B.F.A., A.B.A.

ROTHWELL AND DUNWORTH, MELTON HOUSE, HIGH STREET, DULVERTON, SOMERSET. Prop: M. Dunworth and C. Rothwell. TN: (0398) 23169. Est: 1979. Shop, closed Thursdays and Saturday afternoons. Large stock sec. and antiq. Spec: field sports, literature, antiques. M: A.B.A., P.B.F.A.

MICHAEL STROUD, COWSLIP FARM, LOXTON, AXBRIDGE, BS26 2XF. TN: Edingworth 234, Est: 1968. Private premises, appointment necessary. Medium sec. stock.

SUMMERLANDS BOOKS, 38 HILL HEAD, GLASTONBURY, SOMERSET BA6 8AR. Prop: Brian Williams. TN: (0458) 32843 & (021 777) 4150. Est: 1983. Private premises; appointment necessary. Small stock sec. and antiq. Spec: mysticism, the occult, alternative medicines; Glastonbury. Corresp: Français, Dutch, Italiano. B: Barclays Bank PLC, 21–23 High Street, Glastonbury, Somerset BA6 9HF.

TAUNTON ANTIQUARIAN BOOKSHOP, 27-29 SILVER STREET, TAUNTON, SOMERSET. Prop: M. & P.A. Carter. TN: 89327. Est: 1979. Shop, closed on Tuesdays, Wednesdays and Thursdays. Open during normal business hours. Small stock sec. and antiq. M: P.B.F.A.

WAKEFIELD YOUNG BOOKS, LITTLE BRYMPTON, BRYMPTON D'EVERCY, YEOVIL, SOMERSET. Prop: C. MacTaggart and R. Young. TN: (093 586) 2609. Est: 1970. Private premises; usually available but telephone call advisable. Small stock sec. and antiq. old master, modern and Japanese prints. Children's and illustrated books. Cata: occasionally. M: P.B.F.A.

CHARLES A. WALSH, ELY LODGE, 9 FRENCH WEIR AVENUE, TAUNTON, SOMERSET TA1 1XQ. TN: (0823) 74396. Est: 1974. Private premises; appointment necessary. Medium stock sec. and antiq. books. Cata: general occasionally.

WELLSPRING BOOKSHOP, PENNILESS PORTCH, MARKET PLACE, WELLS, SOMERSET. TN: (0749) 72156X.

H.F.J. WIGRAM, FOXHERNE, BLAGDON HILL, TAUNTON, SOMERSET TA3 7SQ. Prop: H.F.J. Wigram. TN: (0823) 42517. Est: 1980. Private premises; appointment necessary. Small stock sec. and antiq. Spec: the British Empire. Cata: 4 or 5 a year.

WIVEY BOOKSHOP, 4 SILVER STREET, WIVELISCOMBE, SOMERSET. Prop: Mr. and Mrs. R. Barraclough. TN: (0984) 23104. Est: 1983. Shop, closed Tuesday, Wednesday and Thursday. Medium stock sec. and antiq. Spec: transport. B: National Westminster Bank, Wiveliscombe.

PLEASE MENTION THIS DIRECTORY WHEN QUOTING!

50. SURREY

ASHTEAD
BEDDINGTON
CARSHALTON
CATERHAM
CHERTSEY
CROYDON
DORKING
EAST MOLESEY
EPSOM
FARNHAM
GODALMING
GUILDFORD
HASLEMERE
KINGSTON
MILFORD
MITCHAM
MORDEN
NEW MALDEN
PURLEY
REDHILL
REIGATE
RICHMOND
SOUTH NUTFIELD
SUTTON
THAMES DITTON
THORNTON HEATH
WALTON ON THAMES
WEYBRIDGE
WOKING
WORCESTER PARK
WORMLEY

ANTIQUARIAN BOOKSHOP [DORKING] LIMITED, 34 Highdown, Worcester Park, Surrey KT4 7HZ. Prop: H.S. Linfield. Est: 1955. Storeroom at Dorking open by appointment only. Spec: English literature, arts, collectors' subjects, bibliography, books about books, literary biography, social sciences, Victorian and other illustrated books, travel, sets of authors, prints and engravings.

R.S. & N.R. ASPINWALL, 'Stanmore' Ramsden Road, Godalming, Surrey GU7 1QE. Est: 1976. Private premises; appointment necessary. Very small stock sec. and antiq. books; occasional new. Spec: topography and travel. Cata: miscellaneous; British topography, 1 a year.

AVOCET BOOKS LTD. P.O. Box 4, Ashtead, Surrey KT21 2LP. Prop: P.A. Culpin. TN: (03722) 77880. Est: 1979. Private premises; appointment necessary. Very small stock sec. and antiq. Spec: veterinary and farriery, agriculture, Disneyana, old toy catalogues, hawking and falconry. B: Lloyds Bank, Ashtead, Surrey.

BALDUR BOOKSHOP, 44 Hill Rise, Richmond, Surrey. Prop: Eric Barton. TN: (01) 940-1214. Est: 1933. Shop. Large sec. and antiq. stock. Spec: cricket and the 1890's.

BEACON HILL BOOKSHOP, Beacon Hill Road, Hindhead, Surrey GU26 6QL. Prop: S.F. and C.M.S. Jenks. TN: (042873) 6783. Est: 1970. Shop, early closing Wednesdays. Medium stock sec. and antiq.

G. AND G. BEARE, 39 VICTORIA ROAD, KNAPHILL, WOKING, SURREY GU21 2AH. Prop: Geraldine Beare. TN: Brookwood 81264. Est: 1979. Private premises; postal business only. Very small stock sec. and antiq. Spec: illustrated, children's, Strand magazines. Cata: 2 a year. B: Midland Bank, Knaphill, Woking, Surrey.

MRS. P.A. BLUNT, 'TIMBERLEY', 48 HILLSIDE ROAD, ASHTEAD, SURREY. TN: Ashtead 74909. Maps and prints; colouring artist.

BOOKBOX, 122 SOUTH STREET, DORKING, SURREY. Prop: Pat Brown and Connie Fisher. TN: (0306) 886468. Est: 1982. Shop, closed Monday and Wednesday; also private premises, by appointment. Medium stock sec. and antiq. Spec: 19th and 20th century literature, topography. Cata: 1 or 2 a year. Corresp: Français, Italiano. B: Barclays Bank, Station Approach, Tadworth, Surrey.

B.B. BOOKS, 1 SUNDRIDGE ROAD, WOKING, SURREY GU22 9AU. Prop: A.J. Browning. Postal business only. Small sec. and antiq. stock. Spec: cats, dogs, fruit.

DAVID BRISTOW ANTIQUARIAN BOOKSELLERS LIMITED, 32 COMBE ROAD, KINGSTON UPON THAMES, SURREY, KT2 7AG. Prop: Derrick Nightingale. TN: (01) 549-5144. Est: 1974. Shop. Medium stock sec. and antiq. Spec: 19th century fiction. Cata: 12 a year. Corresp: Deutsch, Russian. B: Lloyds Bank, New Malden Surrey. Account 0010045.

EDWARD H. BRYANT, 6 Seaforth Gardens, Stoneleigh, Epsom, Surrey. TN: (01) 393-7752. Spec: travel and exploration (Africa, Asia, Americas, Australasia, Pacific, Polar). Middle East, mountaineering, big game hunting.

P.W. BURDITT Saint Anne's House, Onslow Crescent, Woking, Surrey. Prop: P.W. and J.A. Burditt. TN: Woking 73177. Est: 1977. Private premises; appointment necessary. Spec: out-of-print dog books. Cata: 3 yearly. B: Midland Bank, Walton-on-Thames, 34 High Street. Account 41032429.

CHEAM BOOK SHOP, 32 Station Road, Belmont, Sutton, Surrey SM2 6BS. Prop: William A. Carter. TN: (01) 642-1234. Est: 1970. Shop, closed Wednesdays. Very large stock sec. and antiq. also back-numbers of journals, new books to order, and small antiques and pictures. B: Midland Bank, 2 High Street, Sutton, Surrey, SM1 1HX. Account 70235784. M: B.A.

TREVOR COLDREY, 8 Recreation Road, Guildford, Surrey GU1 1HE. TN: (0483) 33177. Storeroom, private premises; appointment necessary. Large stock sec. and antiq. books. Spec: literary criticism and scholarly books on the arts. Cata: 6 a year.

A.J. COOMBES, 24 Horsham Road, Dorking, Surrey RH4 2JA. Prop: J.A. Coombes. TN: (0306) 880736. Est: 1967. Private premises; appointment necessary. Small stock sec. and antiq. Spec: British topography and local history; ordnance survey maps. Cata: 6 a year. Corresp: Deutsch. B: Lloyds Bank Ltd., 120 High Street, Dorking, Surrey RH4 1BB. M: A.B.A.

RONALD COOPER, 46 Westbury Road, New Malden, Surrey. Prop: Ronald Cooper. TN: (01) 949-1640. Est: 1983. Private premises; appointment necessary. Very small stock sec. and antiq. Spec: British topography, collectors' books, family histories, diabetes. Cata: occasional. Corresp: Français. B: National Girobank, Bootle, Merseyside G1R 0AA. Credit 33 385 2001.

CRANE BOOKSHOP LIMITED, 70a High Street, Haslemere, Surrey. TN: Haslemere 2140. Est: 1955. Shop and storeroom, early closing Wednesday. Large sec. and antiq. stock. Spec: literary periodicals. Cata: on foregoing, irregularly. M: B.A.

H. CROSSLEY, The Old Vicarage, 91 Warwick Road, Thornton Heath, Surrey CR4 7NN. TN: (01) 684-9448. Est: 1960. Private premises; appointment necessary. Spec: early illustrated, atlases, English and foreign topography, trades, costumes.

CROYDON BOOKSHOP, 304 Carshalton Road, Carshalton, Surrey SM5 3QB. Prop: J.C. Burton (Managing Partner), Mrs. P. Reding and P.J. Rogers. TN: (01) 643-6857 (642-7468, after hours). Est: 1954. Shop, open 11.00 a.m. to 5.30 p.m. Large sec. and antiq. stock.

P. DANZEY, 287 The Glade, Shirley, Croydon, Surrey CR0 7UQ.

ELLESMERE BOOKS, 56 Cardinal Avenue, Kingston upon Thames, Surrey KT2 5SB. Prop: Roger and Hilary May. TN: (01) 546-1845. Est: 1980. Private premises; postal business only. Very small stock sec. and antiq. Spec: classical and mediaeval studies, travel and topography. Cata: 2 or 3 a year. M: P.B.F.A.

EVANS THE BOOK, 84 Hill Rise, Richmond, Surrey. Prop: M.I. Evans. TN: (01) 948-0182. Est: 1966. Postal business only. Small sec. and antiq. stock. Spec: modern first editions. Cata: modern first editions, irregularly. B.A.

EXTRA BOOKS, Eastdene, Station Road, Bramley, Near Guildford, Surrey GU5 0DP. Prop: M. Wybrow. TN: (0483) 892744.

FINE AND LIMITED EDITIONS LIMITED, 23 High Path Road, Merrow, Guildford, Surrey. Prop: Cy. Olney. TN: (0483) 574748. Shop, closed Monday and Thursday. Very small sec. and antiq. stock. Fine Limited edition and private press books only.

ALICK FLETCHER, 2 Guildford Park Road, Guildford, Surrey, Est: 1948. Storerooms, appointment necessary. very large sec. and antiq. stock. Spec: scholarly books, rare, fine bindings. Cata: 1–2 a year. A.B.A.

C.P. FLOREY, 18 Whitethorn Gardens, Addiscombe Road, Croydon, Surrey CR0 7LL. TN: (01) 654-4724. Est: 1960. Private premises, appointment necessary. Medium sec. and antiq. stock. Corresp: Français, Deutsch. A.B.A. N.B.L.

ELIZABETH GANT, "Past & Presents", 52 High Street, Thames Ditton, Surrey. TN: (01) 398-0962. Part of shop, closed Monday and Wednesday, appointment necessary. Spec: children's and illustrated books. Corresp: Français, Deutsch. B: Lloyd's Bank, Esher. *Also private premises at* 8 Sandown Close, Esher, Surrey. TN (01) 398-5107.

A. BURTON-GARBETT, 35 THE GREEN, MORDEN, SURREY. TN: (01) 540-2367 TA: Garbo Morden Surrey. Est: 1959. Private premises, appointment necessary. Medium sec. and antiq. stock. Spec: South and Central America, Mexico and Caribbean. Cata: on foregoing. A.B.A.

A. AND M. GIBB, WOOD END, PETWORTH ROAD, WORMLEY, SURREY GU8 5TR. Prop: Alistair Gibb. TN: (042879) 2830. Est: 1978. Private premises; appointment necessary. Small stock sec. and antiq. Spec: banking and numismatics, also back-numbers of journals. B: Royal Bank of Scotland, Bank Street, Elie, Fife, Scotland. Account 160014.

GOLF BOOKS, WOODBINE HOUSE, 12 SPENCER ROAD, SOUTH CROYDON, SURREY CR2 7EH. Prop: Philip Truett. TN: (01) 686-1080. Est: 1974. Private premises; postal business only. Sec. and antiq. books on golf only; no general stock. Cata: 1 a year.

MRS. D.M. GREEN, 7 TOWER GROVE, WEYBRIDGE, SURREY KT13 9LX. TN: Walton on Thames 241105. Est: 1973. Private premises; appointment necessary. Very small stock sec. and antiq. books, medium stock of county maps. Spec: antique maps of British counties. Lists sent.

HIGHBURY BOOKS, 66A EAST STREET, EPSOM, SURREY. Prop: David Johnston. Est: 1981. Shop, early closing Wednesday. Small stock sec. and antiq. Corresp: Français, Deutsch. B: National Westminster Bank, Bridge Street, Leatherhead, Surrey.

ESMOND HOLDEN LIMITED, CLAVERDON, WHITE POST HILL, REDHILL, SURREY RH1 6JN. TN: Redhill 64448. Est: 1933 as Pelican Library. Private premises, appointment necessary. Small sec. and antiq. stock. Cata: fiction and general, occasionally. A.B.A.

W. & A. HOUBEN, 2 CHURCH COURT, RICHMOND, SURREY TW9 1JL. TN: (01) 940-1055. Est: 1947. Shop, early closing Wednesday. New, and medium sec. and antiq. stock, also prints.

PETER HOWARD BOOKS, 347 BRIGHTON ROAD, SOUTH CROYDON, SURREY. Prop: Peter and Barbara Howard. TN: (01) 688-6558 and (01) 681-1627. Shop. Large stock sec. and antiq.

JOHN L. HUNT, 268 CROYDON ROAD, CATERHAM, SURREY. TN: Caterham 43387. Est: 1927. Private premises, trade seen by appointment. Medium sec. stock. Supplier to trade only. Spec: fiction, biography, plays, travel.

IVELET BOOKS LIMITED, 18 FAIRLAWN DRIVE, REDHILL, SURREY RH1 6JP. Directors: Mrs. Elizabeth Ahern and Dr. Alan Ahern (Secretary). TN: (0737) 64520. Est: 1978. Private premises; appointment necessary. Medium stock sec. and antiq. also new books. Spec: the garden, landscape architecture, plant monographs, plant collecting, herbals, early agriculture. Cata: 3 or 4 a year. Corresp: Français. B: Lloyds Bank, 1 London Road, Redhill RH1 1ND. Account 00333665. M: P.B.F.A.

DEREK W. JAMES, CORNER CROFT, 33 OLD LODGE LANE, PURLEY, SURREY, CR2 4DJ. TN: (01) 660-5072. Est: 1946. Private premises; appointment necessary. Small sec. and antiq. stock. Spec: aviation, military, India and Far East. B: National Westminster Bank, High Street, Sutton, Surrey. Account 02113171. A.B.A.

KOHLER AND COOMBES LIMITED, 12 HORSHAM ROAD, DORKING, SURREY RH4 2JL. TN: (0306) 881532. Telex: 21120 (mono.Ref.1393) Est: 1963. Storeroom open normal business hours. Medium stock sec. and antiq. books. Spec: English literature; George Gissing; special collections on specific subjects. Cata: on foregoing, occasionally. A.B.A.

FRED LAKE, 104 KINGS ROAD, WALTON-ON-THAMES, SURREY KT12 2RE. TN: Walton on Thames 27824. Postal business only. Very small sec. and antiq. stock. Spec: archery, bow-hunting, rules of archery clubs, archery periodicals and ephemera. Cata: on foregoing, occasionally.

J. LAWTON LTD., 1 BOUNDSTONE ROAD, WRECCLESHAM, FARNHAM, SURREY. Prop: D.W.E. Burden. TN: Frensham 3615. Est: 1967. Private premises, appointment necessary. Very small sec. and antiq. stock, also maps and prints. Spec: topography, English and foreign maps and prints. Cata: maps and prints, infrequently.

LAPIS LAZULI, 53 GLOUCESTER ROAD, KEW, RICHMOND, SURREY TW9 3BT. Prop: S.N. and A.G. Thomas. TN: (948) 5667. Est: 1978. Private premises; appointment necessary. Very small stock sec. and antiq. Spec: 19th and 20th century literature, children's books, art reference, printing. Catas. Corresp: Français. M: P.B.F.A.

LENS OF SUTTON, 4 WESTMEAD ROAD, SUTTON, SURREY SM1 4JT. Est: 1929. Shop, early closing Wednesdays. Medium stock sec. and antiq. books; also new books. Spec: railways, buses, trams.

LLOYD'S OF KEW, 9 MORTLAKE TERRACE, KEW, RICHMOND, SURREY. Prop: Daniel Lloyd. Shop, closed Wednesdays. Large stock sec. and antiq. also new books. Spec: gardening and botanical. Cata: on this area, 1 a year, price 50p.

LONDINIUM BOOKS, 141 CROYDON ROAD, BEDDINGTON, SURREY. Prop: Eric and Jean Mahoney. Sec. and antiq. Spec: ordnance survey maps, illustrated books, juvenilia.

RICHARD LYON, P.O. BOX 150, KINGSTON UPON THAMES, SURREY KT2 5SZ. TN: (01) 546-6149. TA: Leobro, Kingstonthames. Telex: 943763 (CROCOM G Ref LEOBRO). Private premises; postal business only. Medium stock sec. and antiq. also new books. Spec: Oriental art reference (especially Chinese ceramics and jade), primitive art reference, carpets textiles, Far Eastern travel and history. Cata: 2 a year. Corresp: Français, Español, Italiano, Polish.

J.W. McKENZIE, 12 STONELEIGH PARK ROAD, EWELL, EPSOM, SURREY. TN: (01) 393-7700. Est: 1971. Shop and storeroom; appointment necessary. Very small stock sec. and antiq. books. Spec: cricket, theatre and the performing arts. Cata: cricket, occasionally.

JEAN MAHONEY, 141 CROYDON ROAD, BEDDINGTON, SURREY CR0 4OJ. TN: (01) 688-6670. Est: 1976. Private premises; appointment necessary. Small stock sec. and antiq. Spec: ordnance survey maps, juvenalia. P.B.F.A.

MEADVALE BOOKS, 8 Clarence Road, Meadvale, Reigate, Surrey. Prop: Mr. J. Mole. TN: (073 72) 45631. Est: 1982. Private premises; appointment necessary. Very small stock sec. and antiq. Spec: books on Surrey and Sussex. Cata: 2 a year. B: Midland Bank Ltd., 72 Station Road, Redhill, Surrey.

THE MOLE BOOKSHOP, 81 Walton Road, East Molesey, Surrey KT8 0DP. Prop: Keith Langford. TN: (078 481) 3461. Est: 1975. Shop, closed Monday and Wednesday. Small stock sec. and antiq. Spec: mountaineering, naval. Cata: 3 a year. Corresp: Français, Deutsch. B: Lloyds Bank Ltd., Walton Road, East Molesey, Surrey.

NAPP BOOKS, The Skerries, 13 Pottery Lane, Wrecclesham, Farnham, Surrey. Prop: N. Perry. TN: (0252) 713179. Private premises; appointment necessary.

NICHOLSON KENT P.O. Box 18, Chertsey, Surrey KT16 0LG. Manager: T.G. Kent. TA: Broxville, Chertsey. Est: 1976. Private premises; postal business only. World-wide search service for out-of-print books. Spec: music, popular record catalogues.

THE OLD HOUSE BOOKSHOP, Wagon Yard, Lower Church Lane, Farnham, Surrey GU9 7PS. Prop: D.A. and O.L. Collett. TN: Farnham 714754. Est: 1952. Shop, early closing Wednesday. New, and medium sec. and antiq. stock, also book-binding. Spec: transport—air, road, railway and sea. B.A.

JOHN A. PARKINSON, 130 Farley Road, Selsdon, South Croydon, Surrey CR2 7NF. Prop: John A. Parkinson. TN: (01) 657-3191. Est: 1981. Private premises; appointment necessary. Small stock sec. and antiq. Spec: antiq. music, sheet music and music books. Cata: 3 a year. Corresp: Français, Deutsch. B: Lloyds Bank, Addington Road, Selsdon, South Croydon.

PAST AND PRESENTS, 52 High Street, Thames Ditton, Surrey. Prop: Elizabeth Gant. TN: (01) 398-0962. Est: 1982. Shop, closed Monday and Wednesday. Private premises; appointment necessary. Very small stock sec. and antiq. Spec: children's and illustrated books. Corresp: Français, Deutsch. B: Lloyds Bank, Esher.
Also at 8 Sandown Close, Esher, Surrey. TN: (01) 398-5107.

REIGATE GALLERIES LIMITED, 45a Bell Street, Reigate, Surrey RH2 7AG. Prop: K. & J. Morrish. TN: Reigate 46055. Est: 1948. Shop; closed on Wednesday afternoons. Medium stock sec. and antiq. also picture framers. B: Midland Bank, Central Croydon Branch, 9 Wellesley Road, Croydon. Account 41016083. M: P.B.F.A.

THE RICHMOND BOOKSHOP, 20 RED LION STREET, RICHMOND, SURREY TW9 1RW. Prop: J. Prescott and R. Rey. TN: (01) 940-5512. Est: 1965. Shop, open Fridays and Saturdays only; no postal trade. Large stock sec. and antiq. books. Spec: arts and humanities.

MISS E.P. ROBINSON, 39 BRAY ROAD, GUILDFORD, SURREY GU2 5LH. TN: Guildford 573018. Private premises, appointment necessary. Very small sec. and antiq. stock. Spec: nursing.

R. WILSON ROSE, 275 KING'S ROAD, KINGSTON, SURREY KT2 5JJ. TN: (01) 549-7502. Est: 1964. Private premises; appointment necessary. Medium stock sec. and antiq. books. Spec: social, political and economic history; history of education; history; sociology. Cata: on above and related subjects, 8 a year.

W. SHAER, 6 SIRDAR ROAD, MITCHAM, SURREY CR4 2BX. TN: (01) 646-0123. Est: 1960. Private premises; postal business only. Very small sec. and antiq. stock. Spec: illustrated, antiquarian.

R.H.S. SPAIGHT, 5 KELVIN COURT, MARLBOROUGH ROAD, RICHMOND, SURREY TW10 6JS. Prop: Robin and Patricia Spaight. TN: (01) 948-0643. Est: 1966. Private premises, appointment necessary. Small sec. and antiq. stock and back numbers of military journals. Spec: military (Army and air). Cata: military, 4 a year. B: National Westminster Bank, 1 Saint James's Square, London SW1. Account 13349961. M: A.B.A.

SPIRE BOOKS, 32 ROSEBERRY AVENUE, NEW MALDEN, SURREY KT3 4JS. Prop: T.L. Cooper. TN: (01) 942-2111. Est: 1982. Private premises; appointment necessary. Spec: Ecclesiastical architecture and allied subjects. Cata: several a year. Corresp: Français, Deutsch. B: National Westminster Bank, 125 Great Portland Street, London W1N 6AX.

B.F. STEVENS & BROWN LIMITED, ARDON HOUSE, MILL LANE, GODALMING, SURREY GU7 1HA. TN: Godalming 4391. Telex: 859192. TA: Stebrovens Godalming. Est: 1864. Offices, appointment necessary. Small sec. and antiq. stock. Cata: general, occasionally. A.B.A. B.A. N.B.L.

HENRY STEVENS, SON & STILES, 4 UPPER CHURCH LANE, FARNHAM, SURREY AND AT P.O. BOX 1299, WILLIAMSBURG, VA 23185, U.S.A. TN: Farnham 715416. TA: Mulier Farnham. Shop, closed Saturdays; appointment preferred. Very large sec. and antiq. stock of Americana, old maps and atlases only. Cata: Americana (from Farnham). A.B.A. A.B.A.A.

THEATREMANIA, 66 TRINDLES ROAD, SOUTH NUTFIELD, SURREY RH1 4JN. Prop: Tony Webster. TN: (682) 2651. Est: 1983. Private premises; appointment necessary. Very small stock sec. and antiq. Spec: theatre and performing arts. Cata: infrequent. B: Barclays Bank, 112 Woodcote Road, Wallington, Surrey.

THOMAS THORP, 170 HIGH STREET, GUILDFORD, SURREY GU1 3HP. Prop: H.N., J.H., J.D. and T.C. Thorp. TN: (0483) 62770. Est: 1883. Shop, no early closing. Very large stock sec. and antiq. books; also new books and remainders. Cata: remainders, 5 a year.

CHARLES W. TRAYLEN, CASTLE HOUSE, 49–50 QUARRY STREET, GUILDFORD, SURREY. Prop: C.W. and N.C.R. Traylen. TN: Guildford (0483) 572424. TA: Traylen Guildford. Est: 1945. Shop, closed Mondays. New, and very large sec. and antiq. stock. Cata: general, 3 a year. A.B.A. B.A. N.B.L.

ANTONY WALEY, 14 HIGH STREET, REIGATE, SURREY RH2 9AY. TN: (74) 40020. Est: 1976. Shop, Wednesdays by appointment. Large stock sec. and antiq. books. Spec: illustrated, Folio Society. Corresp: Français. B: Lloyds Bank, Reigate. Account 0167216. P.B.F.A. A.B.A.

VINCENT WATERHOUSE, THE GARDEN FLAT, ADDINGTON PALACE, CROYDON, SURREY CR0 5BB. Prop: Vincent Waterhouse. (01) 656-9194. Est: 1982. Private premises; postal business only. Very small stock sec. and antiq. Spec: modern firsts, private press, illustrated books, bibliography. Cata: 3 a year. B: Williams and Glyn's Bank, Park Street, Croydon.

THE WAVERLEY BOOKSHOP, 97 BRIGHTON ROAD, GODALMING, SURREY. Prop: T.L. Zinn and P. Fennymore. TN: (7979) 6729. Est: 1973. Private premises; appointment necessary. Large stock sec. and antiq. and a few new. Corresp: Deutsch, Français. M: N.B.L.

M.E. WEBB, THE STABLE, GREENLANE, MILFORD, Near GODALMING, SURREY GU8 5BG. Prop: Mrs. M.E. Webb. TN: (048 68) 28896. Est: 1973. Private premises; appointment necessary. Small stock sec. and antiq. books. Spec: topography; country books; children's. Cata: occasionally.

WORLD WAR II BOOKS, P.O. BOX 55, WOKING, SURREY. Prop: Mrs. S.A. Palmer. Est: 1981. Private premises; postal business only. Very small sec. and antiq. stock. Spec: World War II.

51. CORNWALL

BUDE	NEWQUAY
EAST LOOE	PADSTOW
FALMOUTH	PENZANCE
FOWEY	SAINT AUSTELL
HELSTON	SAINT IVES
KILKHAMPTON	SALTASH
LAUNCESTON	TRURO
LISKEARD	WADEBRIDGE

JAMES BAIN LIMITED, TRELOWEN, PENROSE, WADEBRIDGE, NORTH CORNWALL PL27 7TB. Prop: G.D.R. and S.Y. Drake. TN: (084 14) 300. Est: 1816. Private premises; appointment necessary. Small stock sec. and antiq. Spec: bibliography, modern illustrators, Cornwall (including maps and prints). Cata: 1 or 2 a year. Corresp: Français. B: Lloyds Bank, 16 Saint James's Street, London SW1A 1EY. M: A.B.A., N.B.L.

BOOKENDS, 4 SOUTH STREET, FOWEY, CORNWALL. Prop: Jenny Parnwell and Penny Owen. TN: (072683) 2637. Est: 1982. Shop: Closed Wednesday afternoon in winter. Small stock sec. and antiq. Spec: Cornish Books, A. Quiller-Couch, Daphne Du Maurier. Corresp: Français, Sspañol. B: Lloyds Bank, Fowey, Cornwall.

E.K. BROWN, BEVOIS MOUNT, CHURCH STREET, LISKEARD, CORNWALL PL14 3AQ. TN: Liskeard 45128. Est: 1948. Private premises; appointment necessary. New, and medium sec. and antiq. stock on cricket association and rugby football. Cata: on foregoing, occasionally.

CARN COBBA BOOKS, ZENNOR, ST. IVES, CORNWALL TR26 3BZ. Prop: Quinton Quayle. TN: (0736) 796951. Est: 1968. Private premises Large sec. and antiq. stock, also 2000 autograph letters and MSS Spec: early children's books, poetry, novels, detective fiction, first editions of English literature from incunabula to moderns.

CHAPTER ONE, GRENVILLE HOUSE, PENSTOWE, KILKHAMPTON CORNWALL EX23 9QY. Prop: D.R. and O.C. Trumble. TN Kilkhampton 439. Est: 1980. Private premises: appointment necessary Medium stock sec. and antiq. M: P.B.F.A.

PETER DALWOOD, 44 CAUSEWAYHEAD, PENZANCE, CORNWALL. TN Penzance (0736) 3702. Est: 1949. Shop, early closing Wednesday Large sec. and antiq. stock. Spec: English literature and history archaeology, art, Cornwall, ships. Cata: general. A.B.A.

O.M. DAVIES, ROSE COTTAGE, DIDDIES ROAD, STRATTON, BUDE, CORNWALL EX23 9NF. TN: Bude 2585. Est: 1965. Private premises; postal business only. Very small stock sec. and antiq. Spec: Law. No other books kept. Cata: 1 a year. B: Barclays Bank, Bude. Account 80676608.

RICHARD GILBERTSON, ANGEL HILL, LAUNCESTON, CORNWALL. Launceston 3533. Est: 1949 (London). Shop; preferably by appointment. Small stock sec. and antiq. Spec: English children's books. Cata: 3 or 4 a year. Corresp: Français. B: Lloyds Bank, Crediton, Devon. Account 52312.

DENNIS C. GOSNEY, 11 PERHAVER WAY, GORRAN HAVEN, SAINT AUSTELL, CORNWALL. TN: (0726) 842575. Spec: Cornish history and topography, antiquarian.

RONALD C. HICKS, 'DUNROAMIN', 3 CLARE TERRACE, FALMOUTH, CORNWALL. TN: Falmouth 313061. Est: 1964. Private premises, appointment necessary. Very small sec. and antiq. stock. Spec: Cornish histories. Cata: general.

MRS. SHIRLEY LANE, KILTER, COVERACK, HELSTON, CORNWALL TR12 6TN. Prop: Mrs. S.K. Lane. TN: (0326) 280344. Est: 1976. Private premises: appointment necessary. Small stock sec. and antiq. Periodic lists. Corresp: Français. B: Barclays Bank, Helston, Cornwall.

KENNETH LANGMAID, GLENCAIRN HOUSE, GRAMPOUND ROAD, TRURO, CORNWALL. TN: Saint Austell 882280. Est: 1966. Private premises; telephone for appointment. Shop premises: 'Elisabeth', 57A Little Castle Street, Truro. (Books, antiques etc.). Large sec. and antiq. stock. Spec: regional authors, literature, history, sociology, religion. TN: Truro 71345.

JOHN MAGGS, 54 CHURCH STREET, FALMOUTH, CORNWALL. TN: Falmouth 313153. Est: 1900. Shop, early closing Wednesday. Antiquarian print dealers only.

G.W. MOSDELL FINE BOOKS, HILLSIDE, SAINT ISSOY, WADEBRIDGE, CORNWALL. Prop: Gerry Mosdell. TN: (08414) 666. Est. 1963. Stockroom: appointment necessary. Very small stock sec. and antiq. B: Lloyds Bank Limited, Barnstaple, North Devon. M: A.B.A., P.B.F.A.

THE OLD COFFEE HOUSE BOOKS, 29 WESTGATE STREET, LAUNCESTON, CORNWALL. Prop: M.D.F. Ward. Shop. Large stock sec. and antiq.

THE OLD HALL BOOKSHOP AND ART GALLERY, SHUTTA ROAD, EAST LOOE PL13 1BJ. Prop: George H. Jesson. TN: 05036 3700. Est: 1983. Shop, closed on Thursday afternoons (except between June and September). Medium stock sec. and antiq. Spec: natural history, Cornish history and topography, rare maps of Cornwall. Also stocks maps and prints, oil painting and watercolours. Cata: 1 a year. B: Barclays Bank, Lye, Stourbridge, West Midlands. Account 00734004.

IAN PROCTOR, 14 CAUDLEDOWN LANE, STENALESS, SAINT AUSTELL, CORNWALL. TN: (0726) 850435. Private premises; appointment necessary.

THE QUAY BOOKSHOP, QUAY STREET, TRURO, CORNWALL TR1 2HE. Prop: Bruce Burley. TN: Truro 76817. (STD 0872). Est: 1968. Shop, early closing Thursdays in Winter. Medium sec. and antiq. stock, also selected new. Spec: nautical, Cornish books, Devon books, literature. A.B.A.

RAINSFORD RARE BOOKS, 1ST FLOOR ABOVE WILLIAMS-CHEMIST, MARKET PLACE, ST. IVES, CORNWALL. Prop: Victoria Rainsford. Est: 1967. Storeroom, appointment preferred. Medium sec. and antiq. stock, some new. Spec: modern French illustrated, fine arts, bibliography. Cata: on foregoing, 2 a year. N.B.L.

E.R. SLADE, 65 LONGVIEW ROAD, SALTASH, CORNWALL PL12 6EF. TN: Saltash 3834. Est: 1975. Private premises; appointment necessary. Very small stock sec. and antiq. Spec: West Country, in particular Plymouth and Dartmoor. Cata: 1 a year. Corresp: Français, Español. B: Barclays Bank, Liskeard. Account 00809233.

THE STRAND BOOKSHOP, 4 The Strand, Padstow, Cornwall. Prop: D.J. Farquhar, Mrs. M.A. Rowe, Mrs. P.M. Bate and Miss S.A.Rowe TN: Padstow 532236. Est: 1963. Shop, early closing Wednesday in winter only. New, and medium sec. and antiq. stock. Spec: Cornish books; antique maps and prints

COLIN D. TOZER, 75 Fore Street, Saltash, Cornwall PL12 6AB. TN: (07555) 5313. Est: 1978. Private premises; appointment necessary. Very small stock sec. Spec: crime and detective fiction. Large and comprehensive stock of Edgar Wallace. Cata: occasionally.

WELL-HEAD BOOKS, Wellesley Farmhouse, Mitchell, Newquay, Cornwall, Prop: Jo and Derek Godfrey. TN: Mitchell (087 251) 425. Private premises; shop is in Truro Pannier Market, Lemon Quay, Truro, open Wednesdays, Fridays and Saturdays. Large sec. and antiq. stock, some new. Spec: Juveniles, especially Victorian boys' fiction; Cornish books.

52. DEVON

ANGEL HILL BOOKSHOP, 15 Angel Hill, Tiverton, Devon EX16 6PE. Prop: J.N. Segal and R.A. Spiers. Shop: early closing Thursday. Small stock sec. and antiq. Spec: ancient and modern philosophies. M: P.B.F.A.

ANNE'S EMPORIUM 5 The Arcade, Okehampton, Devon EX20 1EX. Prop: Anne Coates. TN: (0837) 3645. Est: 1981. Shop. Small stock sec. and antiq. B: Lloyds Bank, Okehampton.

BAMPTON BOOKS, Franklyn, Deyman's Hill, Tiverton, Devon EX16 4LL. Prop: L.V. Kelly. TN: Tiverton 256170. Est: 1972. Private premises; appointment necessary. Small stock sec. & antiq. Spec: broadcasting and communications. Corresp: Deutsch, Français. Cata: broadcasting–2 a year.

D. BENDING, 12 Cross Park Way, Crown Hill, Plymouth, Devon PL6 5AP. TN: (0752) 772 966. Shop, sec. and antiq. stock. Spec: natural history, topography.

THE BOOKCASE, 28 King Street, Tavistock, Devon PL19 0DX. Prop: Jerry and Jean Harden. TN: (0822) 2410. Est: 1970. Shop, closed Wednesdays during the winter. Medium stock sec. and antiq. books. Large stock of prints. Spec: West Country.

BOOK-ENDS, 2 Rundle Road, Newton Abbot, Devon. Prop. Geoff. Cox. TN: (0626) 68718. Private premises; appointment necessary. Small stock sec. and antiq. Spec: railways and canals.

THE BOOKSHOP, 72 FORE STREET, TOTNES, DEVON. Prop: K.C. Parnell. TN: 864088. Est: 1971. Shop, early closing Thursday. Medium sec. and antiq. stock.

GERARD BROOKES, CROSS PARK, CHAGFORD, DEVON. TN: Chagford 3349. Small stock sec. and antiq. Spec: natural history. Private premises; appointment necessary. Cata.

THE BRUNSWICK BOOKSHOP, BRUNSWICK PLACE, DAWLISH, DEVON. Prop: Gordon Wright. TN: (062 686) 3318. Est: 1956. Shop, closed Thursdays in Winter. Sec. and antiq. stock; also new books and local maps and prints.

PETER BURDICK, RIVERBANK, RETREAT DRIVE, TOPSHAM, EXETER EX3 0LS. Topsham 7296. Est: 1983. Private premises; appointment necessary. Small sec. and antiq. stock.

M. & P.A. CARTER, 34 OXFORD GROVE, ILFRACOMBE, DEVON. TN: (0271) 62924. Formerly of the Old Cinema Bookshop, Ilfracombe. Stock of approximately 5,000 general sec. and antiq. books, plus a selection of Jazz literature. Callers welcome any time, but please telephone first to save a wasted journey.

CASTLE LANE BOOK CORNER, OFF MARKET STREET, TORQUAY, DEVON. Prop: Ivy Earl Smith. TN: (0803) 28991. Est: 1973. Two shops, closed Wednesday afternoons. Very large stock. Spec: Devon and Dartmoor.

CHANTRY BOOKSHOP, 11 HIGHER STREET, DARTMOUTH, DEVON TQ6 9RB. Prop: F.E.W. Merkel. TN: (08043) 2796. Est: 1948. Shop, open business hours or by appointment. Small stock sec. and antiq. books; also fine old prints, maps, watercolours. A.B.A.

COLLARDS BOOKSHOP, 4 CASTLE STREET, TOTNES, SOUTH DEVON. Prop: Belle Collard. TN: home, (054 855) 246. Est: 1970. Shop, early closing Thursdays in Winter. Medium stock sec. and antiq. books. Spec: detective fiction.

ROGER COLLICOTT, 45 DANES ROAD, EXETER, DEVON. Private premises; appointment advised. Small stock sec. and antiq. Spec: West Country topography. P.B.F.A.

COLYTON BOOKS, COLYTON, DEVON. Prop: R. Keen. TN: (0297) 52518. Est: 1971. Shop, early closing Wednesdays. Small stock sec. and antiq. books; also antiques. Spec: law.

CHARLES COX, TWO BELLS, CHAWLEIGH, CHULMLEIGH, DEVON EX18 7HA. Prop: Charles Cox. TN: (07691) 80582. TA: Verso Chulmleigh. Est: 1974. Private premises; appointment necessary. Small stock sec. and antiq. Spec: 19th century literature. Cata: 4 a year. Corresp: Français, Deutsch. B: Lloyds Bank, Tiverton, Devon. M: A.B.A.

THE DARTMOOR BOOKSHOP, 2 KINGSBRIDGE LANE, ASHBURTON, DEVON. Prop: Mrs. E. Lowell. TN: (0364) 53356. Shop. Medium stock sec. and antiq. books.

DICKENS CENTENARY BOOKSHOP, 13 CITY ARCADE, FORE STREET, EXETER EX4 3JE. Prop: R. Parry and R.C. Parry, M.A. TN: (0392) 31587. Est: 1970. Shop. Medium stock sec. and antiq books. Spec: Devonshire. Cata: occasionally. P.B.F.A.

ENIGMA BOOKS, RUINS FIELD, CHURCH LANE, SHELDON, HONITON, DEVON EX14 0QU. Prop: A.E.R.M. Stevens and M.B. Wood. TN: (040 484) 391. Est: 1976. Private premises; appointment necessary. Small stock sec. and antiq. Spec: 19th century fiction, ghost and detective fiction, gothic novels, modern first editions. Cata: 2 or 3 a year. B: National Westminster Bank, High Street, Honiton, Devon.

EXETER RARE BOOKS, GUILDHALL SHOPPING CENTRE, EXETER, DEVONSHIRE EX4 3HG. Prop: R. & R.C. Parry. TN: (0392) 36021. Est: 1977. Shop. Small stock sec. and antiq. Spec: Devon topography. Corresp: German. B: Barclays Bank, Exeter High Street, Exeter. Account 20694738. M: A.B.A. P.B.F.A.

PAUL GIBB, 1A CHAPEL STREET, TIVERTON, DEVON. TN: (088 42) 4595. Private premises; appointment necessary. P.B.F.A.

PETER HAMES, BAKER'S THATCH, CHURCH STREET, BRAUNTON, NORTH DEVON EX33 2EL. TN: (0271) 814095. Private premises; appointment necessary. Spec: topography craft-practical. P.B.F.A.

FREDERICK HARRISON, THE OLD VICARAGE, 43 BRIDWELL ROAD, WESTON MILL, PLYMOUTH, DEVON. TN: (0752) 365595. Private premises; appointment necessary. P.B.F.A.

HOOPER AND MILNE BOOKS, 32 LOWER STREET, DARTMOUTH, DEVON. E.W. Hooper and L.E. Milne. (080 43) 2615. Est: 1981. Shop. Small stock sec. and antiq. B: Lloyds Bank, Spithead, Dartmouth. M: P.B.F.A.

IVYBRIDGE BOOKSHOP, 20 FORE STREET, IVYBRIDGE, DEVON. Prop: James A. Mitchell. TN: Ivybridge (07554) 3666. Shop, closed all day Wednesday and Saturday afternoons. Corresp: Danish. B: Lloyds Bank, 31 Fore Street, Totnes, Devon. Account 0283475. P.B.F.A. (Main premises, James A. Mitchell, North Huish, Devon).

JULIAN'S, 35 VENN GROVE, HARTLEY, PLYMOUTH, DEVON PL3 5PH. TN: (0752) 701740. Prop: Mrs. P.M. Tilbury. Private premises; appointment necessary. Small stock sec. and antiq. Spec: nautical.

RICHARD KEEN, WEST STREET, AXMINSTER, DEVON. TN: Axminster 33785. Est: 1973. Shop, closed Wednesday afternoons. Small stock sec. and antiq. Spec: law, otherwise general stock.

LAST BASTION BOOKSHOP, 75 Fore Street, Bovey Tracey, Newton Abbot, Devon TO13 9AB. Prop: Mr. and Mrs. Huxley. TN: Bovey Tracey 833438. Est: 1979. Shop; closed on Wednesday afternoons: appointments can be made for Wednesday afternoons and Sundays. Medium stock sec. and antiq. Spec: Devon and Dartmoor books. Separate shop for new books. Also bookbinding and translation agency. Cata: 2 a year. B: Midland Bank, Courtenay Street, Newton Abbot. Account 71030345. M: P.B.F.A., B.A.

LINDY'S, 58A Queen Street, Newton Abbot, South Devon. Prop: Duncan and Linda Campbell. TN: (0626) 63221. Est: 1982. Shop; business hours, also by appointment. Medium stock sec. and antiq. Spec: theology. Cata: on subject request.

JOHN LYLE Peeks, Harpford, Sidmouth, Devon EX10 0NH. TN: Colaton Raleigh (0395) 68294. Est: 1952. Private premises, appointment necessary. French and English new, and medium sec. and antiq. stock; also hand printing. Spec: wine, cookery; surrealist movement in art and literature, English and French. Cata: on foregoing, irregularly. M: A.B.A., P.B.F.A., Association of Sn.

DOREEN McCARTHY, Mid-Devon House, South Molton Street, Chulmleigh, Devon EX18 7BW. TN: Chulmleigh 80354. Est: 1979. Stockroom at Eggesford Station; appointment necessary. Small stock of sec. and antiq. books. Cata: occasionally. B: Lloyds Bank, 122 East Street, South Molton, Devonshire. Account 0095504.

MAGIS BOOKS, Cotley House, Dunsford, Devon EX6 7BH. Prop: Mrs. M.A. and I.S. Geikie. TN: (039) 281519. Spec: Occult.

MESSENGERS, 7 Eldertree Gardens, Exeter, Devon EX4 4DE. Prop: Barry Evans. TN: (0392) 213540. Est: 1980. Private premises; appointment necessary. Small stock sec. and antiq. Spec: postal history books and ephemera, overseas guide books, year books, directories, travelogues, military campaigns post 1800, ephemera of all types. Cata: 3 a year. Corresp: Français. B: Barclays Bank, 20 High Street, Exeter. Account 30631035. M: P.B.F.A., Ephemera Society, Manuscript Society.

JAMES A. MITCHELL, 1 THE MANOR, NORTH HUISH, SOUTH BRENT, SOUTH DEVON TQ10 9NQ. TN: South Brent 2288 (STD 03647). Est: 1971. Private premises, appointment requested. Medium sec. and antiq. stock.

MRS. M.C. MOYLE, "MADRAS", 29 FURZEHATT ROAD, PLYMSTOCK, PLYMOUTH, DEVON PL9 8QX. Prop: Mrs. M.C. Moyle. TN: (0752) 42424. Est: 1975. Private premises; appointment necessary. Small stock sec. and antiq. Spec: Devon maps and prints; maps and prints–sporting, naval, military etc. Corresp: Français. M: P.B.F.A.

MR PUNCH'S BOOKSHOP, 5 CHURCH STREET, PAIGNTON, DEVON TQ3 3AF. Prop: E.R. and A.R.A. Wickstead. TN: (0803) 528050 (day) & 63383 (evening). Est: 1979. Shop. Large stock sec. and antiq. B: Lloyds Bank, Higher Union Street, Torre, Torquay.

MIKE NOTT, 17 CATHEDRAL YARD, EXETER EX1 1HB. TN: (0392) 35086. Medium sock sec. and antiq. books, also prints and maps. M: A.B.A.

THE OLD BOOK SHOP [BRIXHAM] LTD. 9 BOLTON STREET, BRIXHAM, SOUTH DEVON. TN: Brixham 4754. Est: 1971. Shop, no early closing. Very large sec. and antiq. stock, also remainders and antique prints.

PANDORA, ANTIQUES CENTRE, 27 NEW STREET, BARBICAN, PLYMOUTH, DEVON PL4 0SP. Prop: William Musgrove. TN: (0752) 61165. Home (0752) 43374. Est: 1971. Stand in antiques market. Small stock sec. and antiq. books; also publishers' remainders, picture postcards, and antiques. Corresp: Français, Español. B: Lloyds Bank, Plymstock Branch, The Broadway, Plymouth. Account 0239527.

PEDLAR'S PACK BOOKS, 4 CIVIC HALL SHOPS, MARKET SQUARE, TOTNES, DEVON. Prop: Martin and Dell Waters. TN: (0803) 866423 (Shop), (036 43)(home). Est: 1981. Shop; closed Thursdays from November to March inclusive. Small stock sec. and antiq. B: National Westminster Bank, Fore Street, Totnes, South Devon. M: P.B.F.A.

ROBIN PITTS, 18 WAVERLEY ROAD, WESTVILLE, KINGSBRIDGE, DEVON. TN: Kingsbridge 2027.

P.M. POLLAK, 29 DRORIDGE, DARTINGTON, TOTNES, SOUTH DEVON TQ9 6JQ. Prop: P.M. Pollak, Ph.D., F.L.S. TN: (0803) 862543. Est: 1973. Shop; small stock sec. and antiq. Spec: science, medicine, technology, natural history. Cata: 8 - 10 a year in specialist subjects. A.B.A.

PORCUPINES, 11 BOUTPORT STREET, BARNSTAPLE, DEVON. Prop: Susan Lowe. TN: (0271) 43641. Est: 1964. Bookroom open Tuesday to Saturday. Small stock sec. and antiq. books. M: P.B.F.A.

MAX POWLING, 10 Darren Road, Kingsteignton, Newton Abbot, Devon TQ12 3DU. TN: Newton Abbot 2922. Private Premises; appointment necessary. Medium stock sec. and antiq. Spec: military & naval history.

QUAYSIDE BOOKSHOP, 43 Northumberland Place, Teignmouth, Devon. Prop: K.E. and J.T. Robinson. TN: (062 67) 5436. Est: 1982. Shop. Small stock sec. and antiq. also new books. B: Lloyds Bank, 4 Regent Street, Teignmouth, Devon. M: B.A.

ROOM AT THE TOP, The Shambles, Fore Street, Kingsbridge, Devon. Prop: Bernard Jacombs. TN: (0548) 6364. Est: 1980 Shop, closed afternoons Thursday and Saturdays. Cata: ocasionally. B: Lloyds Bank, Fore Street, Kingsbridge, Devon.

ROWAN BOOKS, 11 Clifton Hill, Exeter, Devon EX1 2DJ. Prop: Nick Sherington. TN: (0392 216532). Est: 1980. Private premises; appointment necessary. Very small stock sec. and antiq. Spec: first editions of modern English and American literature. Cata: 3 a year.

THE SIMPSON GALLERY, 61 Wolborough Street, Newton Abbot, Devon TQ13. Prop: Bill Simpson. TN: (0626) 66453. Est: 1982. Watercolour gallery, shop, closed Monday. Also open by appointment. Small stock sec. and antiq. also new local interest books. Spec: 19th century literature, railways, motoring, sailing, topography. Cata: scheduled for production. B: Williams and Glyn's Bank Ltd., Strand, Torquay, Devon. M: P.B.F.A.

S.P.C.K., 1-2 Catherine Street, Cathedral Yard, Exeter, Devon EX1 1EX. TN: (0392) 73640. Shop. Medium stock sec. and antiq. also new books. Spec: theology, history, literature. M: B.A., N.B.L.

SOUTH WEST PROGRAMME COLLECTORS (SWCP), 98 Coombe Lane, St. Marychurch, Torquay, Devon TQ2 8EA. Prop: J.F. and J. O'Donnell. TN: 311323. Est: 1979. Private premises; postal business only. Very large stock of antique and modern football programmes. Small stock of better class reference books. Spec: natural history, collecting, topography. Cata: programmes catalogues appromimately every 5 weeks.

TANTALUS ANTIQUES & BOOKS, 36 Rolle Street, Exmouth, Devon. Prop: A.A. and B.K. Dustan Smith. TN: (039 52) 73210. Shop, early closing Wednesdays.

EDWARD THOMAS, "Tinca" Mill Cross, Rattery, Nr. South Brent, Devon TQ10 9LA. TN: South Brent 3494. Est: 1974. Private premises; appointment necessary. Very small stock sec. and antiq. B: National Westminster Bank, Torquay, Strand, Devon. Account 05900921. M: P.B.F.A.

TORRIDGE BOOKS OF LANGTREE, TORRINGTON, DEVON EX38 8NR. Prop: Mary M. Heath. TN: (080 55) 200. Est: 1967. Private premises, but trade welcome any time in business hours. Small sec. and antiq. stock. Spec: West Country; Henry Williamson. Cata: general, 2 a year.

VICTORIA BOOKSHOPS, 14 TEMPLE STREET, SIDMOUTH, DEVON. Prop: J.K. Austin. TN: (039 55) 4461. Est: 1966. Shop, early closing Thursdays in Winter. Large stock sec. and antiq. books; also new books. B.A. (In association with Victoria Bookshop of Swindon.)

WHIDDONS BOOK ROOM, CHAGFORD, DEVON. Prop: Patrick McCormack. TN: Chagford 3237. Shop. Small stock sec. & antiq. also tea rooms.

53. DORSET

BEAMINSTER
BLANDFORD FORUM
BOURNEMOUTH
DORCHESTER
GILLINGHAM
LYME REGIS
POOLE
PUDDLETOWN
SHAFTESBURY
SHERBORNE
VERWOOD
WEYMOUTH
WIMBORNE

A1 CRIME FICTION, 25 Acreman Street, Sherborne, Dorset DT9 3PW. Prop: D.C. Ireland. TN: 814989. Est: 1970. Private premises; appointment necessary. Large stock sec. and antiq. Cata: 12 a year. Corresp: Français. B: Midland Bank, 1 Middle Street, Yeovil, Somerset. Account 01030191.

THE ANTIQUE MAP AND BOOKSHOP, 32 High Street, Puddletown, Nr. Dorchester, Dorset DT2 8RU. Prop: C.D. and H.M. Proctor. TN: (030584) 633. Est: 1976. Shop. Small stock sec. and antiq. Spec: fine bindings, illustrated books, French, German, Italian books pre 1900, literature, topography, maps. Corresp: Deutsch. B: National Westminster Bank, 661 Christchurch Road, Boscombe, Bournemouth. Account 52761436. M: P.B.F.A.

ASHLEY BOOKSHOP, 30b Ashley Road, Boscombe, Bournemouth, Dorset. Prop: Mr. and Mrs. D.J. Horne. Est: 1945. Shop. Very large stock sec. and antiq. books, also postcards, cigarette cards and prints. Spec: Dorset and Hampshire topography.

BARTON BOOKS, Spinneys, Sutton Poyntz, Weymouth, Dorset. Prop: Mrs. A.M.P. Dodge. TN: (0305) 832 189. Private premises; appointment necessary. Spec: poetry, illustrated children's books. M: P.B.F.A.

THE BOOK IN HAND, 17 Bell Street, Shaftesbury, Dorset. Shop, closed Wednesdays.

BOOKLORE. THE SHERBORNE BOOKSHOP, 2 Hound Street, Sherborne, Dorset DT9 3AA. Prop: Mr. and Mrs. J.C. Miller. TN: (0935) 814191. Est: 1975. Shop: closed on Wednesday afternoons. Small stock sec. and antiq. books. New books also stocked. Spec: topography, natural history, travel, poetry. Corresp: Français. B: Barclays Bank, Cheap Street, Sherborne. Account 70654051. M: P.B.F.A., B.A.

BOOKS AFLOAT, 66 Park Street, Weymouth, Dorset DT4 7DE. Prop: John Ritchie. TN: (030 57) 79774. Est: 1983. Shop, closed Mondays. Medium stock sec. and antiq. Spec: naval and maritime.

HENRY BRISTOW 12 Springfield Road, Verwood, Dorset BH21 6HY Prop: V.J.H. Bristow, Iris M. Bristow, David Bristow. TN: (0202) 826979. TA: Bristow Wimborne. Spec: autograph letters, manuscript material, documents, association copies, ephemera and ephemeral publications. Cata: on foregoing.

DAVID BRODIE, 106 CASTLEMAN AVENUE, SOUTHBOURNE, BOURNEMOUTH, DORSET BH6 5EP. TN: (0202) 431997. M: P.B.F.A.

V.I. BURD, THE ELMS, SHAFTESBURY ROAD, GILLINGHAM, DORSET SP8 4JX. TN: (074 76) 2304. Est: 1977. Small general sec. and antiq. stock. Spec: fine illustrated books; West Country topography pre-1930.

MORLEY CASE, 144 WESTERN AVENUE, BOURNEMOUTH, DORSET BH10 6HL. TN: Bournemouth 572573. Est: 1973. Private premises; appointment necessary. Very small stock sec. and antiq. Also old postcards. B: National Westminster Bank, 314 Wimborne Road, Bournemouth BH9 2HJ. Account 02803445. M: P.B.F.A.

COMMIN'S BOOKSHOP [PETER KENNEDY], 100 OLD CHRISTCHURCH ROAD, BOURNEMOUTH BH1 1LT. Prop: Peter Kennedy. TN: (0202) 27504. Est: 1892. Shop. Large stock sec. and antiq. Spec: colour-plate, leather bindings, steel and copper-plate, travel and topography, atlases, maps and prints. Catalogues. M: A.B.A.

H.V. DAY, OLD ROMAN CATHOLIC CHURCH, 25 HIGH WEST STREET, DORCHESTER, DORSET DT1 1UW. OLD ROMAN CATHOLIC CHURCH, 25 HIGH WEST STREET, DORCHESTER, DORSET, DT1 1UW. Prop: H.V. Day and Miss M. Van Noorden. TN: Dorchester 904. Shop, early closing Thursday. Sec. and antiq. stock, also maps and prints. Spec: Dorset. A.B.A.

STEPHEN DUNHILL, 20 EAST STREET, WAREHAM, DORSET BH20 4NP. TN: 2945.

DURWESTON BOOKS, 54–55 DURWESTON, BLANDFORD FORUM, DORSET DT11 0QA. Prop: Mrs. F.E. Penn. TN: Blandford 53223. Est: 1980. Private premises; appointment necessary. Very small stock sec. and antiq. Cata: occasional lists. B: Barclays Bank, Blandford. Account 10333476.

STEVEN FERDINANDO, THE SWAN GALLERY, 51 CHEAP STREET, SHERBORNE, DORSET. Prop: Simon Lamb. (0935) 814465/850210. Est: 1983. Shop: early closing Wednesday. Medium stock sec. and antiq. also maps and prints. Spec: Dorset books, Thomas Hardy, Powys family. M: P.B.F.A.

TREASURE ISLAND BOOKSHOP, 21 WESTBOURNE ARCADE, BOURNEMOUTH, DORSET. TN: Bournemouth 44914. Est: 1947. Shop and storeroom, closed Wednesday. Large sec. stock. No catalogues.

R.E. GREENLAND, CHURCH STREET, DORCHESTER, DORSET OT1 1JN. TN: Dorchester (0305) 62517. Est: 1972. Shop, early closing

Thursday. Medium sec. and antiq. stock. B: Lloyds Bank, Dorchester. Account 0308878.

R.H. & P. HASKELL, The Bookshop, 19 Towngate Place, Poole, Dorset BH15 1PL. TN: (020 13) 70134. Est: 1973. Shop. Mediums stock sec. and antiq. books; also publishers' remainders . Spec: architecture.

HELICON BOOKS, 94 Howeth Road, Bournemouth, Dorset BH10 5ED. Prop: John Howard. TN: (0202) 521764. Est: 1982. Private premises; appointment necessary. Very small stock sec. and antiq. also new books. Spec: poetry and literature. Cata: 3 a year. Corresp: Français, Deutsch. B: Midland Bank, Landsdowne Branch, 7 Royal London House, Christchurch Road, Bournemouth BH1 3LL. A/c No. 01053787. M: P.B.F.A.

BETTY AND R. HYDE, 7 Coy Pond Road, Branksome, Poole, Dorset BH12 1JT. TN: (0202) 766047.

FRED JACKSON 17 North Street, Beaminster, Dorset DT8 3DZ. TN: (0308) 862754. Est: 1973. Private premises; appointment necessary. Medium stock sec. and antiq. books; also new books on local topics and publishing. Spec: educational and political reprints. Cata: occasionally.

PETER KENNEDY, 100 Old Christchurch Road, Bournemouth, Dorset. Prop: Peter Kennedy. TN:(0202) 27504. Est: 1972. Stock can be seen on the first floor of Commin's Bookshop at the same address. Sec. and antiq. Spec: natural history, botany and gardening, fine colour-plate. M: A.B.A.

MARINE-WORKSHOP BOOKSHOP, The Old Bonded Store, The Cobb, Lyme Regis, Dorset DT7 3JF. Prop: Maurice S. Bishop. TN: Lyme Regis 2429. Est: 1962. Shop. Medium sec. and antiq. stock. Cata: occasionally.

A.E. MORRIS (YESTERDAYS BOOKS), 65–67 Bennett Road, Bournemouth, Dorset BH8 8RH. Prop: Mrs. A.E. Morris. TN: (0202) 302023. Shop. Medium stock sec. and antiq. Spec: children's illustrated, travel books with engraved views, coloured plates and maps; leather-bound books.

KENNETH MUMMERY LIMITED, 9 Saint Winifreds Road, Bournemouth, Dorset BH2 6NY. Prop: Kenneth Mummery. TN: Bournemouth 25170. TA: Olmuscus Bournemouth. Est: 1945. Private premises, appointment necessary. Large sec. and antiq. stock. Spec: music. Cata: music, 2 a year. A.B.A.

M. & R. ORCHARD, 74 BRASSEY ROAD, WIMBORNE, BOURNEMOUTH, DORSET. TN: (0202) 531787. Private premises; appointment necessary.

ORCHARDS, 7 WESTBOURNE ARCADE, BOURNEMOUTH, DORSET. Prop: Brian Orchard. Shop, no early closing. Spec: sheet music, films, railways, local history.

JOHN RITCHIE, CLOVER COTTAGE, WONSTON, HAZELBURY BRYAN, NEAR STURMINSTER NEWTON, DORSET. TN: Hazelbury Bryan 411. Spec: Maritime books, also print, paintings, models.

H. & S. ROWAN, 459 CHRISTCHURCH ROAD, BOSCOMBE, BOURNEMOUTH, DORSET. TN: Bournemouth 38820. Est: 1969. Shop, no early closing. Medium sec. and antiq. stock, also remainders, bric-a-brac and prints. Spec: art, Hampshire topography, plate books, prints.

SACKETTS BOOKSHOP, 36A SALISBURY STREET, BLANDFORD FORUM, DORSET. Prop: Terance and Eliza Sackett. TN: (0258) (53654). Est: 1980. Shop, closed Wednesday afternoons. Medium stock sec. and antiq. Spec: crafts, especially embroidery, weaving and textiles. Cata: Lists 4 a year, plus continual specific craft mailings. Corresp: Français. B: Midland Bank, Market Place, Blandford Forum Dorset.

SERENDIP FINE BOOKS, 11 BROAD STREET, LYME REGIS, DORSET. Prop: Mr. & Mrs. C.E.H. Chapman. TN: (029 74) 2594. Est: 1968. Shop, early closing Thursdays. Small stock sec. and antiq. books; also new books, greeting cards and posters. B.A., N.B.L.

EDWARD AND PAMELA PAGET-TOMLINSON, DUNTISH OLD FARM, RUCKLAND NEWTON, DORCHESTER, DORSET. Prop: E. and P. Paget-Tomlinson. Est: 1978. Very small stock sec. and antiq. Private premises; appointment necessary. Spec: model railways, model ships, maritime. Cata: occasional. Corresp: Français, Deutsch. B: National Westminster Bank, Ulverston, Cumbria LA12 7AX.

TREVORS BOOKSHOP, 71 Poole Road, Westbourne, Bournemouth, Dorset. TN: (0202) 762508. Shop. Sec. and Antiq. also new books.

WESTHAM BOOKSHOP, 13 Abbotsbury Road, Westham, Weymouth, Dorset. Prop: J.E. Spooner and S.A. Minns. TN: (030 57) 75660. Est: 1976. Shop, early closing Wednesdays. Medium stock sec. and antiq. books.

CHRISTOPHER WILLIAMS [INCORPORATING CULMUS BOOKS], 23 Saint Leonard's Road, Bournemouth, Dorset BH8 8QL. Prop: Mr. and Mrs. C. Williams. TN: (0202) 519683. Shop, closed Mondays. Spec: the arts, bibliography, topography, cookery and wine.

WIMBORNE BOOKSHOP, 26 West Street, Wimborne Minster, Dorset. Prop: W.H. Hoade. TN: (0202) 887320. Est: 1977. Shop, early closing Wednesdays. Small stock sec. and antiq. books. Spec: archaeological, Dorset maps and prints. Cata: 3 or 4 a year.

WOOLCOTT BOOKS, Peacemarsh, Gillingham, Dorset SP8 EU. Prop: H.M. and J.R. St. Aubyn. TN: Gillingham (Dorset) 2863. Est: 1978. Private premises; appointment necessary. Small stock sec. and antiq. Spec: all military and British colonial subjects. Cata: 2 a year. B: Lloyds Bank, Warminster. Account 0043612.

SIDNEY WRIGHT BOOKSELLERS, 12 and 13 Royal Arcade, Boscombe, Bournemouth, Dorset BH1 4BT. TN: Bournemouth (0202) 37153. Est: 1906. Shop, closed Wednesday afternoons Winter, all day Summer. New, and large sec. and small antiq. stock. M: B.A., N.B.L. N.B.L.

ROSIE AND SUSY YOUNG, Oselhay Farmhouse, Whitchurch Canonicorum, Bridport, Dorset. Prop: Rosie Young. TN: Chidlock (0297) 89710. Private premises; appointment advisable. Medium stock sec. and antiq. books. Spec: juvenile, illustrated. M: P.B.F.A.

54. HAMPSHIRE AND THE ISLE OF WIGHT

ALRESFORD	NEW MILTON
ALTON	PETERSFIELD
ANDOVER	PORTSMOUTH
BASINGSTOKE	RYDE
BEMBRIDGE	RINGWOOD
CHANDLERS' FORD	ROMSEY
CHURCH CROOKHAM	SANDOWN
COWES	SOUTHAMPTON
EMSWORTH	SOUTHSEA
FARNBOROUGH	TOTLAND
LISS	VENTNOR
LYMINGTON	WINCHESTER

ACADEMY BOOKS, 13 Marmion Road, Southsea, Hampshire PO5 2AT. Prop: William H. Robinson. TN: 816632. Est: 1971 (Portsmouth). Shop and stockroom. Spec: theology, church history, also new books on theology. Cata: 2 a year.

ARMSTRONG, 14A York Road, Sandown, Isle of Wight PO36 8ET. Prop: Mrs. B.E. Armstrong. TN: (0983) 406226. Est: 1980. Stockroom and shop; appointment necessary. Small stock sec. and antiq. books, also coins, postcards and stamps. Spec: Isle of Wight. Corresp: Deutsch, Français. B: Lloyds Bank, 14 High Street, Sandown. Account 187297.

AVIATION BOOKS, Mill Race, Old Mill Lane, Sheet, Petersfield, Hampshire GU31 4DA. Prop: G.E. Lott. Private premises; appointment preferred. Small sec. and antiq. stock. Spec: aviation. Cata: occasionally.

VINCENT G. BARLOW, 24 Howerts Close, Warsash, Southampton, Hampshire SO3 6JR. Prop: Vincent Barlow. TN: (04895) 82431. Est: 1981. Private premises; appointment necessary. Very small stock sec. and antiq. Spec: illustrated books, artists monographs, art reference. Cata: occasional. B: Barclays Bank, 1 Shore Road, Warsash, Southampton SO3 6JR.

J.G. BARTON, 84 Old Kennels Lane, Winchester, Hampshire. TN: Winchester 66543. Private premises, appointment necessary. Small sec. and antiq. stock. Spec: British topography, archaeology, history. Cata: on foregoing, occasionally.

BOOK ACADEMY, 13 Marmion Road, Southsea, Hampshire. Prop: W. Robinson. TN: 21041. Est: 1972. Shop. Large stock sec. and antiq.

books; also new books, antiques and pictures. Spec: theology. Cata: general, 2 a year.

BOOKS AND THINGS, 99 Old Milton Road, New Milton, Hampshire BH25 6DN. Prop: A. Keith. TN: (0425) 617521. Est: 1977. Shop; closed Wednesday afternoons. Large stock sec. and antiq. also back numbers of journals. Corresp: Français. B: Lloyds Bank, Station Road, New Milton. Account 0116671.

BOOKSHELVES, 13 University Road, Highfield, Southampton, Hampshire. Prop: Sarah Bossom. TN: Southampton 556009.

THE BOOKSHOP, The Square, Emsworth, Hampshire PO10 7EJ. Prop: Miss D.M. Way. TN: Emsworth 2617. Shop, early closing Wednesday. New, and small sec. and antiq. stock; also stationery and pottery. B.A. N.B.L.

BUFO BOOKS, 9 School Lane, Saint Ives, Ringwood, Hampshire. Prop: Ruth Allen and Peter Hubbard. TN: (042 54) 4442. Est: 1979. Private house; appointment necessary. Small stock sec. and antiq. Spec: children's books, countryside and natural history. Corresp: Français. B: Lloyds Bank PLC., West Cliff (Bournemouth) Branch, 16 Poole Hill, Bournemouth BH2 5PY. M: P.B.F.A.

CAMPBELL'S PICTURECRAFT, Dennett Road, High Street, Bembridge, Isle of Wight. TN: Bembridge 2354. Prop: F. Stockton. Est: 1959. Shop, early closing Thursday. Very small sec. and antiq. stock; also picture framer. Spec: topographical prints of the Isle of Wight, Hampshire, Sussex; maps of the Isle of Wight; sea charts. B: Barclays Bank, High Street, Ryde, Isle of Wight. M: Fine art Trade Guild

JAMES CATNEY, 11 Bath Road, Cowes, Isle of Wight PO31 7QN. TN: 298899. Est: 1977. Shop; closed on Wednesdays. Medium stock sec. and antiq. also back-numbers of journals. Corresp: Français.

T.A. CHERRINGTON, 67A Bedford Place, Southampton, Hampshire SO1 2DS. TN: (0703) 224265. Est: 1976. Shop. Large stock, sec. and antiq. books. Subject lists (S.A.E.)

M. & B. CLAPHAM, Lymcroft, Boldre, Lymington, Hampshire SO4 8PD. Prop: Michael and Barbara Clapham. TN: (0590) 73178. Est: 1978. Private premises; anytime by appointment. Med. stock sec. and antiq. Spec: Australasia. Cata: 6 a year. Corresp: Français, Italiano. B: National Westminster Bank, Lymington. M: P.B.F.A.

COUNTRYSIDE BOOKS, 6 WINCHESTER STREET, ANDOVER, HAMPSHIRE. Prop: Martin Smith. TN: Andover 58254. Est: 1975. Shop, closed Wednesday. Small stock sec. and antiq. Spec: natural history, agriculture, field sports, countryside generally. Cata: 4 a year. B: National Westminster Bank, 9 Bridge Street, Andover, Hants. Account 73 65743. M: P.B.F.A.

A.E. COX, 21 CECIL ROAD, ITCHEN, SOUTHAMPTON, HAMPSHIRE SO2 7HX. TN: Southampton (0703) 447989. Private premises; postal business and book fairs. Small sec. and antiq. stock. Spec: cinema, theatre and all entertainment. Cata: on foregoing, 8 a year. M: P.B.F.A.

IAN CROSS, MAIDENTHORNE COTTAGE, NORTH WALTHAM, BASINGSTOKE, HAMPSHIRE. Prop: Ian Cross. (025 675) 587. Est: 1972. Private premises; appointment necessary. Very small stock sec. and antiq. also remainders. Spec: portrait miniatures and silhouettes. Corresp: Français, Italiano. B: Lloyds Bank, 115 Victoria Road, Aldershot, Hampshire.

PETER M. DALY, REAR OF "SHIPS AND SEALING WAX", 20A JEWRY STREET, WINCHESTER, HAMPSHIRE. Est: 1977. Shop, open Monday, Fridays & Saturdays. Spec: natural history, botany, gardening, birds, travel. B: National Westminster Bank, 105 High Street, Winchester. Account 73264083.

FARNBOROUGH BOOKSHOP AND GALLERY, 26 GUILDFORD ROAD WEST, FARNBOROUGH, HAMPSHIRE GU14 6PU. Prop: P.H. Taylor. TN: Farnborough 518033. Est: 1978. Shop; closed on Wednesdays. Medium stock sec. and antiq. Spec: military history, modern first editions, also picture gallery and picture framing. Cata: 10 a year. Corresp: Français, Italiano, Deutsch. B: Lloyds Bank, 47 Lynchford Road, Farnborough, Hampshire. Account 0231084.

SUSANNA FISHER SPENCER, UPHAM, SOUTHAMPTON, HAMPSHIRE SO3 1JD. TN: DURLEY (048 96) 291. Private premises; appointment necessary. Stock of sea charts and books on hydrography, sailing directions. only. Cata: charts, 3 a year.

H.M. GILBERT & SON, 2½ PORTLAND STREET, SOUTHAMPTON, HAMPSHIRE SO1 0EB. Prop: B.L. and R.C. Gilbert. TN: Southampton 26420. Est: 1859. Shop, no early closing. New, and very large sec. and antiq. stock. B: Lloyds Bank, 19 High Street, Southampton. Account 0151588. A.B.A. B.A.

HENRY MARCH GILBERT, 19 The Square, Winchester, Hampshire. Prop: B.L. & R.C. Gilbert. TN: Winchester 52832. Est: 1895. Shop, no early closing. New, and very large sec. and antiq. stock. A.B.A. B.A.

C & M GREENFIELD, 8 West Heath Road, Farnborough, Hampshire GU14 8QH. Prop: C.D. Greenfield. TN: Farnborough 43121. Est: 1978. Private premises. Postal business only. Small stock sec. and antiq. Cata: occasionally. B: Trustee Savings Bank, 92 Queensmead, Farnborough, Hampshire. Account 77-4922-00567061.

E. CHALMERS HALLAM, Earlswood, 4 Egmont Drive, Avon Castle, Ringwood, Hampshire. TN: Ringwood 3289. Est: 1946. Storeroom, appointment necessary. Large sec. and antiq. stock. Spec: angling, shooting, firearms, archery, falconry, big game hunting, wildfowling and field sports; natural history; arms and armour. Cata: on foregoing, about 4 a year. Corresp: Français.

FRANK HAMMOND, Sowley House, Lymington, Hampshire SO4 8SQ. TN: East End 231. Private premises, appointment necessary. Est: 1938. Medium antiq. stock. Spec: travel. early English books, illuminated manuscripts.

THE HAMPSHIRE BOOKSHOP, Kingsgate Arch, Winchester, Hampshire SO23 9PD. Prop: Mrs. M. Green. TN: (0962) 64710. Est: 1973. Shop, early closing Thursdays. Very small stock sec. and antiq. books; also new books. Spec: fine arts; local history, prints and maps.

MICHAEL HARRINGTON LIMITED, 74 Parchment Street, Winchester, Hampshire SO23 8AT. TN: Winchester 53608. Prop: R.M.H. Lawrence. Shop. Est: 1948. New, and medium sec. stock. Spec: theatre and allied subjects. Cata: 3 a year. M: B.A., N.B.L.

HERITAGE BOOKS LIMITED, 7 Cross Street, Ryde, Isle of Wight PO33 2AD. Director: Reverend D.H. Nearn, B.D., F.R.G.S. TN: Ryde 62933. Est: 1978. Shop, closed on Thursdays. Medium stock sec. and antiq. modern first editions, Isle of Wight, yachting, Africa. Cata: occasionally. Corresp: Français, Portuguese. B: National Westminster Bank, High Street, Ventnor, Isle of WIght.

HUGHES AND SMEETH LIMITED, 1 Gosport Street, Lymington, Hampshire. Prop: Peter Hughes and Sandra Smeeth (Directors). TN: (0590) 76324. Est: 1976. Shop. Medium stock sec. and antiq. Spec: travel, topography, natural history, also stocks antique maps and prints. Cata: 1 a year. B: National Westminster Bank, Blue Boar Row, Salisbury, Wiltshire. M: P.B.F.A., A.B.A.

HARRY E. ILES, 16 SHAMBLERS ROAD, WEST COWES, ISLE OF WIGHT. Est: 1960. Postal business only. Very small sec. and antiq. stock. Spec: military, Isle of Wight. Cata: on foregoing, occasionally. B: Lloyds Bank, High Street, West Cowes, Isle of Wight. Account 0059119.

H.B. JOHN, 26 NEW ROAD, LOVEDEAN, PORTSMOUTH, HAMPSHIRE PO8 9RU. Private premises, postal business only. Small stock sec. and antiq. Spec: applied arts, wireless and television, illustrators, caricaturists, children's books. Cata: occasionally.

A. & S. KEEN 19 PIER STREET, VENTNOR, ISLE OF WIGHT. TN: Ventnor 853706. Est: (in Ventnor) 1972. Shop, early closing Wednesday May to Sept; all day Wednesdays October to April. Medium sec. and antiq. stock. M: A.B.A.

THE LISS BOOKSHOP AND GALLERY, 73 STATION ROAD, LISS, HAMPSHIRE GU33 7AD. Prop: Olive Butler and Mr. A.E. Gabie. TN: Liss 2406. Est: 1978. Shop and gallery. Very large stock sec. and antiq. also back-numbers of journals, cards, art materials, pictures and prints, picture framing. Corresp: Français, Español

THE MEETING HOUSE PRESS, 24, PITREAVIE ROAD, COSHAM, PORTSMOUTH, HAMPSHIRE PO6 2ST. Prop: Donald E.W. Howells. TN: Cosham 374476. Est: 1968. Postal business only. New and small sec. humanism, freethought, rationalism. Cata: on foregoing Spring and Autumn.

MILESTONE PUBLICATIONS, 62 MURRAY ROAD, HORNBEAM, PORTSMOUTH, HAMPSHIRE. Prop: N.J. Pine. TN: (0705) 597440. Est: 1973. Stockroom; appointment necessary. Very small stock dealing only with Goss and Crested China; books only by Goss, and by Llewelyn Jewitt and S.C. Hall. Also new books on the same area. B: Lloyds Bank, High Street, Emsworth, Hampshire.

MOTLEY BOOKS LIMITED, MOTTISFONT ABBEY, ROMSEY, HAMPSHIRE SO5 0LP. TN: Lockerley (0794) 40278. TA: Motbooks Southampton Est: 1963. Postal business only. New, sec. and antiq. stock on theatre Cata: frequently.

OLDFIELD ANTIQUE MAPS AND PRINTS, 34 NORTHAM ROAD SOUTHAMPTON, HAMPSHIRE SO2 0PA. Prop: Anne Downes. TN Southampton (0703) 38916. Est: 1970. Shop. Small stock sec. an antiq. Spec: topographical books, large stock of maps and prints. Cata occasionally. B: Barclays Bank, West Street, Fareham. Accoun 70703222. M: P.B.F.A.

LAURENCE OXLEY, The Studio Bookshop, 17 Broad Street, Alresford, Near Winchester, Hampshire SO24 9AW. TN: Alresford (096273) 2188. TA: Oxley Alresford. Est: 1949. Shop, early closing Wednesday. Large sec. and antiq. stock; also prints, maps, water-colours; picture frame makers (trade and retail); restoration and cleaning of oils and prints. Spec: India and Far East. Lists issued monthly. Also topography, atlases, scrapbooks. A.B.A. B.A. N.B.L. Fine Art Trade Guild.

THE PETERSFIELD BOOKSHOP, 16a Chapel Street, Petersfield, Hampshire. Prop: Frank Westwood. TN: Petersfield 63438. Est: 1918. Shop, no early closing. New, and large sec. and antiq. stock; also picture framing. Spec: Colonial travel and history; angling. Cata: on foregoing and general, 3 a year. A.B.A., B.A., N.B.L., P.B.F.A., B.A.D.A.

PINHORNS, Hulverstone Manor Farmhouse, Newport, Isle of Wight PO30 4EH. Prop: Malcolm Pinhorn, B.A., F.S.G. Est: 1966. Postal business only. Very small sec. and antiq. stock, also publishers. Spec: English architectural, family, and local history. Isle of Wight. Cata: on foregoing, occasionally.

WG. CDR. F.E.F. PRINCE, KILN LODGE, BLACKNEST, ALTON, HAMPSHIRE GU34 4QB. Est: 1967. Private premises; appointment necessary. Medium stock sec. and antiq. books. Spec: aviation. Cata: aviation, 2 a year. A.B.A.

PRINTED PAGE, 2-3 BRIDGE STREET, WINCHESTER, HAMPSHIRE SO23 9BH. Prop: Christopher D. Wright. TN: 54072. Est: 1977. Shop; closed on Mondays. Very small stock sec. and antiq. also picture framing. Spec: Hampshire, canals, antique prints and maps. Cata: occasionally. B: Coutts and Co. 1 Old Park Lane, London W1X 4BS.

A.G. & M.M. PURSER, 12 PEVERELLS ROAD, CHANDLERS FORD, HAMPSHIRE. Prop: A.G. and M.M. Purser. TN: (042 15) 61815. Private premises; telephone appointment necessary. Very small stock sec. and antiq. Spec: colouring and mounting of maps and prints. Also small selection of topographical books.

STANLEY V. RIDDELL, OLD DOWN HOUSE, SWELLING HILL, ROPLEY, ALRESFORD, HAMPSHIRE SO24 0DA. Est: 1951. Postal business only. Very large stock of antique maps and prints. B: National Westminster Bank, Four Marks, Alton, Hampshire.

RUSKINS 2, 27 BELL STREET, ROMSEY, HAMPSHIRE SO5 8GY. Prop: J. Davies. TN: Romsey 516404. Est: 1980. Shop. Medium stock sec. and antiq. Spec: sailing.

J.C. & R.M.P. SANDFORD, 172 READING ROAD SOUTH, CHURCH CROOKHAM, HAMPSHIRE. TN: (025 14) 7235. Est: 1971. Private premises; appointment essential. Small stock sec. and antiq. Spec: field sports (especially shooting), natural history of game animals and birds. Cata: occasionally. Corresp: Français.

SEN BOOKS, GREENWAYS, 177 PACK LANE, KEMPSHOTT, BASINGSTOKE, HAMPSHIRE RG22 5HW. Prop: Sarah and Andrew Duckworth. TN: (0256) 22904. Est: 1974. Private premises; appointment necessary. Medium stock sec. and antiq. books. Cata: general, occasionally.

GILBERT SHEMELD, 9 MARGATE ROAD, SOUTHSEA, HAMPSHIRE. TN (0705) 816245. Est: 1951. Private premises; appointment necessary. Very small stock sec. and antiq. books. Spec: ephemera and rare antiquarian only. Cata: ephemera, 4 a year.

L.J. SKLAROFF, CRAIGLEA, THE BROADWAY, TOTLAND, ISLE OF WIGHT PO39 0BW. Prop: L.J. Sklaroff. TN: (0983) 754960. Est: 1970. Private premises; any time but appointment preferred. Small stock sec. and antiq. Spec: modern first editions, private presses, 20th centur illustrators, Mervyn Peake. Cata: 6 a year. Corresp: Français, Deutsch, Italiano, Español. B: Midland Bank, Freshwater, Isle of Wight. M: P.B.F.A.

SKRIMSHIRE'S BOOKSHOPS, 25 AND 34 NORTHAM ROAD, SIX DIALS, SOUTHAMPTON, HAMPSHIRE SO1 0NZ. Prop: M.E. Kneller. TN: Southampton 22804. Est: 1948. Shop, closed Wednesday Afternoons. Large sec. and antiq. stock. Cata: occasionally.

S.P.C.K., 24 THE SQUARE, WINCHESTER, HAMPSHIRE SO23 9EX. TN: 0962-66617. Shop. Large stock sec. and antiq. Spec: theology, history, literature, also new books and periodicals. M: P.B.F.A., B.A., N.B.L.

TARA ASSOCIATES LIMITED, SOUTH END HOUSE, CHURCH LANE, LYMINGTON, HAMPSHIRE SO4 9RA Directors: Peter and Elizabeth Watson. TN: (0590) 76848 TA: Tara Lymington. Est: 1973. Private Premises and stock room; appointment necessary. Medium stock sec. and antiq. books. Spec: social and economic history; including exploration and trade, fashion and manners, feminism, social philosophy, history of technology. Cata: on foregoing, 5 a year. B: Barclays Bank, High Street, Lymington, Hants. Account 40857300. A.B.A., P.B.F.A.

W.D. TRIVESS, Heathfield House, Meonstoke, Southampton, Hampshire SO3 1ND. TN: Droxford (04897) 326. Est: 1936. Private premises, appointment necessary. Small sec. and antiq. stock. Spec: mainly antiquarian maps and prints. Cata: monthly.

THE TYRRELL BOOKSHOP AND GALLERY LIMITED, 80 Christchurch Road, Ringwood, Hampshire BH24 1DR. Prop: David Bristow. TN: (04254) 4489. Est: 1977. Shop: closed on Monday and Saturday afternoons. Small stock antiq. Spec: Australasia. Cata: 12 a year.

UPCROFT BOOKS LIMITED, 66 Saint Cross Road, Winchester, Hampshire SO23 9PS. TN: (0962) 52679. Telex: 477379. Ref: UBL0023. Private premises; appointment necessary. Small stock sec. and antiq. Spec: history, architecture. Cata: 6 a year. B: National Giro. Account 234 2251

WARSASH NAUTICAL BOOKSHOP, 31 Newtown Road, Warsash, Southampton, Hampshire SO3 6FY. Prop: Alan Obin. TN: (048 95) 2384. Shop, no early closing. Small stock sec. and antiq. books; also new books. Spec: nautical books of all sorts. Cata: on foregoing, 2 or 3 a year. B.A.

55. WEST SUSSEX

ARUNDEL
BOGNOR REGIS
CHICHESTER
CUCKFIELD
EAST GRINSTEAD
EAST PRESTON
HASSOCKS
HAYWARDS HEATH
HORSHAM
LANCING
LITTLEHAMPTON
MIDHURST
PETWORTH
RUSPER
UPPER BEEDING
WORTHING

MICHAEL ARDEN-BROWN AND SONS, 39 Orchard Way, Bognor Regis, Sussex. Prop: Michael Arden-Brown. Est: 1963. Stockroom; appointment necessary. Small stock sec. and antiq. Spec: naval and maritime, the sea and shipping. Cata: several a year. M; A.B.A. P.B.F.A.

ATHLETICA [BOOKS] INTERNATIONAL, 32 Halsbury Road, Worthing, West Sussex BN11 2JP. Prop: G.D. Goodrich. TN: (0903) 200434. Est: 1974. Private premises; appointment necessary. Very small stock sec. and antiq. books. Spec: Olympic Games, Track and Field Athletics, Official and Unofficial Reports onOlympic, Commonwealth and other Games; histories, statistics, golf (instructional before 1925, history and biographies). Cata: on foregoing, occasionally.

MISS M.G. ATKINS, 117 Birdham Road, Chichester, Sussex. TN: Chichester 83446. Est: 1962 (formerly of The Bookshop, Blackheath). Private premises, appointment necessary. Very small sec. and antiq. stock. Spec: early juvenile. Cata: early juvenile and general, occasionally. N.B.L.

BADGERS BOOKS, 8 Gratwicke Road, Worthing, West Sussex BN11 4BH. Prop: Ray Potter and David Crawford. TN: Worthing 211816. Est: 1982. Shop. Small stock sec. and antiq. Spec: natural history; occult and mysticism.

J.R. BATTEN, 9 Windmill Lane, Lewes Road, East Grinstead, West Sussex RH19 3SZ. TN: (0342) 22051. Sec. and antiq. stock: also prints, china and ephemera. Spec: cricket.

BOOK BARGAINS, 130 The Hornet, Chichester, Sussex PO19 4JR. Est: 1960. Shop, closed Mondays and Thursdays. Small sec. and antiq. stock, small amount of new books; prints and British coins. Spec: Sussex, natural history, art & military.

BOOKROOM, Petworth Antique Market, East Street, Petworth, West Sussex GU28 0AB. Prop: Doris Rayment. TN: 42073. Est: 1968. Shop. Small stock sec. and antiq. also antiques. B: Midland Bank, Petworth. Account 60690112.

FRANCES BOOKS, 3 Crescent Road, Worthing, Sussex. Prop: Mr. and Mrs. M. Lee. TN: Worthing (0903) 209693. Est: 1968. Shop, early closing Wednesday. Medium sec. and antiq. stock.

THE BOOKSHOP IN NORFOLK ROAD, 13 Norfolk Road, Littlehampton, Sussex. Prop: Mike and Rosie Jennings. TN: Littlehampton 3638. Est: 1970. Shop, early closing Wednesday. (Closed Tuesday & Wednesday in winter.) Medium sec. and antiq. stock, also bric-a-brac. Spec: police and crime. Cata: on foregoing, occasionally.

BROADWATER BOOKROOM, 20 Broadwater Street East, Worthing, Sussex BN14 9AD. Prop: Mrs. Ursula Powell. TN: (0903) 39708. Est: 1974. Shop, closed Wednesdays. Small stock sec. and antiq. books; also antiques. Spec: Irish interest.

BROWSE AWHILE, Mint Market, Grange Road, Midhurst, West Sussex. Prop: Dalveen and John Taylor. TN: (048 68) 7243. Est: 1980. Shop; open Tuesday, Thursday, Friday 11–4pm., also Saturday. B: Barclays Bank, 87 High Street, Godalming, Surrey. M: P.B.F.A.

BYGONE BOOKS, Axmas Cottage, Rusper, West Sussex RH12 4RF. Prop: G.R. Armstrong. TN: (029 384) 256. Private premises; appointment necessary. Small antiquarian stock. Spec: General literature pre 1800. Cata: occasionally. M: A.B.A.

CASTLETOWN BOOKSHOP, Henfield Road, Upper Beeding, Sussex. Prop: D.J. Barr. TN: (0903) 813048. Shop; open on Wednesdays and Saturdays 9.30 am to 5 pm. Other times by appointment. Small stock sec. and antiq. Spec: illustrated and private press books, natural history.

CHICHESTER BOOKSHOP LIMITED, 33 and 39 Southgate, Chichester, West Sussex PO19 1DP. Prop: George Thompson and John Dent. TN: Chichester 785473. Est: 1966. Shop, closed Thursday afternoons. Large sec. and antiq. stock.

W.D. CRAVEN, 2 Kent Mansions, Brighton Road, Worthing, Sussex BN11 3EH. TN: (0903) 38503. Est: 1950. Private premises; appointment preferred. Small sec. and antiq. stock. Spec: agriculture before 1900; English literature before 1850, first and early editions.

CURIOSITIES, 103 South Street, Lancing, West Sussex BN15 8AS. Prop: J.D. Van Dam. TN: (09063) 2807. Est: 1972. Shop. Medium stock sec. and antiq. also picture framers, restoration, paintings and prints. Corresp: Deutsch, Français, Italiano. B: Barclays Bank, 47 North Road, Account 40902128.

D.L. BOOKS, Whiteways, 28 Lowfield Road, Haywards Heath, Sussex RH16 4DW. Prop: Mr. and Mrs T.E. Fisher. TN: Haywards Heath 59455. Private premises; appointment necessary. Large stock sec. and antiq. A.B.A.

TOM DRIVER AGENCIES, The Old Stable Bookshop, 2 Tarrant Square, Arundel, West Sussex BN18 9DE. Prop: Mr. and Mrs. T. Driver. Est: 1981. Shop, closed Monday and Tuesday. Small stock sec. and antiq. Spec: The Works of Rudyard Kipling. Cata: monthly. M: P.B.F.A.

EPHEMERA, Castle Court, rear of 12 High Street, Arundel, Sussex BN18 9AB. Prop: H. Mitchell Jacob, J.P. TN: Arundel 883120. Est: 1925. Shop. Small sec. and antiq. stock.

W.J. FAUPEL, 3 Halsford Lane, East Grinstead, Sussex RH19 1NY. TN: (0342) 27043. Est: 1980. Private premises; postal business only. Large stock sec. and antiq. maps and views. Spec: Americas (North, Central, South), Carribean.

DONALD GILDEA, 15 Shelley Road, Bognor Regis, Sussex. TN: Bognor Regis (0243) 821266. Est: 1966. Private premises; postal business only. Small sec. stock. Spec. bibliography, gardening, cooking, biography, memoirs, Eng. literature. Cata: occasional lists on foregoing.

W.H. GILLESPIE-BOOKS, Tutts Cottage, Manor Close, The Street, East Preston, West Sussex. Prop: W.H. Gillespie. TN: (090 62) 3471. Est: 1982. Private premises; appointment necessary. Small stock sec. and antiq. also new books. Spec: the Police. Cata: occasional.

HENRY GOULDEN BOOKS, 22 High Street, East Grinstead, Sussex. TN: 22669. Est: 1975. Shop; closed on Wednesdays afternoons. Small stock sec. and antiq. also new books. Corresp: Deutsch. B: National Westminster Bank. Account 34381848. M: B.A.

P.L. HANCOCK, 40 West Street, Chichester, Sussex. TN: 786173. Shop. Medium stock antiq.

HORSHAM BOOK SHOP, 18 MARKET SQUARE, HORSHAM, SUSSEX RH12 1EU. Prop: David and Marilyn Harries. TN: (0403) 52187. Shop. Medium stock sec. and antiq. Spec: 18th century biography, modern fine bindings. Cata: 2 a year on the former. Corresp: Français. B: Williams and Glyn's Bank, 130 Saint James's Street, Brighton BN2 1TH.

KEELE'S, 9 SAINT PANCRAS, CHICHESTER, SUSSEX. Prop: J.M. and T.J.L. Wynne-Tyson (Centaur Press Limited). TN: Chichester 786779. Est: 1977. Shop, closed Mondays & Thursdays. Small stock sec. and antiq. also some new. Spec: Sussex Books.

KIM'S BOOKSHOP, 17 WEST BUILDINGS, WORTHING, SUSSEX BN11 3BS. Prop: M.L. Francombe. TN: Worthing 206282 and 41326. Est: 1972. Shop, closed Wednesdays. B: Lloyds Bank, 233 Tarring Road, Worthing, West Sussex.

BRIAN LANGMEAD, APPLESHORE, SPINNEY LANE, ITCHENOR, CHICHESTER, WEST SUSSEX, PO20 7DJ. TN: Birdham (0243) 512214. Spec: bird books and rural sports.

ANTHONY D. LILLY, 1 NORTH PLACE, WESTERN ROAD, LITTLEHAMPTON, WEST SUSSEX. TN: Littlehampton 4028. Est: 1957. Shop. Small stock sec. and antiq. Spec: natural history. Cata: 2 a year, lists one every 2 months. B: National Westminster Bank, High Street, Littlehampton. Account 63241021. M: A.B.A.

MADELEINE PRODUCTIONS, 15 WALLACE AVENUE, WORTHING, WEST SUSSEX BN11 5RA. Prop: John Skinner. TN: (0903) 503551. Est: 1981. Private premises; postal business, also by appointment. Spec: cinema–biography, theory, film annuals, photo archive. Very small stock sec. and antiq. Cata: occasionally. B: Barclays Bank, 1 Chapel Road, Worthing, West Sussex.

COLIN MEARS' BOOKSHOP, 17 STATION PARADE, TARRING ROAD, WEST WORTHING, SUSSEX. TN: (0903) 504227 and 503530. Est: 1979 (shop) and 1974 (home). Shop; closed all day on Wednesdays. Small stock sec. and antiq. Spec: children's illustrated books (antique and modern), also non-fiction. Cata: 1 or 2 a year. B: Midland Bank, 16 Goring Road, Worthing, West Sussex BN12 4AW. Account 40-4723-91007203.

KIT MOUAT, MERCERS, CUCKFIELD, SUSSEX RH17 5JU. TN: Hayward Heath 54043. Est: 1967. Postal business only. New, and very small sec and antiq. stock. Spec: secular humanism, freethought, rationalism alternative medicine.

MURRAY BOOKS, 44 SUSSEX ROAD, HAYWARDS HEATH, WEST SUSSEX RH16 3DT. TN: (0444) 52727.

THE OLD BOOKSHOP, 52 NORTH STREET, WORTHING, SUSSEX. Prop: R.J. Blossett and C.D. Chiswell. TN: Worthing 202066. Est: 1950. Shop, closed Wednesday. Large sec. and antiq. stock; also remainders, music, records. Spec: music. A.B.A.

PHILLIMORE & COMPANY LIMITED, SHOPWYKE HALL, CHICHESTER, WEST SUSSEX PO20 6BQ. TN: Chichester (0243) 787636. Est: 1897. Spec: local history, genealogy, heraldry and allied subjects.

POST MORTEM BOOKS, 5 STANFORD AVENUE, HASSOCKS, SUSSEX BN6 8JL. Prop: E. Spurrier. TN: Hassocks 2612. Est: 1980. Private premises; appointment necessary. Very small stock sec. and antiq. Spec: detective, mystery and crime fiction. New books of reference works relating to specialist subject. Cata: 3 times a year. Corresp: Français. B: Barclays Bank, Keymer Road, Hassocks, Sussex. Account 50828300.

J.T. RADFORD, BRAMBLINGS, WEST WALBERTON LANE, WALBERTON, ARUNDEL, SUSSEX. TN: (024 368) 2197. Est: 1976. Private premises; appointment necessary. Small stock sec. and antiq. books. Spec: natural history, ornithology, entomology; travel and topography. Cata: on the foregoing, 2 or 3 a year.

A. SEDDON, 53 OLD FORT ROAD, SHOREHAM BY SEA, SUSSEX BN4 5RL. TN: (079 17) 61501. Est: 1978. Private premises; postal business only. Small sec. and antique. stock. Spec: A.C. Swinburne and associated literature. B: National Westminster Bank, Saint James Street, Brighton.

THE STEYNE BOOKSHOP, 5 HIGH STREET, WORTHING BN11 1NY. Prop: C. Francombe and S.Broad. TN: (0903) 206216. Shop. Large sec. and antiq. stock.

HARRIET TRUSCOTT, WHITE GATES, BARNS GREEN, HORSHAM, SUSSEX RH13 7PU. TN: Southwater (0403) 730554. Est: 1965. Private premises, appointment necessary. Medium sec. and antiq. stock. Spec: topography, natural history. Cata: general, occasionally. Corresp: Français. B: Lloyds Bank, Market Square, Horsham. Account 0113798.
[*Shop at* 139 PORTOBELLO ROAD, LONDON W11].

56. EAST SUSSEX

BATTLE	MIDHURST
BEXHILL	NUTLEY
BRIGHTLING	ROTHERFIELD
BRIGHTON	ROTTINGDEAN
CROWBOROUGH	RYE
EASTBOURNE	SAINT LEONARD'S
FOREST ROW	SEAFORD
HASTINGS	SHOREHAM-BY-SEA
HOVE	UCKFIELD
LEWES	UPPER HARTFIELD

AD ORIENTEM LIMITED, 2 CUMBERLAND GARDENS, SAINT LEONARD'S-ON-SEA, SUSSEX. Prop: R.A. Gooch. TN: Hastings (0424) 427186. TA: Oriental St. Leonards. Est: 1964. Private premises, appointment necessary. New, and small sec. and antiq. stock. Spec: Oriental, African. Cata: on foregoing, 3 a year.

AFRICANA ANTIQUARIANS, PENLAN, CROWBOROUGH HILL, CROWBOROUGH, SUSSEX TN6 2EA. Prop: E.R. Frankel and J. Lipkin. TN: (089 26) 2454. TA: Jaylip. Est: 1977. Postal business only. Sec. and antiq. stock. Spec: books on Africa. Cata: Africana, occasionally. A.B.A. P.B.F.A.

ANTHONY ANTIQUES, 138 EDWARD STREET, BRIGHTON, SUSSEX. Prop: Anthony F. Young. TN: Brighton 732418. Est: 1969. Shop, early closing Saturday. Medium sec. and antiq. stock, also antiques. Spec: commemorative books; military.

ANTIQUARIAN & OLD BOOK COMPANY, 36 KINGSTON BROADWAY, SHOREHAM-BY-SEA, SUSSEX. Postal business only. Small sec. and antiq. stock. Spec: Africa, Arctic, Australasia, Pacific, North and South America, Middle East, Europe and general travels and foreign interest. Cata: general, occasionally; and lists on required subjects on foregoing.

ADAM BALL ANTIQUARIAN BOOKS LIMITED, 37A GLOUCESTER ROAD, BRIGHTON, EAST SUSSEX. TN: (0273) 600400. Est: 1979. Shop. Medium stock sec. and antiq. Spec: early Brighton. Fine and Applied Arts etc. Cata: occasionally. M: P.B.F.A.

AUTOMOBILIA, 30 WEST DRIVE, BRIGHTON, EAST SUSSEX. Prop: Kenneth Ball. TN: (0273) 690000. Storeroom; appointment necessary. Spec: automobiles and transport.

BENNETTS, 71A WESTERN ROAD, HOVE, SUSSEX BN3 2JQ. Prop: D. Bennett. TN: (0273) 734084. Shop, selling old prints and postal service booksellers. Spec: fine arts and allied subjects. Frequent lists.

BEULAH HOUSE BOOKSHOP, 18 WEST STREET, ROTTINGDEAN, BRIGHTON, SUSSEX. Prop: Douglas E. Morrison. TN: (0273) 34242. Est: 1976. Shop, closed Monday afternoons and Wednesday all day. Small stock sec. and antiq. Spec: H. Rider Haggard, Strand magazines. B: Lloyds Bank, High Street, Rottingdean.

BIBLE AND BOOK DEPOT, 7 GENSING ROAD, SAINT LEONARD'S-ON-SEA, SUSSEX. Prop: R.S. and D.I. Pile. TN: Hastings 427682. Shop, closed Wednesdays. Small stock sec. Spec: Evangelical theology, Plymouth Brethren books. M: B.A.

BIOSCOPE BOOKS LIMITED, 27 TRAFALGAR STREET, BRIGHTON, EAST SUSSEX BN1 4ED. Prop: Ross MacKinnon. TN: (0273) 684754. Est: 1972. Shop. Medium stock sec. and antiq. books; also new books on the cinema. Spec: cinema; books, stills, posters etc. Cata: cinema, 1 a year.

BOHEMIA BOOKSHOP, 116 BOHEMIA ROAD, SAINT LEONARD'S-ON-SEA, EAST SUSSEX. Prop: Frank Letchford. TN: (0424) 432186. Est: 1958. Shop. Very small stock sec. and antiq. books; also new books. Spec: aviation, aeronautics, aerial combat. Cata: aviation, 4 a year. B.A.

BON-ACCORD BOOKS, FLAT 3, 43 COLLINGTON AVENUE, BEXHILL, EAST SUSSEX TN39 3PX. Prop: George and Joan Collins. TN: Bexhill 219590. Est: 1960. Private premises; appointment necessary. Very small stock sec. and antiq. Spec: furniture reference. Cata: rarely. Corresp: Deutsch, Français. B: Barclays Bank, Gillingham, Kent. Account 80276413. M: P.B.F.A.

BOOKHUNTERS, P.O. Box 36, 2 CLAREMONT, HASTINGS, EAST SUSSEX. Prop: Together & Co. Ltd. TN: (0424) 445775. Est: 1976. Stockroom; postal business only. Small stock sec. and antiq. also new books. Spec: booksearching. Cata: on request. Corresp: Français. B: Lloyds Bank, Hastings.

BOOKMAN'S HALT, 127 BOHEMIA ROAD, SAINT LEONARD'S-ON-SEA. Prop: Clive Linklater. TN: Hastings 421413. Est: 1958. Shop, closed on Wednesdays. Small stock sec. and antiq.

BOOKMARK, 7 POWIS SQUARE, BRIGHTON, SUSSEX BN1 3HH. Prop: Anne Excell. TN: Brighton 23006. Est: 1974. Private premises; appointment necessary. Small sec. and antiq. stock in specialities only. Spec: juveniles. Cata: juveniles and illustrated books, 3 a year.

BOW WINDOWS BOOK SHOP, 128 High Street, Lewes, East Sussex BN7 1XL. Prop: Wm. Dawson & Sons, Limited, Cannon House, Folkestone, Kent. TN: (0273) 472830. TA: Bowbooks, Lewes. Shop; closed all day Saturdays. Large stock sec. and antiq. Spec: natural history, English literature, travel and topography, old maps and some new books. Cata: 4 a year. B: National Westminster Bank, Snith's office, 1 Princes Street, London, E.C. M: A.B.A.

R.A. BRIMMELL, 54 Tower Road West, Saint Leonard's-on-Sea, East Sussex TN38 0RG. Prop: R.A. and A.D. Brimmell. TN: (0424) 423404. Private premises, appointment necessary. Small sec. and antiq. stock. Spec: early children's books and illustrated books only. M: A.B.A.

BRITISH CHESS MAGAZINE LIMITED, 9 Market Street, Saint Leonard's-on-Sea, East Sussex TN38 0DQ. TN: (0424) 424009. Business hours. 09.00 to 13.00 hrs Mondays to Fridays, or by appointment. New, and very small sec. stock. Spec: chess only.

N.F. BROOKES (FORMERLY BARRY'S BOOKSHOP), 12a Queens Road, Brighton, East Sussex. Prop: N.F. Brookes. TN: (0273) 23105 & 772918. Est: 1981. Shop. Large stock sec. and antiq. Spec: English and Polish literature, science fiction, teaching. Corresp: Français, Greek, Español, Polish, Scandinavian languages. B: Allied Irish Bank, 22 Marlborough Place, Brighton.

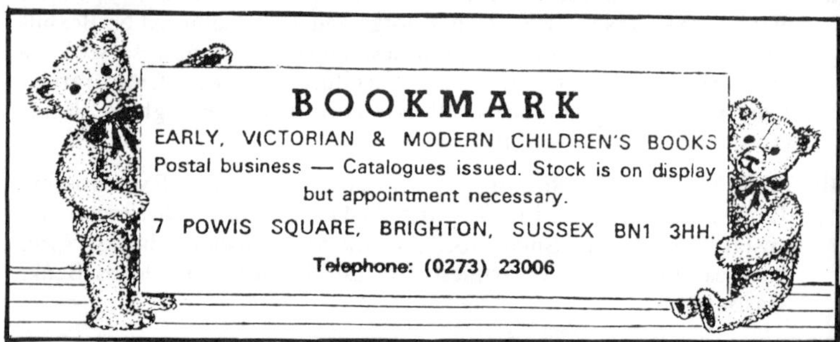

DAVID AND ERNIE CAFFIN, BOOK BARGINS, 130 THE HORNET, CHICHESTER, SUSSEX PO19 4JR.

CHOSEN BOOKS, 10 LAWRENCE ROAD, HOVE, SUSSEX BN3 5OB. Prop: T.F. McWhinnie. TN: (0273) 778612. Est: 1978. Private premises; appointment necessary. Small stock sec. and antiq. Spec: social history, politics, trade Unionism, Women's rights, racialism and related biographies and reminiscences. Cata: 3 or 4 a year. Corresp: Français, Español. B: Midland Bank, 168 Portland Road, Hove. Account 71021370.

CAROLINE CRISFORD, 43A HIGH STREET, LEWES, SUSSEX BN7. TN: (07916) 6060. Spec: applied arts.

COOKS BOOKS, 34 MARINE DRIVE, ROTTINGDEAN, EAST SUSSEX BN2 7HQ Prop: T.A. McKirdy. TN: (0273) 32707. TA: Cooksbooks, Brighton. Est: 1975. Private premises; appointment necessary. Small stock sec. and antiq. books. Spec: cookery, food, drink and related subjects. Cata: on foregoing, 4 to 6 a year.

CROSBY BOOKS, ORLINGBURY HOUSE, FOREST ROW, SUSSEX RH18 5AA. TN: (089277) 353. Est: 1971. Private premises; appointment necessary. Sec. and antiq. Spec: Oriental carpets, books on glass collecting.

CROSLAND AND DENIS, THE LONG CROFT, UPPER HARTFIELD, EAST SUSSEX TN7 4DT. Prop: Margaret Denis. TN: Forest Row 2482. Est: 1978. Private premises; appointment necessary. Small stock sec. and antiq. New books can be ordered. Corresp: Français. B: Barclays Bank, 73–75 Calverley Road, Tunbridge Wells, Kent. Account 30042226.

MARY CRUTCH, 12 HIGH STREET, SEAFORD, EAST SUSSEX. TN: (0323) 892417. Small sec. and antiq. stock. Spec: English literature, memoirs, early children's books. Cata: on foregoing, 4 a year.

A.J. CUMMING, 159 HIGH STREET, LEWES, SUSSEX. TN: (079 16) 2319. Est: 1976. Shop. Medium stock sec. and antiq. books. Spec: English literature; travel, art, illustrated, detective fiction (catalogue only). Cata: detective fiction, occasionally.

RODERICK DEW, 29 SOUTH STREET, EASTBOURNE, EAST SUSSEX BN21 4UP. TN: (0323) 646206. Est: 1975. Shop, closed Wednesdays. Small stock sec. and antiq. books. Spec: art and antiques.

WILLIAM DUCK, THE GLEBE HOUSE, BRIGHTLING, EAST SUSSEX TN32 5HE. TN: Brightling (0424 82) 295. Est: 1963. Private premises; appointment essential. Medium antiq. stock. Spec: art, architecture, townplanning, civil engineering, technology and industry; automobiles, aviation, railways, ships, commerce, International Industrial Exhibitions. Cata: on foregoing, 8 a year. M: A.B.A.

EASTBOURNE BIBLE CENTRE, 91–93 SEASIDE ROAD, EASTBOURNE, SUSSEX. TN: Eastbourne 32070. Est: 1943. New, and small sec. stock. Christian literature. B.A.

RAYMOND ELGAR, 31 CHARLES ROAD WEST, SAINT LEONARD'S-ON-SEA, SUSSEX. TN: (0424) 425405. Postal business only. New, and very small sec. and antiq. stock; also publishing. Spec: musical literature, especially the violin family. Cata: occasionally.

FREDA FARDOE, 19 GENSING ROAD, SAINT LEONARD'S-ON-SEA, SUSSEX TN38 0HE. TN: (0424) 429490. Est: 1966. Shop, closed Wednesdays and Thursdays. Medium stock sec. and antiq. books.

FIFTEENTH CENTURY BOOKSHOP, 99 HIGH STREET, LEWES, SUSSEX BN7 1XH. TN: Lewes 4160. Prop: Eric Blundell. Est: 1955. Shop, early closing Wednesday. Medium sec. and antiq. stock. A.B.A. B.A.

FISHER NAUTICAL, 157 SACKVILLE ROAD, HOVE, SUSSEX BN3 3HD. Prop: S.D. Fisher. TN: (0273) 687480. TA: Fisher Naut, Brighton. Est: 1966. Postal business only. Medium stock sec. and antiq. books. Spec: maritime. Cata: maritime, 4 or 5 a year.

GUY FITZMAURICE, 22 LION STREET, RYE, SUSSEX TN31 7LB. TN: (079 73) 3675. Est: 1974. Shop, early closing Tuesdays. Small stock sec. and antiq. books; also antiquarian maps and prints.

DOUGLAS J. FRYER, 9 DE WARRENNE ROAD, LEWES, SUSSEX. TN: Lewes (07916) 5959. Est: 1958. Private premises; appointment necessary. Very small stock sec. and antiq. Spec: collecting antiques, arms and armour, jewellery. B: Barclays Bank, High Street, Lewes, Sussex.

JOAN GLENVILLE, 16B PALMEIRA COURT, 25–28 PALMEIRA SQUARE, HOVE, SUSSEX BN3 2JP. Prop: Joan Glenville. TN: (0273) 733300. Est: 1980. Private premises; appointment necessary. Small stock sec. and antiq. Spec: illustrated books 19th and early 20th century, London, Victoriana, Lists: irregular. B: Lloyds Bank (Palmeira Branch), 1 Church Road, Hove, Sussex.

J.M. GORTON, 22 CHARLES ROAD, SAINT LEONARDS-ON-SEA, SUSSEX TN38 0QH. Prop: J.M. Gorton. Est: 1981. Private premises;

appointment necessary. Very small stock sec. and antiq. Spec: English literature, chess, mathematics, history, philosophy, English. Cata: 4 a year. B: Barclays Bank PLC., 78 Victoria Street, London SW1E 5JN. (Business account).

A.R. HODGES–BOOKS, 10 LINTON ROAD, HASTINGS, EAST SUSSEX TN34 1TN. Prop: A.R. Hodges. TN: (0424) 434455. Est: 1966. Private premises; postal business only. Very small sec. and antiq. stock. Spec: English literature, first editions, bibliography, book design and illustration, detective fiction. Catalogues issued.

J.F. HOLLEYMAN, 3 PORTLAND AVENUE, HOVE, EAST SUSSEX BN3 5NP. TN: Brighton 410915. Private premises; appointment necessary. Small sec. stock. Spec: photography. Cata: on foregoing, monthly.

HOLLEYMAN & TREACHER LIMITED, 21A & 22 DUKE STREET, BRIGHTON, SUSSEX BN1 1AH. Directors: M.G. Kadwell and D.J. Plumtree. TN: Brighton 28007. (STD 0273). Est: 1937. Shop, no early closing. New, and very large sec. and antiq. stock. Spec: music; archaeology; Sussex; prints and maps. A.B.A.

HOOVEY'S BOOK SERVICE, 10 CLAREMONT, HASTINGS, SUSSEX.

A. HOWARD, 26 BRUNSWICK SQUARE, HOVE, SUSSEX BN3 1EJ. Prop: Mrs. A. Prothero Howard. TN: Brighton 738812. Est: 1973. Stockroom; appointment necessary, also at Bookfairs and Antique Fairs. Very small stock sec. and antiq. Spec: heraldry, illustrated books, juvenilia, Victoriana. Restoration and art work undertaken on old documents. New books on collectors reference ordered. Also stocks old prints, maps, ephemera, Victorian toys, mostly antiquarian. Cata: occasionally. Corresp: Français. B: National Westminster Bank, Portslade and West Hove Branch, 257 New Church Road, Hove, Sussex, BN3 4EL. Account 57074038.

HOWES BOOKSHOP, TRINITY HALL, BRAYBROOKE TERRACE, HASTINGS, EAST SUSSEX TN34 1HQ. Prop: Raymond Kilgarriff. TN: (0424) 423437. TA: Liberwise, Hastings. Shop, early closing Saturdays. Very large stock sec. and antiq. books; also some new. Spec: antiquarian and scholarly works in the humanities; especially literature, history, theology, bibliography. Cata: on foregoing, 3 a year. M: A.B.A., N.B.L.

KEMP TOWN BOOKS, 91 SAINT GEORGE'S ROAD, BRIGHTON, SUSSEX BN2 1EE. Prop: W.V. and G. Hendy. TN: (0273) 682110. Est: 1973. Shop, early closing Wednesdays. Small stock sec. and antiq. books; also new books. Spec: art; literature; politics. Cata: on foregoing, occasionally.

S. KING, 5 HASLAM CRESCENT, PEBSHAM, BEXHILL ON SEA, EAST SUSSEX TN40 2PD. TN: (0424) 219057. Est: 1950. Private premises; appointment necessary. Small sec. and antiq. stock. Spec: Evangelical, theology, Plymouth Brethren books. Cata: Evangelical theory, 1 a year.

KOKORO, 36 DUKE STREET, BRIGHTON, SUSSEX BN1 1AG. Prop: C.G. and B.J. Page. TN: (0273) 25954. Est: 1969. Shop, open 10.00 to 17.30 hrs. Large stock of sec. and antiq. books on Far Eastern arts. Spec: Japanese block-printed material, natural history, topography. Cata: B: Barclays Bank, North Street, Brighton, Sussex. Account 90665177. 4–6 a year.

K. LANE, 52 BLATCHINGTON ROAD, HOVE, SUSSEX BN3 3YH. TN: Brighton 731386. Est: 1960. Shop, early closing Wednesday. Medium sec. and antiq. stock; also stamps. Spec: circus. Cata: circus and general, irregularly.

LANSDOWNE BOOKSHOP, 48 LANSDOWNE PLACE, HOVE BN3 1HH. Prop: M. Wolfe. TN: (0273) 770740.

LONDON & BRIGHTON ANTIQUARIAN BOOKS, 33 TRAFALGAR STREET, BRIGHTON BN1 4ED. Prop: G.B. Carruthers. Est: 1978. Shop. Medium sec. and antiq. stock.

MALTBY BOOKS, 4 THE BROADWAY, CROWBOROUGH, EAST SUSSEX TN6 1DF. Prop: John and Ann Maltby. TN: Crowborough 2409. Est: 1978. Shop. Very small stock sec. and antiq. Spec: natural sciences, travel, literature. Corresp: Français. B: Midland Bank, Crowborough. Account 31032151. M: P.B.F.A.

THE MARLBOROUGH BOOKSHOP, 18 MARLBOROUGH PLACE, BRIGHTON, SUSSEX BN1 1UB. Prop: W. Torrens-Burton. TN: (0273) 688001. Est: 1976. Shop, no early closing. Medium stock sec. and antiq. books; also postcards and sheet music. Spec: Victorian and Edwardian bindings.

J. AND M. MORTON-SMITH, KNOCKHUNDRED HOUSE, KNOCKHUNDRED ROW, MIDHURST, SUSSEX GU29 9DQ. TN: (073081) 5124. Shop. Spec: calligraphy and music.

MOTORMANIA (EAST SUSSEX) LIMITED, 76 LONDON ROAD, SAINT LEONARD'S-ON-SEA, EAST SUSSEX TN37 6AS. Prop: W.F. Smith. TN: (0424) 422579. Est: 1960. Private premises; appointment necessary. Small stock sec. and antiq. Spec: motor cars and motor cycles. Back-numbers of journals stocked. Cata: 2 annually. B: Midland Bank, Norman Road, Saint Leonard's-on-Sea. Account 81006681.

JOHN NIXON, 6 PENDRILL PLACE, COCKMOUNT LANE, WADHURST, EAST SUSSEX.

THE ODD VOLUME, 53 UPPER GLOUCESTER ROAD, BRIGHTON, EAST SUSSEX. Prop: D.J. Brewer, J.S. Dodds and A. Miller. TN: Brighton 27845. Est: 1979. Shop. Medium stock sec. and antiq. also new books. Spec: literature, history, modern first editions, politics, feminism. Cata: 4 a year. M: P.B.F.A.

OLD HASTINGS BOOKSHOP, 15 GEORGE STREET, HASTINGS, SUSSEX TN34 3EG. Prop: Brian Riches. TN: 425989. Est: 1976. Shop, closed on Wednesdays. Medium stock sec. and antiq.

PHYLLIS HASTINGS ANTIQUARIAN BOOKSHOP, BATTLE, EAST SUSSEX, TN33 0AN. Prop: Phyllis Hastings. TN: Battle 3729. Est: 1978. Shop; open Thursdays, Fridays and Saturdays. Medium stock sec. and antiq.

PICTURE BOOKS, 88 SAINT JAMES'S STREET, BRIGHTON, SUSSEX BN2 1TD. Prop: Camilla Francombe and Stuart Broad. TN: (0273) 697381. Est: 1976. Shop, no early closing. Large stock sec. and antiq. books. Spec: modern illustrated; juvenilia. Cata: various, occasionally. B: National Westminster Bank, 5 Broadwater Street East, Broadwater, Worthing. Account 58099514.

PUBLIC HOUSE BOOKSHOP, 21 LITTLE PRESTON STREET, BRIGHTON BN1 2HQ. R. Cupidi. (0273) 28357. Est: 1971. Shop. Very small stock sec. and antiq. also new books. Spec: North American Indian Studies. Cata: 1 or 2 a year. Corresp: Italiano, Dutch, Français, Deutsch. B: Barclays Bank, North Street, Brighton. M: B.A.

P.J. RADFORD, SHEFFIELD PARK, near UCKFIELD, SUSSEX. TN: Dane Hill (8025) 790531. TA: Atlas Uckfield. Est: 1938. Gallery, open normal business hours, Very large stock of early maps, atlases, old prints; Cata: on foregoing, 7 a year, and lists. A.B.A. B.A.D.A.

RENAISSANCE BOOKS, 275 DYKE ROAD, HOVE, SUSSEX BN3 6PD. Prop: C.J. and D.J. Walton. Est: 1979. Private premises; postal business only. Small stock sec. and antiq. Out-of-print booksearch service. Spec: poetry. Lists: occasional. B: Co-operative Bank, Brighton, Sussex BN1 1AB. A/C no. 22299705.

ROTHERFIELD BOOKSHOP, 5 HIGH STREET, ROTHERFIELD, EAST SUSSEX TN6 3LL. Prop: Col. H.D. Muggeridge. TN: Rotherfield 2719. Est: 1979. Shop. Medium stock sec. and antiq.

CLIFFORD RUSH, 99 MARINA, SAINT LEONARDS-ON-SEA, SUSSEX TN38 0BP. Prop: C. and C.G. Rush. TN: (0424) 423980. (STD 0424). Est: 1946. Private premises, appointment necessary. Very small sec. and antiq. stock. Spec: English literature, prints, Orient.

SAINT NICHOLAS BOOKSHOP, 18 LANSDOWN PLACE, LEWES, SUSSEX. Prop: Mary Harman. TN: (079 16) 2669. Est: 1968. Shop, open Friday, Saturday 10 a.m. to 5 p.m., other days by appointment. Small sec. and antiq. stock. Spec: English literature; illustrated books, topography, children's books.

STEPHEN SAMUELSON, BOOKSELLER, 20 CLAREMONT, HASTINGS, EAST SUSSEX TN34 1HA. TN: (0424) 421149. Est: 1972. Shop; closed on Wednesdays. Medium stock sec. and antiq. Spec: art, natural history. New books also stocked. Cata: 6 a year. B: Barclays Bank, Harold Place, Hastings. Account 40778257. M: P.B.F.A.

SCORPIO BOOKSHOP & GALLERY, 50 HIGH STREET, BATTLE, EAST SUSSEX. Prop: Mr. and Mrs. Hook, Mr. and Mrs. Peppiatt. TN: (042 46) 3403. Est: 1983. Shop, closed Wednesday afternoon. Very small stock sec. and antiq. also new books and original art. B: National Westminster Bank, 16 High Street, Battle, East Sussex TN33 0AG. M: B.A.

RAYMOND SMITH, 30 SOUTH STREET, EASTBOURNE, SUSSEX BN21 4XB. (Late J.G. Glover and Daughter.) TN: (0323) 34128. Est: as J.G. Glover 1897, change of ownership 1963. Shop, closed Wednesdays. New, and large sec. and antiq. stock; also remainders, old maps and prints, framed and unframed. Spec: English and foreign literature, the arts; theology; railways. M: A.B.A., B.A., N.B.L.

SOUTHERN BOOKSELLERS & PUBLISHING COMPANY, 84 BOHEMIA ROAD, SAINT LEONARDS-ON-SEA, SUSSEX. Prop: C.W. and A.H. Steggell. TN: Hastings 28565. Postal business only. Spec: cricket; ornithology. Cata: on foregoing, occasionally.

BRIAN T. STOW, ALCHORNES COTTAGE, BELL LANE, NUTLEY, EAST SUSSEX TN22 3PD. Prop: Brian T. Stow. TN: (082571) 2691. Est: 1962. Private premises; postal business only. Medium stock sec. and antiq. Spec: topography. Cata: 10 to 12 a year. M: P.B.F.A.

TAMARISK BOOKS, 80 HIGH STREET, HASTINGS, EAST SUSSEX TN34 3EL. Prop: Laurie and Ann Taylor. TN: (0424) 420591. Shop.

THEATRE BOOKSHOP, 26 NEW ROAD, BRIGHTON, SUSSEX BN1 1UG. Prop: Ryman Atkinson. TN: (0273) 681405. Est: 1962. Shop, no early closing. Medium stock sec. and antiq. books. Spec: illustrated books, literature, modern first editions. M: A.B.A.

A.B. TOWNLEY, FLAT 2, 26 BRUNSWICK SQUARE, HOVE, SUSSEX BN3 1EJ. TN: (0273) 738812. Postal business only. Private premises; but shows at book fairs etc. Very large sec. and antiq. stock; also undertakes specialist catalogues, inventories etc. for librarians and auctioneers. Cata: 2 a year.

TOGETHER AND CO. LIMITED, 3 Claremont, Hastings, Sussex. Est: 1976. Stockroom; postal business only. Medium stock sec. and antiq. Spec: Egyptology, Tibet, books on banking, bonds, collecting banknotes. Corresp: Français.
Also trading as: Claremont Books, Papyrus and Ptah Meri Books.

THE TRAFALGAR BOOKSHOP, 44 Trafalgar Street, Brighton, Sussex. Prop: David Boland. TN: (0273) 684300. Est: 1979. Shop. Medium stock sec. and antiq. Spec: field sports and colour plate books. Back-numbers of journals stocked. B: Barclays Bank, 144 London Road, Brighton, BN1 4LD.

G.W. WALKER, The Shop, 13 Prospect Place, Hastings, Sussex TN34 1LN. Est: 1962. Shop and storeroom, no early closing. small sec. and antiq. stock. Spec: Australia; topography, poetry, antiquarian books, Victoriana, 18th and 19th century magazines, prints.

MRS. ELIZABETH WHITE, 80a Springfield Road, Brighton, Sussex BN1 6DE. TN: (0273) 65604. Est: 1968. Private premises; postal business only. Very small stock sec. and antiq. books. Spec: gardening. Cata: occasionally.

WILBURY BOOKSHOP, 69a Church Road, Hove, Sussex BN3 2BB. Prop: Philip and Wendy Pegler. TN: (0273) 772115. Est: 1975. Shop, no early closing. Medium stock sec. and antiq. books. Spec: national health and oriental philosophy.

57. KENT

ASHFORD	PETTS WOOD
BECKENHAM	RAMSGATE
BEXLEY	ROCHESTER
BROADSTAIRS	SANDWICH
BROMLEY	SEVENOAKS
CANTERBURY	SIDCUP
CRANBROOK	SITTINGBOURNE
DEAL	SWANLEY
FAVERSHAM	TENTERDEN
FOLKESTONE	TONBRIDGE
HILDENBOROUGH	TUNBRIDGE WELLS
MAIDSTONE	WESTERHAM
ORPINGTON	WHITSTABLE

ABBEY BOOKS, 9 Gatefield Lane, Faversham, Kent ME13 8NX. Prop: Russell Long. TN: (0795) 533040. Est: 1967. Stockroom; appointment necessary. Small stock used. Spec: ships, shipping, maritime and naval history. Cata: 2 a year. B: Barclays Bank, Court Street, Faversham, Kent ME13 7AW. Account 90589748. M: P.B.F.A.

ALBION BOOKSHOP, 28 Albion Street, Broadstairs, Kent. Prop: A. Kemp. TN: Thanet 62876. Shop. Sec. and antiq. stock.

ASHBOURNE BOOKS, 128 High Street, Tenterden, Kent TN30 6HT. Prop: R.D. Sexton. (TN): (058 06) 4892. Shop. Small stock sec. and antiq. B: National Girobank, Account 32 450 8107. M: P.B.F.A.

THE ATTIC [SEVENOAKS], LIMITED, The Village House, Brasted, Westerham, Kent. Prop: Mr. & Mrs. James Brydon. TN: Westerham 63507. Est: 1953. Private premises, appointment preferred. New, and small sec. and antiq. stock. Spec: travel, biography. Cata: occasionally.

BELL HARRY BOOKS, 110 Northgate, Canterbury, Kent. Prop: Jack and Elizabeth Hubbard. TN: Canterbury 53481. Shop. Medium stock sec. and antiq. books.

BETHSAIDA CHRISTIAN BOOKSHOP, 9 Tower Parade, Whitstable, Kent CT5 2BJ. Prop: Derek H. Johnson. TN: (0227) 265961. Est: 1980. Shop, closed all day on Wednesdays. Large stock sec. and antiq. Spec: protestant and nonconformist. Some back-numbers of journals and new books stocked, foreign Bibles and New Testaments, Sunday school and Welsh interest books. Cata: 4 a year. Corresp: Italiano, Deutsch, Cymraeg, Dansk. B: National Westminster Bank, Canterbury. Account 54875250.

THE BIOGRAPHY BOOKROOM, 45 STATION ROAD, SWANLEY, KENT BR8 8ES. Prop: A.R. Mills and Margaret Lomas. TN: Swanley 63858. Est: 1970. Private premises; telephone or postal business only. Office: 45 Station Road, Swanley, Kent BR8 8ES. TN: (82) 63858. Small stock sec. and antiq. books. Spec: biography and autobiography. Free search service on all subjects. B: Midland Bank, 38 High Street, Dartford, Kent. Account 01066056.

J. AND S.L. BONHAM, AVERENG ROAD, FOLKESTONE, KENT, CT19 5HT. Prop: John and Suzanne Bonham. TN: (0303) 52557. TA: Bonbook, Folkestone. Est: 1980. Private premises; appointment necessary. Small stock sec. and antiq. Spec: Australiana, general travel and topography. Cata: 4 a year. Corresp: Deutsch, Français. B: Williams & Glyn's Bank, Folkestone, Kent. Account 11155292. M: P.B.F.A.

BIRD BOOKS OF SEVENOAKS, 19 CHURCH ROAD, SEAL, SEVENOAKS, KENT. Prop: G. Demar. TN: (0732) 62155. Est: 1977. Shop, closed Mondays, Tuesdays and Wednesdays; appointment recommended. Small stock sec. and antiq. books; also new books. Natural history only. Cata: natural history, 2 a year.

P.M. BLEST, LITTLE CANON COTTAGE, WATERINGBURY, MAIDSTONE, KENT. TN: (0622) 812577 and 812940. Est: 1974. Storeroom premises; appointment necessary. Medium stock sec. and antiq. books. Spec: natural history (especially ornithology, domestic animals, gardening, hunting, shooting, fishing, dogs etc.). Cata: 2 a year. Corresp: Français. M: P.B.F.A.

THE BOOKSHOP [FAVERSHAM], 119 WEST STREET, FAVERSHAM, KENT. Prop: C.M. Ardley. Est: 1975. Medium stock sec. and antiq. books.

BRIDGE, CONACHAR, SAINT DAVID'S BRIDGE, CRANBROOK, KENT TN17 3HJ. Prop: Mr. and Mrs. I.R. Bell. TN: (0580) 713683. TA: Colophon Cranbrook Kent. Est: 1966. Shop, closed Tuesdays and Wednesdays. Large stock sec. and antiq. books. Spec: English literature. Cata: literature, first editions, 3 a year.

MRS. J.C. BROADLEY SPRINGHILL, FORDCOMBE MANOR, NEAR TUNBRIDGE WELLS, KENT TN3 0SE. TN: (089 274) 359. Private premises.

CANTERBURY BOOKS, St. Peter's Gate Antiques & Crafts Market, 20 St. Peter's Street, Canterbury, Kent. Prop: David Beaney. Shop. Illustrated books only in the fields of fiction, children's, antiquarian, topography, natural history & bound periodicals. Cata: 4 per year.

CHALYBEATE BOOKS, 34 Cambridge Street, Tunbridge Wells, Kent TN2 4SJ. Prop: David and Victoria Strauss. TN: (0892) 36376. Est: 1977. Private premises; appointment necessary. Small stock sec. and antiq. Spec: British diaries and letters, arts, literature, lives and letters. Social history of 18th and 19th centuries. Cata: 2 to 3 times a year. B: National Westminster Bank, 32 Mount Pleasant, Tunbridge Wells, Kent. Account 71657959. Small stock sec. and antiq. Spec: British diaries and letters, arts, literature, lives and letters. Cata: 2 to 3 times a year. B: National Westminster Bank, 32 Mount Pleasant, Tunbridge Wells, Kent. Account 71657959.

CHAPTER ONE, 343 High Street, Rochester, Kent ME1 1DA. Prop: Geraldine S. Waddington and John Brook. TN: (0634) 812973. Est: 1982. Shop. Medium stock sec. and antiq. Spec: wood engraving, papermaking. Cata: occasional.

THE CHAUCER BOOKSHOP, 6 Beer Cart Lane, Canterbury, Kent CT1 2NY. Prop: Robert Leach. TN: (0227) 53912. Shop, no early closing. Medium sec. and antiq. stock.

CHRISTIE-BATEMAN BOOKS, Swale View, Lady Margaret Manor, Doddington, Sittingbourne, Kent ME9 0NT. Prop: M.E. Theobald and Shaun Christie-Theobald. TN: Doddington 079586, 270. Est: 1976. Private premises; postal business only. Very small stock used. Spec: natural history, rural literature, gardening and illustrated books. Some back-numbers of horticultural journals stocked, also a few new numbers stocked. Cata: occasionally. Corresp: French. B: Barclays, Sittingbourne. M: P.B.F.A.

CYNARA BOOKS, 34 London Lane, Bromley, Kent BR1 4HD. Prop: Michael and Geraldine Seeney. TN: (01) 460-4548. Est: 1977. Private premises, appointment necessary. Small stock sec. and antiq. books. Spec: 19th and 20th century English literature.

DARTFORD HEATH BOOKS, 21 OLD BEXLEY LANE, BEXLEY, KENT DA5 2BL. Prop: W.S. Heywood. TN: (2) 526155. Est: 1980. Shop, closed Mondays. Telephone call advised, shop open Tues–Sat, 1 p.m. to 6 p.m. Medium stock sec. and antiq. Cata: irregularly. Corresp: Français, Deutsch. B: Barclays Bank PLC, Crayford. M: P.B.F.A.

WM. DAWSON AND SONS LIMITED, CANNON HOUSE, FOLKESTONE, KENT. TN: Folkestone 57421. TA: Dawbooks Folkestone. Storeroom, open normal business hours. Small sec. and antiq. stock, very large stock learned journals. Spec: books, bibliography, reference and related subjects, journals, sciences and humanities. Cata: periodicals occasionally, books occasionally.

MRS. IRIS M. EADE, 3 PRIORY AVENUE, PETTS WOOD, ORPINGTON, KENT BR5 1JE. TN: Orpington 30554. Est: 1965. Mainly postal business. Medium sec. stock.

P.M.E. ERWOOD [BOOKS FOR ASTRONOMERS], 95 WALTON ROAD, SIDCUP, KENT DA14 4LL. TN: (01) 300-7980. Est: 1950. Storeroom and house premises; appointment necessary. Small stock sec. and antiq. books. Spec: astronomy and related subjects (space travel, physics, optics etc). Cata: on foregoing, about 12 a year.

ESTUARY BOOKS, THE SCHOOL HOUSE, HOLYWELL LANE, UPCHURCH, NEAR SITTINGBOURNE, KENT. Prop: Malcolm John. TN: (0634) 43884. Est: 1976. Private premises; postal and book fairs only. Spec: transport (buses), British topography, freemasonry. Cata: occasionally. M: P.B.F.A.

FELSTEAD BOOKS, PHILDON LODGE, SEAL HOLLOW ROAD, SEVENOAKS, KENT TN13 3SL. Prop: E.R. Smith. TN: (0732) 456928. Est: 1979. Private premises; appointment necessary. Small stock sec. and antiq. Spec: Peerage and Baronetage, Landed Gentry.

MALCOLM GARDNER, BRADBOURNE FARMHOUSE, SEVENOAKS, KENT. Prop: Charles Allix. TN: (0732) 451311. TA: Horologias Sevenoaks Kent. Est: 1934. House premises; open Mondays to Fridays or any time by appointment. Medium stock sec. and antiq. books. Spec: virtually every worthwhile book on clocks and watches. Cata: on foregoing, annually.

GUNYON'S BOOKSHOP, 49–51 HIGH STREET, SANDWICH, KENT CT13 9EG. Prop: D.S. Gunyon. TN: 612457. Est: 1951. Shop, closed Mondays. Small stock sec. and antiq. books. Spec: Kent, educational, childrens. Corresp: Français. B: Midland Bank, 10 Cattle Market, Sandwich, CT13 9AQ. Account 90401153.

HALL'S BOOKSHOP, 20–22 CHAPEL PLACE, TUNBRIDGE WELLS, KENT. Prop: Elizabeth Bateman. TN: Tunbridge Wells 27842. Est: 1898. Shop, closed Wednesday, open weekdays 9.30–1; 2.15–5. Large sec. and antiq. stock. No catalogues. A.B.A.

T. & L. HANNAS, 33 FARNABY ROAD, BROMLEY, KENT BR1 4BL. Prop: Torgrim and Linda Hannas. TN: (01) 460-5702. TA: Hannas, Bromley. TA: Hannas Bromley Kent. Est: 1954. Private premises; appointment necessary. Small stock sec. and antiq. books. Spec: English literature before 1850; Scandinavia. Cata: on foregoing, 3 a year. A.B.A.

HOFMANN & FREEMAN [ANTIQUARIAN BOOKSELLERS] LIMITED, 8 HIGH STREET, OTFORD, SEVENOAKS, KENT, TN14 5PQ. TN: (095 92) 2430. TA: Hofmann, Sevenoaks. Est: 1962. Shop and offices; appointment necessary. Small antiq. stock. Spec: 17th and 18th century English literature; English literary and historical manuscripts and autographs. Cata: on foregoing, occasionally. A.B.A.

KEITH HOGG, 82 HIGH STREET, TENTERDEN, KENT TN30 6JJ. TN: (058 06) 2050 Est: 1953. Business by appointment only. New, sec. and antiq. stock. Spec: bibliography, typography and related subjects. Cata: on foregoing only. A.B.A.

PAUL HOLCOMBE, 5 NORTH LANE, CANTERBURY, KENT. Prop: Paul Holcombe. TN: (0227) 57913. Est: 1978. Shop. Very large stock sec. and antiq. Spec: business studies, Canadiana. Cata: 2 a year. B: Barclays Bank, Terminus Street, Harlow. Canadian Account.

DAVID G. H. HORNAL, ANWOTH, 1 WOODLAND WAY, DYMCHURCH, KENT. TN: (0303 82) 2389.

MICHAEL HOSKING, THE GOLDEN HIND BOOKSHOP, 85 BEACH STREET, DEAL, KENT CT14 6JB. TN: (0304) 375086. Est: 1974. Shop, closed Wednesdays and Thursdays. Medium stock sec. and antiq. books. Spec: modern first editions; literature; Kentish topography. Cata: modern first editions and miscellaneous, about 4 a year. M: A.B.A.

LEWIS BOOKSHOP, 7 GEORGE LANE (NEAR CURZON CINEMA), FOLKESTONE, KENT. Prop: Mrs. J. Lewis. TN: (0303) 53287 and 50709. Shop. Small stock sec. and antiq. books. Spec: war books. Cata: (1) war; (2) travel and natural history; (3) general, 6 a year on each.

LLOYD'S BOOKSHOP, 27 HIGH STREET, WINGHAM, NEAR CANTERBURY, KENT CT3 1AW. Prop: Mrs. Jane Morrison. TN: Wingham 774. Est: 1959. Shop. Large stock sec. and antiq. books. Spec: children's, music. M: A.B.A.

HORNAL'S of TENTERDEN and DYMCHURCH

MEDICINE · SCIENCE · PHYSICS
NATURAL HISTORY

Please quote any important books on

HOMOEOPATHIC MEDICINE

DAVID G. H. HORNAL

"ANWOTH" I Woodland Way, Dymchurch,
Romney Marsh, Kent.

Tel. 0303-82 2389 & Tenterden 058-06 3585

85 BEACH STREET,
DEAL, KENT CT14 6JB

Telephone:
Deal (0304) 375086

Modern First Editions
General secondhand and
antiquarian stock.
Occasional catalogues.

G. & D. I. MARRIN & SONS

KENTISH TOPOGRAPHY.
NATURAL HISTORY.
Good Antiquarian Books
Catalogues Issued

149 SANDGATE ROAD
FOLKESTONE.
TEL. 53016

RICHARD MacNUTT LIMITED, 29 MOUNT SION, TUNBRIDGE WELLS, KENT TN1 1TZ. TN: Tunbridge Wells 25049. TA: Musicana Tunbridge Wells. Est: 1929. Private premises, appointment necessary. Spec: music, music literature, manuscripts, autographs, prints. Cata: on foregoing, occasionally. A.B.A.

MELROSE BOOKS, 35 DORNDEN DRIVE, LANGTON GREEN, TUNBRIDGE WELLS, KENT. Prop: Stuart Collins. TN: (089 286) 2078. Est: 1982. Private premises; appointment necessary. Small stock sec. and antiq. Cata: occasional. Corresp: Français. B: Lloyds Bank, Pantiles Branch, 1 London Road, Tunbridge Wells, Kent.

DAVID MILES, THE COTTAGE, SPRING LANE, FORDWICH, CANTERBURY, KENT CT2 0DY. TN: (0227) 712176. Private premises; appointment necessary. Medium stock sec. and antiq. Spec: early children's books, juvenalia, illustrated books. Cata: 2 a year. B: National Westminster Bank, Albert Embankment, London SE11. M: P.B.F.A.

MARTIN ORSKEY, LTD., LITTLE GAINS HOUSE, ELMSTED, ASHFORD, KENT TN25 5JU. TN: (023 375) 204. Est: 1964. Private premises, appointment necessary. Small antiq. stock. ABA.

G. & D.I. MARRIN & SONS, 149 SANDGATE ROAD, FOLKESTONE, KENT. TN: Folkestone 53016. Est: 1940. Shop and showrooms. Medium sec. and antiq. stock; prints and paintings. Spec: Kent and South East England topography. Cata: general, regularly, free. A.B.A.

MOUNT EPHRAIM BOOKS, 25/27 MOUNT EPHRAIM, TUNBRIDGE WELLS, KENT. Prop: Laureen Banwell and Vic Prior. (0892) 21888. Est: 1982. Shop, closed Wednesdays. Small stock sec. and antiq. B: National Westminster Bank, St. John's Road, Tunbridge Wells, Kent.

PATRICK AND MARY MULLEN, ANTIQUARIAN BOOKDEALERS, STABLINGS COTTAGE, GOODWIN ROAD, RAMSGATE, KENT CT11 0JJ. TN: Thanet (0843) 587283. Est: 1978. Private premises; appointment necessary. Medium sec. and antiq. stock. Spec: railways, all aspects, all countries books and ephemera. New books supplied to order. Cata: railwayana 6 a year. B: Midland, Ramsgate, Kent. Account 21036807. M: P.B.F.A.

THE OLD RAMSGATE BOOKSHOP, ADDINGTON STREET, RAMSGATE, KENT CT11 9PT. Prop: Owen T. Williams. TN: (0843) 586377. Est: 1981. Shop, open Fridays and Saturdays, also Sunday mornings 10–1 p.m. Small stock sec. and antiq. Spec: literature, topography and travel. Cata: lists in Bookdealer only. B: National Giro.

P.J. PARR, 2 ARDMORE COTTAGE, BISHOPS DOWN PARK ROAD, TUNBRIDGE WELLS, KENT TN4 8XX. Prop: Mr. P.J. Parr. TN: (0892) 23767. Est: 1982. Private premises; appointment necessary. Medium stock sec. and antiq. Spec: Mysticism, The Occult, Philosophy, Psychology, Religion and all related subjects. Cata: every 6 weeks. B: Lloyds Bank, The Pantiles, 1 London Road, Tunbridge Wells, Kent. M: P.B.F.A.

PERIWINKLE PRESS, CHEQUERS HILL, DODDINGTON, SITTINGBOURNE, KENT ME9 0BN. Prop: E.R. and A. Swain. TN: Doddington 246. Est: 1968. Shop and workshop, early closing Saturdays. Small stock sec. and antiq. books, also mount cutting and picture framing. Spec: Kent topographical, prints, maps and plates.

J.J. RIGDEN BOOKS, 17 BEVERLEY ROAD, CANTERBURY, KENT CT2 7EN. Prop: Mrs Juanita J. Rigden. TN: (0227) 69911. Est: 1976. Private premises, appointment necessary. Medium sec. and antiq. stock. Spec: juveniles 1850–1980. Cata: juveniles, 6 a year. "100 years of children's books" alternate months. B: National Giro Account 32 494 4004 and Lloyds Bank, Saint Dunstans, Canterbury. Account 0134347.

H.T. RODDA, 52 RADNOR PARK ROAD, FOLKESTONE, KENT CT19 5AY. TN: (0303) 58905. Est: 1977. Private premises; appointment necessary. Small stock sec. and antiq. books.

THE SANDWICH BOOKSHOP, 13 STRAND STREET, SANDWICH, KENT CT13 9DX. Prop: Mrs. Iona Bown. TN: (030 46) 3192. Est: 1973. Shop, early closing Wednesdays. Medium stock sec. and antiq. books, also antiquarian prints. Cata: general, 4 a year.

SANDGATE BOOKS, 33 SANDGATE HILL, FOLKESTONE, KENT CT20 3AX. TN: (0303) 38141. Private premises; appointment necessary.

JULIA SESEMANN, 10 KEMERTON ROAD, BECKENHAM, KENT BR3 2NJ. Prop: Julia Sesemann. TN: (01) 658-6123. Est: 1977. Private premises; appointment necessary. Small stock used. Spec: children's books, fiction and illustrated, Enid Blyton specialist. Cata: 2 a year. B: National Westminster: Coulsdon South Branch, 150 Brighton Road, Coulsdon. Account 01730428.

GEOFF. SHAW, 32 COLLEGE ROAD, BROMLEY, KENT BR1 3PE. Est: 1972. Postal business only. Very small stock sec. and antiq. books. B: National Giro account 32 229 4207.

ROGER SHEPPARD, 117 KENT HOUSE ROAD, BECKENHAM, KENT BR3 1JJ. TN: (01) 778-0534. Est: 1973. Postal business only. Small stock sec. and antiq. books; also publishing (Trigon Press). Cata: English literature; modern first editions. 2 a year.

J.D. SMALL, 54 TONBRIDGE ROAD, HILDENBOROUGH, KENT. Prop: J.D. Small. TN: (0732) 833105. Est: 1983. Private premises; appointment necessary. Very small stock sec. and antiq. Corresp: Français, Españtol. B: Barclays Bank Ltd., High Street, Tonbridge, Kent.

S.P.C.K. 7 SAINT PETER'S STREET, CANTERBURY, KENT. TN: Canterbury 64237. Est: 1925. Shop, closed Thursday. Medium sec. and antiq. stock.

NICK SPURRIER, 79 WHITSTABLE ROAD, CANTERBURY, KENT CT2 8EA. Nick Spurrier. TN: 62764. Est: 1977. Private premises; appointment necessary. Small stock used. Spec: Russia, China, socialism and communism, trade unions, economic history, pacifism. Cata: monthly lists. B: National Westminster, 51 St. Dunstan's Street, Canterbury, Kent CT2 8BS. Account 70388164.

CHRISTINE SWIFT, 45 SCOTT STREET, MAIDSTONE, KENT. Prop: Robert and Christine Swift. TN: (0622) 677577. Est: 1975. Shop. Medium stock sec. and antiq. Spec: topography. Cata: 1 a year. B: National Westminster Bank, Kentish Branch, Maidstone, Kent.

W. DAVENPORT TAYLOR, ASHOVER, GILHAM GROVE, DEAL, KENT KT14 9AX. Prop: D. Davenport Taylor. TN: Deal 4462. Est: 1949. Private premises, open to trade only by appointment. New and sec. stock. Spec: juveniles, Library supply and textbook (Sales) service to schools. Corresp: Deutsch, Français.

JOHN THORNTON, 6 LONDON ROAD, TUNBRIDGE WELLS, KENT. TN: Tunbridge Wells 27364.

THOMAS BECKET BOOKS, 2 SEA STREET, WHITSTABLE, KENT. Est: 1964. Private premises; appointment necessary. Medium sec. and antiq. stock. Spec: theology, bygone Kent. Cata: general, occasionally. Corresp: Français. B: Trustee Savings Bank, High Street, Whitstable. Account 307365.

THOMAS J. WATSON, GROSVENOR BOOKSHOP, 69 GROSVENOR ROAD, TUNBRIDGE WELLS, KENT. TN: Tunbridge Wells 22322. Est: 1957. Shop, early closing Wednesday. Large sec. and antiq. stock; also stationery. Cata: general, occasionally. B.A.

WEALDEN BOOKS, 39 ADISHAM DRIVE, MAIDSTONE, KENT ME16 0NP. Prop: Alfred and C.A. King. TN: Maidstone (0622) 62581. Est: 1980. Private premises; appointment necessary. Small stock sec. and antiq. Spec: Kent, topography and local fiction. Cata: 12 a year. B: Barclays Bank, Middle Row, Maidstone, Kent.

ANTHONY WHITTAKER, FOUR SEASONS, CHILLMILL GREEN, BRENCHLEY, TONBRIDGE, KENT TN12 7AL. Prop: A. Whittaker. TN: (089 272) 3494. Est: 1980. Private premises and storeroom; appointment necessary. Small stock sec. and antiq. Spec: children's and illustrated, fine and applied arts, natural history, Kent topography.

WINTERDOWN BOOKS, WINTERDOWN, ACRISE, FOLKESTONE, KENT CT18 8LW. Prop: Guy Meynell. TN: 030-389-3110. Private premises; stock cannot be seen. Medium stock used. Spec: medicine, biology and related history and biography. Cata: 2–3 a year. Corresp: French and Italian. B: National Giro 00 372 4352.

MARTIN WOOD, 2 SAINT JOHN'S ROAD, SEVENOAKS, KENT. Prop: Martin Wood. TN: (0732) 457205. Est: 1970. Stockroom and private premises; business hours and by appointment. Closed odd days during the Cricket Season. Spec: cricket. Cata: about every 9 months. B: Midland Bank PLC, 69 High Street, Sevenoaks, Kent.

58. AUSTRALIA

THE ANTIQUE BOOKSHOP AND CURIOS, 322B MILITARY ROAD, CREMORNE, N.S.W. 2090. Prop: Peter and Maureen Tinslay. Medium stock sec. and antiq. books, also maps, theatre programmes etc. Cata: occasionally.
(*Also at SSydney Antiquarian Books, 31 George Street, The Rocks, Sydney, N.S.W.*).

PETER ARNOLD, ANTIQUARIAN BOOKSELLERS PTY. LTD. 463 HIGH STREET, PRAHRAN, VICTORIA 3181, AUSTRALIA. TN: (03) 529-2933. Est: 1969. Shop. Medium sec. and antiq. stock. Spec: Australiana, Australian literature. Cata: 4 a year. A.B.A. A.N.Z.A.A.B.

AUSTRALASIAN FINE BOOKS, P.O. BOX 531, WODEN, ACT 2606, AUSTRALIA. Prop: P.J. Rusbridge. TN: (062) 314485. Est: 1980. Private premises; appointment necessary. Very small stock sec. and antiq. Spec: Australiana pre-1914, British colonial and military history pre-1918. Cata: 2 a year. Corresp: Français, Deutsch, Russian. B: Commonwealth Trading Bank, Woden, Act 2606, Australia. Account 153-540.

CONRAD BAILEY, 15 Melrose Street, Sandringham, Victoria 3191, Australia. TN: 598-3025. TA: Conbail, Melbourne. Est: 1965. Shop, open most afternoons, mornings by appointment. Large stock sec. and antiq. books on Australia, the South Pacific and South East Asia. Cata: on foregoing, about 12 a year.

BEAR BOOKS, P.O. Box 22, Lyons Street, Williamstown, Victoria, Australia. (4 Watson Court, Altona, Victoria, Australia.) Prop: T.R. Ferris. TN: 398 2622 397 6466. Est: 1968. Private premises; appointment necessary. Small stock sec. and antiq. also new books. Spec: Australiana, Australian literature and children's books. Cata: 2 a year. B: U.K. Lloyds Bank Ltd., Guildford Branch, 147 High Street, Guildford, Surrey GU1 3AG, England.

BECK BOOK COMPANY PTY. LIMITED, 53 Pulteney Street, Adelaide, South Australia 5000. TN: 223-5213. Est: 1932. Shop, early closing Saturday. New, and medium sec. and antiq. stock. Spec: Australiana. Cata: Australiana.

BERKELOUW, Bendooley, Hume Highway, Berrima, N.S.W. 2577. Est: in Holland 1812, in Australia 1949. Large sec. and antiq. stock. Spec: Australiana, Pacific, anthropology, Africa, America, natural history. Cata: on foregoing, 6–10 a year. A.B.A.

BOOKFELLOW, 106 Harrington Street, Hobart, Tasmania. Prop: Fullers Bookshop Pty Ltd. Est: 1920. Shop; closed Saturdays. Medium stock sec. and antiq. also a few new. Spec: Australiana, Tasmaniana, modern first editions.

BOOKS OF YESTERYEAR, 5 Hunter Street, Sydney 2000, N.S.W. Prop: L. Vanbeugen. TN: 233 5714. Est: 1975. Stockroom; appointment necessary. Medium stock sec. and antiq. Spec: Australiana, Pacific, New Zealand, New Guinea. Cata: 10 -12 a year. B: Commonwealth Trading Bank, Sydney, Australia.

BRADSTREETS BOOKS, P.O.Box 442, Hawthorn 3122, Melbourne, Victoria.

KAY CRADDOCK, Suites 1-4 (First Floor), 401 Saint Kilda Rd, Melbourne, Vict. 3004. Prop: Kay and Muriel Craddock. TN: (03) 267-3152. Est: 1965. Shop, closed Saturday afternoons. Medium stock sec. and antiq, also a few specialised new. Spec: English literature, private press and illustrated, books on books. M: A.B.A.

JAMES DALLY, G.P.O. Box 1932, Adelaide, South Australia 5001. Est: 1960. Private premises; appointment necessary. Medium stock sec. and antiq. books; some selected new books. Spec: Australia and the Pacific. Cata: on foregoing. 2 a year. A.B.A.

ROBERT DOUWMA, 283 Toorak Road, South Yarra, Victoria 3141.

DIAL-A-BOOK, 15 Robertson Road, Newport, N.S.W. 2106.

PAUL FRANCE FINE AND RARE BOOKS, P.O. Box 663, Alice Springs, N.T. 5750.

RUTH GOOCH, 44 View Street, Clayton, 3168, Victoria.

JUDY HASTINGS, 9 Kahibah Road, Mosman, N.S.W. 2088. TN: 969 1697. Spec: antique books, maps, prints, engravings.

KENNETH HINCE, 138–140 Greville Street, Prahran, Victoria 3181. TN: 51-5231. Est: 1959. Shop, no early closing. Very large sec. and antiq. stock. Spec: Australiana; literature and criticism. Cata: on foregoing and general, irregularly. M: A.B.A., S.L.A.M., A.N.Z.A.A.B.

LOUELLA KERR BOOKS, 17 Palace Street, Petersham, N.S.W. 2049. TN: (02) 569 0156. Private premises; appointment necessary. Spec: Australiana, literature, domestic economy and female travel and education, juvenile. Cata.

LAWTONS BOOK PTY LTD. 68 Wollongong Street, Fyshwick, Canberra, A.C.T., Australia. Prop: Ron Winch. TN: 805304. Est: 1975. Shop. Very large stock sec. and antiq. Also new Australian publications. Spec: Australiana, Pacificiana, militaria. Cata: 2 a year. B: Westpac Banking Group, Wollongong Street, Wychwick, A.C.T. 2609.

ANNE McCORMICK, 2 Regent Street, Paddington, Sydney, N.S.W. 2021, Australia. TN: 357-6541. Est: 1970. Shop. Medium stock sec. and antiq. books. Spec: Australiana. M: A.B.A., Antique Dealers Association of New South Wales, A.N.Z.A.A.B.

TIM McCORMICK, 53 QUEEN STREET, WOOLLAHRA, 2025, N.S.W., AUSTRALIA. Prop: Tim McCormick. Est: 1970. Small stock sec., and antiq. Spec: Australiana. Cata: occasional. Corresp: Français, Italiano, Deutsch. B: West Pacific, Oxford Street, Paddington 2021, Sydney, Australia. M: A.B.A., A.N.Z.A.A.B.

ROBERT MUIR 24 STIRLING HIGHWAY, NEDLANDS, WESTERN AUSTRALIA 6009. TN: 86-5842 and 86-6103. Old and rare books.

PENN'S BOOKSHOP, 123 LITTLE COLLINS STREET, MELBOURNE, VICTORIA 3000, AUSTRALIA. Prop: Peter and Joan Stewart. TN: 63-5134. Est: 1964. Shop, closed Saturdays; (appointment necessary on Saturdays). Stock of 30,000 volumes sec. and antiq.; also new books, and prints. Spec: Australiana; natural history; the arts; Cata: on foregoing, 2 a year. Australian Booksellers Association.

HARRI AND CAROL PELTOLA, 11 GLORIANA STREET, MORNINGSIDE, QUEENSLAND 4170.

PIONEER BOOKS, P.O. BOX 57, OAKLANDS PARK, SOUTH AUSTRALIA, 5046. Prop: Paul Depasquale, Judith Crabb and Monica M. Depasquale. TN: (298) 4645 and (43) 3338. Est: 1974. Shops (2), irregular hours, weekdays and appointment necessary. Large stock used. Spec: South Australiana, children's books (British and Australasian of the 19th and 20th centuries), back-numbers of journals kept, also publishers and entrepreneurs. Cata: frequently. Corresp: Deutsch, Français, Italiano. B: Bank of New South Wales, Marion, South Australia.

READ'S RARE BOOK SHOP, 42 ELIZABETH STREET, BRISBANE, QUEENSLAND, AUSTRALIA. Prop: Harri Peltola. TN: (07) 229 3278. Est: 1928. Shop. Medium stock sec. and antiq. Spec: Australiana, all subjects. B: Australian and New Zealand Banking Group Ltd., Boundary Street, West End 4101, Australia.

GASTON RENARD, 51 SACKVILLE STREET, COLLINGWOOD, VICTORIA 3066. TN: (03) 417 1044. Est: 1945. Large stock sec. and antiq. Spec: Australia and Pacific: Natural history; medicine; science; Old and rare. Cata: frequently. M: ABA. ANZABA.

ROSEVILLE ANTIQUARIAN BOOKSHOP, 100 PACIFIC HIGHWAY, ROSEVILLE, SYDNEY, N.S.W. 2069. Prop: Margaret Woodhouse. TN: 46-3339. Est: 1962. Shop, early closing Saturdays. Medium sec. and antiq. stock. Spec: Australiana, Pacific. Cata: on foregoing, 8 a year. M: A.B.A. Records.

SERENDIPITY BOOKS, 80 HENSMAN ROAD, SUBIALO, W.A. 6004. Prop: Dr. I.K. & Mrs. I.M. McGill. TN: 381 6519. Est: 1973. Very large stock. Storeroom; appointment necessary.

SPECIALITY BOOKS, 3 LOS ANGELES COURT, SAINT KILDA, VICTORIA 3182, AUSTRALIA. Prop: Carl Herzog. TN: 91-1939. Est: 1974. Private premises; appointment necessary. Small stock sec. and antiq. books. Spec: gardening; architecture; trades; decorative arts.

STANDARD BOOK, 136 RUNDLE MALL, ADELAIDE, SOUTH AUSTRALIA 5000. Manager: Jon F. Napier. TN: (08) 223 5380. Est: 1935. Shop (department in a large store). Medium stock sec. and antiq. M: Australian Booksellers' Association.

MICHAEL TRELOAR, 13 PAYNHAM ROAD, COLLEGE PARK, SOUTH AUSTRALIA 5069. TN: (08) 42 7325. Est: 1976. Shop. Medium sec. and antiq. stock. Cata: occasionally. M: A.N.Z.A.A.B.

TYRRELL'S BOOK SHOP PTY LTD. 328 PACIFIC HIGHWAY, CROW'S NEST, SYDNEY, N.S.W. 2065, AUSTRALIA. Prop: W.T. Tyrrell. TN: 43-5920 and 439 3658. Est: 1906. Shop. Stock of over 30,000 sec. and antiq. books, also new books, art materials and records. Spec: Australiana, art, technical, educational, classics. M: N.S.W. Booksellers Assoc.

WEEKEND GALLERY BOOKS PTY LTD. 5 BIRDWOOD STREET, HUGHES, CANBERRA, A.C.T. AUSTRALIA 2605. TN: 062-812745. Est: 1971. House premises; open Saturdays and Sundays, other days by appointment. Medium stock sec. and antiq. books, antique maps and prints. Cata: occasionally. M: A.N.Z.A.A.B.

Also at THE OLD BOOKROOM, BELCONNEN CHURCHES CENTRE, BENJAMIN WAY, BELCONNEN, A.C.T. 2617. TN: 062-515191. Open Monday to Friday 10 a.m.–5.30 p.m., Friday nights until 8 p.m. and Saturday 10 a.m.–5 p.m.

WHORTLEBERRY BOOKS, 48 LISTON STREET, BURWOOD, VICTORIA 3125. Prop: C.R. McGillivery. TN: (03) 29 6094. TA: Whortle, Melbourne.

59. NEW ZEALAND

AUCKLAND
CANTERBURY
CHRISTCHURCH
DUNEDIN
WELLINGTON

ARNOLD BOOKS, P.O. BOX 22, LINCOLN, CANTERBURY, NEW ZEALAND. Prop: M.C. and J.A. Palmer. TN: Christchurch 487643. Est: 1978. Private premises; appointment necessary. Small stock used. Spec: natural history, biological sciences, gardening, domestic animals. Back-numbers of journals stocked. Cata: 4 a year. Corresp: French. B: Bank of New South Wales, High Street, Christchurch. Account 030813: 065493;02. M: Booksellers Association of New Zealand.

CITY BOOKSHOP, P.O. BOX NO. 5453, 21–23 MORAY PLACE, DUNEDIN, NEW ZEALAND. Prop: Elizabeth Poole and Anthony Reeder. TN: 773379. Est: 1976. Shop and stockroom; closed on Saturdays. Open during normal business hours. Medium stock used. Spec: New Zealand books. New New Zealand books also kept. Cata: occasionally. M: Booksellers' Association of New Zealand.

ANAH DUNSHEATH RARE BOOKS, 6 HIGH STREET, AUCKLAND 1, NEW ZEALAND. (P.O. BOX 4181, AUCKLAND). Prop: A. Dunsheath. TN: 790 379. or after hours 543–788. Est: 1969. Shop, closed on Saturdays. Large stock sec. and antiq. books. Spec: travel (New Zealand, Australia, South Pacific). Cata: on foregoing, 4 a year. M: A.B.A., A.N.Z.A.A.B.

SMITH'S BOOKSHOP LIMITED, 34 MERCER STREET, WELLINGTON 1, NEW ZEALAND. Prop: R.E. Reynolds. TN: 724075. Est: 1900. Shop. Large sec. and antiq. stock. Spec: Pacific books. Cata: Pacific books, about 2 a year. M: A.B.A., A.N.Z.A.A.B.

JOHN SUMMERS BOOKSHOP, 224 TUAM STREET, CHRISTCHURCH, NEW ZEALAND. TN: 798-656. Est: 1958. Shop, no early closing. Large sec. and antiq. stock; also new books and prints.

60. SOUTHERN AFRICA

CAPE TOWN
CONSTANTIA
FLORIDA
JOHANNESBURG
VEREENIGING

G. BAKKER, 84 LOVEDAY STREET, JOHANNESBURG, SOUTH AFRICA. TN: 834–7340. Est: 1943. Shop. New, and small sec. and antiq. stock. Spec: Africana. Cata: Africana, 2 a year.

CLARKE'S BOOKSHOP, 211 LONG STREET, CAPE TOWN 8001, SOUTH AFRICA. Prop: P. Mills and H. Dax. TN: 235739. TA: Chapbooks Cape Town. Shop, early closing Saturday. Large sec. and antiq. stock, Spec: Africana, also maps and prints, travel, natural history, literature, history and other scholarly works. Cata: general, 3-4 a year. A.B.A.

STANLEY CLINGMAN, 206 MONTROSE, 36 PRITCHARD STREET, JOHANNESBURG, SOUTH AFRICA 2001. TN: 435589. Est: 1977. Shop, early closing Saturdays, appointment preferred. Small stock sec. and antiq. books; also some new. Spec: travel, Africana, natural history, maps and prints. Cata: general, 3 a year.

CONSTANTIA BOOKS, P.O. BOX 186, CONSTANTIA, SOUTH AFRICA 7848. Prop: P.V. Mills. TN: (021) 742334. Est: 1974. Shop, early closing Saturday; appointment preferred. Small stock sec. and antiq. books. Spec: Africana (especially Southern Africa, all subjects). Cata: Africana, 4 a year.

DAVID CROCKER, AFRICANA BOOKS, P.O. BOX 482, FLORIDA 1710, SOUTH AFRICA. TN: 672-1011. Stock at shop 4, Pica Centre, Cotswold Road, Florida Hills. Shop; open Mondays - Fridays 8 am to 4 pm; Saturdays: 9 am to 1 pm. Spec: Africana books. These can also be seen at 505 Union Castle Building, Corner Commissioner and Loveday Streets, Johannesburg. (834-1563). Cata: lists frequently.

EXCLUSIVE BOOKS (PTY.) LIMITED, 48 PRETORIA STREET, HILLBROW, JOHANNESBURG, SOUTH AFRICA. TN: 642-5068, 642-5069 and 642-5060. Est: 1950. Shop, no early closing, open all week-end. New, remainder, also stationery, etc. South African Booksellers' Association.

JUSTUS BOOK ROOM, 25–28 J.B.S. BUILDING, VOORTREKKER STREET, VEREENIGING, SOUTH AFRICA. Prop: H.J. Gregory. TN: 22-1696. Est: 1960. Shop, early closing Saturday. New, and large sec. and antiq. stock; also Continental magazines. Spec: Africana; Napoleonica; Churchilliana; Continental magazines and books. Cata: Africana and occasionally Napoleon and Churchill.

JEFFREY SHARPE RARE BOOKS, P.O. Box 261372, Excom, Johannesburg, South Africa. Prop: Jeffrey Sharpe. TN: 37 8138. Est: 1982. Shop. Small stock sec. and antiq. Spec: fine bindings, Africana. Cata: 2 a year. B: Barclays Bank, Eloff Street South, Box 3401, Johannesburg, S.A. Account 1154419.

FRANK R. THOROLD [PTY.] LIMITED, P.O. Box 241, Johannesburg 2000. (4th Floor, S.A. Fire House, 103 Fox Street, Johannesburg, South Africa.) TN: 838-5903. TA: Afribooks Johannesburg. Shop, early closing Saturday. New, and large sec. and antiq. stock; also prints, maps and paintings of South African interest. Spec: Africana and South African legal. Cata: Africana, irregularly. Corresp: Deutsch, Français, Hollandse, Portuguese. B: Nedbank, Fox Street Branch, Johannesburg. Account 1908-051-787. A.B.A. South African Antique Dealers' Association.

61. WEST AFRICA

FREETOWN (SIERRA LEONE).

E. & K. DENNY, P.O. Box 805, Freetown, Sierra Leone. TN: Freetown (from U.K. 010-232) 024 365. and antiq. stock. Spec: books and maps relating to Africa.

62. EAST AFRICA

NAIROBI (KENYA)

A. ABELL, P.O. Box 25277, Nairobi, Kenya. Prop: Alec and Alison Abell. TN: Nairobi 566-662. Est: 1972. Private premises; appointment preferred. Small stock sec. and antiq. books on Africa. Spec: Kenya, East Africa, big game hunting, African natural history. Cata: on foregoing, 2 a year.

63. SOUTH EAST ASIA

BANGKOK (THAILAND)

CHARLEMNIT, 1–2 Erawan Arcade, Bangkok, Thailand. Prop: M. Jumsai. TN: 252-8759, 391-2115. Est: 1953. Shop and storeroom (108 Sukhumvit, Soi 53, Madee Paidee, Bangkok), open Monday to Saturday 9 a.m. to 6 p.m. New and large sec. stock. Spec: South East Asia. Cata: Thailand and own publications, irregularly.

A LIST OF DEALERS
IN SECONDHAND AND ANTIQUARIAN BOOKS
ARRANGED ALPHABETICALLY

The index numbers refer to the sections in the Geographical List

A

A1 Crime Fiction, 25 Acreman Street, Sherborne, Dorset DT9 3PW. 814989 . . . 53
À La Mode, 1 Oakwood Park Road, London N14. (01) 785-6911 43
Abacus Books, 24 Regent Road, Altrincham, Cheshire. (061 928) 5108 . . . 18
Abbey Antiquarian Books, Abbey Old House, Cowl Lane, Winchcombe, Near Cheltenham, Gloucestershire GL54 5RA. (0242) 602589 32
Abbey Books, 36 Sopwell Lane, Saint Albans, Hertfordshire AL1 1RR. (0727) 32514 36
Abbey Books, 9 Gatefield Lane, Faversham, Kent ME13 8NX. (0795) 533040 57
Abel (Guy)=Greenway Books, London SW2 46
Abell (A.), P.O. Box 25277, Nairobi, Kenya. Nairobi 566-662 62
Aberdeen Rare Books, Slains House, Collieston, Ellon, Aberdeenshire AB4 9RT. (035 887) 275 4
Abington Books, Little Abington, Cambridgeshire CB1 6BQ. (01) 267 2701 . 30
Abrams (Peter)=Hourglass Books, Haverfordwest 6
Abramski (Y. + Mrs. D.)=Cyclamen Books, Leicester 24
Academy Books, 13 Marmion Road, Southsea, Hampshire PO5 2AT. 816632 54
Acorn Books, 12 Forteviot Gardens, Garlieston, Newton Stuart DG8 8BL . 5
Acres of Books, Trinity Square, South Woodham Ferrers, Essex CM3 5JX. (0245) 323 585 37
Ad Orientem Limited, 2 Cumberland Gardens, Saint Leonard's-on-Sea, Sussex. Hastings (0424) 427186 56
Adab Books, Moody's Yard, Claypath, Durham DH1 1RG. (0385) 63309 . . 9
Adams (Mrs. D.), 25 Broad Street, Bath, Avon 38
Adams (J.G.), 32 Cropthorne Road, Shirley, Solihull, B90 3JN. (021) 744-1754 26
Adamson and Associates (Gareth), 108 High Street, Newmarket, Suffolk CB8 8JP. 0638-68934 31
Adrian (J.)=Holborn Books, London WC2 48
Aeschlimann (Christopher John)=Abbey Antiquarian Books, Winchcombe . 32
Africana Antiquarians, Penlan, Crowborough Hill, Crowborough, Sussex TN6 2EA. (089 26) 2454 56
Ahern (Elizabeth and Alan)=Ivelet Books, Redhill 50
Ailsa Books, 10 Walker Street, Paisley. 041-887-9446 5
Aird (P.S.)=Garrick Bookshop, Stockport 14
Aitchison (Lesley)=Ambra Books, Clifton 38
Albany Books, 113 Albany Road, Cardiff CF2 3NS. (0222) 498802 6
Albatross Bookshop (The), 12 Mariners Square, Haverfordwest, Pembrokeshire, Dyfed. (06467) 475. (after hours) 6
Albion Books, 72b Fellows Road, London NW3 3LJ. (01) 722-4738 and (01) 722-6708 44

B

Backus Limited (Edgar), 44–46 Cank Street, Leicester LE1 5GU. (0533) 58137 . . . 24
Baddeley (F.H.)=The Cottage Bookshop, Penn . . . 34
Baddiel (Sarah), 43 Kendal Road, Gladstone Park, London NW10 (01) 452-7243 . . . 44
Badgers Books, 8 Gratwicke Road, Worthing, West Sussex BN11 4BH. Worthing 211816 . . . 55
Bailey (Conrad), 15 Melrose Street, Sandringham, Victoria 3191, Australia. 598-3025. TA: Conbail, Melbourne . . . 58
Bailey Hill Bookshop, Fore Street, Castle Cary, Somerset BA7 7BG. (0963) 50917 . . . 49
Bailey (L.W.)=Coffeebooks, Stratford-upon-Avon . . . 28
Bailey's Books, 13 Horse Street, Chipping Sodbury, Avon BS17 6DA. (0454) 313399 . . . 38
Bailey (Brian L.), Westbourne Antique Arcade, 113 Portobello Road, London, W11. (01) 229-1692 . . . 47
Bain Limited (James), Trelowen, Penrose, Wadebridge, North Cornwall PL27 7TB. (084 14) 300 . . . 51
Bainbridge (S.R.)=Offa's Dyke Books, Ludlow . . . 22
Baines (Mr. & Mrs. Edward)=The Rutland Bookshop, Uppingham . . . 24
Baines (Jack)=Anglesey Books, Anglesey . . . 6
Baker—Fine Books (C.G.), 22 Forester Road, Bath, Avon. (0225) 64095 . . . 38
Baker (Mrs. Gwen)=The Guernsey Bookshop, Guernsey . . . 1
Bakker (G.), 84 Loveday Street, Johannesburg, South Africa. 834–7340 . . . 60
Baldur Bookshop, 44 Hill Rise, Richmond, Surrey. (01) 940-1214 . . . 50
Baldwin (M. & M.), 98 Kenyon Street, London SW6 6LB. (01) 385-2036 . . . 46
Ball Antiquarian Books Limited (Adam), 37A Gloucester Road, Brighton, East Sussex. (0273) 600400 . . . 56
Ball (John)=Horse and Groom Bookshop, Cheltenham . . . 32
Ball (Kenneth)=Automobilia, Brighton . . . 56
Bampton Books, Franklyn, Deyman's Hill, Tiverton, Devon EX16 4LL. Tiverton 256170 . . . 52
Banbury Bookshop, White Lion Walk, Banbury, Oxon OX16 8UD. (0295) 52002 & 50731 . . . 33
Bancroft (A. & B.), Springfields, Ogbourne, Colerne, Near Chippenham, Wiltshire SN14 8DJ. (0225) 742156 . . . 39
Bannatyne Books Limited, 6 Bedford Road, London N8. (01) 340-1953 . . . 43
Banwell (Laureen)=Mount Ephraim Books, Tunbridge Wells . . . 57
Bar Bookstore (The), Unit A1, Chapman's Yard, Waterhouse Lane, Scarborough, North Yorkshire YO11 1DP . . . 11
Barber Fine Books and Search Service (Michael), Culver Street West, Colchester, Essex. (0206) 66663 . . . 37
Barbican Bookroom, 28 Market Place, Durham, (0385) 63041 . . . 9
Barbican Bookshop, 24 Fossgate, York. York (0904) 53643 . . . 11
Barbican Bookshop, 1 Franklin Road, Harrogate. Harrogate (0423) 55620 . 11
Barlow (Vincent G.), 24 Howerts Close, Warsash, Southampton, Hampshire SO3 6JR. (04895) 82431 . . . 54
Barn Books, 1a Highbury Park, Islington, London N5 . . . 43

Barnard Gallery, Grange Farm, Everton, Doncaster. (077 786) 324 17
Barnard (P.N.), Bag End, Hurley, Maidenhead, Berkshire SL6 5NB. (062 882) 4337 40
Barnes (William), 86 Saint Dion's Road, Parson's Green, London SW6. (01) 736-5860 46
Baron (H.), 136 Chatsworth Road, London NW2 5QU. (01) 459-2035 . . . 44
Barr (D.J.)=Castletown Bookshop, Upper Beeding 55
Barraclough (Mr. & Mrs. R.)=Wivey Bookshop, Wiveliscombe 49
Barrett (John)=Albany Books, Cardiff 6
Barrett (R.F.), The Bookshop, 3 Eyre Street, Clay Cross, Chesterfield, Derbyshire. (0246) 865880 19
Barrie's Bookshop, 4 Montpellier Walk, Cheltenham, Gloucestershire GL50 1SD. (0242) 515813 32
Barrott (H.N.)=West Port Books, Edinburgh 4
Barrow Books Limited, Leitholm by Coldstream, Berwickshire TD12 4JN. Leitholm 277 4
Barstable Books, 28 Ravensbourne Drive, Chelmsford, Essex CM1 2SJ. (0245) 58649 37
Barton Books, Spinneys, Sutton Poyntz, Weymouth, Dorset. (0305) 832 189 . 53
Barton (Eric)=Baldur Bookshop, Richmond 50
Barton (J.G.), 84 Old Kennels Lane, Winchester, Hampshire. Winchester 66543 54
Bass (Ben), Greyne House, Marshfield, Avon. (022124) 279 38
Bass (Fred)=The Bookshop, London 48
Bass (Fred)=The Booksmith, London 47
Bate (Mrs P.M.)=The Strand Bookshop, Padstow 51
Bateleur Books, Perryfield, Sollers Hope, Hereford HR1 4RN. (098 986) 226 27
Bateman (Elizabeth)=Hall's Bookshop, Tunbridge Wells 57
Bath Book Exchange, 35 Broad Street, Bath, Avon BA1 5LP. (0225) 5514 . 38
Batstone Books, 24 Gloucester Street, Malmesbury, Wiltshire SN16 0AA. (06662) 3072 39
Batten (J.R.), 9 Windmill Lane, Lewes Road, East Grinstead, West Sussex RH19 3SZ. (0342) 22051 55
Batterham (David), 36 Alexander Street, London W2. (01) 229-3845 . . . 47
Baume (Louis C.)=Gaston's Alpine Books, Bloxham 33
Baverstock Books and Bygones, 31 Lynn Road, Snettisham, Near King's Lynn, Norfolk. (0485) 41680 25
Baxter (A.L.)=D. Mellor and A.L. Baxter, London W8 47
Baxter, The 647 Gallery (B. & R.), 647 King Street, Aberdeen AB2 1SB. 45416 4
Baxter–Books (Eddie), 88 Benedict Street, Glastonbury, Somerset BA6 9EZ. (0458) 31662 49
Bay Bookshop, 14 Seaview Road, Colwyn Bay, Clwyd. (0492) 31642 6
Baynton-Williams, 18 Lowndes Street, Belgravia, London SW1X 9EY. (01) 235-6595 46
Bayntun (George), Manvers Street, Bath, Avon. (0225) 66000 38
Beach (D.M.), 52 High Street, Salisbury, Wiltshire. Salisbury 3801 39
Beacon Hill Bookshop, Beacon Hill Road, Hindhead, Surrey GU26 6QL. (042873) 6783 50
Beagle Books, 21 Derwent Avenue, Ickenham, Uxbridge, Middlesex. (71) 39189 44

C

Crozier (Robert), 2 Park View, Larkhall, Lanarkshire ML9 2JJ. 883272 . . 5
Crutch (Mary), 12 High Street, Seaford, East Sussex. (0323) 892417 . . . 56
Cselik (F.), 26 Risingholme Road, Harrow, Middlesex HA3 7ER 44
Cuddihy (Padraig S.)=The Antiquarian Bookshop, Tramore 2
Culpin (P.A.)=Avocet Books Ltd., Ashtead 50
Cumming (A.J.), 159 High Street, Lewes, Sussex. (079 16) 2319 56
Cumming (John), 22 Conway Street, London, W1P 5HP. (01) 388-3029 . . 47
Cupidi (R.)=Public House Bookshop, Brighton 56
Curiosities, 103 South Street, Lancing, West Sussex BN15 8AS. (09063) 2807 55
Curraun Books. Belfarsad, Curraun, Achill, Co. Mayo, Eire. Achill Sound 94 2
Curruthers (G.B.)=London & Brighton Antiquarian Books, Brighton . . . 56
Cyclamen Books, P.O.Box 69, Leicester LE1 9EW. (0533) 551795. TA: Cyclabook, Leicester 24
Cynara Books, 34 London Lane, Bromley, Kent BR1 4HD. (01) 460-4548 . 57

D

D'Arcy Books, The Chequers, High Street, Devizes, Wiltshire SN10 1AT. (0380) 6922, after hours Bromham (0380) 850319 39
D.L. Books, Whiteways, 28 Lowfield Road, Haywards Heath, Sussex RH16 4DW. Haywards Heath 59455 55
Dakin (Alec N.)=The Kingsley Bookshop, Bath 38
Dalby (Richard), 4 Westbourne Park, Scarborough, North Yorkshire YO12 4AT. (0723) 77049 11
Dalian Books, 81 Albion Drive, London Fields, London E8 4LT. (01) 249-1587 41
Dally (James), G.P.O. Box 1932, Adelaide, South Australia 5001 58
Dalton (B.)=Offstage Theatre Shop and Gallery, London NW1 44
Dalwood (Peter), 44 Causewayhead, Penzance, Cornwall. Penzance (0736) 3702 51
Daly (Peter M.), Rear of "Ships and Sealing Wax", 20A Jewry Street, Winchester, Hampshire 54
Dance Books Ltd. 9 Cecil Court, Charing Cross Road, London WC2N 4EZ. (01) 836-2314 48
Daniels (Miss Diana)=Individual Books, Mill Hill 44
Daniels (J.W.), 98 Foxberry Road, London SE4. (01) 274-4728 45
Danzey (P.), 287 The Glade, Shirley, Croydon, Surrey CR0 7UQ 50
Darby (Alan)=Lotus Press Limited, Anglesey 6
Dartford Heath Books, 21 Old Bexley Lane, Bexley, Kent DA5 2BL. (2) 526155 57
Dartmoor Bookshop (The), 2 Kingsbridge Lane, Ashburton, Devon. (0364) 53356 52
Davenport (Lewis), 51 Great Russell Street, London WC1. (01) 405-8524 . 48
David (G.), 3 & 16 Saint Edward's Passage, Cambridge CB2 3PJ. (0223) 354619 30
David's Bookshop, 14 Eastcheap, Letchworth, Hertfordshire. (046 26) 4631 . 36
Davidson Books, 34 Broomhill Road, Spa, Ballynahinch, Co. Down, Northern Ireland. (0238) 562502 2
Davies (Mrs A.C.)=Honeyfields Books, Ashbourne 19

E

F

Forsling (Mrs. S.)=Decor Books, Highgate 43
Forster (W.), 83a Stamford Hill, London N16. (01) 800-3919 43
Forwood (Kemys & Sally)=The Clocktower Bookshop, Hay-on-Wye . . . 6
Foster-Cherrington, 39 Clarence Gate Gardens, Glentworth Street, London NW1 6BA. (01) 262-7201 44
Foster (J.A.)=Park Book Shop, Wellingborough 29
Foster (W.A.), 134 and 183 Chiswick High Road, London W4. (01) 995-2768 and 994-1610 47
Foulkes (L.)=Out-of-Print Book Service, Cardiff 6
Fountain (Andrew)=Hermes Books, Cheltenham 32
Four Pages (The), 34 Woodhall Drive, Pinner, Middlesex HA5 4TQ. (01) 428-7868 44
Four Shire Books, 17 High Street, Moreton-in-Marsh, Gloucestershire GL56 0EA. (0608) 51451 32
Fox (Frank & Maureen), 1 Ashley Villas, Box, Corsham, Wiltshire SN14 9AD. Box 742775 39
Foyle Limited (W. & G.), 119 Charing Cross Road, London WC2. (01) 437-5660 48
France Fine and Rare Books (Paul), P.O. Box 663, Alice Springs, N.T. 5750 . 58
Francis (P.W.)=Bateleur Books, Sollers Hope 27
Francombe (Camilla)=Picture Books, Brighton 56
Francombe (M.L.)=Kim's Bookshop, Worthing 55
Frankel (E.R.)=Africana Antiquarians, Crowborough 56
Franks (T.E. & J.), 30 Reresby Crescent, Rotherham S60 4DW. (0709) 541166 17
Fraser (Donald), 48 Dalkeith Road, West Dulwich, London SE21. (01) 670-3274 45
Freeman (L.)=Barn Books, Islington 43
Freeman (Peter)=Green Knight Bookshop, London WC2 48
Freer (Henry), i6 Sycamore Road, Birstall, Leicester LE4 4LT. Leicester 674719 24
Frew (R.C.)=Primrose Hill Books, London, N.W.1. 44
Friend (John)=Camden Passage Sites Limited, Islington 43
Frizzell (Alex M.), Castlelaw, West Linton, Peebles-shire. (0968) 60450 . . 4
Frognal Rare Books, 18 Cecil Court, London WC2N 4HE. (01) 240-2815. TA: Finresbook, London, W.C.2 48
Frost (Jenifer), Hill House, Gresham, Norwich NR11 8RB. Matlaske 338 . 25
Fulford Bookshop and Cartoon Gallery, 90 Main Street, Fulford, York. (0904) 641389 11
Fuller D'Arch Smith, 37b New Cavendish Street, London W1M 8JR. (01) 722-0063 47
Fullers Bookshop Pty Ltd=Bookfellow, Hobart 58

G

Gabie (Mr. A.E.)=The Liss Bookshop and Gallery, Liss 54
Gabrielle Simon, 5 Church Street, Abbey Green, Bath, Avon. Bath 61687 . . 38
Gage Postal Books, P.O. Box 105, Westcliff-on-Sea, Essex SS0 8EQ. (0702) 715133 37
Gall (James), 49 Anderson Avenue, Aberdeen AB2 2LR. Aberdeen 0224-491716 4

Gibbons (R.H.)=Piers-Gibbons Books, Leamington Spa 28
Gibbs Bookshop Limited, 10 Charlotte Street, Manchester M1 4FL. (061) 236-7179 14
Gilbert (B.M.), Dunsford House, College Avenue, Grays, Essex RM17 5UW. (0375) 72187 37
Gilbert (Henry March), 19 The Square, Winchester, Hampshire. Winchester 52832 54
Gilbert (Philip)=The Little Bookshop, Oxford 33
Gilbert (R.A.), 4 Julius Road, Bishopston, Bristol, Avon BS7 8EU. (0272) 46936 38
Gilbert's, Langford Manor, Lower Swell, Fivehead, Taunton, Somerset TA3 6PH. (046 08) 457 49
Gilbert & Son (H.M.), 2½ Portland Street, Southampton, Hampshire SO1 0EB. Southampton 26420 54
Gilbertson (Richard), Angel Hill, Launceston, Cornwall. Launceston 3533 . 51
Gildea (Donald), 15 Shelley Road, Bognor Regis, Sussex. Bognor Regis (0243) 821266 55
Gilham Books, 4 Saint Austell Road, London SE13. (01) 852-1905 45
Gili (J.L. & E.H.)=The Dolphin Book Co., Limited, Cumnor 33
Gill (Clifford), Springfield Lodge, Rolleston, Newark, Nottinghamshire NG23 5SH. Southwell 81-3104 20
Gill (Michael & Nicole)=Childhood Books, London SE18 45
Gillespie–Books (W.H.), Tutts Cottage, Manor Close, The Street, East Preston, West Sussex. (090 62) 3471 55
Gillespie (E. & W.H.)=The Bookshop in Norfolk Road, Littlehampton . . . 55
Gillies (Benny), 31 Victoria Street, Kirkpatrick Durham, Castle Douglas, Kirkcudbrightshire DG7 3HQ. (055 665) 412 5
Gilmorehill Books, 43 Bank Street, Hillhead, Glasgow. (041) 339-7504 . . . 5
Gilpin (D.T.)=Railwayana Limited, Sheffield 17
Gladman (M.)=The History Bookshop, London, N11 1ER 43
Glendale (M. & R.), 9a New Cavendish Street, London W1. (01) 487-5348 . 47
Glenton (F.I. and A.M.)=Northstead Books, Leicester 24
Glenville (Joan), 16B Palmeira Court, 25–28 Palmeira Square, Hove, Sussex BN3 2JP. (0273) 733300 56
Globe Bookshop (The), 21 Saint Margarets Green, Ipswich, Suffolk 31
Gloucester Road Bookshop, 123 Gloucester Road, London SW7. (01) 370-3503 46
Glover (Charles & Betty)=The Hayes Bookshop, Hayes 44
Glover (E.G.) 20 Chatsworth, Sutton-in-Ashfield, Nottinghamshire NG17 4GG. (0623) 59352 20
Godfrey (Alan), 57–58 Spoor Street, Dunston, Gateshead NE11 9BD. Dunston 608546 9
Godfrey's Old Newspaper Shop (David), 37 Kinnerton Street, London SW1X 8ED. (01) 235-7788 46
Godfrey (Jo & Derek)=Well-Head Books, Newquay 51
Godfrey Limited (Thomas C.), 32 Stonegate, York YO1 2AP. (0904) 24531 . 11
Godsmark (N.H.)=Doric House Books, Scarborough 11
Golden Age Books, . Valldemosa, 28 Saint Peter's Road, Malvern, Worcestershire WR14 1QS 27
Golden Ball Books, 45 Healey Avenue, High Wycombe, Buckinghamshire HP13 7JR. (0494) 442869 34

Golden Dawn Books, 35 Atwood Road, Manchester M20 0TA. (061) 434 1308 14
Golding (Eric), 11 and 12 North Brink, Wisbech, Cambridgeshire PE13 1JR. Wisbech 582927 30
Goldmark Books, 14 Orange Street, Uppingham, Leicestershire. (0572) 822694 24
Goldscheider (Gaby), 29 Temple Road, Windsor, Berkshire SL4 1HP. (95) 61517 40
Goldschmidt & Company, Ltd. (E.P.), 64 Drayton Gardens, South Kensington, London SW10 9SB. (01) 373-2266 46
Golf Books, Woodbine House, 12 Spencer Road, South Croydon, Surrey CR2 7EH. (01) 686-1080 50
Golfiana Miscellanea Limited, Hampden House, 84 Kingsway, London WC2. (01) 405-5323 48
Gooch (Ruth), 44 View Street, Clayton, 3168, Victoria 58
Gooch (R.A.)=Ad Orientem Limited, Saint Leonards-on-Sea 56
Good News Bookshop Limited, 67 Wright Street, Hull HU2 8JD. (0482) 28135 16
Good News Media, 3a Forum Building, Saint James' Parade, Bath BA1 1UG. (0225) 66092 38
Goodden (Peter)=The Avon Bookshop, Bath 38
Goodinson (Lorraine), Cragwell House, Hesleyside, Bellingham, Hexham, Northumberland. (0660) 20345 7
Goodramgate Books, Maps and Prints, 58 Goodramgate, York. (0484) 46833 11
Goodrich (G.D.)=Athletica (Books) International, Worthing 55
Gorton (J.M.), 22 Charles Road, Saint Leonards-on-Sea, Sussex TN38 0QH 56
Gosford Books, 116 Gosford Street, Coventry CV1 5DL. (0203) 20813 . . . 26
Gosney (Dennis C.), 11 Perhaver Way, Gorran Haven, Saint Austell, Cornwall. (0726) 842575 51
Gough Books (Simon), 3 Fish Hill, Holt, Norfolk. (026 371) 2650 or (026 387) 603 and 2761. TA: Books, Holt 25
Goulden Books (Henry), 22 High Street, East Grinstead, Sussex. 22669 . . 55
Grahame (Major Iain), Daws Hill, Lamarsh, Bures, Suffolk CO8 5EX. (078-729) 213. TA: Dawshall, Bures 31
Grange Bookshop, 186–188 Causewayside, Edinburgh EH9 1PN. (031) 667-2759 4
Grant Books, Victoria Square, Droitwich, Worcestershire. (029 923) 680 or (0905) 778155 27
Grant (John), 13C & 15A Dundas Street, Edinburgh EH3 6QG. (031) 556 9698 4
Graphic Allegra Limited=The Attic Gallery 44
Gray (T.B. & J.N.), The Old Market Garden, Tealby, Market Rasen, Lincoln LN8 3YB. (067 383) 436 21
Grayling Books, Lyvennet, Crosby Ravensworth, Penrith, Cumbria CA10 3JP. Ravenworth 282 8
Grayling (D.)=Stricklandgate Antiques, Kendal 8

PLEASE MENTION THIS DIRECTORY WHEN QUOTING

H

Haas (Otto), 49 Belsize Park Gardens, London NW3 4JL. (01) 722-1488 . . 44
Hab Books, 35 Wellington Road, Ealing, London W5 4UJ 47
Habraszewski (T.)=Hab Books, Ealing 47
Hackett (R.G.)=Boer War Books, York 11
Hackett (R.P. & B.L.)=Old Curiosity Shop, Frome 49
Haddan's Bookshop, 30 Benedict Street, Glastonbury BA6 9EX. Glastonbury 31753 49
Hadfield (G.K.), Blackbrook Hill House, Tickow Lane, Shepshed, Loughborough LE12 (0509) 503014 24
Hagley Bookshelf (The), 30 Cavendish Drive, West Hagley, Stourbridge DY9 0LS. (0562) 884816 26
Haldane (J.)=Abington Books, Abington 30
Halewood (M.H.)=Preston Book Company, Preston 12
Halewood & Sons, 37 Friargate, Preston, Lancashire, PR1 2AT. Preston (0772) 52603 12
Hall (Anthony C.), 30 Staines Road, Twickenham, Middlesex TW2 5AH. (01) 898-2638 44
Hall (Dennis)= Hanborough Books, Church Hanborough 33
Hall (Dorothy)=Invicta Bookshop, Newbury 40
Hall (Mrs. D.M.)=The Needwood Bookshop, Burton-on-Trent 23
Hall (G.)=Bolton Book Centre, Bolton 14
Hall (Ian)='Q' Books, Telford 22
Hall (J.)=J. Clarke-Hall Limited, London, EC4 8DU 42
Hall's Bookshop, 20–22 Chapel Place, Tunbridge Wells, Kent. Tunbridge Wells 27842 57
Hall (Victor), 44 Harcourt Terrace, London SW10 9JR 46
Hallam (E. Chalmers), Earlswood, 4 Egmont Drive, Avon Castle, Ringwood, Hampshire. Ringwood 3289 54
Hallett (R. & I.)=Southmoor Books, Sandford Saint Martin 33
Halter (Lionel), 7 Hale Lane, Mill Hill, London NW7 3NU. (01) 959-2936 . 44
'Hamakrik' Book & Binding Company, 45 Craven Walk, London N16. (01) 800-5655 43
Hambleton Books, 43 Market Place, Thirsk, North Yorkshire YO7 1HA. (0845) 22343 11
Hames (Peter), Baker's Thatch, Church Street, Braunton, North Devon EX33 2EL. (0271) 814095 52
Hamilton (Gabrielle & Simon)=Gabrielle Simon, Bath 38
Hamilton (S.), Parc, Caio, Llanwrda, Dyfed SA19 8PF. (055 85) 405 . . . 6
Hamlyn (Martin)=Peter Murray Hill (Rare Books) Limited, Highgate . . . 43
Hammersmith Books, Lifford's Place, Barnes High Street, London SW13. (01) 876-7254 46
Hammond (Frank), Sowley House, Lymington, Hampshire SO4 8SQ. East End 231 54
Hammond (J.C.G.), Crown Point, 33 Waterside, Ely, Cambridge CB7 4AU. (0353) 4365 30
Hampshire Bookshop (The), Kingsgate Arch, Winchester, Hampshire SO23 9PD. (0962) 64710 54
Han-Shan Tang Limited, 717 Fulham Road, London SW6 5HL. (01) 731-2447. TA: Hanshanbooks 46

Heywood (L.G.), Usher House, 30 Mill Street, Ludlow, Shropshire. (0584) 2658 22
Heywood (W.S.)=Dartford Heath Books, Bexley 57
Hickman (T.C.)=Brewhouse Press, Melton Mowbray 24
Hicks: Bookseller (Robert), 5 Saint John Road, Old Fletton, Peterborough PE2 8BL. (0733) 65996 30
Hicks (Ronald C.), 'Dunroamin', 3 Clare Terrace, Falmouth, Cornwall. Falmouth 313061 51
Higham (S.P.C.K.), (Charles), Holy Trinity Church, Marylebone Road, London NW1 4DU. (01) 387-5282 44
Highbury Books, 66a East Street, Epsom, Surrey 50
Hilgrove Books, 22b Hilgrove Street, Saint Helier, Jersey, Channel Islands. 0534-31947 1
Hill Books (Alan), 130 Whitham Road, Sheffield, S10 2SR. 665768, 747721 17
Hill (A.G.M.)=Bracken Books, Sutton Coldfield 26
Hill Limited (G. Heywood), 10 Curzon Street, London W1Y 7FJ. (01) 629-0647. 47
Hill (G.H.)=Linden Books, Doncaster 17
Hill [Rare Books] Limited (Peter Murray), 35 North Hill, Highgate, London N6. (01) 340-6959 43
Hillyers, 301 Sydenham Road, London SE26. (01) 778-6361 and (01) 777-2506 (Home) 45
Hince (Kenneth), 138–140 Greville Street, Prahran, Victoria 3181. 51-5231 . 58
Hinchliffe (B.)=Railwayana Limited, Sheffield 17
Hinchliffe Books, Clematis Cottage, 15 Castle Street, Thornbury, Bristol, Avon BS12 1HA. (0454) 415177 38
Hinde (P.T.)=Ystwyth Books, Aberystwyth 6
Hine (James & Margaret)=Gresham Books, Tring 36
Hirschler (B.), 62 Portland Avenue, London N16. (01) 600-6395 43
History Bookshop (The), 2 The Broadway, Friern Barnet Road, London N11 1ER. (01) 368-8568. TA: Histybooks 43
Hoade (W.H.)=Wimborne Bookshop, Wimborne Minster 53
Hodges–Books (A.R.), 10 Linton Road, Hastings, East Sussex TN34 1TN. (0424) 434455 56
Hodges (Lesley)=Costume and Fashion Bookshop, London, SW3 66J . . . 46
Hodges (Ronald C.)=The Border Bookshop, Galashiels 4
Hodgkins and Company Limited (Ian), Mount Vernon, Butterow, Rodborough, Stroud, Gloucestershire GL5 2LP. Stroud 4270 32
Hodgkins (John R.)=Clifton Books, Southend 37
Hofmann & Freeman [Antiquarian Booksellers] Limited, 8 High Street, Otford, Sevenoaks, Kent, TN14 5PQ. (095 92) 2430 57
Hogg (Keith), 82 High Street, Tenterden, Kent TN30 6JJ. (058 06) 2050 . . 57
Hoggarth (John R.), Thorneywaite House, Glaisdale, Whitby, North Yorkshire YO21 2QU. (0947) 87338 11
Holborn Books, 14 Charing Cross Road, Leicester Square, London WC2. (01) 240-2337 48
Holcombe (Paul), 5 North Lane, Canterbury, Kent. (0227) 57913 57
Holdan Books Limited, 15 North Parade Avenue, Oxford OX2 6LX. (0865) 57971 33

Holden Limited (Esmond), Claverdon, White Post Hill, Redhill, Surrey RH1 6JN. Redhill 64448 50
Holder (Don), The Marchmont Bookshop, 39 Burton Street, London WC1 . 48
Holdfast Books, 54 Old Street, Upton-on-Severn, Worcestershire WR8 0HW. (06846) 2134 27
Holland Brothers, Barn House, New Street, Ledbury, Herefordshire HR8 2DX. (0531) 2825 27
Hollett and Son (R.F.G.), 6 Finkle Street, Sedbergh, Cumbria LA10 5BZ. Sedbergh (0587) 20298 & 20286 8
Holleyman (J.F.), 3 Portland Avenue, Hove, East Sussex BN3 5NP. Brighton 410915 56
Holleyman & Treacher Limited, 21a & 22 Duke Street, Brighton, Sussex BN1 1AH. Brighton 28007. (STD 0273) 56
Hollywood Road Bookshop, 8 Hollywood Road, London SW10 46
Holman (M.)=Anglebooks Limited, London 48
Holtom (Christopher), Esperanza, Aust, Bristol, Avon BS12 3AX. (04545) 2557 38
Honeyfields Books, 5 Hazel Close, Ashbourne, Berbyshire DE6 1HX. (0335) 43823 19
Hook (Mr. & Mrs.)=Scorpio Bookshop & Gallery, Battle 56
Hooker (John), Cortes, Kirk Wynd, Abernethy, Perthshire PH2 9JD. (073) 885-325 4
Hooper and Milne Books, 32 Lower Street, Dartmouth, Devon. (080 43) 2615 52
Hoovey's Book Service, 10 Claremont, Hastings, Sussex 56
Hopgood (J.)=The Quarto Bookshop, Saint Andrews 4
Hoppen Limited (Stephanie), The Studio, 17 Walton Street, London SW3. (01) 589-3678 46
Hopwood (Tony)=Holdfast Books, Upton on Severn 27
Horne (Mr. & Mrs. D.J.)=Ashley Bookshop, Boscombe 53
Hornsby (M.), 36 Burton Road, Ashby-de-la-Zouch, Leicestershire. Ashby 6734 24
Hornung (Robert), 23 Meadow Way, Letchworth, Herts. SG6 3JB. (046 26) 6334 36
Horrobin (P.J.)=The Carneforth Books1aa arnforth 12
Horse and Groom Bookshop, 310 Saint George's Place, Cheltenham, Gloucestershire 32
Horsham Book Shop, 18 Market Square, Horsham, Sussex RH12 1EU. (0403) 52187 55
Horsnell (Bryan)=Footballana, Tilehurst 40
Hosking (Michael), The Golden Hind Bookshop, 85 Beach Street, Deal, Kent CT14 6JB. (0304) 375086 57
Houben (W. & A.), 2 Church Court, Richmond, Surrey TW9 1JL. (01) 940-1055 50
Hourglass Books, 6 Dew Street, Haverfordwest, Dyfed 6
Housmans Bookshop Limited, 5 Caledonian Road, King's Cross, London N1. (01) 837-4473 43
Howard (A.), 26 Brunswick Square, Hove, Sussex BN3 1EJ. Brighton 738812 56
Howard Books (Peter), 347 Brighton Road, South Croydon, Surrey. (01) 688-6558 and (01) 681-1627 50
Howard of Wellingborough (Carl), 84 Cedar Way, Wellingborough, Northamptonshire. (0933) 67808 29

Howard (Mrs. H.M.)=Harrow Bookshop, Harrow 44
Howard (John)=Helicon Books, Bournemouth 53
Howe (K. & J.), 14 New Station Street, off Boar Lane, Leeds 15
Howells (Donald E.W.)=The Meeting House Press, Portsmouth 54
Howes Bookshop, Trinity Hall, Braybrooke Terrace, Hastings, East Sussex TN34 1HQ. (0424) 423437 56
Hoy (I.)=Ian Hodgkins and Company Limited, Stroud 32
Hubbard (Clifford L.B.)=Doggie Hubbards Bookshop, Aberystwyth 6
Hubbard (Jack & Elizabeth)=Bell Harry Books, Canterbury 57
Hubbard (Peter)=Bufo Books, Ringwood 54
Hudson (E.)=Good News Media, Bath 38
Hudson's Bookshops Limited, Hudson's University Bookshop, The New Refectory, University of Birmingham, Birmingham (021) 472-3034 . . 26
Hughes and Smeeth Limited, 1 Gosport Street, Lymington, Hampshire. (0590) 76324 54
Hughes (David E.), 21 Madoc Street, Llandudno. 77700 6
Hughes (G. & M.) 19 Graham Place, Stromness, Orkney KW16 3BZ. Stromness (0856) 850428 4
Hughes Rare Books (Spike), Leithen Bank, Leithen Road, Innerleithen, Peeblesshire EH44 6HY. (0896) 830019 4
Humber Books, 688 Beverley Road, Hull, North Humberside, HU6 7JH. (0482) 802239 16
Humm (Robert), 6 Fairlawn Grove, London W4 5EH. (01) 995-5005 . . . 47
Hunnings (P.J.M.)=Penn Barn Bookshop, Penn 34
Hunt (John L.), 268 Croydon Road, Caterham, Surrey. Caterham 43387 . . 50
Hunt (R.)=Vintage Motorshop, Batley 15
Hutchinson (A.P. and M.)=Demetzy Books, London, W.11. 47
Hutton Books, Barnfield, The Pavement, Brewood, Stafford ST19 9BZ. (0902) 850229 23
Huxley (William C.), The Book Corner, Wellington Market, Salop TF1 1DT. (0743) 4506 22
Huxley (Mr. and Mrs.)=Last Bastion Bookshop, Newton Abbot 52
Huxter (R.I. & S.)=Walsall House, Barmouth 6
Hyde (Betty and R.), 7 Coy Pond Road, Branksome, Poole, Dorset BH12 1JT. (0202) 766047 53
Hyde Park Bookshop, 8 and 10 Headingley Lane, Leeds 6. (0532) 782689 . . 15
Hyland (C.P.), The Old Rectory, Wallstown, Castletownroche, Mallow, Co. Cork, Eire. Mallow (022) 25217 2
Hyslop (D.W.), 17 & 19 Guthrie Street, Edinburgh EH1 1VG. (031) 225-4061 4

I

Iles (Harry E.), 16 Shamblers Road, West Cowes, Isle of Wight 54
Images, 16 Cecil Court, Charing Cross Road, London WC2N 4HE. (01) 836-8661 48
Inch's Books, 3 Saint Paul's Square, York YO2 4BD. (0904) 29770 11
Individual Books, 9 Hammers Lane, Mill Hill, London NW7 4BY. (01) 959-1089 44
Inland Pool Book Service, 5 Cornhill, Wellington, Somerset. (0823 47) 2650 . 49

J

K

L

Mc and Mac

M

Mair Wilkes Books, 3 Saint Mary's Lane, Newport-on-Tay, Fife. Newport-on-Tay 542352 or 542167 4
Majid (Abdul)=The Bookshop, Glasgow 5
Mallon (E.)=Cathair Books, Wicklow 2
Mallorn Books, 58 Waldeck Street, Reading, Berkshire. (0734) 863525 . . . 40
Maltby Books, 4 The Broadway, Crowborough, East Sussex TN6 1DF. Crowborough 2409 56
Malvern Bookshop (The), 7 Abbey Road (at the Priory Steps), Malvern, Worcestershire. Malvern 5915 27
Malynowsky (R.W.), 18 Doughty Street, London WC1 48
Mansfield (Judith), 60a Dornton Road, London SW12. (01) 673-6635 . . . 46
Map House (The), 54 Beauchamp Place, Knightsbridge, London SW3 1NY. (01) 589-4325 and (01) 589-9821 46
Marathon Books, 23 Greenway Close, Sale, Cheshire. (061) 969-4594 . . . 14
Marbeck Books, 2 Marbeck Close, Windsor, Berkshire. (95) 64354 40
Marcet Books, 4a Nelson Road, Greenwich, London SE10. (01) 853-5408 . . 45
Maric Books, Hampstead House, 5b Dene Road, Northwood, Middlesex HA6 2AE. (65) 21337 44
Marine Books, "Nilcoptra", 3 Marine Road, Hoylake, Wirral, Cheshire L47 2AS. (051) 632-5365 18
Marine-Workshop Bookshop, The Old Bonded Store, The Cobb, Lyme Regis, Dorset DT7 3JF. Lyme Regis 2429 53
Marjon Books, 16 Mannering Gardens, Westcliff-on-Sea, Essex SS0 0BQ. (0702) 347119 37
Marks Limited (Barrie), 5 Princes Avenue, Muswell Hill, London N10 3LS. (01) 883-1593 43
Marlborough Bookshop (The), The Parade, Marlborough, Wiltshire. (0672) 54074 39
Marlborough Bookshop (The), 18 Marlborough Place, Brighton, Sussex BN1 1UB. (0273) 688001 56
Marlborough Rare Books Limited, 35 Old Bond Street, London W1X 4PT. (01) 493-6993 47
Marrin & Sons (G. & D.I.), 149 Sandgate Road, Folkestone, Kent. Folkestone 53016 57
Marriott (R.A.), 24 Thirlestane Road, Far Cotton, Northampton NN4 9HD. (0604) 65190 29
Marsden (Francis), c/o 140–142 King's Road, Chelsea, London SW3 4UX. (01) 735-8570 46
Marshall (Anthony)=County Bookshop, Rutland 24
Marshall (Bruce), Garstang, Stair, near Mauchline, Ayrshire. Trabboch 283 and Ayr 284505 5
Marshall (B.), 24 River Street, Ayr, Ayrshire. Ayr 84505 5
Marshall & Daughters (E.A.), Isel Cottage, Isel, near Cockermouth, Cumbria CA13 0QG. (09404) 608 8
Martin (A.A.)=Woodford Bookshop 36
Martin (John), 14 Walker Lane, Hyde, Cheshire. (061) 368 1406 18
Martin Music Books (Philip), 22 Huntingdon Road, York YO3 7RL. York (0904) 36111 11
Martin (R.A.), 83 Crumlin Road, Seacash, Crumlin, Co. Antrim, Northern Ireland. (08494) 53453 2

PLEASE MENTION THIS DIRECTORY WHEN QUOTING

Montpelier Books, 32 Alma Vale Road, Clifton, Bristol, Avon BS8 2HY. (0272) 742690 38
Moon's Bookshop (Michael), 41–43 Roper Street, Whitehaven, Cumbria. Whitehaven 62936 8
Moore (Eric T.), 24–25 Bridge Street, Hitchin, Hertfordshire. Hitchin 50497 36
Moore (Peter), P.O. Box 66, 200a Perne Road, Cambridge CB1 3PD. 211846. TA: Antipodes, Cambridge, England 30
Moorhead Books, Suffield Cottage, Moorhead, Gildersome, Leeds LS27 7BA. (097 330) 852264 15
Moorland Books, Unit 5, Alexander Craft Centre, High Street, Uppermill, Oldham, Greater Manchester. Saddleworth (045 77) 5214 and 3095 . . 14
Morgan (Eiddon), Laburnums, Heronsgate, Rickmansworth, Hertfordshire WD3 5DB. (260) 2786 36
Morgan (H.J.), 25 Oaklands Avenue, Brookmans Park, Hatfield, Herts. AL9 7UH. (77) 52640 36
Morgan (Hugh & Rosemary)=Turret House Books, Wymondham 25
Morgan (Paul)=Coch-y-Bonddu Books, Machynlleth 6
Morley (R. & R.)=Bay Bookshop, Colwyn Bay 6
Morrell & Company Limited (W.T.), 2, 3 4 and 5 Sackville Street, Piccadilly, London W1X 2DP. (01) 734-0308 47
Morrell (Robert W.), 443 Meadow Lane, Nottingham NG2 3GB 20
Morris (Marian)=The Bookshop, Wells 49
Morris (Philip), 31 Highgate, Beverley, North Humberside HU17 ON. (0482) 869453 16
Morris (A.E.), (Yesterdays Books) 65–67 Bennett Road, Bournemouth, Dorset BH8 8RH. (0202) 302023 53
Morrish (K. & J.)=Reigate Galleries Limited, Reigate 50
Morrison (Alan), 4 Warton Cottages, Warton, near Rothbury, Northumberland 7
Morrison (Douglas E.)=Beulah House Bookshop, Rottingdean 56
Morrison (Mrs. Jane)=Lloyd's Bookshop, Wingham 57
Morten [Booksellers] Limited (E.J.), 2, 4, 6, 8 and 9 Warburton Street, Didsbury, Manchester M20 0RA. (061 445) 7629 14
Morten's Bookshops Limited, 50-52 Chestergate, Macclesfield. (0625) 23679 18
Mortlake and Co. (Harold), 28 Ferry Road, Barnes, London SW13 9PR. (01) 748-9675 46
Morton (B.) and M. Jones, Downwood, Dusthouse Lane, Bromsgrove, Worcestershire. (0527) 73449 and 73797 27
Morton (G.B.)=Staffs Educational Book Company, Lichfield 23
Morton-Smith (J. and M.), Knockhundred House, Knockhundred Row, Midhurst, Sussex GU29 9DQ. (073081) 5124 56
Mosdell Fine Books (G.W.), Hillside, Saint Issoy, Wadebridge, Cornwall. (08414) 666 51
Mostly Books, 247 Rawlinson Street, Barrow-in-Furness, Cumbria LA1 4DW. (0229) 36808 or 25097 8
Motley Books Limited, Mottisfont Abbey, Romsey, Hampshire SO5 0LP. Lockerley (0794) 40278 54
Motormania (East Sussex) Limited, 76 London Road, Saint Leonard's-on-Sea, East Sussex TN37 6AS. (0424) 422579 56
Mouat (Kit), Mercers, Cuckfield, Sussex RH17 5JU. Haywards Heath 54043 55

N

O

Old Book Shop [Brixham] Ltd. (The) 9 Bolton Street, Brixham, South Devon. Brixham 4754 . . . 52
Old Bookshop (The), 52 North Street, Worthing, Sussex. Worthing 202066 . 55
Old Coffee House Books (The), 29 Westgate Street, Launceston, Cornwall . 51
Old Cricket, 6 Buckingham Road, Hampton, Middlesex TW12 3J. (01) 941-6150 . . . 44
Old Curiosity Shop, 15 Catherine Hill, Frome, Somerset BA11 1BZ. (0373) 4482 . . . 49
Old Hall Bookshop and Art Gallery (The), Shutta Road, East Looe PL13 1BJ. 05036 3700 . . . 51
Old Hall Bookshop (The), 32 Market Place, Brackley. (0280) 704146 . . . 29
Old Hastings Bookshop, 15 George Street, Hastings, Sussex TN34 3EG. 425989 . . . 56
Old House Bookshop (The), Wagon Yard, Lower Church Lane, Farnham, Surrey GU9 7PS. Farnham 714754 . . . 50
Old Ramsgate Bookshop (The), Addington Street, Ramsgate, Kent CT11 9PT. (0843) 586377 . . . 57
Oldfield Antique Maps and Prints, 34 Northam Road, Southampton, Hampshire SO2 0PA. Southampton (0703) 38916 . . . 54
Oldham (Mrs Anne)=Ashley Books, Crymmych . . . 6
Oldham (Dr. Tim)=Wyseby House Books, Newbury . . . 40
Oley (Richard), 6 Station Road, South Shields, Tyne and Wear NE33 1ED. (0632) 551963 . . . 9
Oliver (J.E.), Malt Cottage, Croft Yard, Wells-Next-The-Sea, Norfolk. (0328) 711128 . . . 25
Ollerhead (P.)=Copnal Books, Crewe . . . 18
Olley (Leonard J.)=Pillar-Box Books, Eastwood . . . 37
Olney Books, 22 Bridge Street, Olney MK46 4AB . . . 34
Olney (Cy.)=Fine and Limited Editions Limited, Merrow . . . 50
Omniphil Limited, Germain's Lodge, Fullers Hill, Chesham, Buckinghamshire. (0494) 771851 . . . 34
On The Shelf, The Lanes, London Road, Hadleigh, Benfleet, Essex. (0702) 556275 . . . 37
Orbis Books (London) Ltd., 66 Kenway Road, London SW5 0RD. (01) 370-2210 . . . 46
Orchard Books, Orchard Neville House, Baltonsborough, Glastonbury, Somerset. (0458) 50443 . . . 49
Orchard (M. & R.), 74 Brassey Road, Wimborne, Bournemouth, Dorset. (0202) 531787 . . . 53
Orchards, 7 Westbourne Arcade, Bournemouth, Dorset . . . 53
Orient Books, Little Blakes, Halse, Taunton, Somerset TA4 3AG. (0823) 432466 . . . 49
Orman (Roger H.)=Newnham Bookshop, Newnham . . . 32
Orskey, Ltd. (Martin), Little Gains House, Elmsted, Ashford, Kent TN25 5JU. (023 375) 204 . . . 57
Orta Books, 5 Oakwood Avenue, Henleaze, Bristol, Avon BS9 4NS. (0272) 623656 . . . 38
Otway (R. & S.), Dutch Barton Cottage, Church Street, Bradford-on-Avon, Wiltshire BA15 1LN. (022 16) 3885 . . . 39
Out-of-Print Book Service, 17 Fairwater Grove East, Cardiff. (0222) 569488 6

PLEASE MENTION THIS DIRECTORY WHEN QUOTING

P

Q

R

PLEASE MENTION THIS DIRECTORY WHEN QUOTING

S

Scoresby House Bookshop, 13 Flowergate, Whitby, North Yorkshire. Whitby (0947) 605116 11
Scorpio Bookshop & Gallery, 50 High Street, Battle, East Sussex. (042 46) 3403 56
Scott (Cyril), 1 Church Street, Mere, Wiltshire BA12 6DS. (747) 860 297 . 39
Scott (Graham K.) 68–69 Saint John's Street, Bury Saint Edmunds, Suffolk IP33 1SJ. (0284) 3933 31
Scott (R.J.), 26a Coniscliffe Road, Darlington, County Durham. 63911 & 53767 9
Scott (T.F.S.), Flat 3, 32 Eton Avenue, London NW3 3HL. (01) 794-6640 . 44
Scowen (B.A. & H.R.)=Acres of Books, South Woodham Ferrers 37
Scowen (R.S. and P.A.), 9 Birchwood Grove, Hampton, Middlesex TW12 3DU. (01) 979-7429 44
Scurfield (G.B. & C.), 1 Wells Road, Fakenham, Norfolk NR21 9EG. (0328) 2450 25
Sea Books, 1 Cambridge Street, Harrogate, North Yorkshire. (0423) 500341 (evenings only) 11
Seafarer Books, 24 Market Courtyard, Riverside, Haverfordwest, Dyfed. Home: after 18.00 hrs. (0646) 600675 6
Seal Books, 2 Coningsby Road, London W5 4HR. (01) 567-7198 47
Searle (E.A.)=The Bookroom, Cambridge 30
Sears (M.)=M. & R. Glendale, London, W.1. 47
Seaton (A.V.)=Bewick Books, Newcastle 9
Second Edition, 9 Howard Street, Edinburgh. (031) 552-1850 4
Seddon (Alan & Maureen)=Browzers, Manchester 14
Seddon (A.), 53 Old Fort Road, Shoreham by Sea, Sussex BN4 5RL. (079 17) 61501 55
Seeney (Michael & Geraldine)=Cynara Books, Bromley 57
Segal (J.N.)=Angel Hill Bookshop, Tiverton 52
Sen Books, Greenways, 177 Pack Lane, Kempshott, Basingstoke, Hampshire RG22 5HW. (0256) 22904 54
Sephton (A.F.), 16 Bloemfontein Avenue, Shepherds Bush, London W12 7BL. (01) 749-1454 47
Serendip Fine Books, 11 Broad Street, Lyme Regis, Dorset. (029 74) 2594 . 53
Serendipity Books, 80 Hensman Road, Subialo, W.A. 6004. 381 6519 . . . 58
Serif Books, Harrow House, Chipping Campden, Gloucestershire GL55 6DY. (0386) 840558 32
Sesemann (Julia), 10 Kemerton Road, Beckenham, Kent BR3 2NJ. (01) 658-6123 57
Sever (T.P.)=Books, Manchester 14
Sexton (R.D.)=Ashbourne Books, Tenterden 57
Seydi (Sevin), 80 Marquis Road, London NW1 9UB. (01) 485-9801 44
Shaer (W.), 6 Sirdar Road, Mitcham, Surrey CR4 2BX. (01) 646-0123 . . 50
Shapero (Bernard J.), Gray's Antique Market, 58 Davies Street, London, W.1. (01) 449-4340 47
Shaw (Alan)=Moorland Books, Oldham 14
Shaw (D.M.)=Clifton Books, Wigan 12
Shaw (Geoff.), 32 College Road, Bromley, Kent BR1 3PE 57
Shaw (Norman), 84 Belvedere Road, London SE19 2HZ. (01) 771-9857. 45

PLEASE MENTION THIS DIRECTORY WHEN QUOTING

Theatre Bookshop, 26 New Road, Brighton, Sussex BN1 1UG. (0273) 681405 56
Theatremania, 66 Trindles Road, South Nutfield, Surrey RH1 4JN. (682) 2651 50
Thesaurus [Jersey] Limited, 20 Sand Street, Saint Helier, Jersey, C.I . . . 1
Thesaurus [Jersey] Limited, 1 Sunshine Avenue, Saint Helier, Jersey, C.I. 77016 1
Thesaurus [Jersey] Limited, 15–16 Tudor House, Mill Street, Saint Peter Port, Guernsey, C.I. 20217 1
Thesaurus [Jersey] Limited, 30 Sand Street, Saint Helier, Jersey, C.I. 37045 1
Thin (James) 53-59 South Bridge, Edinburgh EH1 1YS. (031) 556-6743 . . 4
Thoemmes Antiquarian Books, 1a College Court, Gloucester, Gloucestershire GL1 2NJ. (0452) 500776. Telex: 437244 CMINTL 32
Thomas Becket Books, 2 Sea Street, Whitstable, Kent 57
Thomas (Mrs. D.L.A.)=Haddan's Bookshop, Glastonbury 49
Thomas (Edward), "Tinca" Mill Cross, Rattery, Nr. South Brent, Devon TQ10 9LA. South Brent 3494 52
Thomas (S.N. & A.G.)=Lapis Lazuli, Richmond 50
Thomas, Wyn (E.), Old Quarry, Miners' Lane, Old Colwyn, Clwyd. (0492) 515336 6
Thompson (George)=Chichester Bookshop Limited, Chichester 55
Thompson (M. & A.C.), Unit 3, 1 Town Green, Wymondham, Norfolk NR18 0PN. (0953) 602244 25
Thompson (Ray)=Timeslip, Newcastle upon Tyne 9
Thompson's Book Shop, Dunstall House, Park Street, Cirencester GL7 2BX. (0285) 5239 32
Thorne's Bookshop, Percy Street, Newcastle upon Tyne. (0632) 326421 . . 9
Thornhill (John & Margaret)=Candle Lane Books, Shrewsbury 22
Thornton (John), 6 London Road, Tunbridge Wells, Kent. Tunbridge Wells 27364 57
Thornton & Son (J.), 11 Broad Street, Oxford OX1 3AR. Oxford (0865) 42939 33
Thorold [Pty.] Limited (Frank R.), P.O. Box 241, Johannesburg 2000. (4th Floor, S.A. Fire House, 103 Fox Street, Johannesburg, South Africa.) 838-5903 60
Thorp (Thomas), 9 George Street, Saint Albans, Hertfordshire AL3 4ER. (0727) 65576 36
Thorp (Thomas), 170 High Street, Guildford, Surrey GU1 3HP. (0483) 62770 50
Thredder [Books] (P.), Bourtswell Cottage, The Bourts, Upper Lydbrook, Gloucestershire GL17 9QB. (0594) 60187 32
Tilbury (Mrs. P.M.)=Julian's, Plymouth 52
Tilleys Bookshop, 29/31 South Street, New Whittington, Chesterfield, Derbyshire. (0246) 473047 19
Timbrell (P.)=Stepping Stones Bookshop, Lealholme 11
Timeslip, 20 Pink Lane, Newcastle upon Tyne. (0632) 328616 9
Tinslay (Peter & Maureen)=The Antique Bookshop and Curios, Cremorne, N.S.W. 58
Titcombe (Philip)=Gard Books, York 11
Titles Old and Rare Books, 15/1 Turl Street, Oxford OX1 3DQ. (0865) 727928. TA: Titles, Oxford, England 33

U

V

W

PLEASE MENTION THIS DIRECTORY WHEN QUOTING

Wray (David), Fortunes Well, Sheepscombe, Stroud, Gloucestershire GL6 7RL. Painswick 812386 32
Wray (L. & P.L.)=Pandion Books, Ripon 11
Wright (Christopher D.)=Printed Page, Winchester 54
Wright (D.)=The Globe Bookshop, Ipswich 31
Wright (Gordon)=The Brunswick Bookshop, Dawlish 52
Wright (M.N.), 137 Hedonsley Road, Consett, County Durham. (0207-50) 5560 9
Wright Booksellers (Sidney), 12 and 13 Royal Arcade, Boscombe, Bournemouth, Dorset BH1 4BT. Bournemouth (0202) 37153 53
Wright (Vivian), Fennelsyke, Raughton Head, Carlisle, Cumbria. (069 96) 431 8
Wrigley (John R.), 185 The Wheel, Ecclesfield, Sheffield S30 3ZA. (0742) 460275 17
Wybrow (M.)=Extra Books, Bramley 50
Wycherley (Stephen), 508 Bristol Road, Selly Oak, Birmingham B29 6BD. (021) 471 1006 26
Wylie (Malcolm James)=Cathay Books, Edinburgh 4
Wynne-Tyson (J.M. & T.J.L.)=Keele's, Chichester 55
Wynter Limited (Harriet), 50 Redcliffe Road, London SW10 9NJ. (01) 352-6494. Telex 21879. ATT: Harriet 46
Wyseby House Books, Siver Birches, Oxdrove, Burghclere, Newbury, Berkshire RG15 9JS. (063) 527 232 40

Y

Yablon (C. & A.)=Ian Hodgkins and Company Limited, Stroud 32
Yaffey (M.)=Cratchit's Bookshop, Carmarthen 6
Yesterday's News, 43 Dundonald Road, Colwyn Bay, Clwyd LL29 7RE. Colwyn Bay (0492) 31195 6
Yesterday's Paper, 102 Walmgate, York. (0904) 27715 11
Young (Anthony F.)=Anthony Antiques, Brighton 56
Young (B.R. & E.M.B.)=Corn Exchange Bookshop, Stirling 5
Young (P.)=Youngs Antiquarian Books, Tillingham 37
Young (Rosie and Susy), Oselhay Farmhouse, Whitchurch Canonicorum, Bridport, Dorset. Chidlock (0297) 89710 53
Youngs Antiquarian Books, Tillingham, Essex. (062187) 351 37
Yoxford Bookshop, High Street, Yoxford, Saxmundham, Suffolk. (072 877) 309 31
Ystwyth Books, 7 Princess Street, Aberystwyth, Dyfed SY23 1DX. (0970) 617511 6

Z

Zeno, 6 Denmark Street, London WC2H 8LP. (01) 836-2522 48
Zentner (Fred)=The Cinema Bookshop, London 48
Zinn (T.L.)=The Waverley Bookshop, Godalming 50
Zographos (M.P.)=Zeno, London 48
Zwemmer Limited (A.), Litchfield Street, London WC2. (01) 836-4710 . . 48

SPECIALTY SECTION

Specialties are arranged under the following heads:

AGRICULTURE which includes horticulture and gardening.

AUTOGRAPHS AND MANUSCRIPTS.

BIBLIOGRAPHY which includes all books about books.

BIOGRAPHY which includes all life stories, memoirs and reminiscences.

COLLECTING such items as coins, stamps, clocks, antiques.

CRAFTS AND USEFUL ARTS such as cookery and photography.

ENTERTAINMENTS which includes cinema, theatre and all branches of public entertainment.

FICTION which includes fantasy, weird and similar stories.

FINE AND RARE EDITIONS which includes all books sought because they are old, first or limited editions, private press books, fine printing or binding, miniature books and incunabula.

FOREIGN which includes all books in any language other than English.

HISTORY which includes folklore and genealogy.

JUVENILE.

LAW AND CRIMINOLOGY.

MEDICINE.

MUSIC which includes scores and books about music.

NATURAL HISTORY which includes archaeology, ornithology and zoology.

PERIODICALS.

PICTORIAL ART AND ART REFERENCE which includes all books about or illustrative of the pictorial arts, colorplates, fine illustrations and prints.

POETRY.

RELIGION AND PHILOSOPHY (1) which includes general religious literature, theology, psychology, rationalism and freethought and philosophy.

RELIGION AND PHILOSOPHY (2) which includes astrology, occult and psychic.

SCIENCE.

SOCIOLOGY which includes political and social movements, freemasonry, political economy, government.

SPORT AND PASTIMES.

TECHNICAL, INDUSTRIAL AND COMMERCIAL which includes engineering, journalism, manufacturing, military and naval, transport.

TEXT BOOKS AND OTHER EDUCATIONAL WORKS.

TOPOGRAPHY AND AMERICANA.

TOPOGRAPHY AND TRAVEL general and foreign.

DEALERS IN SECONDHAND AND ANTIQUARIAN BOOKS ARRANGED ACCORDING TO THEIR SPECIALITIES

The index numbers refer to sections in the Geographical List

AGRICULTURE

includes HORTICULTURE, GARDENING

Aberdeen Rare Books, Slains House, Collieston, Ellon, Aberdeenshire AB4 9RT—*agriculture* 4
Acorn Books, 12 Forteviot Gardens, James Allan—*gardening* 5
Acres of Books, Trinity Square, South Woodham Ferrers, Essex CM3 5JX —*gardening* 37
Arnold Books, P.O. Box 22, Lincoln, Canterbury, New Zealand—*gardening* . 59
Beagle Books, 21 Derwent Avenue, Ickenham, Uxbridge, Middlesex —*gardening* 44
Mary Bland, Augop, Evenjobb, near Presteign, Powys—*gardening and botany* 6
P.M. Blest, Little Canon Cottage, Wateringbury, Maidstone, Kent —*gardening* 57
Mr. Mick Boddy [Lily Book Dealer], 21a Lowfield Road, West Hampstead, London NW6 2PP—*lilies, (lilium and hybrid species only)* 44
The Book Shelf, 16 Albert Street, Mansfield, Nottinghamshire—*gardening* . 20
Bookstack at The Lodge, The Lodge, Wightwick Manor, Near Wolverhampton, West Midlands—*gardening* 26
Chantrey Books, 24 Cobnar Road, Sheffield S8 8QB—*gardening* 17
Christie-Bateman Books, Swale View, Lady Margaret Manor, Doddington, Sittingbourne, Kent ME9 0NT 57
Ciderpress Books, The Cottage, Kingsbury Episcopi, Martock, Somerset TA12 6AU—*gardening* 49
M. & R. Clark, 67 Lowther Road, Preswich, Manchester M25 8GP —*gardening* 14
Cottage Books, Gelsmoor, Coleorton, Leicestershire—*agriculture rural life* . 24
Countryside Books, 6 Winchester Street, Andover, Hampshire—*agriculture* . 54
W.D. Craven, 2 Kent Mansions, Brighton Road, Worthing, Sussex BN11 3EH—*before 1900* 55
Peter M. Daly, Rear of "Ships and Sealing Wax", 20A Jewry Street, Winchester, Hampshire 54
Mrs. Assia Doyle, Teffont, Salisbury, Wiltshire, SP3 5QP 39
Donald Gildea, 15 Shelley Road, Bognor Regis, Sussex—*gardening* 55
T.B. & J.N. Gray, The Old Market Garden, Tealby, Market Rasen, Lincoln LN8 3YB—*agriculture,country subjects* 21

AUTOGRAPHS AND MANUSCRIPTS

BIBLIOGRAPHY

BIOGRAPHY

includes ALL BOOKS BY OR ABOUT INDIVIDUALS

COLLECTING

CRAFTS AND USEFUL ARTS, FOOD AND DRINK

EDUCATIONAL

includes SCHOOL AND UNIVERSITY TEXTS, ECONOMICS

ENTERTAINMENTS

J.W. McKenzie, 12 Stoneleigh Park Road, Ewell, Epsom, Surrey—*theatre, performing arts* 50
Madeleine Productions, 15 Wallace Avenue, Worthing, West Sussex BN11 5RA—*cinema* 55
Motley Books Limited, Mottisfont Abbey, Romsey, Hampshire SO5 0LP . . 54
Offstage Theatre Shop and Gallery, 37 Chalk Farm Road, London NW1 8AJ —*the performing arts, particularly theatre* 44
C.D. Paramor, 25 Saint Mary's Square, Newmarket, Suffolk CB8 0HZ . . 31
The Portman Bookstore, Portman House, 17 Brodrick Road, London SW17 7DZ—*cinema* 46
Read, 48a Charing Cross Road, London WC2H 0BB—*performing arts* . . . 48
Spread Eagle Bookshop, 8 Nevada Street, Greenwich, London SE10—*cinema and theatre* 45
Theatremania, 66 Trindles Road, South Nutfield, Surrey RH1 4JN—*theatre and performing arts* 50
Robert Vaughan, 20 Chapel Street, Stratford-upon-Avon, Warwickshire —*theatre and other performing arts* 28
Vintage Magazine Shop Limited, Vintage House, Great Windmill Street, London WC2. (Corner of 39–41 Brewer Street)—*film, theatre* 48
Peter Wood, 20 Stonehill Road, Great Shelford, Cambridge CB2 5JL—*all performing arts* 30

FICTION

includes FANTASY, WEIRD, WITCHCRAFT

R. Andrews, 138 Kingswood Chase, Leigh on Sea, Essex SS9 3BG—*crime, detective, thriller* 37
Avocet Books Ltd. P.O. Box 4, Ashtead, Surrey KT21 2LP—*Disneyana* . . . 50
Bell, Book & Radmall Limited, 4 Cecil Court, London WC2N 4HE—*fantasy* 48
Black Bird Books, 24 Grampian Gardens, London NW2—*detective, thrillers, mysteries* 44
David Bristow Antiquarian Booksellers Limited, 32 Combe Road, Kingston upon Thames, Surrey, KT2 7AG—*19th century* 50
N.F. Brookes (Formerly Barry's Bookshop), 12a Queens Road, Brighton, East Sussex—*science fiction* 56
Button's Ltd, 21 Smith Street, Saint Peter Port, Guernsey, C.I—*Channel Islands: modern out-of-print, fiction* 1
Childhood Books, 132 Macoma Road, London SE18 2QZ—*fantasy* 45
Collards Bookshop, 4 Castle Street, Totnes, South Devon—*detective* 52
A.J. Cumming, 159 High Street, Lewes, Sussex—*detective fiction* 56
Richard Dalby, 4 Westbourne Park, Scarborough, North Yorkshire YO12 4AT—*fantasy fiction* 11
Anthony Dyson, 57 Saint John's Road, Oldbury, Warley, West Midlands B68 9SA—*detective* 26
C.R. Eastwood, 32 Riverton Road, Puriton, Bridgwater, Somerset—*19th century* 49
Toby English, c/o The Gallery, Lamb Arcade, Wallingford, Oxfordshire —*science fiction and fantasy* 33
Enigma Books, Ruins Field, Church Lane, Sheldon, Honiton, Devon EX14 0QU—*19th century, ghost, detective, gothic novels* 52
Ferret Fantasy, 27 Beechcroft Road, Upper Tooting, London SW17 7BX —*science, detective, Victorian* 46

FINE AND RARE EDITIONS

includes ALL BOOKS SOUGHT BECAUSE THEY ARE OLD, FIRST OR LIMITED EDITIONS, PRIVATE PRESS BOOKS, FINE PRINTING OR BINDING, MINIATURE BOOKS, INCUNABULA

FOREIGN

includes ALL BOOKS IN LANGUAGES OTHER THAN ENGLISH, DICTIONARIES, GRAMMARS

HISTORY

includes FOLKLORE, GENEALOGY, HERALDRY

JUVENILE

LAW AND CRIMINOLOGY

MEDICINE

MUSIC

includes SCORES AND BOOKS ABOUT MUSIC

NATURAL HISTORY

includes ARCHAEOLOGY, ORNITHOLOGY, ZOOLOGY, GEOLOGY, GEOGRAPHY

PERIODICALS

PICTORIAL ART

includes ALL BOOKS ABOUT OR ILLUSTRATIVE OF THE PICTORIAL ARTS, COLOUR PLATES, FINE ILLUSTRATIONS

POETRY

PRINTS AND MAPS

RELIGION AND PHILOSOPHY (1)

includes GENERAL RELIGIOUS LITERATURE, THEOLOGY, PSYCHOLOGY, RATIONALISM AND FREE THOUGHT, PHILOSOPHY

RELIGION AND PHILOSOPHY (2)

includes ASTROLOGY, OCCULT, PSYCHIC

REMAINDERS

NEW BOOKS, OVERSTOCKS, ETC. SOLD CHEAPLY BY PUBLISHERS TO CLEAR REMAINDER OF AN EDITION

SCIENCE

SOCIOLOGY

includes POLITICAL AND SOCIAL MOVEMENTS, FREEMASONRY, POLITICAL ECONOMY, GOVERNMENT

John Mead, Post Box No. C06 5DX, Belsize Cottage, 3 Broad Street, Boxford, Suffolk—*rural life, English social history, radical politics* 31
Ming Books, 115 High Street, Berkhamsted, Herts. HP4 2DJ—*politics* . . . 36
Stanley Noble, 24 Gladwell Road, London N8 9AB—*economics, world politics* 43
The Odd Volume, 53 Upper Gloucester Road, Brighton, East Sussex—*politics* 56
Pickering & Chatto Limited, 16 and 17 Pall Mall, London SW1Y 5NB —*economics* 46
Leslie Robert, 74 Devonport, Sussex Gardens, London 47
R. Wilson Rose, 275 King's Road, Kingston, Surrey KT2 5JJ 50
The Social Sciences Bookshop Limited, 74 Park Chase, Wembley, Middlesex HA9 8EH—*social services, local government, economics* 44
Nick Spurrier, 79 Whitstable Road, Canterbury, Kent CT2 8EA—*socialism, communism, trade unions, economic history* 57
Tara Associates Limited, South End House, Church Lane, Lymington, Hampshire SO4 9RA—*social and economic, women studies* 54
Frank Turner Rare Books, c/o Barclays Bank, King Street, Ludlow, Shropshire—*17th and 18th century; rural life* 22

SPORT, GAMES AND PASTIMES

Albany Books, 113 Albany Road, Cardiff CF2 3NS—*chess* 6
J.A. Allen & Co. [The Horseman's Bookshop] Limited, 1 Lower Grosvenor Place, Buckingham Palace Road, London SW1W 0EL—*horses, horseriding, racing, breeding, driving, polo and other horse sports* . . . 46
Denis W. Amos, 10 Mill Lane, Cheshunt, Waltham Cross, Hertfordshire EN8 0JH—*ball games and athletic sports especially tennis* 36
Anglebooks Limited, 2 Cecil Court, London WC2—*angling* 48
Anglesey Books, 5 Church Street, Llangefni, Anglesey, Gwynedd —*mountaineering* 6
S.E. Arthur, 4 Ty Brith Gardens, Usk, Gwent NP5 1BY—*golf* 6
Ashley Books, Rhychydwr, Crymmych, Dyfed SA41 3RB—*Caving, potholing, speleology* 6
Athletica [Books] International, 32 Halsbury Road, Worthing, West Sussex BN11 2JP—*Olympic Games, track and field athletics* 55
Sarah Baddiel, 43 Kendal Road, Gladstone Park, London NW10—*golf, motoring* 44
Bibliagora, P.O. Box 7, Hounslow, Middlesex TW3 2LA—*skill and chance, bridge* 44
P.M. Blest, Little Canon Cottage, Wateringbury, Maidstone, Kent—*field sports* 57
The Book Shop, 36 Gordon Road, Enfield, Middlesex—*doll and toy books* . . 43
Books Etc., 3b Wharf Road, Stamford, Lincolnshire—*philatelic* 21
J.K. Books [Sporting], 90 Shay Lane, Ovenden, Halifax, West Yorkshire —*hunting, racing, the horse, field sports and sporting* 15
The Border Bookshop, 64 High Street, Galashiels, Selkirkshire—*field sports* . 4
British Chess Magazine Limited, 9 Market Street, Saint Leonard's-on-Sea, East Sussex TN38 0DQ—*Chess* 56
E.K. Brown, Bevois Mount, Church Street, Liskeard, Cornwall PL14 3AQ —*cricket, association and rugby football only* 51
Mrs. I.J. Burlingham, 11 Geneva Gardens, Stranmillis Road, Belfast BT9 5FY, Northern Ireland—*cricket, golf* 2

TECHNICAL, TRANSPORT AND MILITARY

includes ENGINEERING, MANUFACTURING, MILITARY, NAVAL AND TRANSPORT

TOPOGRAPHY AND TRAVEL (1)

BRITISH ISLES

TOPOGRAPHY AND TRAVEL (2)

GENERAL AND FOREIGN

DISPLAYED ADVERTISEMENTS
List of Advertisers